A MONUMENT TO BLACKNESS

A MONUMENT TO BLACKNESS

Murals and Black Liberation,
from the Harlem Renaissance to Black Lives Matter

Hannah Jeffery

THE UNIVERSITY OF
GEORGIA PRESS
Athens

© 2026 by the University of Georgia Press
Athens, Georgia 30602
www.ugapress.org
All rights reserved
Set in 9.5/14 Quadraat Regular
by Rebecca A. Norton

Printed digitally

EU Authorized Representative
Easy Access System Europ—Mustamäe tee 50, 10621 Tallinn, Estonia,
gpsr.requests@easproject.com

Library of Congress Cataloging-in-Publication Data

Names: Jeffery, Hannah, 1990– author
Title: A monument to Blackness : murals and black liberation,
from the Harlem Renaissance to Black Lives Matter / Hannah Jeffery.
Description: Athens : The University of Georgia Press, [2026] |
Revision of the author's thesis (doctoral)—University of Nottingham, 2019. |
Includes bibliographical references and index.
Identifiers: LCCN 2025028735 | ISBN 9780820366302 hardback |
ISBN 9780820375229 paperback | ISBN 9780820375236 epub |
ISBN 9780820375243 pdf
Subjects: LCSH: African American mural painting and decoration—
20th century | African American mural painting and decoration—
21st century | Art—Political aspects—United States—History—20th century |
Art—Political aspects—United States—History—21st century
Classification: LCC ND2639.3.A35 J44 2026
LC record available at https://lccn.loc.gov/2025028735

For James and Cora,
my rocks and my sources of laughter.

CONTENTS

ILLUSTRATIONS

ACKNOWLEDGMENTS

Everyone always says it takes a village to write a book, and that couldn't be truer. This book has gotten over the line thanks to a host of amazingly generous people I've been lucky enough to have in my life. My heartfelt thanks must first go to the inspirational powerhouse that is Celeste-Marie Bernier. I watched her give a lecture at a University of Nottingham taster session back in 2007, and that lecture inspired me to go to Nottingham and have her as my lecturer. She then became my PhD supervisor in 2015, my postdoctoral mentor in 2020, and my wonderful friend throughout. This book has been guided by her. She has helped me navigate new intellectual, ideological, and artistic terrains, and *A Monument to Blackness* is richer because she shared her expertise and passions with me. I also owe a debt of gratitude to my amazing all-female PhD team from the University of Nottingham. Zoe Trodd plucked me from obscurity during a fourth-year undergraduate module and saw something in me that at the time I didn't see in myself. She championed me to continue studying a topic I dearly love. I am grateful for her generosity and can-do attitude. Stephanie Lewthwaite enthusiastically joined the team a year in, and her unwavering support and encyclopedic knowledge, along with her kindness, passion, and generosity of spirit, were constant sources of motivation. My thanks also go to staff members in the Department of American and Canadian Studies at the University of Nottingham, who always stopped to have a chat with me, offered sage advice, stood by the postgraduate community when we needed it, and were a great laugh to be around. I was at Nottingham for nine years, and I couldn't imagine a better group of people to be surrounded by as I began my research for this book. My thanks also go to Alan Rice, whose work is a real source of inspiration and has informed some conceptualizations throughout this book—thank you for your feedback and for being a cheerleader.

On a personal note, I'd also like to thank my brilliant and inspiring friends. My profound thanks go to Hannah-Rose Murray, Nick Batho, Katherine Burns, and Krysten Blackstone. Academia can be a tricky, daunting, and confusing place to navigate at times, but finding friends who create a warm, engaging, and friendly space to share is fundamental, and you've joyously provided this space for me. To Meghan, currently fighting the good fight in Washington, D.C. She takes time out of her day to check my stress levels, Venmo me money to buy pizza to make sure I feed myself, and selflessly read pages and pages of my work under the pretense of wanting to learn more—thank you for your unwavering support, friendship, and inspiring enthusiasm. To Rosie, who keeps me calm and makes me laugh during every FaceTime, inspiring me in ways that I definitely don't articulate enough. And to Cat and Rachel, whose joy, humor, hard work, and tenacity inspire me daily.

My thanks also go to the Arts and Humanities Research Council (AHRC) for their studentship. The AHRC not only allowed me to undertake my PhD at the University of Nottingham but also provided research grants that gave me the opportunity to conduct international research in the United States. I am grateful to the Smithsonian Institution for awarding me a Baird scholar-in-residence postdoctoral fellowship. My research in the Archives of American Art at the Smithsonian helped strengthen the archival bedrock of this book immeasurably. I also thank the Leverhulme Trust for an Early Career Fellowship, which granted me the space to turn my manuscript into a fully formed book.

One of the most inspirational and memorable experiences of writing this book was making contact with giants in the field—not only writers, photographers, and documentarians but also muralists. This book would not be what it is today without the help of each and every person who either sat with me in person in New York, spoke to me for hours over Skype, or constantly replied to my inordinate number of questions through email. My thanks go to Jim Prigoff, who wrote the seminal book on Black muralism and talked with me for hours about his experience of writing and publishing his book. Alan Barnett sat on the phone telling me stories of his days as an activist in the 1960s and how he went on to create the most comprehensive study of protest murals in the United States. Tim Drescher provided me with the contacts for many muralists and graciously offered to house me the next time I'm in Berkeley. Jeff Huebner shared manuscripts, photographs, names, contacts, and much needed wisdom with me and kindly showed me around the old mural stomping grounds of Chicago—I will forever remember that day. I thank muralist and writer Jane Weissman, whom I met in London years ago and who has been corresponding with me ever since. She has introduced me to amazing figures in the art world. I've also been so fortunate to speak with and interview many muralists: Eugene "Eda" Wade, Dana Chandler, Dewey Crumpler, Dindga McCannon, Tomie Arai, Susan Kiok, and Susan Caruso-Green. Your words and stories are the most important part of this book. I would not have attempted it without your help, and I can only hope I've done justice to your experiences and your work.

This book is dedicated to my family, Mum, Dad, Sam, Sophie, Jax, Gran, and Ron. You've all been my rock throughout this, and I wouldn't be where I am today without the sacrifices you've made and the unwavering support you've given me. Your selflessness knows no bounds, and I truly can't thank you enough for everything. To Nana and Jack, who instilled in me a sense of adventure, a passion for reading, and a love of America. Finally, I dedicate this book to James and Cora. Thank you doesn't seem enough, but I am truly grateful for your care, compassion, and support in the final few months while I finished this book. Thank you for the laughter you constantly fill the house with, for the love you continually share, and for the encouragement you provide on a daily basis. You are my rocks.

A MONUMENT TO BLACKNESS

The People's Art

Murals and the Black Community

It's difficult to keep feelings of depression and defeat at bay, but our histories, perceived in all their dynamism, their resistance and resilience, can give us heart and direction. —*Cedric Robinson, professor*

Murals—the largest and, by extension, the most compelling genre of the visual arts—are celebrations of scale, intelligence, ingenuity, imagination, and spirit that form an important thread in black America, inspiring and shaping a culture of hope. —*Floyd Coleman, artist*

Horrific distortion and misrepresentation have been transmuted into a counternarrative celebrating the triumph of the imagination and the power of the spirit. These dynamic forces are the engine of African American mural making. —*Edmund Barry Gaither, curator and art historian*

This book tells a story of empowerment. It tells a story of activism, resilience, interaction, engagement, protest, self-love, community love, and Black pride. It shows us how people in neighborhoods and cities across the United States gained a deeper sense of self through public art. It gives us a snapshot into how Black communities strengthened relationships not only among themselves but also within the physical spaces in which they lived. It shows us just how powerful and pervasive Black murals have been in the movements for Black liberation throughout the twentieth and twenty-first centuries.

"The *Wall of Dignity* stands as a monument to Blackness," the East Side Voice of Independent Detroit (ESVID) wrote in its April 22, 1968, community newspaper, *The Ghetto Speaks.* "It is our firm hope that it may help inspire our Black youth today to match and even excel the accomplishments of the great personages depicted there," the article continued.[1] In 1968 the city of Detroit, reeling in the aftermath of a violent racial rebellion from the previous year, was enveloped by stories of hurt, anger, and destruction. To alter this ongoing narrative etched into the surface of the city, muralists Bill Walker and Eugene "Eda" Wade traveled to Detroit to create a mural, along with several local artists, that lionized Blackness across the diaspora. It included portraits of rich and prosperous lands of Benin City and Ife, Nigeria; likenesses of leaders such as Malcolm X, Sojourner Truth, Marcus Garvey, and Martin Luther King Jr.; and smaller vignettes of enslavement and freedom fighters surrounding the emblazoned white title, WALL oF DiGNiTY, painted onto the surface.

Wall of Dignity was more than just a colorful painting on a wall. It stood proudly on the city's commemorative landscape, etching Black history into its foundations and challenging the pervasive racist imagery that lived throughout the nation's mainstream. "To the Black ghetto school child, [the wall] confronts the 'Imagery' of 'Little Black Sambo' and projects a far different Image than that of which so many Black people today are conscious," ESVID wrote. The wall recuperated Black memories and bodies so frequently erased by a racist national imagination, destroying "the 'traditional' Image of the lazy head-scratching, shuffling Negro" and replacing it with projections of Black empowerment, Black truth, Black history, and Black pride.[2] As the mural presided evocatively over Mack Avenue and Lillibridge Street in Detroit's Black East Side community, it offered—finally—a counternarrative of triumph and the power of Black resilience. "It remained difficult to find images of blacks winning," Black artist Michael D. Harris spoke of the lack of Black representation in mainstream society throughout the twentieth century. "It was difficult to find images of blacks on television, in print media, or in film. It was also difficult to find images by blacks in museums, galleries, or art texts."[3] So murals like *Wall of Dignity* offered up a way to finally showcase and celebrate Black life and history from a Black perspective in a Black space.

Thinking of the movement for Black liberation in the United States conjures up a full spectrum of images. We might think of Martin Luther King Jr. marching throughout the South with members of the Southern Christian Leadership Conference and Student Nonviolent Coordinating Committee, singing "We Shall Overcome," or the haunting declarations that "everybody knows about Mississippi goddamn," sung out by the rich voice of Nina Simone. We might think farther back, to the radical abolitionist freedom fighters and makers of history from the eighteenth and nineteenth

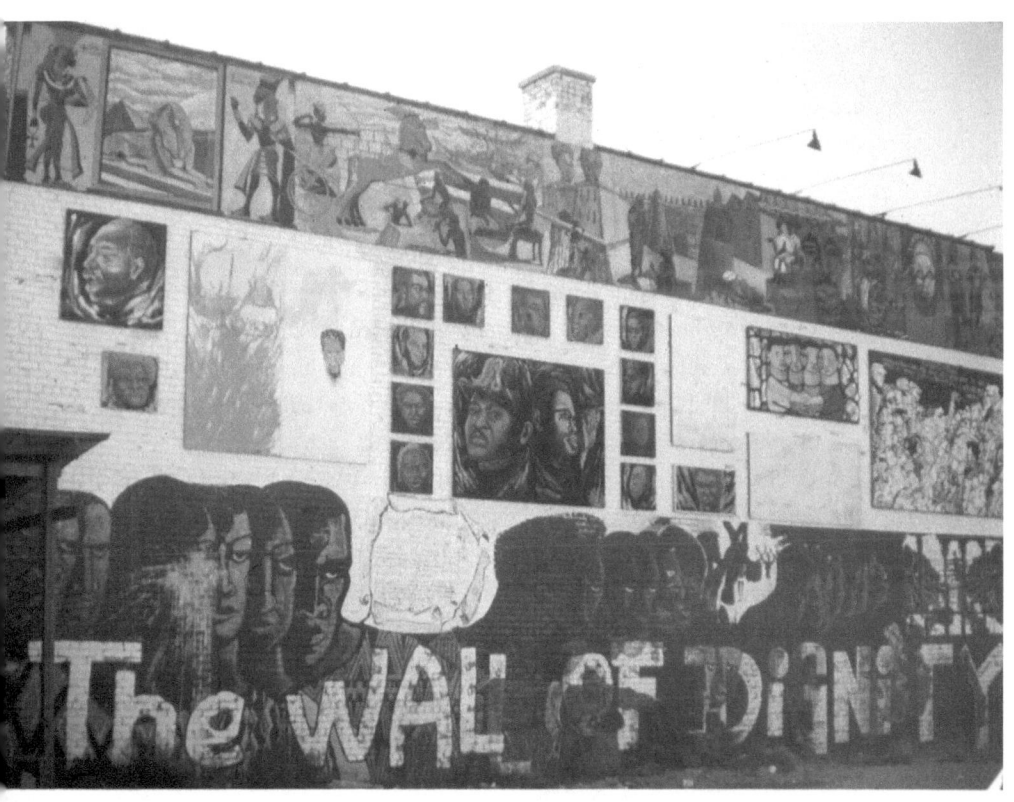

Wall of Dignity (1968), Mack Avenue and Lillibridge Street, Detroit, Mich. Painted by William Walker, Eugene "Eda" Wade, Edward Christmas, Eliot Hunter, Al Saladin Redmond, and others. Photograph by Georg Stahl. Courtesy of the Georg Stahl Mural Collection, University of Chicago Visual Resources Center Luna Collection.

centuries, such as Frederick Douglass, Harriet Tubman, David Walker, Sojourner Truth, Martin Robison Delany, and Nat Turner. The phrase "Black liberation" might conjure up famed images of Malcolm X preaching to energized crowds in Harlem or the Black Panther Party for Self-Defense stepping out in leather uniforms and berets wielding guns and chanting, "Free Huey" and "Off the Pigs!" And these images might cause us to cast our minds back to the brandished fists of Black Power ubiquitous throughout the 1960s and 1970s. In fact, we might not even need to look to the past at all but instead just out our windows today to the far-reaching protests crying out at the Black lives being lost at the hands of police, vigilantes, and white-supremacist structures embedded deep within the fabric of everyday life. When we think of the movement for Black liberation across the United States, it seems unlikely that we'd initially think of Black murals and public art. But they were (and still are) there, lining the streets and public buildings throughout the movement for Black liberation, curating sites of hope, solidarity, peace, transformation, imagination, strength, commemoration, education, and ritual in the heart of the grassroots, standing powerfully and uncompromisingly in the face of white supremacy.

The cultural landscape of the Black liberation movement is vast and has given birth to a host of responses. It has witnessed the emergence of spirituals and the evolution of jazz, blues, funk, soul, and hip-hop. It has been the muse of Black poets, cultural theorists, authors, painters, sculptors, and playwrights, giving rise to artistic movements such as the Harlem Renaissance of the 1920s and 1930s and the Black Arts Movement (BAM) of the 1960s and 1970s. And nestled deep into each and every decade of the last hundred years, among the poetry, novels, films, sculptures, artwork, and music, are murals. Although commonly overlooked as a potent cultural part of the movement for Black liberation, murals have been integral in the visual battle for Black representation and truth throughout the last hundred years. They live in communities—in streets and inside public buildings—and as powerful tools of expression, communicating messages and rebutting racist and derogatory imagery used to maintain power within society. They live—brave and unyielding—on and inside buildings to inspire overlooked and segregated (both de facto and de jure) community residents, giving them imagery and representation they seldom receive in their day-to-day lives.

Black murals of the last hundred years have always elevated Blackness. Whether through commemorating figures of Black history (Angela Davis, Stokely Carmichael, James Baldwin, W. E. B. Du Bois, and Mary McLeod Bethune), heralding the bountiful lands of a precolonized African diaspora, capturing the painful scenes of enslavement and self-emancipation of unnamed Black heroes of history, or offering narrative displays of Black survival across the nation, these public works of art have always placed Black history and life at the forefront. But as you'll see throughout this book, no two murals are the same. While they may share similar themes or faces of history, be created by the same artist, or be in a similar location, each mural is distinct and unique. They are mirrors of the communities in which they exist, usually democratically created in collaboration or discussion with residents. Each mural, created for the people of each neighborhood, strives to reflect the moods and ideologies of the people living in the artwork's presence. These murals respond to the political, social, and racial upheaval of the times—sometimes global events such as the rise of the Cold War, oftentimes national events such as the growth of the Black Power movement, or frequently localized news stories such as the death of Oscar Grant in Oakland, California, in 2009.

This book stands as one of the first in-depth studies of the national Black mural movement. It shows how Black murals—painted inside government buildings and at Historically Black Colleges and Universities (HBCUs) during the Harlem Renaissance and New Deal era and in the streets from the 1960s to the present day—play an overlooked role in the movement for Black liberation. While they might not effect change on a large scale or formally shape bills and laws, these murals make a difference in communities across the country. When white-supremacist power structures throughout the last hundred years built and maintained officially and unofficially segregated Black enclaves across the nation, keeping neighborhoods distinct and removed from the main arteries of the city through targeted measures such as poor public transportation, segregated school systems, and lack of employment opportunities, muralists turned to the walls of public buildings not only to contest the deeply embedded structural racism scaffolding the social makeup of the United States but also to assert a proud and living Black presence in and on the city. If Black America was going to be kept "separate and unequal," as the 1967 Kerner Commission concluded in a report that tried to understand the wave of racial rebellions sweeping the nation in the mid-1960s, then these local communities would claim these spaces and beautify them with images that heralded Blackness and showcased a Black experience in the country as it really was.

Throughout history, Black murals have transformed walls of buildings into sites of community interaction. These murals became arenas of learning and education when they displayed heroes of history seldom mentioned in history books; they became spaces of commemoration, immortalizing the likenesses of Black martyrs, leaders, and victims of supremacist violence; they invited acts of ritual and performance at their threshold, inspiring dance, poetry, music, and photography; and they stood as mementos of the given period's Black consciousness, reflecting the ideologies of the time back to the community.

"What we are against tends to take precedence over what we are for," historian Robin D. G. Kelley tells us. "It is a testament to the legacies of oppres-

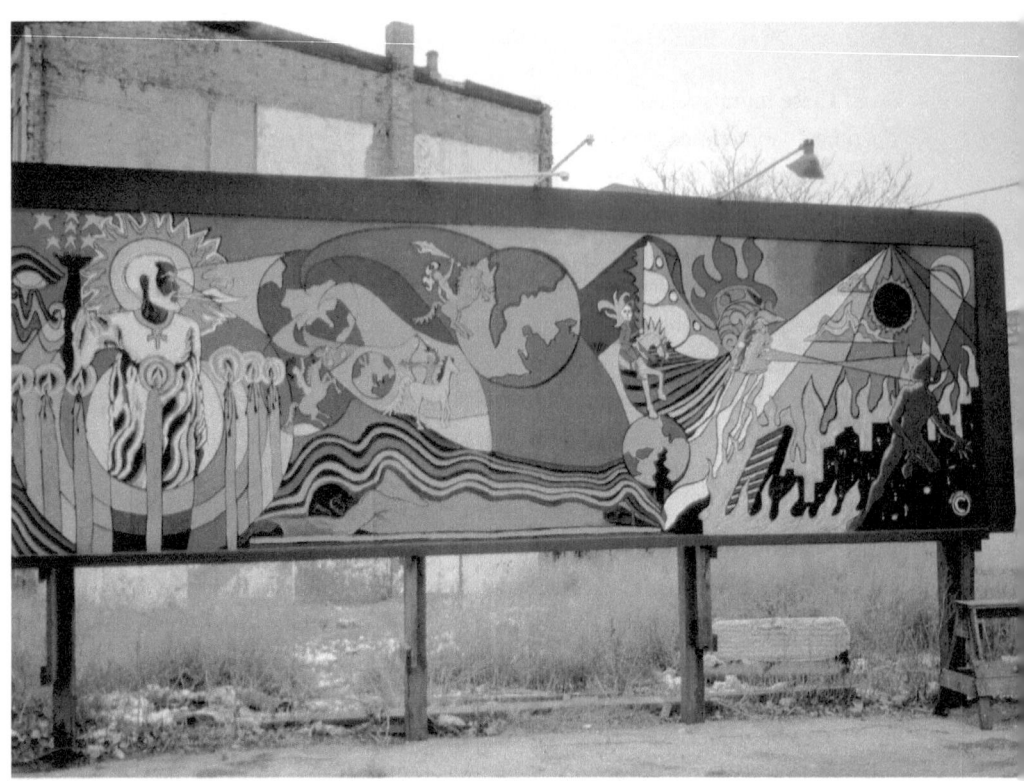

Nation Time (1971), 4141 S. Cottage Grove, Chicago, Ill. Painted by Mitchell Caton. Photograph by Georg Stahl. Courtesy of the Georg Stahl Mural Collection, University of Chicago Visual Resources Center Luna Collection.

sion that opposition is so frequently contained, or that efforts to find 'free spaces' for articulating or even realizing our dreams are so rare and marginalized."[4] But murals don't let these legacies of oppression win. Throughout this book, we see how murals created "free spaces" for envisioning freedom. This book tells us how murals changed public spaces into sites of imagination and empowerment; into arenas where Black viewers could see themselves, their history, and their ancestors on the walls of Black America; and into spaces where Black residents were able to renegotiate their sense of self and place in the world. The movement for Black liberation was "more than sit-ins at lunch counters, voter registration campaigns, and freedom rides; it was about self-transformation, changing the way we think, live, love, and handle pain," as Kelley describes poet Askia Muhammad Touré's perception of the Black liberation movement.[5] And in the pages that follow, we see how murals were and still are an integral part of this introspective, deeply reflective, and transformative movement for liberation from deep within the heart of Black communities.

It might seem that an ephemeral and guerrilla art form would have little importance in a liberation battle that was striving to end legal segregation, demanding the right to vote, and fighting for economic and racial freedom across the country. But "too often our standards for evaluating social movements pivot around whether or not they 'succeeded' in realizing their visions," Kelley tells us, "rather than on the merits or power of the visions themselves."[6] The potency and gravitas of murals, then, does not lie in their tangible "success" in achieving the measurable goals of a civil rights or a Black Power movement, for example. Instead, their "success" lies in the responses from the Black community—in the poetry, prayer, dance, and music performed at their threshold; in the tours of the walls given by excitable young schoolchildren; in the elevation of these children's minds after seeing themselves reflected upon the wall; in the dedication ceremonies that bestow a mural unto a community; and in the pilgrimages made by visitors from far and wide.

When Black murals were painted into the streets for the first time against the backdrop of the Black Power movement, their presence "was a testimony to the many exposed walls and buildings in need of attention in black communities," Black artist Nelson Stevens said. "These were harsh environments, often overcrowded yet filled with vacant lots, abandoned cars, and drab buildings in need of paint and repair."[7] But through the vibrancy of color and elevation of Blackness in their visual content, murals provided a place of hope and inspiration, a place that spiritually nourished the community. "Most of the art that blacks came in contact with at that time was detrimental to their mental health," Stevens believed, and in many ways, murals responded to this, becoming a form of ocular therapy.[8]

MEMENTOS OF A MOVEMENT

Black public art and murals have been a part of the movement for Black liberation since the days of enslavement, from when the formerly enslaved William Wells Brown created his traveling panorama, *Panoramic Views of the Scenes in the Life of an American Slave* in 1849, or from when artist Robert S. Duncanson painted antislavery panoramas, portraits of abolitionists, and expansive murals at the homes of wealthy white elites to demonstrate how artistic skill in the fine arts was proof of Black humanity during the days of slavery. Since 1619, when people were stolen from their homeland in Africa and brought to the United States in chains, those enslaved on the nation's soil constantly produced creative ways of expressing themselves, their culture, their identity, and their history. Artistic traditions of personal and public representations of Blackness and the self took root in the eighteenth and nineteenth centuries through panoramas, portraits, quilts, linocuts, lithographs, pottery, sculpture, dance, song, music, and printmaking. And murals stand on this cultural landscape as yet another way Blackness has been celebrated and asserted in the face of oppression.[9]

This book begins in the 1930s, during the crest of the race-conscious New Negro / Harlem Renaissance movement, when artist Aaron Douglas resurrected the revolutionary likeness of Harriet Tubman in his Bennett College mural, *Harriet Tubman (Spirits Rising)* (1930), giving rise to large-scale, public-facing murals of Black resistance, Black life, and Black struggle.[10] Focusing solely on the twentieth and twenty-first centuries, this book charts the largely undocumented lineage and evolution of Black murals from the 1930s to Black Lives Matter. It begins with the interior artwork of the Harlem Renaissance and New Deal era, when artists such as Douglas, Hale Woodruff, Charles White, Charles Alston, Georgette Seabrooke, John Thomas Biggers, William Edouard Scott, Vertis Hayes, and John Wilson painted the walls of libraries, halls, and student union buildings, commonly at HBCUs in the South. These revolutionary works of art beautifully illustrated a historic and contemporary Black experience in the United States while simultaneously standing against the tightening grip of Fascism and economic bondage on the world stage in the 1930s and 1940s. And as the number of Black interior murals began to dwindle during the height of the Cold War, street murals were waiting in the wings, ready to take center stage.

In 1967, during the cradle of the Black Power movement, Black muralism emerged in the streets. But this spatial shift didn't usher in a distinct and separate artistic movement. When murals became a street phenomenon, they didn't break from the past; instead, they evolved and grew from their earlier interior predecessors. Seeking to reflect diasporic Black life and history in a similar vein to Harlem Renaissance and New Deal era interior murals, street murals became their counterparts. Following on from the 1930s, 1940s, and 1950s, *A Monument to Blackness* continues to weave throughout the 1960s and 1970s to show not only the spread of the Black community mural movement across the country but also the power these murals yielded in

Black America's backyard. Although the revolutionary flames of Black Power began to dim in the late 1970s, street murals remained, proving they weren't just a visual sponsor of this radical movement. As the political pendulum swung far right into the 1980s and 1990s, ushering in a rising tide of neoconservatism and unshakeable austerity, street murals—as we'll see throughout this book—persisted, lining the streets of the communities stung most strongly by the era's right-wing policies. And today in the age of Black Lives Matter, as the close of this book shows, the artistic mural movement continues, this time wallpapering the streets with the portraits of people killed by the police and vigilantes. My aim when undertaking this research and writing this book was not only to show the revolutionary resilience and radical potency of these murals and their responses to racial injustice but also to add breadth and depth to our currently limited understanding of Black muralism by showing it not as isolated moments of public art emerging at various points in history but as one connected, enduring, and evolving artistic movement arcing across the decades, from the Harlem Renaissance to Black Lives Matter today.

While murals have stood as powerful markers on the nation's cultural landscape throughout history, they have repeatedly been overlooked, marginalized, and shunned for their failure to adhere to the norms of established galleried or high-class art. "Too often the spokesman of the official art world conveniently pigeonholed the new murals as 'protest art,' 'minority art,' and 'poor art for poor people' in order to dismiss them from serious consideration," muralists and activists Eva Cockroft, John Pitman Weber, and John Cockroft wrote in *Towards a People's Art: The Contemporary Mural Movement*. The writers used their seminal 1977 book as a way to break through the "near blackout of critical attention" surrounding the stigmatized community murals.[11] "Despite the artistic richness and social significance of the mural movement, only a handful of established art critics have given the community murals attention," they argue. "The literature on public art in general is scant," they go on to say, reflecting the "privatistic focus of the art market. . . . [F]ew critics are prepared to deal with the aesthetic, art-historical, or social issues involved in discussing public art forms."[12] But books such as *Towards a People's Art* and Alan Barnett's groundbreaking and encyclopedic anthology, *Community Murals: The People's Art* (1984), laid the essential foundations for future studies on murals, ensuring that these critical and ephemeral works of art didn't simply become shadows of a distant past.

These geographically and racially diverse texts, covering the full remit of community murals in the United States until the mid-1980s, set the stage for books yet to come (including the one you're currently reading). Throughout the last three decades, we've seen the publication of Tim Drescher's *San Francisco Murals: Community Creates Its Muse, 1914–1990* (1991); the more racially focused *Walls of Heritage, Walls of Pride: African American Murals*, by Jim Prigoff and Robin Dunitz (2000); Stacy Morgan's *Rethinking Social Realism: African American Art and Literature, 1930–1953* (2004); Janet Braun-Reinitz and Jane Weissman's *On the Wall: Four Decades of Community Murals in New York City* (2009); Abdul Alkalimat, Romi Crawford, and Rebecca Zorach's *The Wall of Respect: Public Art and Black Liberation in 1960s Chicago* (2017); Jeff Huebner's *Walls of Prophecy and Protest: William Walker and the Roots of a Revolutionary Public Art Movement* (2019); and Zorach's *Art for People's Sake: Artist and Community in Black Chicago, 1965–1975* (2019).

The "near blackout" of critical attention received by murals, especially Black murals, in the 1970s and 1980s is becoming gradually more transparent today thanks to these works. The inspirational research done by these writers and archaeologists of history has helped shape and inform the new stories that come to life in the following pages. Morgan's *Rethinking Social Realism* offers an incomparable exploration into the relationship between social realism and interior murals of the 1930s, 1940s, and 1950s, helping us understand why African American cultural workers sustained such an engagement with this artistic style. Because of Huebner's book, *Walls of Prophecy and Protest*, as well as Alkalimat, Crawford, and Zorach's *The Wall of Respect* and Zorach's *Art for People's Sake*, we now understand the genesis of the Black mural movement in Chicago and how public art can be "a staging ground for debates about community and identity" in Black communities across the city.[13]

But as Huebner acknowledges in his instrumental opus on Black muralist Bill Walker, "socially conscious outdoor 'street' murals are a significant but often overlooked feature of Chicago's cultural legacy," and the same can be said for the legacy of Black murals—both interior and street—across the country, which is why I have written this book. "Critics and scholars have tended to downplay the contributions of the mural movement," Huebner continues, "missing the chance to demonstrate its relevance and current concerns with performance and community cooperation."[14] So this book tries to stand as a new contribution, offering one of the first comprehen-

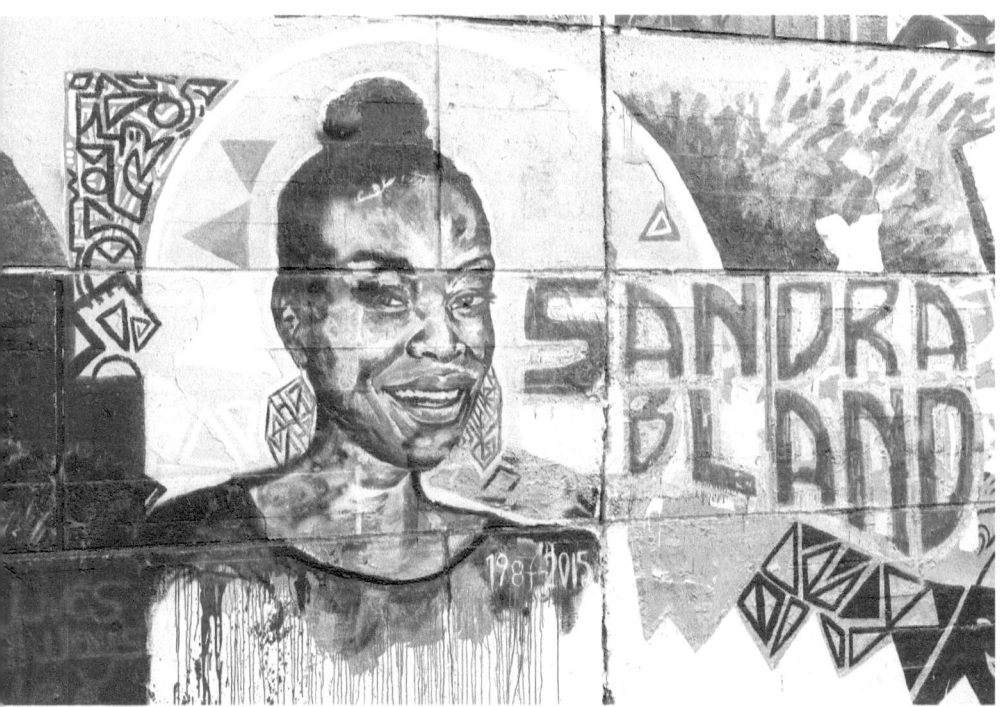

Sandra Bland Mural (2015), Slater Street, Ottawa, Canada. Painted by Kalkidan Assefa and Allan Andre. Image from Flikr, taken by Robert Fairchild, CC BY-NC 2.0. No changes made to image.

sive examinations of the mural movement from the Harlem Renaissance to Black Lives Matter today. It tells us more about the interactive and transformative roles murals have played in Black communities across time, highlighting how murals are edifying, educational, ritualistic, performative, and rehumanizing works of art and community protest embedded into the streets.

Murals are complex to study, which perhaps helps explain their lack of acknowledgment in scholarship. They straddle the boundaries of street, guerrilla, radical, high, contemporary, galleried, commemorative, and ephemeral art, defying any form of categorization. And quite rightly, too. It feels wrong to try and categorize an art form so proudly antiestablishment and so beautifully standing for the people. Murals live defiantly in the face of corporate power structures, democratizing in their creation, anticapitalist in their existence, and "for the people" of the community as their purpose. So attempting to tell the stories of community murals, as mural documentarian Tim Drescher acknowledges, requires an awareness and an in-depth understanding of "multiple simultaneous contexts, including local history, art history, and mural history, as well as images, design, content, and relation to its space on the wall on which it is painted."[15] Essentially, as Drescher is saying here, to have a firm grasp on the significance of murals in communities across the country, one needs to scratch below the surface, to dig into not only the minutiae of the mural itself and the context of the Black art world but also the local context of the neighborhood, the national context of the country, and sometimes even the international context on a global scale.

To do this, I've turned to a myriad of inspirational and groundbreaking scholarship that has helped me not only uncover new ways to understand and frame Black liberation but also provide a rich and fertile ground upon which to layer my own research, expanding the boundaries of Black Power scholarship, given that murals and public art don't typically fall under its remit. Seminal books such as Amy Abugo Ongiri's *Spectacular Blackness: The Cultural Politics of the Black Power Movement and the Search for a Black Aesthetic* (2009); Peniel Joseph's *Waiting 'Till the Midnight Hour: A Narrative History of Black Power in America* (2006), *The Black Power Movement: Rethinking the Civil Rights–Black Power Era* (2006), and *Dark Days, Bright Nights: From Black Power to Barack Obama* (2010); Komozi Woodard's *A Nation Within a Nation: Amiri Baraka (LeRoi Jones) and Black Power Politics* (1999); and William L. Van Deburg's *A New Day in Babylon: The Black Power Movement and American Culture, 1965–75* (1993) have enhanced my understanding of Black Power and its reach both geographically and temporally, illuminating the gaps where murals so perfectly fit but are less documented currently. The role of Black women in the movement for Black Power has also been better understood thanks to the excellent books and articles "Black Women, Urban Politics, and Engendering Black Power" (2006), by Rhonda Y. Williams; "Black Feminists Respond to Black Power Masculinism" (2006), by Kimberly Springer; and Ashley D. Farmer's *Remaking Black Power: How Black Women Transformed an Era* (2017).

This book occasionally skirts the fringes of urban history, and this could not have been done without the influential studies of Arnold Hirsch and Mary Pattillo-McCoy. Hirsch's *Making the Second Ghetto: Race and Housing in Chicago, 1940–1960* (1983) and Pattillo-McCoy's *Black Picket Fences: Privilege and Peril Among the Black Middle Class* (1999) and *Black on the Block: The Politics of Race and Class in the City* (2007) were invaluable in helping me understand the growth of urban centers. They were also instrumental in informing my own theories around how Black murals emerged out of racial confinement in the urban North.

And to help contextualize the Black art world, I've consulted books such as Romare Bearden and Harry Henderson's *A History of African-American Artists: From 1792 to the Present* (1993); Elsa Honig Fine's *The Afro-American Artist: A Search for Identity* (1982); Amy Helene Kirschke's *Aaron Douglas: Art, Race, & the Harlem Renaissance* (1994); Lizzetta LeFalle-Collins and Shifra M. Goldman's *In the Spirit of Resistance: African-American Modernists and the Mexican Mural School* (1996); Sharon Patton's *African-American Art* (1998); Richard Powell and Jock Reynold's *To Conserve a Legacy: American Art from Historically Black Colleges and Universities* (1999); Samella Lewis's *African American Art and Artist* (2003); Celeste-Marie Bernier's *African American Visual Arts* (2008) and *Characters of Blood: Black Heroism in the Transatlantic Imagination* (2012); and Susan E. Cahan's *Mounting Frustration: The Art Museum in the Age of Black Power* (2016). These books all stand as giants in their field and have been significant in helping me uncover radical overtones and undertones of early Black muralism in new and exciting ways.

LIVING BLACK HISTORY

I write this book against a backdrop of turmoil. The years I spent researching, conceptualizing, and writing it have been marked by unimaginable assaults on civil and human rights, by political and racial strife, and by economic turbulence. Embryonic during the final years of Obama's presidency, the planning stages of this book began in what felt like a different era. It didn't seem possible in those moments that the next eight (plus) years would witness the political pendulum swing farther right than ever before, that a presidential administration would be marked by a Muslim ban, family separation policies, an emboldening and catalyzing influence over right-wing ideologies among the body politic, and the growing spread of domestic extremism across the country. After white supremacists walked the streets of Charlottesville in 2017 under a banner to "Unite the Right," chanting "blood and soil," and after one of them killed Heather Heyer after running her over with a car, President Trump stood in the lobby of Trump Towers in New York and told the news cameras gathered around him that there were "fine people on both sides."[16]

Writing about historical protest movements in the United States while living through a time when sexism, racism, homophobia, transphobia, and

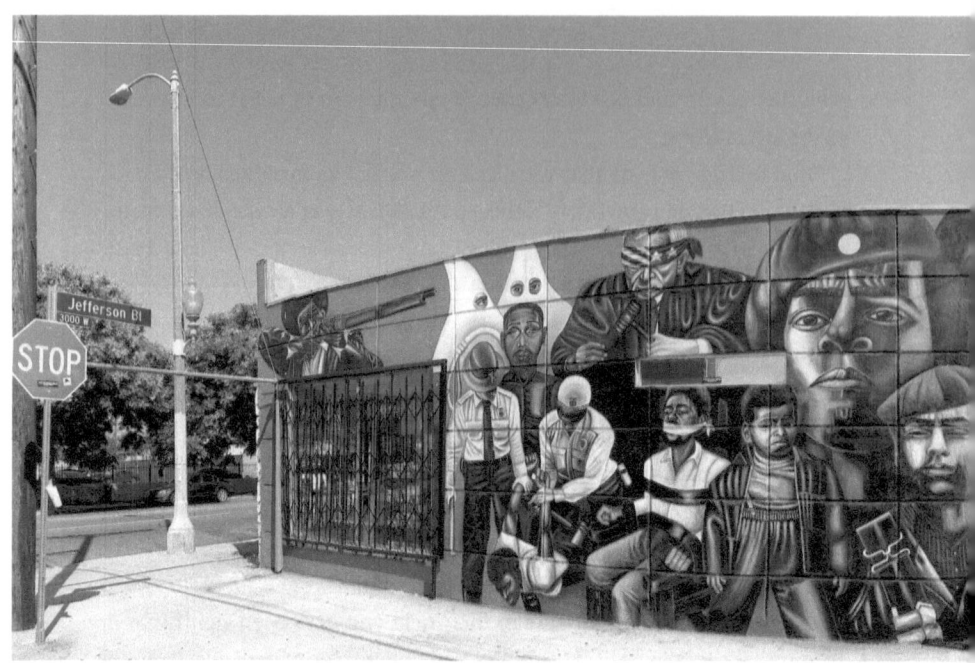

xenophobia are ubiquitous in society feels uncomfortable and, in many ways, quite haunting. And writing about a movement for Black liberation when the names of individuals such as Antwon Rose Jr., Atatiana Jefferson, Breonna Taylor, Elijah McClain, Ahmaud Arbery, and George Floyd join the list of police brutality victims stretching back into the depths of history is both jarring and harrowing. Living through this period of economic, social, and racial depression, where any strides toward justice and equality feel like they're being made in quicksand, has caused me to write, rewrite, and rewrite again the chapters that follow. So much has happened in the last few years, prompting me to continually adjust, reframe, edit, and sometimes remove elements of this book. But the most important reckoning that has happened when writing this book is my own positionality as a white female writer reporting on artistic movements of Black history. I acknowledge my position as a white writer operating in this space and fully recognize the enduring domination of systemically racist structures that not only seek to maintain a terrain of whitewashing and white dominance in the mainstream but also indirectly lead to a proliferation of white writers documenting Black history. While I write about a space and lived experience removed from my own in this book, I remain cognizant of the issues attached to this. I can never know these stories, never live this history, and never feel the

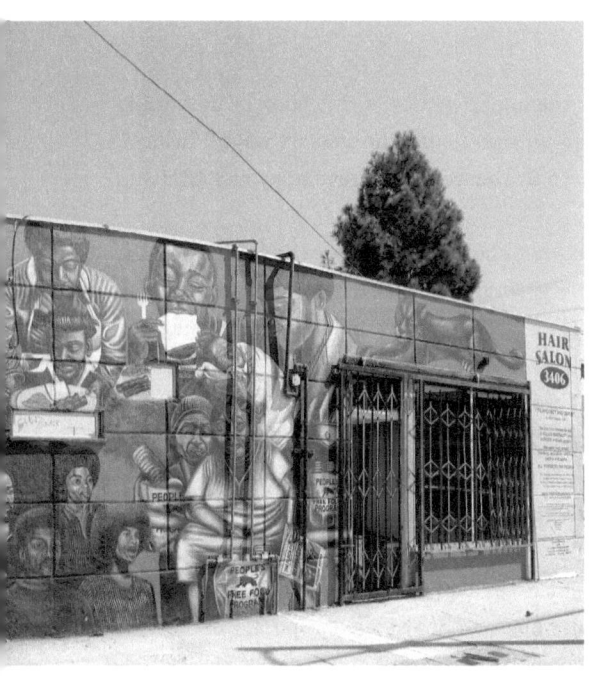

To Protect and Serve (1995–96), 3406 11th Avenue, Los Angeles, Calif. Painted by Noni Olabisi. Image from Flikr, taken by waltarrrrrr, CC BY-NC-ND 2.0. No changes made to image.

emotions directly felt off the back of such entrenched and endemic racism. I try throughout this book to act simply as a canvas on which to tell these stories not yet heard.

In 2006 Manning Marable set a task to writers and researchers to create a "living Black history." "Precious documents, transcripts of important speeches, and crucial manifestos written by African Americans, produced by generation after generation, have been largely scattered, destroyed, and lost," he writes in his book of the same name.[17] Archival materials, speeches, letters, and physical sites of history are getting lost and demolished, he continues, and as time slowly passes, it takes the makers of history and those holding on to stories we are yet to hear with it. We writers have a duty to recreate this hidden, fragmented, or precarious past, he says, and we can do this through gathering film, photography, activist, and artist testimony.

This book seeks to do just that. *A Monument to Blackness* isn't a strict history, art, or even art history book. It draws from and straddles many fields to tell a story of a Black mural movement infrequently documented. I am guided by Marable's declaration that African Americans are the principal actors who must tell the story "from their own vantage point," and I therefore refrain from importing structured frameworks, methodologies, and theories that would detract from the untold stories of this book or that would attempt to categorize them in unnatural and unnecessary ways.[18] Instead, the heart of this work is driven by the words and testimony of artists and activists.

This book wouldn't work—nor should it—without the input from the multiple artists who graciously gave up their time to speak with me and tell me their stories, or without the countless invaluable interviews conducted by others working to shed a light on these overlooked tales. I stand next to writers in this space such as Celeste-Marie Bernier, coming to grips, as she so correctly summarizes, with "the stark reality that the Black artist's search for a new visual language is an artistic and political necessity in the face of the stranglehold exerted by a scopic black—or more accurately white—hole of misrepresentation."[19] Artists are the best theorists of their work, so to assist in refocusing dominant lenses that try to perpetually whitewash the languages employed to discuss Black art across the diaspora, I use artists' words as the anchor of this book, in tandem with the works of Black scholars, activists, cultural theorists, and sociologists from each historic time period discussed.

But I acknowledge that I haven't, and can't, cover everything in this book. Writing on a grassroots history that has only a handful of books to build upon leaves large unfilled (and unfillable) gaps. As Rebecca Zorach acknowledges in *Art for People's Sake*, residents in these communities have passed away without leaving a trace of their thoughts on the murals painted, and if those residents are still alive, it remains a near impossible task to track them down. To try and navigate these lacunae of information, then, I turned to vital secondary sources, as well as newspaper articles, television interviews, news reports, and oral history testimony. I also tested the memories of the artists I was fortunate enough to interview. I used this array of sources to try and build up—in the most comprehensive way possible—the clearest and most accurate record of the time, but I have sometimes had to draw my own conclusions and analysis where these gaps of research remain impenetrable. I understand the possible risks and challenges that come with this process, and I feel conflicted in much the same way Lucy Lippard does when speaking of her book *Mixed Blessings: New Art in a Multicultural America* (2000). "Sometimes I'm saying things I cannot really know," she writes. "Despite the best intentions to make *Mixed Blessings* an egalitarian collage, I still find myself, paradoxically, speaking for others whose voices I am hoping to make heard. Yet another contradiction, since I am all too aware of the history of such co-optations."[20]

This book doesn't stand as a complete and finished product. Much like Prigoff and Dunitz wrote in *Walls of Heritage, Walls of Pride*, this book is also a work in progress waiting to be expanded upon. It's a starting point and a threshold into a commonly overlooked artistic world. Prigoff and Dunitz wanted their investigation to "stimulate interest to ensure that the documentation becomes even more complete," and while I hope my book offers a complementary companion to their work, adding complexity to the movement they capture in theirs, I also wish the same of *A Monument to Blackness*.[21] I hope this book incites discussion and encourages others to expand our understanding of the Black mural movement. This book doesn't cover every Black community mural out there—that remains an impossible task for anyone to undertake, given the ephemeral nature of murals. But in the pages that directly follow, I've included a brief one-hundred-year summary of the Black mural landscape, highlighting the main artists, features, geographical spread, and funding resources, to give a contextual grounding for the remaining chapters. In the remaining chapters, I have selected a handful of examples that perfectly encapsulate the interactive nature of Black murals and their power, malleability, and pervasiveness in communities across the country.

The murals in this book have been chosen because of their close relationship with the communities they serve; they typically invite communal or individual interactions from locals. There's obviously a wealth of murals I could not include in the pages that follow purely due to lack of space, so I have deliberately structured this book around a smaller number of in-depth case studies to capture, in more intimate detail, the minutiae of these murals, their call-and-response interactions with their neighborhoods, and the roles they play in the movements for Black liberation. When conceptualizing this book and deciding whether to structure it around broad readings of many murals or in-depth readings of fewer murals, it felt more natural (and important) to do the latter. I wanted to capture these intricate dynamics that beautifully tell a story of strength and relationship building. I do, however, supplement these larger examples with smaller ones from each time period to try and illustrate the spread of murals across the country throughout the twentieth and twenty-first centuries, and I move between reporting close microhistories from deep within specific communities and streets to zooming out farther and layering these histories into the broader local and national contexts to show how embedded these murals are into movements for social justice.

Although this book documents a racialized mural movement, it also operates on the fringes of intersectionality by inherently discussing an antiestablishment, class-oriented artistic practice. In "What Is This Black in the Black Radical Tradition?," George Lipsitz tells us that "artistic creation has helped the Black working class to decorate the way to other worlds," and this is precisely what murals do.[22] Transformative and interactive, murals are an art of the disenfranchised, an art of the community, and an art of the people, and while this book doesn't use class as the main artery running throughout it, it intrinsically lives in the background of every story told in the following pages.

This book also consciously brings female artists into the discussion. In 1977 Chicago-based muralist Justine DeVan wrote a report that documented the gender-based discrimination experienced by female muralists. Men failed to respond to women's negotiations and communications about creating community walls, citing a lack of interest and confidence that "a group of women could do such a project," DeVan recorded.[23] As Kimberlé Crenshaw's groundbreaking work on intersectionality shows us, racism and sexism overlap, creating multiple levels of social injustice, and the Black female muralists of the community mural movement, as recognized by DeVan, felt this. "The consequences of not having intersectional politics when thinking about feminism and antiracism," Crenshaw states, is that "when feminism doesn't contest the logic of racism, and when racism refuses to take up questions of patriarchy, they often wind up reinforcing each other."[24] The Black community mural movement throughout history has been undeniably male-centric, and working tirelessly against the injustices of not only racism but also sexism and misogyny were fearless and inspirational women such as DeVan, Sharon Dunn, Myrna Weaver, Florence Hawkins, Kathryn Akin, Vanita Green, Barbara Jones-Hogu, Carolyn Lawrence, Dindga McCannon, members of the Black Women's Mural Project in Chicago, and countless others whose names haven't been recorded.

This book acknowledges the overrepresentation of men not only in the volume of Black male artists working during this time but also in mural content; many of the likenesses portrayed on the walls are male figures of history. When this proves not to be the case, this book makes sure to highlight

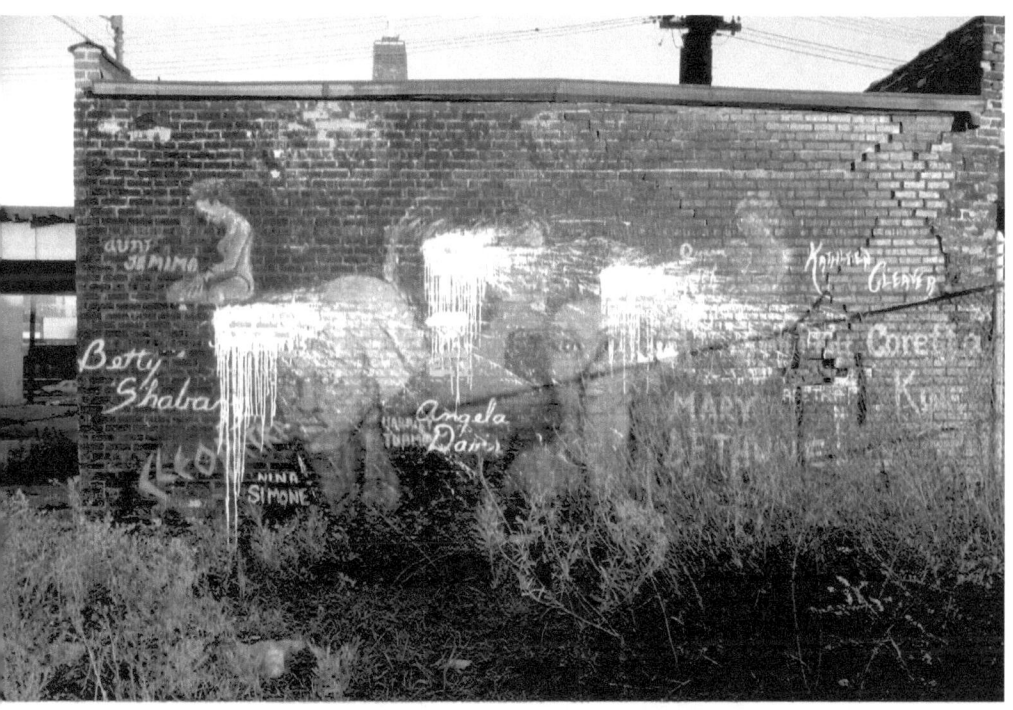

Black Women (Racism) (1970), 861 N. Orleans, Chestnut and Orleans, Chicago, Ill. Painted by Vanita Green. Photograph by Georg Stahl. Courtesy of the Georg Stahl Mural Collection, University of Chicago Visual Resources Center Luna Collection.

these female heroes. Although I am situating murals in the movement for Black liberation, the smaller presence of female artists is not emblematic of the instrumental and still overlooked role Black women played and continue to play in the fight for Black freedom. "Black female heroism must, first and foremost, be understood on its own terms rather than in conjunction with a black male continuum of resistance," writes Bernier.[25] Therefore, while Black female artists are an undeniable and seminal part of the Black mural movement that is layered into this book, their contribution necessitates a more thorough and comprehensive study than what is offered in *A Monument to Blackness*.

This book is about communities and neighborhoods, and as Zorach points out, "community" can take many forms and involve many different groups that, in turn, bring both contrasting and united ideologies and viewpoints.[26] Black communities are not monolithic, and while I use the term "community" to discuss the geographical space inhabited by a group of residents, I acknowledge and understand the gamut of political thought that may live among the neighborhoods discussed throughout this book. These are multifaceted neighborhoods, united through location, race, and class and divergent in political and cultural opinion, so when I speak of "community," I seek not to flatten out the range of beliefs throughout these areas but to acknowledge their multivocality. As such, I try, where research and interviews permit me, to texture mural analysis with counternarratives, complex community discussions, and any disputes among residents or artists. I do this to make sure that the power of murals isn't overexaggerated. While the murals in this book undeniably helped shape individual and collective identity and transform public space, not every mural was always successful, and not every resident was enamored with, or inspired by, its presence.

Chapter 1 begins in the 1930s and sets the stage for the birth of this artistic protest tradition arcing across the twentieth and twenty-first centuries. Set against the backdrop of the Harlem Renaissance and New Deal era, the chapter shows us how murals became bastions of Black artistic agency for the first time in the twentieth century. Empowering in content, these interior murals became renegotiated as vessels of protest, creating unprecedented visual languages of revolution and radicalism that challenged the pervasive iconographies and ideologies of white supremacy across the nation. Pinpointing the arrival of Black murals in the street in 1967, chapter 2 stands as a largely contextual and introductory chapter for the following chapters, which are set against the backdrop of Black Power. It offers an understanding of why Black street murals emerged during the 1960s with *Wall of Respect* (1967). Through a reading of this mural, this chapter tells us more broadly about the unprecedented role murals played in communities, why they were so unique and important in the fight for cultural and racial self-definition during the crusade for Black Power, and how the *Wall of Respect* became an inspiration (and in some cases a template) for subsequent street murals. This chapter works closely with chapter 1 to demonstrate how street murals of the 1960s were a continuation of and evolution from their interior predecessors of the 1930s and 1940s, embedded into the fight for Black emotional, physical, intellectual, and spiritual liberation.

Expanding more specifically upon the context of chapter 2, chapter 3 looks more closely at some of the interactive roles Black murals played in communities across the country during the 1960s and 1970s. Delving into the artistic and sacred celebrations of Blackness inspired by murals, the chapter focuses on the intricate relationship murals have with ritual. Murals invigorate the streets and its residents, and this chapter looks at how murals are used to heal physical and emotional space in the aftermath of racial rebellions and how they inspire individual and communal performances at their site. Closely tied to chapters 2 and 3 and continuing to explore the radical 1960s, chapter 4 looks in detail at how murals could be didactic and educative when artists used community walls as sites of communication and teaching. By confronting the threat to erase Black history and culture from every facet of American life, murals stood on the nation's public landscape to promote truth and pride, telling Black communities about a Black history overlooked and about Black news not reported.

Moving forward in time, then, chapter 5 is set against the backdrop of the 1980s and 1990s, against a deepening neoconservatism, and against a racial reckoning with the wins and losses of both the civil rights movement and the Black Power Movement. This chapter documents how artists of the 1980s and 1990s used murals to confront the new racial, social, political, and economic hurdles of the decades but to still heal, inspire, transform, and educate Black communities. This book ends in the present day—in the age of Black Lives Matter. In the Black mural tradition stretching across the twentieth and twenty-first centuries, we find ourselves today in a new moment that began in 2009 with the killing of Oscar Grant, and this chapter looks not only at how these murals fit into the broader mural movement of the last hundred years but also at how they are used against the assaults on Black life to commemorate, rehumanize, and immortalize their memories so often distorted in the mainstream media.

This book tells the story of Black muralism from the days of racial segregation and the laws of Jim Crow during the 1930s to the present, when those hired to lawfully protect American citizens perpetuate new forms of fatal racial violence in the streets. As we've moved through the last hundred years striving for Black liberation, murals have lined the streets along the way. From Southern lynchings at the beginning of the twentieth century to moments of contemporary lynchings in the streets of Black America today, murals have stood as monuments to Blackness, reminding the nation of the indelible and irreplaceable presence of Black history, culture, and memory throughout the country.

Murals and Movements

A Brief History

This section documents the main evolutions in artists, context and movements, content and style, location, and funding across the last hundred years. While the mural movement has adapted and grown organically between the 1930s and the present day, the shifts documented here are by no means an exhaustive discussion of how the movement has developed across time—and there are always exceptions to these broader characteristics. I provide an overview of the ways in which the movement has, more generally, expanded and evolved from the 1930s and 1940s, into the movement for Black Power, through the post–civil rights era of the 1980s and 1990s, and into the Black Lives Matter movement today. This overview shows in more detail the sheer spread of Black murals and how murals in each era build upon their predecessors to add complexity to the movement as it advances through time, responding to new social, racial, political, and economic turbulence.

This section also acts as a foundation and a bird's-eye view of the mural movement more broadly, discussing key artists and murals of each era. It highlights the breadth of this movement and situates the in-depth examples of murals and their respective contexts in the following chapters. In other words, what you see here is the expansive forest before the individual trees in the chapters to come.

1930s–1950s

As we'll see in the following chapter, the 1930s to the 1950s was a deeply complex period of warring ideologies, a second world war, the rise of the Cold War, and an economic recession. It was a period when modernism and social realism dominated the cultural milieu and when Black muralists began showcasing and celebrating figures of Black history, radical and revolutionary imagery, and the likenesses of ordinary, everyday people. Modernist mural series such as Aaron Douglas's *Aspects of Negro Life* (1934) at the

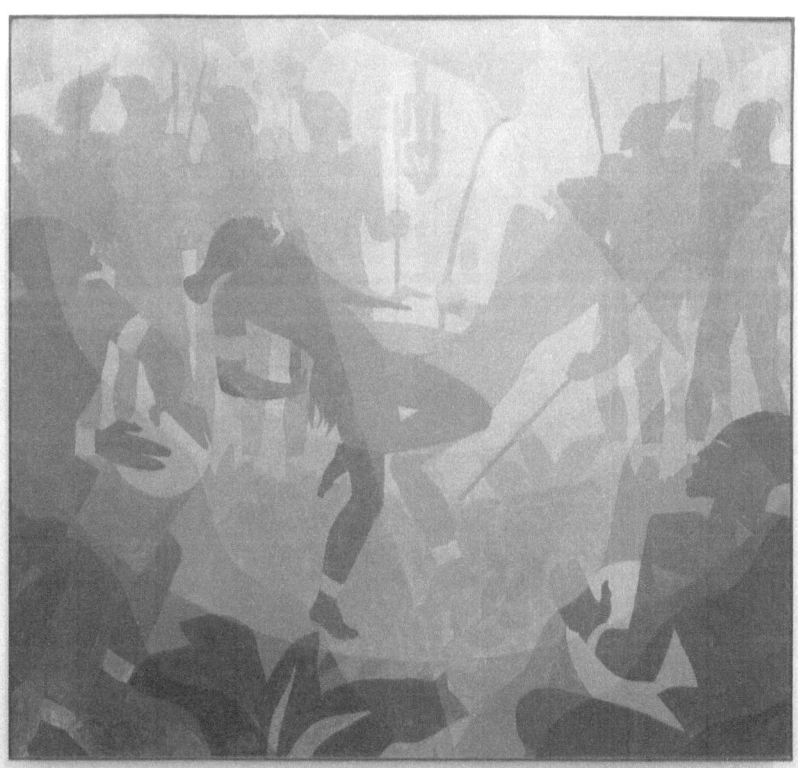

Aspects of Negro Life: The Negro in an African Setting (1934), Schomburg Center for Research in Black Culture, Art and Artifacts Division, New York, N.Y. Painted by Aaron Douglas. Image courtesy of the New York Public Library Digital Collections.

New York Public Library in Harlem and Charles White's social realist mural *Contribution of the Negro to Democracy in America* (1943) at Hampton Institute were some of the most important painted during this period, as we'll see in chapter 1, but they didn't stand alone.

Aaron Douglas's murals punctuated the era. In 1927 he painted a mural called *Jungle and Jazz* at a Harlem nightclub, Club Ebony, on 129th Street and Lenox Avenue. This mural animated the space of the nightclub and mimicked the vibrant and dynamic dance performances inside. Although the mural has been either lost or destroyed (most likely the latter), reviews and newspaper articles give us a brief snapshot into what it may have looked like. We learn from an article in the *Kansas City Call* that the mural was— much like Douglas's later murals—full of "tropical settings of huge trees and flowers, figures of African tom-tom players and dancers, pictures of the American Negro with a banjo and in cakewalk," and on the main panel,

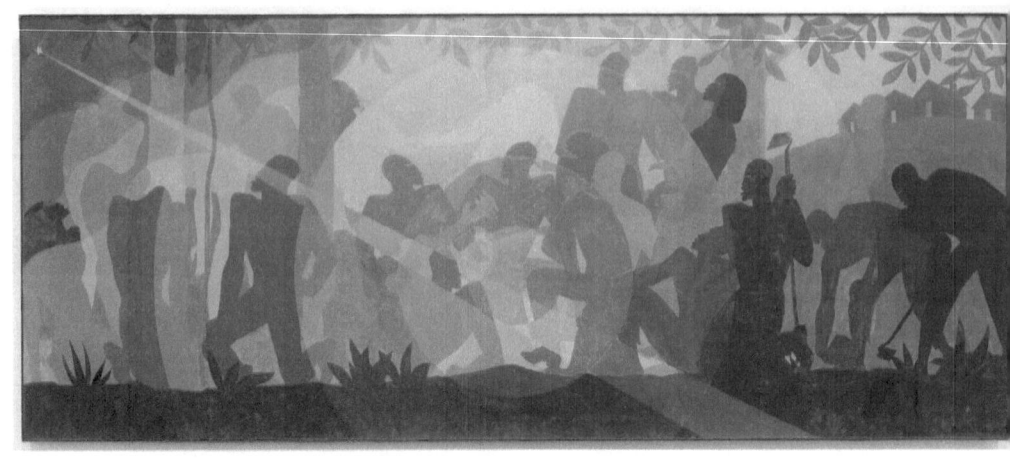

Aspects of Negro Life: An Idyll of the Deep South (1934), Schomburg Center for Research in Black Culture, Art and Artifacts Division, New York, N.Y. Painted by Aaron Douglas. Image courtesy of the New York Public Library Digital Collections.

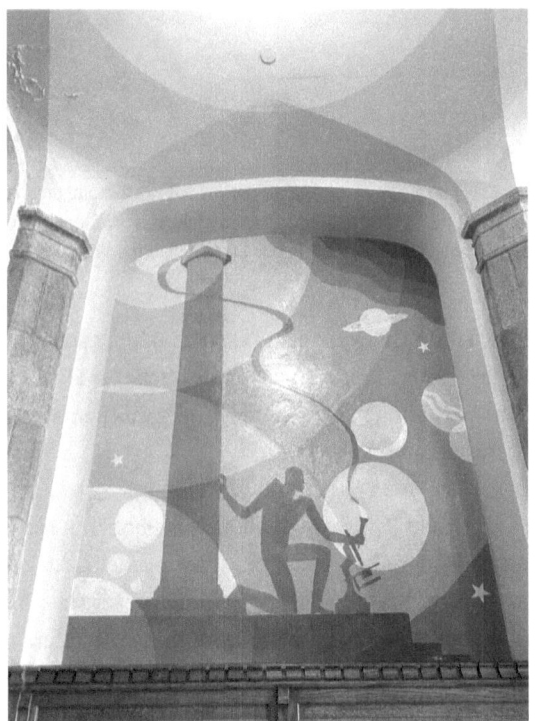

Cravath Hall murals (1930), Cravath Hall, Fisk University, Nashville, Tenn. Painted by Aaron Douglas. Photograph taken by the author.

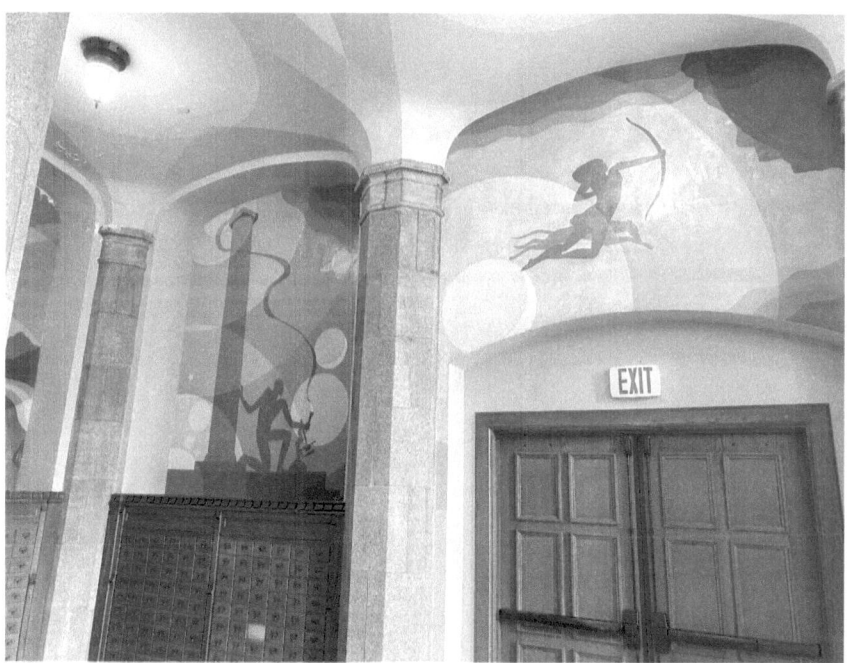

Cravath Hall murals (1930), Cravath Hall, Fisk University, Nashville, Tenn. Painted by Aaron Douglas. Photograph taken by the author.

"silhouetted against a background of modern skyscrapers are the forms of contemporary race dancers and musicians."[1]

Three years later, Douglas was commissioned to create a mural at the Sherman Hotel called *Dance Magic*. He then worked on multiple projects at Black colleges in the South, completing a series of murals—*Negro in Africa, Negro Labor, Negro in America, Spirituals, Inspiration,* and *Night*—at Cravath Library (now Cravath Hall) at Fisk University in Nashville, as well as his mural *Harriet Tubman (Spirits Rising)* at Bennett College in Greensboro, North Carolina. Dominating the early 1930s, he continued to paint murals such as his 1934 *Aspects* series in Harlem before being commissioned to create a series at the Texas Centennial Exposition in Dallas in 1936 (discussed in detail in the following chapter).

The following year, 1936, artist Charles Alston led around thirty assistants—including Georgette Seabrooke, Vertis Hayes, and Beauford Delaney—in painting the Harlem Hospital mural series, where his seventeen-by-six-foot panels, *Mystery and Magic* and *Modern Medicine,* stood at the heart of the project in the Women's Pavilion lobby at 506 Malcolm X Boulevard. For this project, Seabrooke also created her own panel for the nurses' recreation room called *Recreation in Harlem*. A year later, under his work for the Federal Art Project (FAP), artist Archibald Motley painted a mural for a post office in Wood River, Illinois, titled *Stagecoach and Mail*. While the mural is painted in Motley's signature vibrant style, the content itself is more generic, depicting men riding in a horse-drawn carriage and delivering mail across the country. The following year, 1938 (after studying in Mexico with Diego Rivera in 1936), Hale Woodruff embarked on a social realist revolutionary mural series at Talladega College in Alabama that detailed the institution's rich cultural history and told an inspiring story of enslavement, revolution, and liberation. His six-part series begins with the *Amistad* rebellion and subsequent trials before detailing the founding of Talladega College.

The closing year of the 1930s saw the creation of a mural by John Wilson painted at the Roxbury Boys Club, as well as Charles White's first mural, *Five Great American Negroes*, for the Chicago Public Library. Sponsored by the Works Progress Administration (WPA), White's social realist mural calls upon the figures of Sojourner Truth, Booker T. Washington, Frederick Douglass, George Washington Carver, and Marian Anderson to reclaim narratives of Black dignity, history, and resilience and to celebrate Black life. "Because the white man does not understand the history of the Negro, he misunderstands it," White believed, and he used this ethos as an undercurrent throughout much of his work, especially in the 1930s and 1940s.[2]

The dawning of the 1940s saw many more murals created across the country. In 1940, six years before he went to study at the Escuela Nacional de Pintura y Escultura and the Taller de Gráfica Popular in Mexico City, White was commissioned by the Associated Negro Press to create his next mural, *History of the Negro Press*, for the Negro Exposition at the Chicago Coliseum. Three years later, he created perhaps his most prolific and recognizable mural, *Contribution of the Negro to Democracy in America* (detailed in the following chapter). That same year, William Edouard Scott, with sponsorship from the U.S. Treasury Department of Fine Arts, created *Frederick Douglass Appeals to President Lincoln* at the Recorder of the Deeds Building in Washington, D.C. The mural depicts a historical meeting between the abolitionist and the president in which Douglass advises Lincoln to enlist Black soldiers into the Union army during the Civil War. The closing of the decade also saw a famous mural collaboration between Woodruff and Alston, who were commissioned to create a mural for the Golden State Mutual Life Insurance

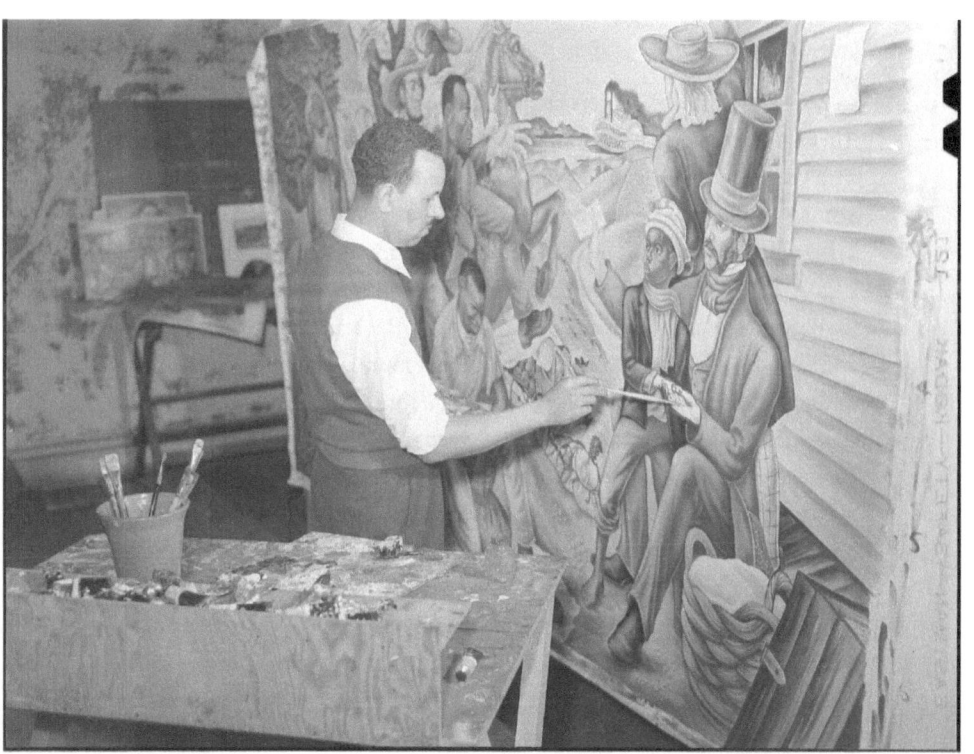

Amistad Mural Series: Underground Railroad (1942), Talladega College, Talladega, Ala. Painted by Hale Woodruff. Image courtesy of the Library of Congress Prints and Photographs Division. Farm Security Administration / Office of War Information photograph collection.

Company titled *The Negro in California History*, which consisted of two panels, *Exploration and Colonization* and *Settlement and Development*.

It was during this decade, too, that muralist John Biggers emerged from under the tutelage of Charles White and Viktor Lowenfeld at Hampton Institute. "I watched his [White's] every step, became his helper, made myself as useful as I could to him," Biggers said of his time spent assisting White on *Contribution of the Negro to Democracy in America* in 1943, a year after he created *Dying Solider*, which depicts the inevitability of military service and the emotional, physical, and mental effects of war.[3] "Pearl Harbor affected us all to such an extent that many dropped out of school that Sunday morning to join the service. The soldier in that drawing is me," Biggers said of the mural. "I was thinking about all I would lose, and I just began to draw my thoughts."[4] The following year, after the success of *Dying Soldier*, which went on to be displayed in the Young Negro Art exhibition at the Museum of Modern Art in New York in 1943, Biggers created his second mural, *Community Preacher*. This mural speaks to the power of the preacher in the Black community and, in a traditional call-and-response fashion, the genuine emotions evoked among a congregation during a sermon. Three years later, in 1946, the powerful mural was bought by the United Transport Service Employees in Chicago, where it was displayed following an unveiling ceremony.

Biggers's murals continued to punctuate the artistic landscape up until the 1990s, with some of his most potent murals emerging in the 1940s and 1950s. He created *U.S. Navy Mural* (1945) for the U.S. Naval Gymnasium, inspired by his time in the service between 1943 and 1945. During his four years at Penn State University between 1946 and 1949, he painted around a dozen murals, including *Burial*, *Sharecroppers*, *Baptism*, *Day of the Harvest*, and *Night of the Poor*. Following his time in Pennsylvania, he then migrated down south, back to his roots. "I went to Greenwich Village very early and found I didn't have anything in common with the people there," he admitted. "I felt that if I had anything to say, I would have to say it in the South. I wanted to come where I felt the black people's roots really are—and they are in the South."[5] Settling in Houston, Texas, Biggers agreed to establish an art department at the Texas State College for Negroes. During his time there, he continued mural painting, creating works such as *Harvesters and Gleaners* (1952), *Contribution of Negro Women to American Life and Education* (1953), *History of the International Longshoreman's Local* (1957), and *Web of Life* (1958).

But Biggers wasn't the only artist creating murals into the 1950s. In 1950–51 Hale Woodruff painted his *Art of the Negro* series in Trevor Arnett Hall at Clark Atlanta University. The mural series is made up of six panels, *Native Forms*, *Interchange*, *Dissipation*, *Parallels*, *Influences*, and *Muses*, and is a "token of my esteem for African art," Woodruff explained. "I wanted it to be something of an inspiration to the students who go to the library, to see something about the art of their ancestors," he continued. "There are many artists and other people today who believe that we have no part of Africa's history. I look at the African artist certainly as one of my ancestors regardless of how we feel about each other today. I've always had a high regard and respect for the African artist and his art."[6]

While this is by no means an exhaustive list of every mural painted between the 1930s and the 1960s, it certainly shows us the pervasiveness of these large-scale forms of public art in colleges, government buildings, and public institutions across the country. But this burgeoning artistic medium didn't just survive for thirty-plus years because of its magnetic and unprecedented visual content. It also needed funding to sustain itself. During this period, patronage took many forms, sometimes drawing criticism and sometimes impacting the visual content (more on this in the following chapter). It ranged from official government sources such as the Works Progress Administration and Federal Art Project, established under the umbrella of the New Deal (discussed in chapter 1); to formal philanthropic sources; to Black colleges and universities; and even to independent sources such as wealthy individual white patrons during the Harlem Renaissance, including Carl Van Vechten and Charlotte Osgood Mason. Sometimes even Black businesses, such as the Los Angeles Golden State Mutual Life Insurance Company, would put up funding for murals, as they did for Woodruff and Alston's *Negro in California History.*

White philanthropic sources such as the Julius Rosenwald Fund, the William E. Harmon Foundation, and the Barnes Foundation were major players on the funding landscape during this era. In the 1930s and 1940s many African American artists and writers such as Charles Alston, Chester Himes, Arna Bontemps, Zora Neale Hurston, Ralph Ellison, James Baldwin, Gordon Parks, Margaret Walker, and Jacob Lawrence had notable success securing funding from the Rosenwald Fund. Established by the Jewish businessman Julius Rosenwald, part owner of Sears, Roebuck and Company, the fund was initially set up in 1917 to further the "general wellbeing of mankind, primarily through an ethic of self-help roughly akin to that advocated by Booker T. Washington."[7] Rosenwald was apparently moved after reading Washington's *Up from Slavery* and sought to help African American communities across the country. Between 1917 and 1924 he gave $4 million to build 5,000 elementary schools, 195 teachers' homes, 103 workshops, and 5 industrial high schools.[8] In 1932, however, under the direction of Edwin Rogers Embree following the death of Rosenwald, the foundation shifted its platform slightly, moving more toward an "increasingly liberal agenda" by funding Black university endowments, the construction of law and medical schools, fellowships, and a vast number of works in the visual arts and literature.[9] In the early 1930s, for example, Hale Woodruff used his fellowship funds to paint a series of landscapes on soil erosion. Charles White used his Rosenwald Fellowship in part to create his *Contribution of the Negro to Democracy in America* mural at Hampton Institute. And in 1946 artist Elizabeth Catlett used her fellowship to develop a linocut series, *The Negro Woman*, which enabled her to study at the Taller de Gráfica Popular in Mexico City.

A few years after the Rosenwald Fund was established, in 1922 self-made real estate tycoon William E. Harmon created the Harmon Foundation. With a great love for and admiration of African American culture, Harmon was invested in finding ways to help individuals "who had not previously had any offers of assistance or reward."[10] Similar to the Rosenwald model, the Harmon Foundation funded ventures such as playgrounds across the country, educational programs for nurses, tuition assistance, and vocational guidance for students. It also funded large-scale events such as the Texas Centennial Exposition in Dallas (including Aaron Douglas's mural series) and individuals such as Countee Cullen, Laura Wheeler Waring, Sargent Johnson, and Langston Hughes for his award-winning novel, *Not Without Laughter* (1930). A few years after the foundation was established, Harmon organized exhibitions across the country to showcase the talent the foundation had accumulated because of its fellowships.

These forms of philanthropic patronage, however, while successful on the surface, were not without critique. In 1933, for example, when the Harmon Foundation closed its annual African American art exhibitions, Black artists spoke up about the patronizing attitude of the foundation. "It has encouraged the artist to exhibit long before he [sic] has mastered the technical equipment of his medium," artist Romare Bearden stated in 1934. "By its choice of the type of work it favors, it has allowed the Negro artist to accept standards that are both artificial and corrupt."[11] The foundation rushed artists, Aaron Douglas agreed, thrusting them into the spotlight prematurely. "Harlem was sifted," he argued. "Neither streets, homes nor public institutions escaped. When unsuspecting Negroes were found with a brush in their hands they were immediately hauled away and held for interpretation. They were given places of honor and bowed to with much ceremony. Every effort to protest their innocence was drowned out with big-mouthed praise. A number escaped and returned to a more reasonable existence. Many fell in with the game and went along making hollow and meaningless gestures with brush and palette. But . . . the Negro artists have emerged."[12]

Patronage, especially from white donors, brought with it a level of complexity and a level of control, according to many critics. During the Harlem Renaissance, individual wealthy white patrons such as Van Vechten and Mason had a particular fascination with "primitivism" and urged Black artists (writers, painters, poets, etc.) to explore this theme through the work they funded. One of the most notable critics of this form of patronage comes from Nathan Huggins in his 1971 book, *Harlem Renaissance*: "By 1926, then, white Americans, were prepared to patronize the Negro. After a history of struggle, of being an outcast, of being viewed with contempt or pity, the Negro was now quoted and cultivated by cultured whites. How grand it was to be valued not for what one might become—the benevolent view of uplift—but for what was thought to be one's essential self, one's Negro-ness."[13]

A more moderate argument on the role of patronage, however, comes from David Levering Lewis's *When Harlem Was in Vogue* (1979):

> White capital and influence were crucial, and the white presence, at least in the early years, hovered over the Negro world of art and literature like a benevolent sensor, politely but pervasively setting the outer limits of its creative boundaries. The motives of the whites, however, was as varied as those of the African American intelligentsia were single minded, and the whites' disunity provided room to play fast and loose along the borders of the arts or for raids even into the heartland of racism. Not being taken seriously—or taken seriously for the wrong reasons—had advantages, so long as leaders like Charles Johnston, James Weldon Johnson, and W. E. B. Du Bois knew what they were doing, were cautious about it, and adroitly manipulated their white patrons and allies.[14]

Lewis's point regarding the subversion and manipulation of Black artists speaks to how Black recipients were able to instead control white patrons for the artists' own artistic gains. It speaks directly to Douglas's conception of the Harlem Renaissance, where he emphatically rejects the notion of white control over Black artists: "There were certain white people at that time that came in contact with blacks and helped make it possible for them to reach a level from which they could create, but this was not something dictated by white culture. They were handling it, looking at it, seeing this thing going on there, but *we* were the ones that were creating this."[15]

This debate around white patronage during the 1920s, 1930s, and 1940s is a long and complex story that is touched upon again in the following chapter but that is analyzed in more depth in works such as *Harlem Renaissance Reader*, edited by David Levering Lewis (1994); Nathan Irvin Huggins's *Harlem Renaissance* (1971); David Levering Lewis's *When Harlem Was in Vogue* (1979); and Amy Helene Kirschke's *Aaron Douglas: Art, Race & the Harlem Re-*

naissance (1995). It is important to understand here, though, the multiple and diverse funding streams that were available (with potential restrictions and caveats) to Black artists, particularly Black muralists, during this era. With philanthropic organizations, governmental agencies, independent white patrons, Black businesses, and Black institutions such as the Hampton Institute and Talladega College offering support to artists, muralists had a handful of avenues through which they could subvert, manipulate, reclaim, and thus create their groundbreaking and radical celebrations of Blackness.

1960s–1970s

The murals of John Biggers and Hale Woodruff continued to line the walls of Black institutions deep into the 1950s, but as the decade wore on, the mural movement was bracing itself for an evolution. As will be discussed in detail in chapter 2, the social, political, and racial climate of the late 1950s and early 1960s set the stage for the next iteration of murals. As the funding landscape changed, as residential segregation deepened, and as the ideological permeations of a burgeoning new Black Power and Black consciousness began to grip communities across the country, murals could no longer be contained inside public buildings. They evolved to become large-scale works of art in the streets of Black America, wallpapering neighborhoods from border to border and coast to coast, continuing to assert Blackness and make statements about the world around them. These murals would be democratizing in nature because they were made and created in dialogue with neighborhood residents. In similar fashion to their artistic forebears, they had a thematic focus on Black beauty, consciousness, and pride; on sharing the headlines of the day, no matter how bleak or upsetting; and on commemorating Black history. But unlike their earlier counterparts, they were able to have a greater sense of immediacy and availability because they were painted on the outside walls of buildings in Black neighborhoods for passersby to contemplate at all hours of the day and night.

In many ways, street murals of the 1960s and 1970s seem much less "official." Their frequent lack of a formal setting (e.g., in an alley instead of a library) perhaps accounts at least in part for why the number of murals grew exponentially during this period. Issues around securing a location could be much more direct and casual by simply asking the owner of the building if they'd agree to the mural. What happened during the 1960s and 1970s, then, against a backdrop of Black Power, the Vietnam War, a countercultural

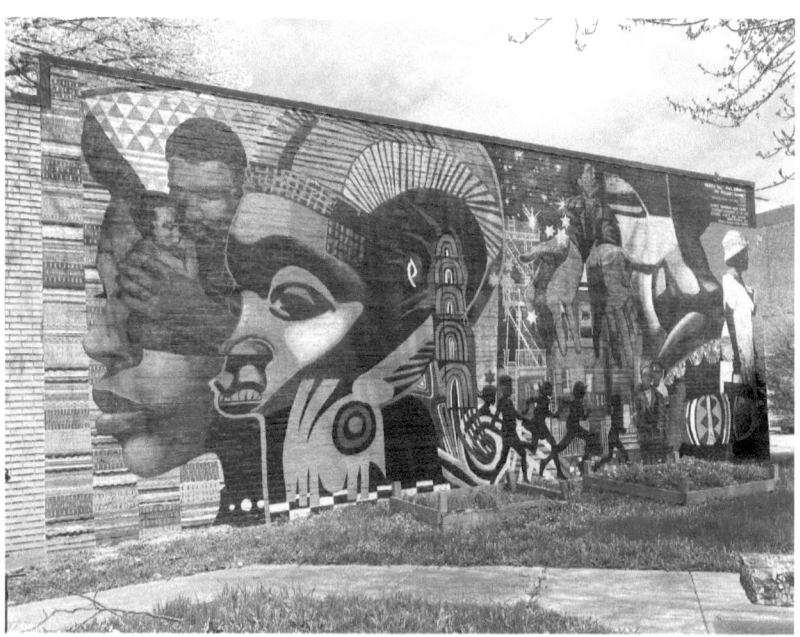

Another Time's Voice Remembers My Passion's Humanity (1979), Elliot Donelley Youth Center Community Art Garden, 3947 S. Michigan Avenue, Chicago, Ill. Painted by Mitchell Caton and Calvin Jones. Restored by Bernard Williams and Damon Lamar Reed in 1998 and 2018. Photograph taken by the author.

revolution, and a host of political assassinations across the globe, is a large sweep of Black murals across the country. Starting in the epicenter of the Midwest and rippling down the East Coast, across the South, and up the West Coast, a series of artists used walls as a form of public demonstration.

While Chicago is well known for its groundbreaking (and first) Black street mural, the *Wall of Respect*, created by Bill Walker and members of the Organization of Black American Culture (OBAC) (and later Eugene "Eda" Wade), the city played host to many other prominent muralists working during the 1960s and 1970s. Don McIlvaine, for example, created a series of murals on both the south and west sides of the city. In 1969 he painted *Into the Mainstream* at Lawndale Avenue and 16th Street, and the following year he created one of his most well-known murals with the gang the Conservative Vicelords titled *Black Man's Dilemma*, which detailed "street scenes—the kinds of things that went on in the community."[16] Working at the same time was muralist Mitchell Caton, who created murals such as *Nation Time* (1971) at 4141 South Cottage Grove Avenue and *Wall of Self-Awareness* (1974), as well as collaborative murals such as *Rip-Off / Universal Alley* with C. Siddha Sila

Webber (discussed in chapter 3), *Prescription for Good Health Care* (1975) with Caryl Yasko and Georg Stahl, *Wall of Daydreaming / Man's Inhumanity to Man* (1975) with Walker and Santi Isrowuthukal, *A Time to Unite* (1976) with Calvin Jones and Justine DeVan, and *Another Time's Voice Remembers My Passion's Humanity* (1979) with Calvin Jones, still standing at the Elliott Donnelley Youth Center on South Michigan Avenue. In 1977 Justine DeVan decorated a street in Cottage Grove with her empowering mural *Black Women Emerging* (1977, discussed further in chapter 2), and Bill Walker continued to create a vast number of murals across the city alongside artists such as C. Siddha Sila Webber, Calvin Jones, Bernard Williams, and Eugene "Eda" Wade.[17] Also emerging in Chicago during this period was the Chicago Mural Group (now the Chicago Public Art Group), which was founded in 1972 by Bill Walker and white Chicago muralist John Pitman Weber.

The tremors of the Black mural movement were felt throughout the Midwest—south in the city of St. Louis in 1968 with the mural *Wall of Respect*, painted by LeRoy White, and eastward in the city of Detroit. Here, murals across the city depicted proud images of Blackness by artists such as Walker and Wade (discussed in chapter 3); LeRoy Foster, who created *Life and Times of Frederick Douglass* (1973); and Jon Onye Lockard, who painted a Pan-African mural with the figure of Shaka Zulu titled *Continuum* (1980) at Manoogian Hall, Wayne State University.

The mural movement was also in action up and down the East Coast in cities such as Boston, where artist Sharon Dunn created one of the first women's murals in the country at Yarmouth Street and Columbus Avenue in South Boston titled *Maternity* (1970) and James Brown painted *The Third Nail* (1971), depicting a Black child shooting up, on the side of a rehabilitation center. Also painting in Boston during the 1960s and 1970s were Arnold Hurley, Dana Chandler, and Gary Rickson, the latter of whom collaboratively created *Exodus Building Mural* (1968), *Segregation B.C.*, and *Stokely and Rap* (1968), as well as their own individual murals. In 1969 Gary Rickson created *Africa Is the Beginning* (1969) at the YMCA in Roxbury, and Dana Chandler painted *Knowledge Is Power: Stay in School* (1972) at Ziegler and Warren Streets, Roxbury, and *The Black Worker* (1973) before joining forces that same year with Nelson Stevens to create *Work to Unify African People* (1973) at the United Construction Workers Labor Temple, also in Roxbury.

In New York City, collaborative interracial mural groups (which began to spring up during this era) such as Smokehouse Associates and Cityarts

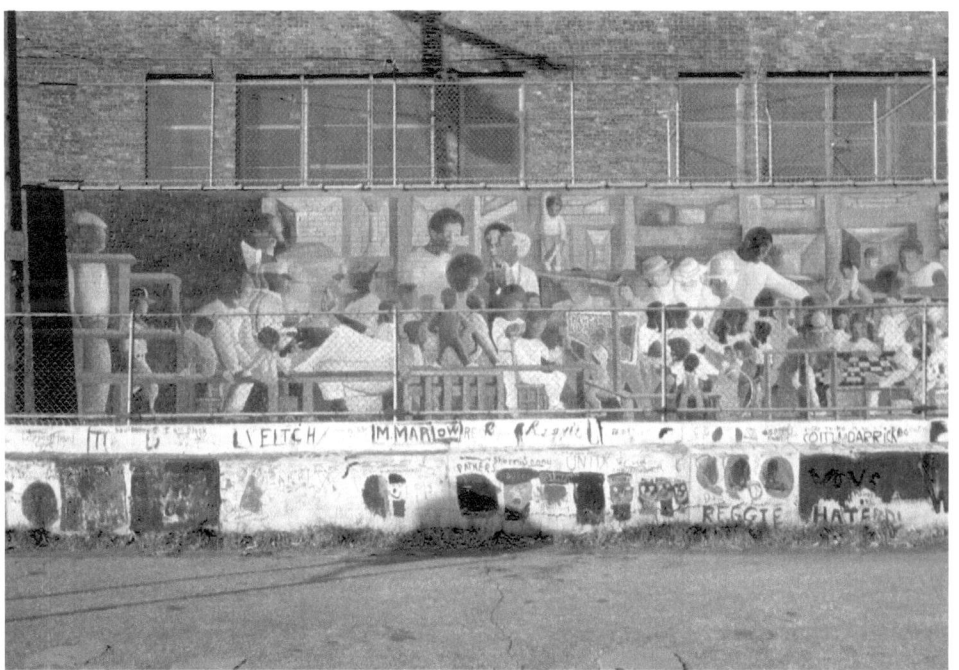

Black Love (1971), 515 W. Oak, Opportunities Industrial Center, Chicago, Ill. Painted by William Walker. Photograph by Georg Stahl. Courtesy of the Georg Stahl Mural Collection, University of Chicago Visual Resources Center Luna Collection.

emerged. Smokehouse Associates included artists such as William T. Williams, Melvin Edwards, Guy Ciarcia, and Billy Rose, and Cityarts included Susan Kiok, Susan Caruso Green, Tomie Arai, Joe Stephenson, and Alan Okada.[18] At the same time and south of New York in the nation's capital, James A. Padgett began creating murals in 1968 with his first piece, *Fine Art, Art, Music, Drama, Past, and Present*, displayed externally at the Fine Arts Building at Howard University. He continued creating murals the following year at the Anacostia Museum and produced *The Aspect of Music*.

In Philadelphia, murals created in the 1960s and 1970s showed Black history, Black consciousness, and Black pride through a myriad of ways. In the late 1960s, artist Justine DeVan, who would go on to create murals in Chicago and become part of the Chicago Mural Group, was approached by Fellowship House, a Quaker social service agency, to paint a series of transportable murals detailing Black heroes throughout history. These murals would be displayed at schools around the Philadelphia.[19] In 1971 Bernard Young designed a mural for 57th Street and Haverford Avenue, in Haddington, Pennsylvania, that was painted by the Haddington Leadership Association. Titled *Wall of Consciousness* but pulling thematic and compositional inspiration heavily from Chicago's *Wall of Respect*, the mural had a backdrop of red, green, and black—symbolizing Black liberation—and upon it were the faces of Black figures such as Jesse Jackson, Malcolm X, Wilt Chamberlain, and Black Jesus. That same year, Clarence Wood and Gary Small, along with artists and local children, painted an untitled mural at the James Rhoads School on 50th Street and Parrish that depicted, in similar fashion to the *Wall of Respect*, the likenesses of Black heroes such as Adam Clayton Powell, Muhammad Ali, Marian Anderson, and Shirley Chisholm.

While the South wasn't necessarily a hotbed for mural activity in the same way the Midwest was, there were still artists working throughout the region in the 1970s, and some of them continued to draw inspiration from the 1967 *Wall of Respect*. In 1976 Amos Johnson, Vera Parks, and Nathan Hoskins created a mural by the same name in downtown Atlanta. Beautifully painted in hyperrealistic detail, the mural depicted the likenesses of Black heroes Angela Davis, Muhammad Ali, W. E. B. Du Bois, Malcolm X, Frederick Douglass, and Martin Luther King Jr. alongside an Egyptian pharaoh, African masks, and a clenched and opening fist. Also in the South and in similar celebratory fashion but with a much more intricate composition, Charles Davis and George Hunt painted the first community mural in Memphis, *A Tribute to Beale Street* (1980), on Second and Beale Streets. The mural depicts the history of Black music and included figures such as Father of the Blues, W. C. Handy, and Memphis politician Boss Crump. The keys of an elongated piano stretch across the mural and morph into the strings of a guitar, around which are a host of narrative scenes of history, as the mural tells a story from African music, to enslavement, to the evolution of Black music in America.

The West Coast emerged as another stronghold of Black muralism and muralism in general. California in the 1960s and 1970s was a complicated and multilayered bastion of political and cultural ideology and identity, and it was home to a countercultural revolution of peace, free love, and mind expansion, with groups such as the Haight Ashbury Muralists creating collaborative murals. Gaining real prominence along the West Coast and happening in tandem with the Black mural movement was the Chicano/a mural movement, which gave rise to national landmarks such as San Diego's Chicano Park from 1970. In many ways (as was happening across the country), "Black, Chicano, and Puerto Rican artists [and later Asian American artists] learned from each other."[20] With all ethnic groups experiencing both insidious and overt forms of racism across the country, many artists used the mural form to reclaim neighborhoods and reaffirm a sense of cultural pride through public artworks.[21]

In large urban centers such as Los Angeles, San Francisco, and Oakland, Black muralists began using walls just as they had done throughout the country—to assert a Black presence and to celebrate Black history. In 1969 Chicago-born muralist David Bradford (who had spent a few days working on the Chicago *Wall of Respect*) was approached to create a series of interracial murals for the East Oakland Development Center, a building that would go on to become Merritt College, where Huey P. Newton and Bobby Seale met and founded the Black Panther Party. He created these murals with prominent Chicano artists Malaquías Montoya and Manuel Hernández Trujillo. In Bradford's panels, we see lines of African American figures, some in colorful clothing, some in suits, and some in dashikis, and below them are figures huddled in a basement, discussing a plan, with guns piled to the side.

Five years later, Bradford created another powerful mural, this time in the Fillmore District of San Francisco. Titled WAPAC Mural, the mural stood as a rebuttal to urban renewal in the Fillmore area. In the 1970s, run-down buildings in the neighborhood were redeveloped into fancy housing for rich elites, provoking confrontation between the local Black community and the Redevelopment Agency. The Western Addition Project Area Commission (WAPAC), acting on behalf on the Black residents of Fillmore, argued that housing should be provided for displaced residents and that residents should be used in renovation and construction work.[22] The Redevelopment Agency paused demolition and listened to the demands of the WAPAC, inspiring Bradford's mural, which shows an empowered central figure liberating himself by ripping apart his shackles and holding his unbound hands aloft above local landmarks and the Victorian houses currently slated for renovation. In front of him stand figures of history—Malcolm X, Billie Holiday, Martin Luther King Jr., Nat Turner, John Coltrane, Duke Ellington, and Jonathan Jackson, who is wielding a machine gun as he raids a Marin County courtroom in an attempt to free his brother George Jackson. Nestled between the figures are a series of steps labeled with the names Tubman, Turner, Garvey, Lumumba, Malcolm, King, and Jackson.

Also working in San Francisco at the same time as Bradford was Robert

Gayton, who painted *Cultural Black Folks* in 1972 on the wall of a warehouse that had been condemned for dereliction in the Fillmore District. In similar fashion to the *Wall of Respect*, his mural brought together notable figures of history such as Joe Louis, Frederick Douglass, Angela Davis, and Malcolm X. Four years later and also in the Fillmore District, Gayton created his 1976 panoramic mural, *Blacks from Egypt to Now*. Upon a clean white backdrop he painted the portraits of Egyptian sphinxes, Queen Nefertiti, and King Tutankhamun along a timeline before adding figures of Black history in the United States. Dewey Crumpler, who is covered extensively in chapter 4, was also working in San Francisco during the 1970s and created *Education Is Truth* (1971) and *The Fire Next Time I* (1977) and *II* (1984) around the Bayview–Hunters Point area of the city, as well as *Multi-Ethnic Heritage: Black, Asian, Native / Latin American* (1974), a mural at George Washington High School in the Richmond District of San Francisco.

Murals of the 1960s and 1970s were a lot more pervasive than their interior predecessors. These murals saw a shift in physical location, being painted directly into the streets. But they also continued physically in the image of their artistic forebears inside institutional buildings, much like Jack Jordan and Jean Paul Hubbard's *Contributions of Blacks to Louisiana History* (1975) mural at Southern University in New Orleans, and Horace Washington and Caleb Williams's 1976 mural, *Crispus Attucks: The Boston Massacre*, painted in the auditorium of the William de Avila Elementary School in San Francisco. During this era, murals also sprang up not only in the streets and not only in schools, universities, and municipal buildings but also in places of worship. In her seminal 2016 book, *Painting the Gospel: Black Public Art and Religion in Chicago*, Kymberly Pinder documents how "black imagery in African American churches has become more common in the last few decades."[23] She discusses Black public art across the city of Chicago, such as Bill Walker's *All of Mankind: The Unity of the Human Race* (1971), at Old Stranger's Home Missionary Baptist Church, and Bernard Williams's *Hagar and Eunuch* (1996) murals at Saint Edmund's Episcopal Church. In the same way that *A Monument to Blackness* seeks to show the importance of the Black mural movement and its attendant artwork, Pinder's book highlights how this religious form of public art "has allowed many socially or economically disenfranchised people of color in the city to see themselves in the source of their salvation, internalizing the equation 'divinity equals blackness,' which transforms their 'nobodiness' into 'somebodiness.'"[24]

It's also worth noting that Black murals of the 1960s and 1970s saw an evolution in style and composition. Many artists subscribed to Charles White's formula of documenting figures of Black history, and they did so in a multitude of ways. Street murals of this era initially followed the *Wall of Respect*'s template (and sometimes name) to show a visually unconnected pantheon of Black heroes across a wall, oftentimes reading like a yearbook of Black history. While this format continued into the 1970s and even beyond, artists also began searching for more complex and intricate ways of telling a broader story about Black life in America, with some still feeling the need to reference Black figures of history. Visual narratives were on the rise, and artists began to create vast, complex stories that drew on imagery from the diaspora and placed it alongside flames, sunbeams, clenched fists, patterned backdrops, psychedelic figures, African masks, Pan-African flags, depictions of music, the birth of the next generation, and images of guns.

From the late 1960s and early 1970s, imagery of defiance and Black self-defense dominated the mural scene. The movements of modernism and social realism were largely left in the past too, but it's important to avoid stylistically pigeonholing artists of the 1960s and 1970s into certain artistic movements. Many artists were working in a host of styles, sometimes dabbling in abstraction, sometimes venturing into cubism, sometimes reviving modernist tendencies, and sometimes resurrecting social realist compositions. This created, in many ways, a new way of painting, a coalition of styles beautifully formulated to explode color and life upon walls in Black communities.

Again, while it's too complex to capture every artist and mural in existence during this period of the 1960s and 1970s, I've tried to show the spread of murals across the country, murals that were inspired by the 1967 *Wall of Respect*, and murals that sprang up because the art form gave artists the room and the physical space to say something other mediums perhaps didn't allow. The era saw the exponential growth of the mural movement in sheer numbers of murals alone; it saw an expansion of style, theme, and composition; and it also gave rise to interracial collaborative mural groups that formed across the country, such as Cityarts Workshop, the Chicago Mural Group, Smokehouse Associates, and the Haight Ashbury Muralists. But in much the same way that mural artists of the 1930s, 1940s, and 1950s had to contend with funding, so too did murals of the 1960s and 1970s.

"As the mural movement was reaching the period of its greatest activity in expansion, it was also undergoing serious stresses," Alan Barnett wrote in *Community Murals: The People's Art* (1984). "One of the key and persistent threats was the difficulty of funding."[25] While most funding for the interior mural movement came from formal sources such as philanthropic fellowships, the WPA and FAP under the New Deal, and Black colleges, the structure of patronage during the 1960s and 1970s was a little different. Support came from a wide variety of sources, including contributions from individuals, churches, local businesses, community organizations, donated equipment and labor from artists, volunteers, apprentices, schools, and colleges, and, like the artists' earlier counterparts, government sources.[26]

Murals of the 1960s and 1970s were grassroots—created by the people, created for the people, and, importantly, created *from* the people. As Barnett estimates, "More than half the funding has been grassroots, coming from local community organizations, merchants and residents."[27] In many instances, muralists were donated walls, paints, scaffolding, and food and drink, and volunteers offered their time to work collaboratively to create murals in their neighborhood. And working in tandem with this grassroots funding was a more official financial channel. In 1965 the National Endowment for the Arts (NEA) was established amid Lyndon B. Johnson's Great Society programs, which aimed "to provide encouragement and financial assistance to the arts."[28] By 1968 the NEA had become involved in inner-city arts programs in an effort to "cool out" areas home to racial rebellions during the long hot summers. (Dana Chandler and Gary Rickson were recipients of these programs through Boston's Summerthing program.) By 1970 the NEA had begun funding outdoor murals through its subprogram Art in Public Places, which directed $5,000 to Boston and $4,000 to Chicago. Three years later, however, funding and support were cut back. "The principal explanation must be the decline of riots and militancy in the inner city together with a recession that began in 1974," Barnett argues. It was racial rebellions that catalyzed federal support in the first place. Muralists knew that "although some of its backers in government were serious about community arts, the main motivation for the NEA money . . . was cooling out the long hot summers."[29] By 1975, however, these artists were able to access another stream of government funding, this time coming out of the Department of Labor. The Comprehensive Employment and Training Act (CETA) began providing training and grants for muralists who were receiving around $700 a month, but by 1981 this funding source had been eliminated entirely.[30]

As is discussed at length in chapter 5, the 1980s, 1990s, and 2000s grappled with the wins and losses of both the civil rights and Black Power movements. It was also an era of austerity and political conservatism marked by unimaginable political assaults on the nation's poor and people of color. Given this sweep of neoconservatism across the national stage under the Republican presidencies of Ronald Reagan and George H. W. Bush and within Bill Clinton's conservative Democratic administration, it's perhaps unsurprising that Reagan's administration sought to cut funding for the National Endowment for the Humanities (NEH) and its subgroup, the NEA, igniting discussions over how history is taught across the nation and in schools.[31] "There are enduring enmities between those who favor a government role in supporting our national cultural life, and those, who for a variety of reasons, do not," Cynthia Koch recounted in her 1998 report, "The Contest for American Culture: A Leadership Case Study on the NEA and NEH Funding Crisis."[32] In 1982 the NEH lost around 14 percent of its $151.3 million budget. The NEA, however, due to an effective lobbying network and dedicated institutional base of arts organizations, was able to maintain a steady stream of funding, although it was hampered by inflation.[33]

Nationally, then, throughout the 1980s, 1990s, and 2000s there was a swell of mural support coming from both private and government funding as well as a push for school mural programs. But while the purse strings remained somewhat loose, the strings of control were tightened in a way they hadn't been during the previous two decades. "Nothing about violence, nothing critical, nothing politically left," mural documentarian Tim Drescher lamented. "Organizations, not artists, controlled imagery, and critical politics was shunned in favor of affirmation."[34] Given the rise of a tempered visual content, "marketing, advertising, and mural painting often overlapped," artist Michael D. Harris argued. "Large advertisements in New York's Times Square, or on well-travelled streets in West Hollywood, California, became like murals and some murals became more like advertisements." He continued by asking, how were passersby supposed to distinguish between "a Michael Jordan Nike ad and the 1988 three-story portrait of Julius Erving in a suit done by non-black artist Kent Twitchell in Philadelphia, or the 1999 mural ad of Michael Jordan and Dennis Rodman along a Chicago Expressway?"[35]

The democratizing call-and-response—a staple characteristic of the 1960s and 1970s mural-making process—began to lessen, and the mural movement visually saw a decline in artwork detailing Black radicalism and revolutionary fervor. Images of clenched fists, guns, and self-liberating figures breaking apart their shackles were steadily waning (although they do remain in some murals of the era such as *Freedom Won't Wait* by Noni Olabisi and Brandan Odums's *ExhibitBE* project, discussed in chapter 5). In 1984, for example, Roderick Sykes created his mural *Unity* on the Harbor Freeway in Los Angeles with sponsorship from the Los Angeles Olympic Organizing Committee. Sykes's semiautobiographical mural vibrantly details his own personal journey of aspiring to be an Olympic runner. "In the front panel is my face, me as a kid in St. Louis. . . . I used to run track, and I always wanted to go to the Olympics. But as time went on, someone was always faster than I was," he stated in an interview in 1994. "The mural's statement is all about getting rid of the generation gap and the color gap, as well as my joy at being involved with the Olympics."[36] The mural depicts two young boys running along a red-and-yellow track that radiates, like a sunbeam, from the eye of a fragmented, colorful face. On the other side of the mural are three faces representing the ageing process—a young boy, an adult, and an older man. Through these faces, Sykes tried to depict the pain he felt, "the agony of struggle in the faces, my culture, my race of people here in America, what it takes to be a warrior."[37]

Black muralists of the 1980s, 1990s, and 2000s still detailed a Black experience in America. They also continued to reclaim space in Black neighborhoods to assert a proud Black presence, and they still used murals to celebrate heroes of Black history. In 1989, for example, Isaka Shamsud-Din and Paul Odighizuwa painted *The Time Is Now, Now Is the Time* at N.E. Shaver Street and N.E. Martin Luther King Jr. Boulevard in Portland, Oregon, sponsored by the Oregon Arts Commission. "I wanted to create a project in public art that would provide training for young African American artists in this community," Shamsud-Din explained. Much like its artistic predecessors, his mural deals with "education, self-knowledge, history, the African past and the living Africa," and it depicts the portraits of Black figures such as Martin Luther King Jr., writer Zora Neale Hurston, and South African playwright Selaelo Maredi, alongside children reading and graduating.[38] Similarly, in 1991 Alice Patrick created her nine-by-sixteen-foot mural, *Women Do Get Weary but They Don't Give Up*, at the National Council of Negro Women at

3720 West 54th Street in Los Angeles to depict nine "larger-than-life African American women" such as Mary McLeod Bethune, Dorothy Height, Josephine Baker, Oprah Winfrey, Sarah Vaughan, Florence Griffith Joyner, and the artist herself.[39]

By the 1990s, Harris argues, "many city centers and public buildings were colorized and invigorated by various murals just as decaying neighborhoods had been vitalized a generation earlier."[40] Although sometimes hampered by an institutional curtailment of inflammatory imagery, murals of the 1980s, 1990s, and 2000s still continued in the vein of their artistic forebears, responding to the turmoil of the decades, only growing and adding greater complexity to the movement through the addition of some new "toned-down" murals. These thematically toned-down murals even introduced a new topic for artists to work with. While most of the Black mural movement centered around Black history and the present day, muralists of the 1980s, 1990s, and 2000s used their murals to look to the future as well, at the next generation of Black Americans carrying their proud ancestral past into a new day, as we see in Keith Williams's 1991 mural, *Becoming Conscious*. Painted at the Martin Luther King Jr. Recreation Center on Orange Avenue and 19th Street in Long Beach, California, and sponsored by the Public Corporation for the Arts, Williams's mural stands—in his words—as a "visual menagerie."[41] Depicting children reading and learning together, he presents for his viewers (which he hopes are children) "a quick little history" for them to learn from and to carry forth with them.[42]

Murals of this era were also even more complex in their composition than ever before. Take *Memory Masks and Images of Reality: Building a More Unified Future* (1995), by Marcus Akinlana and John Yancey, for example. While part of their collaborative mural is made up of a traditional long narrative piece that was painted at eye level and that wraps around the building, just above their detailed scene are large individual panels, each cut out in the geometric shape of a face to symbolize the "Memory Masks." These faces have the physical features of lips, eyes, and a nose, but layered on top of them are individual portraits. "The blue mask represents the African American," Akinlana explained. "The standing figure is the deity Ausar (Osiri) from ancient Egypt (Khemit). . . . The next mask is the Latino and it's based on St. Barbara. . . . The third mask is for European Americans that came to Chicago with the onset of the Industrial Revolution."[43]

Just as the number of murals increased exponentially in the 1960s, then,

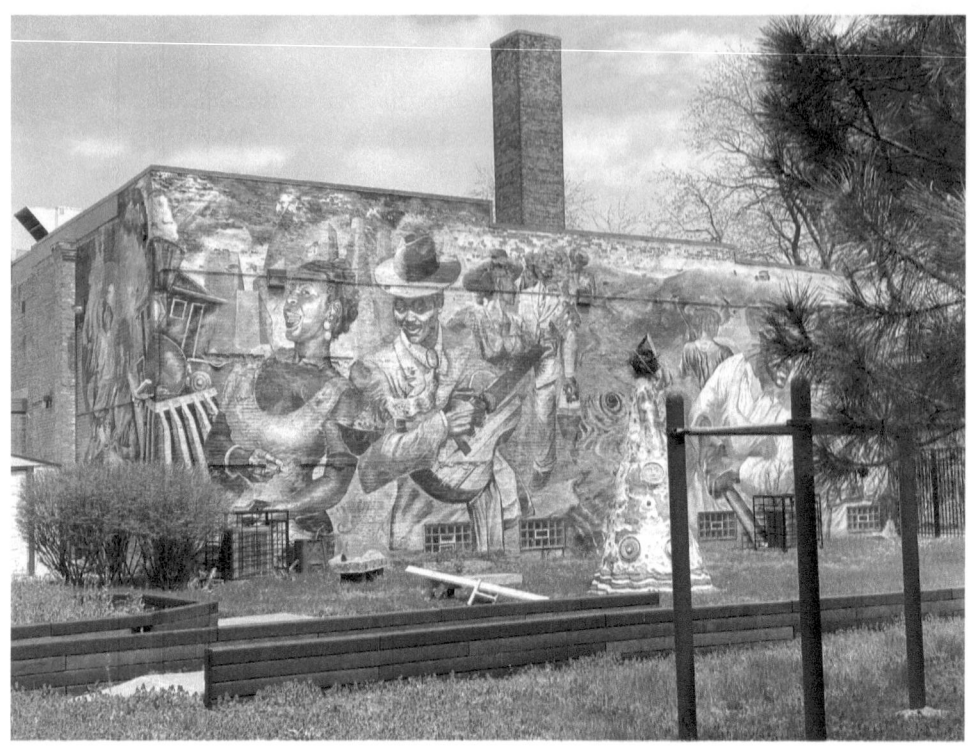

The Great Migration (1995), Elliot Donelley Youth Center Community Art Garden, 3947 S. Michigan Avenue, Chicago, Ill. Painted by Marcus Akinlana and assisted by Juan Angel Chavez, Dorian Sylvain, and community members. Photograph taken by the author.

so too did murals of the 1980s, 1990s, and 2000s. The era ushered in a wealth of artists from border to border and coast to coast who created murals just like those of the 1960s in Black communities and on the walls of Black businesses; in the same vein as those of the 1930s and 1940s in Black colleges and municipal buildings; and in newer places such as playgrounds and elementary schools, including *Peace, Love and Unity* (1985) by Eddie L. Edwards at Martin Luther King Jr. Elementary School in San Diego.

Artists working during the 1960s and 1970s also continued working deep into the 1990s. Bill Walker, C. Siddha Sila Webber, Calvin Jones, and Mitchell Caton continued creating murals across Chicago: Walker's *Wall of Community Respect* (1985) at 47th and Calumet; Webber's *Untitled* (1985) at 1031 Cottage Grove; and Jones and Caton's *Bright Moments, Memories of the Future* (1987) at the New Regal Theater at 79th and Stony Island. But Chicago and the vibrant Midwest more broadly also saw the rise of new Black muralists during this period. Artists such as Charles McGee began painting in Detroit; Ta-coumba T. Aiken worked in Minnesota; Spencer Taylor and Solomon Thurman painted in St. Louis; Ras Ammar Nsoroma created murals in Milwaukee; and Nina Smoot-Cain, Marcus Akinlana, John Yancey, and Bernard Williams painted in Chicago.

While this book focuses specifically on the Black mural movement, it would be remiss to overlook the rise of graffiti art, which is covered in chapter 5. Although emerging in Philadelphia in the 1960s, graffiti became a prominent form of public art in the 1980s that was ubiquitous in cities across the country, but was nowhere more prevalent than New York City. Covering trains, buses, subway stations, and any and every wall in impressively inaccessible locations, graffiti proudly displayed the pen names of artists—names such as Quik, Noc, BLADE, and Kase 2. It became a public art form concerned with getting one's name up in vast quantities across the city, but it was also about using the spray can to make innovative shapes, letters, characters, and backgrounds. And just like community murals, graffiti was not only a form of protest but also an affirmation of the identity of people.[44] Its new and highly stylized writing even influenced muralists of the decades who would sometimes incorporate it into their own murals, such as *L.A.-Berlin Exchange* (1994) on South Vermont Avenue in Los Angeles, by Toons, DruOne, A-One, Mith, Hex, and young German youths, who blended graffiti-style writing around narrative scenes of a downtown Los Angeles cityscape.

Murals of the 1980s, 1990s, and 2000s are complex. While general trends emerged across the decades, murals of this period didn't follow a simple theme or compositional structure or even stick to the same artistic materials. Many murals even stood in the streets as a contradiction to these broader trends, refusing to be categorized. The Black mural movement of the 1980s, 1990s, and 2000s instead evolved and expanded upon all that had come before it. It added greater breadth and depth to a powerful movement of Black art and ushered in new visual content, an expansion of stylistic choices, and an exponential growth in the sheer number of murals by Black artists across the country. And what happened in Black muralism in the 1980s, 1990s, and 2000s continued to happen beyond the millennium and into the present day.

Murals today are everywhere—in the streets and in public buildings across America just like their artistic forebears, but this time in unimaginable quantities. Contemporary Black murals still have a message to share and still have a story to tell about Black history and life in America, only today this message has a new movement to support. As is covered in depth in chapter 6, in America today and across the world more broadly, Black Lives Matter murals line the streets to demand justice, accountability, and recognition for the Black lives being lost at the hands of the police and vigilante groups. They line the walls of neighborhoods across the country to show the resilience of Black life in America. And just like the murals of Charles White, Hale Woodruff, Bill Walker, Justine DeVan, Alice Patrick, Isaka Shamsud-Din, and all those who came before, they live in the streets to show that Black lives have, do, and will always matter.

"I Had to Fight with My Brushes"

Radical Imagery and Interior Black Murals

Art has been for the few, but it should be for the many.
—*Hale Woodruff, artist*

Paint is the only weapon [that] I have with which to fight what I resent.
If I could write, I would write about it. If I could talk, I would talk about it.
Since I paint, I must paint about it. —*Charles White, artist*

We hail the monumental expression of art because such art is public
property. —*David Alfaro Siqueiros, artist*

Harriet Tubman stands atop the barrel of a smoking cannon, casting off the
chains shackling her freedom, in *Harriet Tubman (Spirits Rising)* (1930), by
Aaron Douglas. Traditional and modern healing practices are interwoven to
depict the history of medicine from Africa to America in *Harlem Hospital Murals* (1936), by Charles Alston. Luminous Black skin glistens on the muscular
bodies of ten enslaved men led by Joseph Cinqué as they brandish machetes
and pin down their white enslavers aboard the *Amistad* slave vessel in *Mutiny
Aboard the Amistad 1839* (1939), by Hale Woodruff. A lynched figure hangs
from a tree surrounded by several interlocking narratives that depict the
plotting of a protest inspired by John Brown in *Technique to Serve the Struggle*
(1940–41), by Charles White. And a soldier, falling to his knees, is enmeshed
in a fence of barbed wire while the clothes are torn from his lacerated body
during the bloody conflict of war in *Dying Soldier* (1942), by John Biggers.

The advent of the Wall Street crash in 1929 through to the mid-1950s
saw the rise of a new and unprecedented moment in Black mural art in the
United States—subversive, radical, unshackled, and liberated mural art that
celebrated Blackness for the first time. Emerging during the Harlem Renaissance and cresting in the era of the New Deal and slowly enveloping tide of
the Cold War, Black murals became bastions of Black artistic agency. These

murals were concerned with revolution and radicalism. They celebrated Blackness—Black freedom, Black love, Black heroes, Black life, Black history, and Black struggle—visualizing exceptional acts of Black self-determination and liberation. These Black murals of the early twentieth century became vessels of protest. Artists spoke through them, creating unprecedented images of revolution and radicalism that challenged the pervasive iconographies and ideologies of white supremacy throughout the nation. The decades stretching from the Great Depression to the Cold War shook the lives of African Americans on both domestic and international fronts. The rise and fall of the Harlem Renaissance, the deeply entrenched laws of Jim Crow and proliferation of lynching in the South, the status of economic bondage as a form of neoslavery, the enveloping cloak of Fascism, the threat and later reality of another world war, and the rising tide of Communism and Marxism across the United States left much for Black artists to paint, protest, and support.[1]

From the 1930s to the 1950s, Douglas, Alston, Woodruff, White, Biggers, Georgette Seabrooke, William Edouard Scott, Vertis Hayes, and John Wilson curated a moment in Black muralism to depict and celebrate unrestrained Blackness and to protest the racist and capitalist world around them. As artists and activists dedicated to racial and social justice, they were drawn to the mural as a creative form because of its expansive scale and public-facing nature. Aaron Douglas's reach as an artist and advocate for racial justice, for example, was intimately tied to the public arenas he chose to display his work. By creating empowering and radically crafted artwork for journals, books, and public walls, Douglas was able to "speak and teach about the struggles that he and fellow Black Americans faced."[2] With the same goal to reach a mass Black audience, Charles White turned to murals "to get [his] work before common ordinary people." To White, "a work of art was meant to belong to people. . . . Art should take its place as one of the necessities of life, like food, clothing and shelter."[3] Art is not "for artists and connoisseurs alone," he said in a 1943 interview with the Communist Party's *Daily Worker* newspaper. "It should be for the people. A mural on the wall of a commonly used building is there for everyone to see and read its message."[4]

But while White's artistic interests were piqued by the communal reach of muralism, it was the potential size of murals that fine-tuned his attention as well: "The most important thing . . . for me has always been to say something that is meaningful, and much more important than the media

I use. And whatever media that I could do it strongest, that's the media I've always used. That's why murals are extremely important to me, even though it's hard to get mural commissions these days, but murals I've always felt very strong to because it's allowed me the room to say the kinds of things . . . [and] try to deal with truth."[5] As an art form that could "capture the attention of a mass audience much more readily than could easel painting," murals gave artists the perfect public platform to tell their radical messages.[6] This meant that Black murals sprang up in hospitals, at state fairs, and in HBCUs to protest the national and international threats of white supremacy on Black lives from a Black perspective. By using murals in this way, artists created visual stories of revolution and Black history, stories that overthrew white oppression through rebellion and self-emancipation. But during this thirty-year period, from the Harlem Renaissance up to the Cold War, muralists navigating this powerfully unique art form were met with external and unavoidable constraints around patronage, audience, and location. As artists were deciding what they wanted to say and how they wanted to say it, they had to ask themselves, Where will this mural be displayed? Who's sponsoring it? And who is the audience—Black, white, or both? These answers usually impacted the radical undertones or overtones of such murals.

To demonstrate and unpick this complicated web of forces at play, this chapter looks at Douglas's *Harriet Tubman (Spirits Rising)* mural and his *Aspects of Negro Life* (1934) series and focuses closely on *Into Bondage* (1936), his state-sponsored mural for the Texas Centennial Exposition in Dallas. This mural is placed alongside Charles White's *Contribution of the Negro to Democracy in America* (1943), sponsored by the Julius Rosenwald Fund and displayed at Hampton Institute, an HBCU in Virginia. There are many murals of this era that deserve in-depth studies of their own, but this chapter focuses on just a handful that perfectly demonstrate the intricate dynamics between the interlocking forces of patronage, audience, location, and personal politics. Oftentimes in murals painted at HBCUs, artists had a lot more freedom, meaning that images of resistance were overt and displayed explicit radical imagery of Black revolution, much as *Contribution* does. But the dictates of white patronage and the politics of the mural's location occasionally prevailed too, which meant that artists such as Douglas embedded messages of revolution within historical allegory, coded symbolism, and imprints of socialist imagery, as in *Into Bondage*.

Getting to the heart of this movement in Black mural history is complex.

It spans three decades of warring ideologies, oppositional artistic styles, an economic recession, and the precipice, entrance, and culmination of World War II. But through exploring the process and content behind the modernist murals of Aaron Douglas and the social realist murals of Charles White, we can better understand the intricacies at play within this unique moment of Black mural history. By looking at how artistic style, location, patronage, and personal politics were navigated to create radical and revolutionary imagery that protested Fascism, racism, and capitalism on the national and international stages, we can see how murals, for the first time, became a powerful medium of radical Black protest in the early twentieth century.

FIGHTING ON MANY FRONTS

Empowering and radical imagery in Black murals was a new phenomenon in the 1930s and 1940s. In *Recreation in Harlem* (1937), by Georgette Seabrooke, Black women take center stage for the first time in public art. Scenes of women dancing, singing, conversing with friends, and going about their daily life dominate the mural in joyful harmony. Painted in the 1930s, the mural shows women not as subservient foils to their husband's happiness but as leaders of their own life—proud, content, and independent. Creating her mural for the nurse's recreation room at the Harlem Hospital Center, Seabrooke used her artwork "to give nurses something to look at, something which they could partake in and find interesting rather than their own personal work which in a recreation room might not be as exciting as a subject apart."[7] Two years later, at an HBCU in Alabama, Hale Woodruff curated a radical mural series that chronicled the *Amistad* rebellion and subsequent trial in New Haven, Connecticut. The six-part Talladega College mural series broke artistic and iconographic boundaries when panel 1, *Mutiny Aboard the Amistad, 1839,* showed for the first time in public art "a black man *winning,*" as ten formerly enslaved men revolt against their overseers in an act of mutiny, as the title suggests.[8]

When the artwork of Black artist Robert S. Duncanson tapered to a natural end in the early twentieth century, a new vanguard of Black artists emerged, evolving Black muralism into a movement concerned with protest and agency. Peaking, plateauing, and overlapping from the 1920s to the 1950s was the rise and fall of the New Negro and Harlem Renaissance movement, World War II, a growing interest in Communism within Black communities, a national economic depression and subsequent recovery plan, strong artistic influences from Mexican socialist murals, and the ever-pervasive threat of Fascism. The volatile climate of the early to mid-twentieth century then gave much for Seabrooke, Douglas, White, Woodruff, Alston, Hayes, Scott, and Biggers to protest and to paint.

In 1925 the Harlem Renaissance—synonymous with the term "the New Negro," popularized by philosopher, writer, and educator Alain LeRoy Locke—emerged as a new, modernist movement of Black empowerment, responding to and pushing against the ubiquitous paternalistic imagery of subservient, enslaved African Americans in the national culture. Confined to depictions of servants and laborers, African Americans were a mere foil in mainstream artwork of the nineteenth century that highlighted the philosophy of white superiority.[9] The Harlem Renaissance, therefore, was a way for African Americans to find "a new soul," according to Locke.[10] "The mind of the Negro seems suddenly to have slipped from under the tyranny of social intimidation and to be shaking off the psychology of imitation and implied inferiority," he wrote in his seminal book, The New Negro. "The day of 'aunties,' 'uncles' and 'mammies' is equally gone. Uncle Tom and Sambo have passed on. . . . The popular melodrama has about played itself out, and it is time to scrap the fictions, garret the bogeys and settle down to a realistic facing of facts."[11]

The Harlem Renaissance provided a fertile ground for Black artists and writers to reclaim Black history, memory, and culture from the supremacist stereotypes of the nineteenth century. It was a "spiritual emancipation," continued Locke.[12] Creating a cultural movement that reclaimed the warped, subservient depictions of Black American life and challenging the widespread myth that "Africans couldn't paint," New Negro artists created works of art that finally foregrounded a Black experience. They placed African Americans back into the broader context of American life and, more importantly, reflected Black culture, Black life, and Black identity to Black viewers from a Black perspective.[13]

But by the mid-1930s the renaissance started to fade, its death knell signaled largely by the Great Depression following the Wall Street crash of 1929. Economic bondage and vast unemployment rates, although widespread across the country following the crash, were felt most severely in northern Black communities already overcrowded after the influx of Black migrants from Southern states during the Great Migration. African Americans from the South moved north to escape the horrors of supremacist violence such as lynchings and Jim Crow laws, but they also migrated in the hope of finding reliable work in the ever-expanding industrial North. Racism was not a Southern phenomenon, though, and white supremacy still had a stronghold in northern institutions, so this, coupled with mass overcrowding in northern cities, meant Black employees were typically the last hired and first fired from industrial jobs. At the same time, downwardly mobile whites displaced many Black workers from even those menial service-sector jobs that African Americans had previously occupied, leading to Black unemployment rates around three times greater than those of whites.

To many Americans, Communism offered an antidote to these oppressions. With sixty-five thousand members at the height of the Depression, the Communist Party of the United States of America (CPUSA) fought militantly to "establish such familiar and illustrious institutions as rent stabilization, public housing, Social Security . . . , and even small-farm subsidies." So by the early 1930s the party had emerged from obscurity, especially in Black enclaves such as Harlem.[14] Playing a decisive role in the movement for Black liberation, the party galvanized Black support in urban centers once it began showing concern for fighting discrimination on both racial and economic fronts, which quickly placed Harlem as an epicenter for the organization. To remedy dwindling membership subscriptions in the late 1920s, Black party members Cyril Briggs and Richard B. Moore focused on transforming the CPUSA—an organization composed almost exclusively of white immigrants—into a group capable of "smashing through the barriers that subordinated blacks."[15]

Black support for the CPUSA grew in the 1930s when African Americans realized that Franklin D. Roosevelt wasn't doing much to alleviate Black poverty.[16] When the president entered the Oval Office in 1933 he promised "a new deal for the American people" that would promote economic recovery. He established the Civilian Conservation Corps (CCC), the National Recovery Administration (NRA), the Federal Deposit Insurance Corporation (FDIC), the Federal Reserve System (FRS), the Securities and Exchange Commission (SEC), and the Agricultural Adjustment Administration (AAA). These programs aimed to give a much-needed injection into the nation's economy by stimulating temporary employment, short-term aid, construction, and agricultural production. One of the most popular and important economic recovery programs was the Public Works of Art Project (PWAP), which would later become the Works Progress Administration (WPA). In 1934 the PWAP was established under the premise that artists "should be held to the same standards of production and public value as workers wielding shovels in the national parks."[17] By May 1935 the PWAP had evolved into a more structured format under the WPA, employing millions of jobseekers to carry out public works projects in the field of construction. Run as a subdivision of the WPA was the Federal Art Project (FAP), which remedied the unemployment levels specifically of artists—one of the most hurt groups in the country.[18] But despite this range of initiatives pioneered by Roosevelt, the New Deal was unpopular with the CPUSA, in part due to its failure to address the lack of socioeconomic advancement for Black Americans and the detrimental effects this had on Black life. Roosevelt's ineffectual response to racial inequality, then, turned Black Americans on to the CPUSA.[19]

As the decade wore on and James Ford headed up the Harlem Communist Party from 1933, the CPUSA expanded toward a popular and cultural front in 1935.[20] Shifting away from the party's early 1930s isolationist stance, which supported the "Black Belt thesis" and argued for Black self-determination in the South, the party adopted a more broadly inclusive, coalition-based strategy that focused on the importance of culture "as one arm, or front, of a widening campaign for social, political and racial equality."[21] With growing support from cultural workers, the mid-1930s saw Black aesthetics become aligned with the aims and aspirations of the popular front, so much so that in a session at the 1940 National Negro Congress (NNC), artist and writer Gwendolyn Bennett proposed that the NNC spend "more time, space, and effort on the cultural front."[22] After all, an audience member declared, "it is the cultural things that keep us from going stark crazy."[23]

As a result, the 1930s and 1940s saw an explosion of literature, plays, poems, and artwork from Black artists, allying leftist themes and iconography with a Black experience in the United States. While artists such as Aaron Douglas, Hale Woodruff, Charles Alston, and Charles White are sometimes referenced in scholarship of this period, greater consideration is typically given to prolific writers and actors—Richard Wright, Ralph Ellison, Paul Robeson, and Claude McKay. These figures had an undeniably complex and important relationship with the cultural front, creating momentous works of art, literature, and music that changed the cultural landscape. But the role of visual artists creating murals of Black protest is equally significant but more overlooked during this period. Visual artists and muralists were at the vanguard of creating Black culture, producing grand-scale murals that lambasted the systemic, social, political, and racial supremacy scaffolding the country. "Landscapes and still life interest me," Black muralist John Wilson argued, "but I feel that because I have the ability to paint rather well and forcefully, I can use this to try to express something maybe more directly functional and concrete as far as it relates to our present social setting."[24] And it was this same impulse that guided the work of many artists of the era, including Aaron Douglas.

In February 1936, at the height of the cultural front, the first American Artists' Congress Against War and Fascism was held in New York City. Over four hundred leading artists, academics, modernists, and social realists were in attendance, including Mexican muralists José Clemente Orozco and David Alfaro Siqueiros and Black artist Aaron Douglas. In front of the four hundred delegates, Douglas spoke to the responsibility of all artists in America. "I should like to close this paper with a sincere appeal to every artist of this congress and to every lover of liberty and justice everywhere, to fight against the rising tide of Fascism," he began.[25] "If there is anyone here who does not understand Fascism let him ask the first Negro he sees in the street. The lash and iron hoof of Fascism have been a constant menace and threat to the Negro ever since his so-called emancipation," he continued.[26] Like John Wilson, Douglas was allied to the radical and honest content of Black art in the United States, proclaiming to his audience: "What the Negro artist should paint and how he should paint it can't be accurately determined without reference to specific social conditions."[27] He continued: "In America, race discrimination is one of the chief props on which Fascism can be built. One of the most vital blows the artists of this congress can deliver to the threat of Fascism is to refuse to discriminate against any man because of nationality, race, or creed."[28]

As many artists took heed of Douglas's clarion call to create artwork of content and critique, some, including Douglas himself, used murals to do so. But this wasn't always a simple endeavor. As an artist working in the 1930s, especially as a Black artist, Douglas sometimes relied on sponsorship from white patrons. This meant he not only had to figure out how to create radical murals in a world threatened by Fascism and neoslavery but also how to navigate an art world constrained by the dictates of white patronage. Working under the remit of modernism, Douglas found a way to embed a coded inspirational and revolutionary message within his murals. In the 1930s artists began pushing the conceptual boundaries of Black muralism, and the murals of Douglas show not only their scope and subversiveness but also how artists traversed the complicated terrains of patronage and audience to create, for the first time, powerful Black public art full of Black life and history that combated the oppressive social, political, and racial injustices shackling the nation.

WORKING ON THIS INNATE BLACKNESS

Born in Topeka, Kansas, in 1899, Aaron Douglas migrated east to New York in 1925 to become one of the most prolific artists of the Harlem Renaissance. Inspired to move to the Eastern Seaboard, Douglas was in search of kindred spirits who shared the growing race consciousness he was cultivating in the Midwest. Douglas stayed in New York for twelve years, from 1925 to 1937, with a year's hiatus in Paris in 1931. Returning from France in 1932, he spent five more years in and out of Harlem before accepting a full teaching position at Fisk University in Nashville in 1937. Rising to prominence during the Harlem Renaissance, Douglas developed close relationships with writers, activists, and philosophers such as Charles S. Johnson and W. E. B. Du Bois, as well as the Bavarian artist Winold Reiss, who became somewhat of a mentor to him. Although he led a rich and varied life, it is Douglas's tenure in Harlem that is of most importance here for two reasons: This was the period when his interest in Communism and Marxism was strongest, and this was the period when he created his beautiful canon of murals.[29]

During the Harlem Renaissance, Douglas was, in his words, "beginning to realize how good it is to be black."[30] He celebrated Blackness and used it to consume his artwork. "I was the first one to give this thing something of a Negro content," he said of his work in the late 1920s. "They [the people of Harlem] had a feeling this isn't something that was done by a Caucasian person. This is a black person. Here at last it is a black person doing this thing. He isn't criticizing his people; he isn't placing them in a situation that they would not normally have."[31]

Producing artwork that rebutted the supremacist iconography of the nineteenth- and early twentieth-century art world, Douglas created groundbreaking imagery by depicting radical portrayals of Black life and reality in his murals, a Black world full of emotion and truth. "Let's bare our arms and plunge them deep through laughter, through pain, through sorrow, through hope, through disappointment," he wrote, "into the very depths of the souls of our people . . . and drag forth material crude, rough, neglected. Then let's sing it, dance it, write it, paint it. . . . Let's create something transcendentally material, mystically objective."[32]

Turning Black pain into Black power, Douglas celebrated Blackness through his artwork, bringing forth from the deep a Black life, history, feeling, reality, and love so overlooked in the artistic mainstream. "Negro life appeared to be limited to a kind of 'shantytown' on the outskirts of the American dream," Douglas told an audience at Dillard University in 1971. It was a tangible yet intangible space that was separated, unequal, and over-looked, a space where "every door was shut" against Black women and men, he recounted.[33] So while entrenched and systemic racism scaffolded the so-cial, racial, and economic makeup of the country, leaving African American life in a "shanty" on the outskirts of the American dream, Douglas argued, he would use his murals to undo this reality in the Black imagination.

Douglas was dubbed the creator of "an original modern black art," and his work during the 1920s and 1930s became synonymous with modernism. But modernism during this period, especially among Black artists, wasn't monolithic.[34] Some "avoided [modernism] in favor of more artistic modes, while others embraced it quite visibly," and not all artists agreed on the sig-nificance and relevance of it. Modernism meant different things in literature just as it did in the visual arts, and many African Americans were ambivalent toward it because of its association with the white, Eurocentric art world. But to Douglas, modernism offered a lens to articulate and depict the world of Black America. He endorsed its utopianism and the potential of its ab-straction: "I just now opened the book [Ruskin, *Ten Lectures in Art*] at random and found this sentence which is the very antithesis of what the modernists are after. I'll quote it, 'You are, in drawing, to try only to represent the ap-pearances of things, never what you know the things to be.'"[35]

To Douglas, modernism wasn't about strict narrative representations—something that came later under social realism. It was instead a period of artistic experimentation and metaphorical representation. Douglas under-stood the important relationship between murals and allegory, and mod-ernism offered him an experimental drawing board ripe with possibilities to explore the brutal topics of bondage and oppression.[36] Modernism flirted with cubism and abstraction, so while flourishing in the era of the New Ne-gro, Douglas and other Black artists fused their understanding of modern-ism's utopia with motifs from an African visual tradition.

In a 1925 letter to Langston Hughes, Douglas expressed the contours of

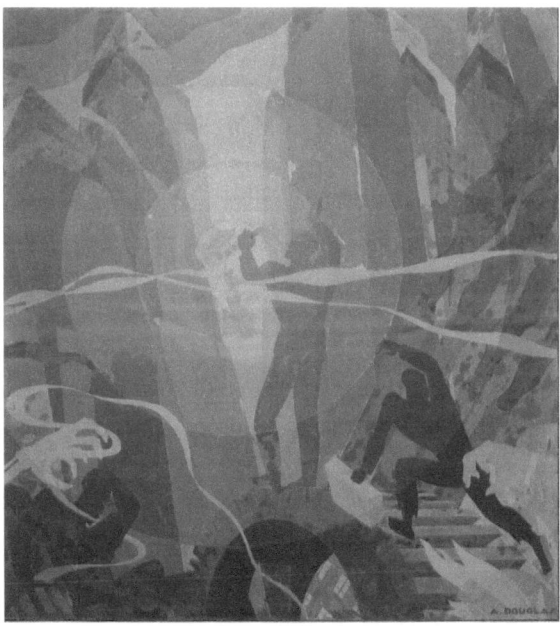

Aspects of Negro Life: Song of the Towers (1934), Schomburg Center for Research in Black Culture, Art and Artifacts Division, New York, N.Y. Painted by Aaron Douglas. Image courtesy of the New York Public Library Digital Collections.

what modernism meant not only to himself but also to African Americans during the Harlem Renaissance. Black artists need to "conceive, develop, establish an art era. . . . Not white art painted black" but a modernist aesthetic centered on something "earthy. Spiritually earthy. Dynamic," Douglas told Hughes.[37] To Douglas, operating in a modernist style offered him a somewhat abstracted terrain to depict his understanding of the restless, racially fractured world around him. With modernism in Douglas's mind predicated upon the belief that it should be Black art painted Black, he used public walls to weave a Black experience of oppression, pain, culture, and pride alongside a vision of a utopian future through geometric silhouettes and diasporic iconography.

Douglas used his craft to celebrate Black culture and reclaim warped, sanitized, and stereotyped accounts of a Black experience. But the Harlem Renaissance and its accompanying culture have been critiqued. "The Renaissance depended on and answered the needs of whites rather than blacks," making it in a way "as much a white creation as it was black," Nathan Huggins argues. Artistically constrained by the fantasies of white patrons, the Renaissance was "merely a taxi trip to the exotic for most white

New Yorkers," he continues.[38] This scathing critique of the Renaissance taps into one of the most documented criticisms of the cultural movement as a whole: the role of patronage. "White capital and influence were crucial," David Levering Lewis writes, "and the white presence, at least in the early years, hovered over the New Negro world of art and literature like a benevolent censor, politely but pervasively setting the outer limits of its creative boundaries."[39]

Douglas, however, although embroiled in a short-term patronage relationship with Harlem Renaissance "sponsor" Charlotte Osgood Mason, emphatically rejected these notions. "There were certain white people at the time that came in contact with blacks and helped make it possible for them to reach a level from which they could create," he stressed, but "it was not something dictated by white culture. It stemmed from Black culture. We were constantly working on this innate blackness at that time that made this whole thing important and unique."[40] Yet while Douglas strongly objected to the notion that Black artists were merely puppets for the entertainment and fantasies of individual white patrons, he was undeniably aware of the artistic constraints placed on Black artists from government funding bodies.

In 1934 Douglas completed his four-part mural series, Aspects of Negro Life, sponsored by the state-funded PWAP, for the Harlem branch of the New York Public Library. The four panels—The Negro in an African Setting, From Slavery to Reconstruction, An Idyll of the Deep South, and Song of the Towers—reveal the evolution and lineage of Blackness and Black life in the United States, from life in Africa, to enslavement, to emancipation, and finally to the reclamation of African traditions on American soil. Created in a typical Douglas color palette, the murals are painted in earthy tones—umbers, yellows, browns, greens, and plum purples—and show silhouetted figures toiling in the fields, breaking shackles, dancing, playing music, and attempting to summit the wheel of industrialism and capitalism. While the mural series beautifully celebrates Black resilience and strength in America, "the artist touches on a subject which brought instant objections from his PWA [sic] superiors," journalist T. R. Poston wrote for the New York Amsterdam News, and that subject matter is the subtle hint to Marxism.[41] "Those who view Aaron Douglas' new mural at the 135th street branch library will hardly suspect the influence of Karl Marx on the delicately-beautiful decoration. But the patron saint of Revolution has left his mark there" in the final panel of the mural, Song of the Towers.[42]

This panel is the most somber of the series. Skyscrapers loom imposingly over three silhouettes: one who stands atop the industrial wheel; one who attempts to climb it with a briefcase in hand; and a third in the bottom left-hand corner of the mural whose contorted frame looks down, holding his head in anguish, as the Statue of Liberty stands faintly in the background. "I was very careful to associate my figures so that they looked like the working people," Douglas spoke of the silhouettes in his murals. "You would not confuse them with the aspiring middle-upper-class, not that I had any antagonism, but that I felt that here is the essence of this Negro thing, here among these people. So I tried to keep it there with simple devices, such as giving the clothing . . . ragged edges, you know, so as to keep the thing realistic."[43]

The natural browns and oranges of the mural are counteracted by an unnatural shade of lime green that curves into smoke-like shapes of industrialism, bisecting the mural. Two dismembered clawing hands, also in lime green, extend from the bottom corners of the mural, seeking to envelop the figures, who try to continue living their lives. "Mr. Douglas is openly apologetic about the note of defeat upon which his mural ends," Poston wrote in his article. "As a student of Marx, and an artist who has been 'bolshevized by conditions,' he knows that he has not finished the picture."[44]

In response to the growing threat of Fascism in 1934 and his personal relationship with Communism following the Scottsboro incident, Douglas wanted to create a fifth panel for the *Aspects* series that would depict "the way out for the Negro . . . the one . . . outlined by Karl Marx and his disciples— the unity of black and white workers in the class struggle."[45] Such an image was never created, but if it had been, "the whole mural would undoubtedly have been rejected by the PWA authorities," Poston argued, citing Douglas's statement: "Under our present system . . . the artist must paint what his employer wants, if he is to keep his own self-respect, however, he must try to maintain a certain honesty and present the picture as he sees it."[46] Caught between wanting to stay true to his artistic, political, and moral inclinations and painting something that wouldn't draw the ire of his patrons, Douglas believed he had compromised his honesty as an artist by leaving the *Aspects* series unfinished, and he apologized to his audience for the sanitized, uninspiring end to the mural series. "Under a SOVIET America," however, according to Poston, "Mr. Douglas believes the artist could have more freedom for expression, more honesty."[47] Although the United States in 1936 was a far cry from the "SOVIET America" Douglas was aspiring to, by the mid-1930s he had discovered a way to bypass the politics around white sponsorship without compromising his own honesty when he created a mural for the Texas Centennial Exposition in Dallas.

As part of the "recovery process of the nation" during the Great Depression, Roosevelt approved $3 million in support of the Texas Centennial Exposition.[48] Running from June until November 1936, it comprised exhibitions and parades held across fifty buildings at Fair Park in Dallas, all of which celebrated the state's history, rich resources, and growing social structure while concurrently laying out the promise of a bright future for the state beyond the depression.[49] Costing around $25 million and attracting over six million attendees, including Roosevelt himself, the fair was hailed as "a tribute to the past, an exposition of the present, and a herald of tomorrow."[50]

The Texas legislation, however, failed to sponsor a Black exhibit for the fair, leading African Americans to lobby the federal government for funds to create a dedicated space for the celebration of Black culture, a space that told of the African American contribution to the nation's identity from a Black perspective. After much lobbying, the Hall of Negro Life was built at Fair Park, marking the first recognition of Black culture at a world's fair. The inclusion of a Black exhibition space had the trappings of progressivism—it provided a space for Black Americans to supposedly "rearticulate their racial and national identities and to reshape historical memory in the public space" during the height of Jim Crow—but many critics of the "racially inclusive" exposition took issue with the physical location of the hall.[51] As Renée Ater's instrumental research into the centennial and Douglas's murals shows us, the hall was contradictory in nature, separated and physically isolated from the main path of the fair, fenced in and obscured by a row of cedar trees and shrubs. While the presence of the hall gave the pretense of governmental interest in Black welfare, life, and culture, it simultaneously upheld the *Plessy v. Ferguson* doctrine of separate but equal.[52] But despite the physical and symbolic location of the hall on the periphery of the exposition, it nonetheless provided a space for Black Americans to finally tell their story from their perspective to both Black and white Americans. Of the 400,000 people visiting the Hall of Negro Life, 275,000 were white.[53]

Aaron Douglas contributed to this retelling of a Black experience by framing the entrance to the hall with four of his murals, only two of which have survived.[54] Creating a mural series for a government-sponsored state fair in the South that aimed to "restore popular faith in the vitality of the nation's economic and political system" meant that Douglas would once again have to navigate the constraints of white patronage, but this time he would do it differently.[55] On the surface, Into Bondage, one of the surviving murals, presents a despairing, sorrowful narrative of enslavement on the untamed, tropical West African coast. Viewers gaze upon nine shackled figures moving from freedom in Africa to enslavement in America. Seven of the nine people walk solemnly toward two tilted ships faintly anchored on the straight horizon line of the wailing sea, their heads bowed in silence. Two shackled but dominant figures defy the procession drifting past them when instead they occupy the center and left-hand side of the panel: A man stands atop a terra-cotta-colored box, and a woman raises her manacles toward the sky in the direction of a red star. The star cascades a deliberate beam of light onto the face of the central figure as he too glances in its direction. The mural, ornamented on each side of the frame with wild foliage differing in tone but of the same earthy palette of blues, greens, and dark pinks, places the viewer as either a manacled figure waiting in the curved line of imprisoned individuals moving toward the ship or a figure of resistance seeking refuge in the tropical undergrowth. As the string of shackled figures tread their final steps on freedom's soil, the raised figure in a visually superior position holds an open palm to his right side. On a surface level, this mural tells a one-dimensional story, the story of the transatlantic slave trade, a story of people being transported from Africa, quite literally, into bondage. But beneath the surface of the artwork runs an ulterior narrative, one embedded into historical allegory, imprinted symbolism, and Communist iconography.

During this period in his life, Douglas embraced Communism as an answer to "the legitimate and significant problems of American society," and the embedded messages in Into Bondage address the racism in America, Fascism on the world stage, and the role Communism might play in remedying the plight of the working class and people of color.[56] Given that "the lash and iron hoof of Fascism have been a constant menace and threat to the Negro ever since his so-called emancipation," Douglas believed, African Americans were "destined to save the 'soul' of America."[57] In the mid-1930s economic depression deepened, Jim Crow violence was still on the rise, and unemployment plagued the country, disproportionately affecting African

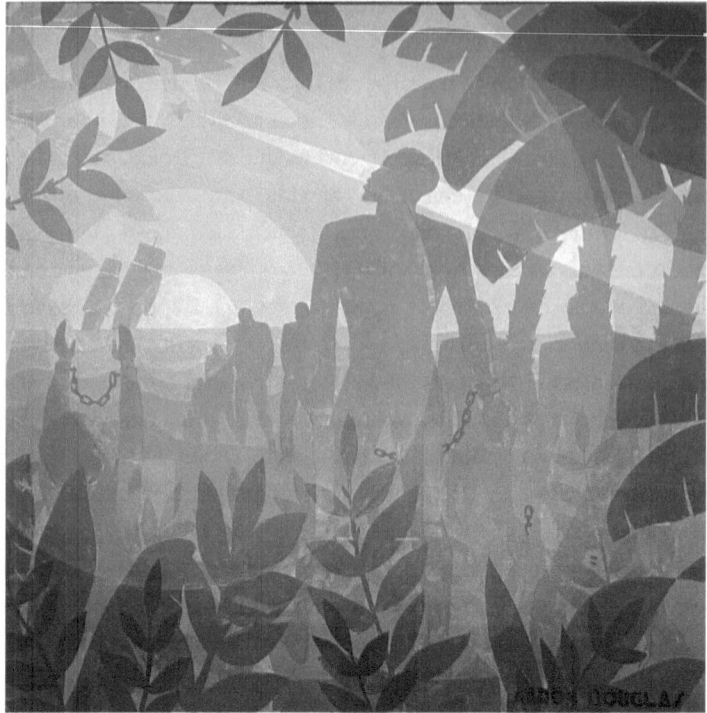

Into Bondage (1936), originally located in the Hall of Negro Life, Texas Centennial, Dallas, Tex. Painted by Aaron Douglas. Photograph taken by the author at the National Gallery of Art, Washington, D.C.

Americans. "We don't have a physical slavery, but an economic one," Jacob Lawrence, one of the most well-known Black painters and modernists of the twentieth century, declared in 1936.[58] Through an in-depth reading of *Into Bondage*, then, we can see how Douglas navigated government sponsorship at a predominantly white state fair to create a mural that championed Communism and protested the intense racial climate and growing threat of Fascism in America.

Exploring the contours of the mural as a medium for Black protest, Douglas encrypted a visual language of resistance through embedded references to liberation: the function of the physical stance of the central figure, the North Star, and the imprint of revolutionary figures from Douglas's earlier canon of murals. He perhaps layered his message of resistance and self-emancipation so deeply into his murals at the Texas Centennial Exposition, however, that white audiences insisted they simply couldn't have been painted by a Black artist, leading a sign to be displayed next to them that read: "These murals were painted by Aaron Douglas, a Negro artist of New York City."[59]

An alternative reading of Into Bondage tells an almost opposite story to the surface-level freedom-to-slavery narrative assumed by many viewers. As seven shackled figures march toward a faint and distant slave ship, the bordering foliage was carefully constructed by Douglas to draw the viewer's focus directly to the manacled figures in the center and left-hand side of the frame, leaving the shackled procession fading into the background as their shadowed bodies are enveloped by the green and unforgiving sea. The procession line isn't the focal point in this mural, nor are the ships looming menacingly in the distance. Instead, these elements of the artwork are peripheral background layers functioning to elevate the central figure that refuses to look down and instead stands strongly, decisively, and fearlessly in an act of defiance. His dissident body language is incongruous to that of his shackled brothers and sisters, who drop their heads in despair as he raises his, unable or perhaps unwilling to watch as their journey into bondage begins. His powerful, broad stance is silhouetted against the bright sky as he starts to pull apart his manacles, dropping hints to the audience of his revolutionary plan. Standing illuminated against the bright green background, his outline offers a stark reminder of the racist silhouettes used to display Black bodies and physiognomies during the eighteenth and nineteenth centuries, except that Douglas's incorporation of this primed and commanding shadowed outline counters such racist connotations.

The light obscures the physical features of this revolutionary man; instead, only the manacles binding his wrists are illuminated when he searches for meaning, hope, and salvation in the dark tropical thicket. Douglas painted this figure with his enlightened head held high, and his body language counters the drooped, shadowed faces of the manacled parade that stomps past him in a ghostly manner as they move from pronounced, defined figures into obscurity. The procession travels past the raised central body, while the thud of footsteps against the thick tropical mud reverberates throughout the image in the form of pulsing off-center concentric circles. Frequently used by Douglas to depict sound and songs of the enslaved—which also contained coded messages of emancipation—the circles vibrate with the weight of despair and fear as each drumming step takes the figures farther from home and closer to the hell that awaits them. But he refuses to take forced steps upon the soft undergrowth of his homeland, where each step would strip him further of his freedom, body, and voice. Instead, he stands ready atop a box, perhaps to deliver a radical oration akin to the revolutionary words from a Denmark Vesey, a Nat Turner, or a Gabriel Prosser.

As this figure stands affirmatively with tension coursing through his muscles, he stares at the brightly colored star in the sky to further unlock—especially for Black viewers—Douglas's concealed message in the mural. To many attendees at the Hall of Negro Life, the sight of a star could be viewed as an homage to the Lone Star, a symbol of pride in the state of Texas. When viewing Into Bondage in 1936, Alonzo J. Aden said: "The star in the design is the 'Lone Star of Texas.'"[60] But considering the content and context of the mural and Douglas's desire to evade artistic lily-whitism, the star has a second meaning, especially for Black audiences. Douglas described the stars of his murals as "radiating star[s] of Emancipation"—a not so subtle hint to their position as the North Star.[61] The North Star guided enslaved people on the Underground Railroad by pointing the direction from Mobile, Alabama, to the Ohio River and through to freedom. In covert acts of resistance, enslaved individuals sang songs such as "Follow the Drinking Gourd" to share instructions on how to find the North Star in the sky and thus escape:

> The riva ends a-tween two hills,
> Foller the drinkin' gou'd;
> 'Nuther riva on the other side
> Follers the drinkin' gou'd.[62]

The "drinking gourd," a code name for the Big Dipper constellation, was used as a reference point to find the North Star. So by creating a glowing star with an informative beam of light fixed into the mind of the central figure, Douglas hinted at resistance and escape and did so during a period in the 1930s when the revolutionary memories of slavery and emancipation were prominent due to the centennial celebrations of Nat Turner's rebellion and the development of "Negro historical weeks" in Harlem, which commemorated Turner, Vesey, and Toussaint Louverture.[63] Myths of the Old South were dismantled during this period and replaced instead with versions of slavery that foregrounded militant resistance. "If these people [the enslaved], who were so much worse off than the people today, could conquer their slavery, we can certainly do the same thing," Jacob Lawrence suggested.[64]

But the presence of the shining star is multifunctional, not only representing the North Star. The red star, which was a common trope in Douglas's depression-era murals such as *Idylls of the Deep South* (1934), *Creation* (1935), and *Aspirations* (1936), is weighted with Communist symbolism as well. In the years preceding World War II, a red star was widely used by anti-Fascist resistance parties, the Workers' and Peasants' Red Army in the Soviet Union, and the Communist Party. Depicting a red star in *Into Bondage* at a moment in time when red stars had become a symbol of anti-Fascism, Douglas subtly drew upon these connotations for audience members aware of these implications, gesturing toward Communism as an alternative political ideology for the liberation of African Americans. Douglas had included this same connotation in his *Aspects* series two years earlier. Through the powerful figure's gaze and the depiction of the North Star—a symbol of emancipation and, more specifically, Communism—viewers are given the tools to piece together an alternate and encoded meaning for the image. When the star is coupled with the elevated stance of the central figure, he can be read as formulating his rebellious escape by using the star as his guide, a plan the female figure on the left side of the mural is also aware of. She too raises her face and manacled wrists to the sky in preparation for an emancipatory plan that will lead to the reclamation of their shackled bodies.

The final key to unlocking Douglas's coded narrative in the mural is his allusions to revolutionary figures from other murals in his canon of work. The two dominant figures of *Into Bondage*, both with their gaze locked on the North Star, are adapted imprints from previous murals that also depict resistance, emancipation, and liberation. When artist Betye Saar discussed the imprints of painful memories of enslavement through her mixed-media installation *Diaspora* (1992), she spoke the words, "That slave ship imprint is on all of us."[65] She conceptualized and reconfigured the uses of evocative slave imagery through its ability to traverse time and space by living as an omnipresent imprint "on all of us." And in the same way that imagery of enslavement is imprinted on us all, as Saar suggests, Douglas, although not working directly with the haunting imagery of the slave ship, which does find its way into the background of *Into Bondage*, engaged in a similarly spectral process by flirting with the contours and boundaries of his artistic canon and reinvigorating the memory of two revolutionary figures from *Harriet Tubman (Spirits Rising)* (1930) and the *Aspects* series (1934).

Painted in 1930–31, *Harriet Tubman (Spirits Rising)* was a tribute to its namesake and depicts, in Douglas's words, "a superior type of Negro wom-

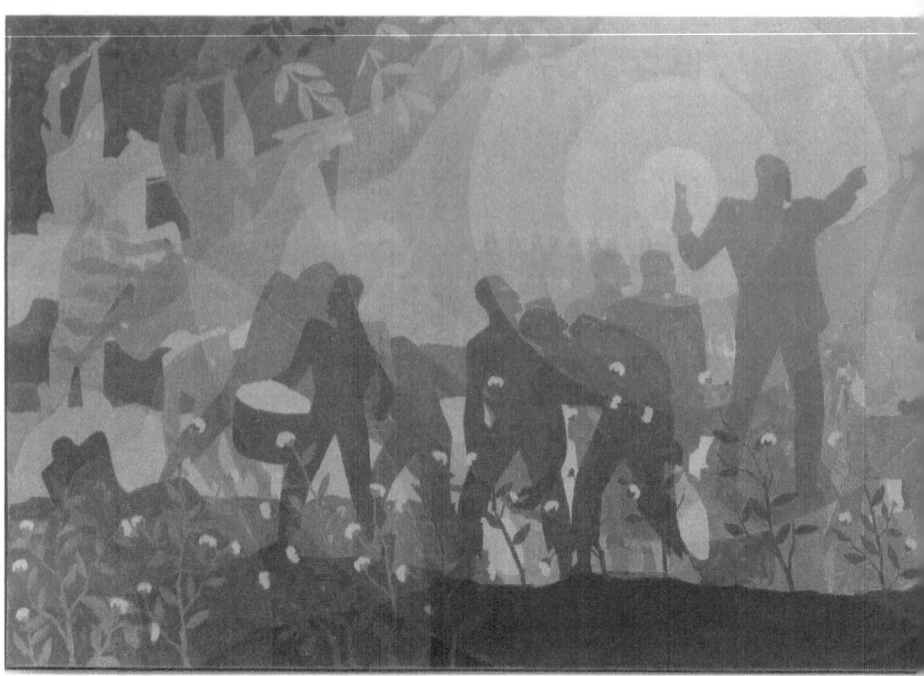

anhood."[66] Douglas painted the silhouetted figure of Tubman with her arms outstretched in an act of defiant resistance, breaking the shackles that rob her of her freedom as she stands atop the barrel of a smoking cannon with a watchful audience scattered around her. Douglas painted this mural, which was sponsored by Alfred K. Stern, son-in-law to philanthropist and Black art sponsor Julius Rosenwald, at Bennett College for Women, an HBCU in North Carolina, and he was afforded significantly more freedom to depict outwardly radical imagery. This revolutionary symbol of Tubman lives on in *Into Bondage*. Douglas invoked her defiant spirit onto the off-center manacled female figure, who raises her chained wrists, ready to break free and fulfill the emancipatory potential depicted by her spectral sister from *Harriet Tubman*.

Similarly, an influence from the panel *From Slavery Through Reconstruction*, from Douglas's 1934 mural series, *Aspects of Negro Life*, lives in *Into Bondage* through the raised central figure. *From Slavery Through Reconstruction*, the third panel of *Aspects*, shows the incongruous meeting of several groups of people. Hooded Klansmen, Union army soldiers, musicians, and a top-hatted figure occupy the space, while an orator stands on a raised platform in the center of the mural reading Abraham Lincoln's Emancipation Proclamation. At first glance, the box on which the central figure stands in *Into*

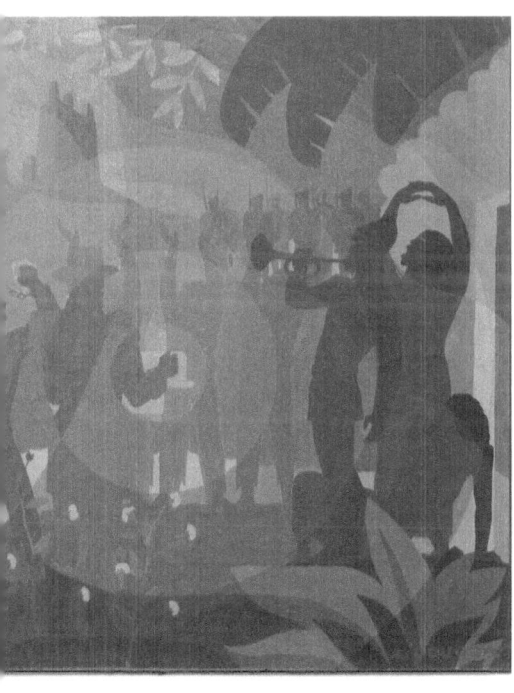

Aspects of Negro Life: From Slavery to Reconstruction (1934), Schomburg Center for Research in Black Culture, Art and Artifacts Division, New York, N.Y. Painted by Aaron Douglas. Image courtesy of the New York Public Library Digital Collections.

Bondage reminds audiences of an auction block, foreshadowing his potential life in enslavement. But invoking the memory of the elevated figure from *Aspects*, who symbolizes "the careers of outstanding Negro leaders during this time," intensifies the radical narrative running under the surface by placing the central figure as leader of a revolution.[67] Unable to create overtly challenging iconography in 1934 to depict "a way out for the Negro," Douglas left *Aspects* unfinished, only to resurrect the memory of the "outstanding Negro leader" reading the Emancipation Proclamation two years later in *Into Bondage*. He wanted the final panel of *Aspects* to show "the unity of black and white workers in the class struggle," and by imprinting the memory of the Emancipation Proclamation into a mural covertly championing Black revolution, Douglas united the acts of emancipation in both murals to finish what he was unable to complete two years earlier.[68]

Douglas's murals were "part of a heroic endeavor by black historians and fair organizers to counter the effacement of a black presence from the main exposition," writes Ater. Although this statement is certainly true, Douglas's murals actually go beyond contesting erasure at the fair. Treating *Into Bondage* as a visual palimpsest with instructional memories layered into the artwork enables us to uncover an encoded visual language within the mural that circumvented the issues of location and patronage. In his brave and bold modernist murals for the Texas Centennial Exposition, Douglas layered an alternate message of revolution into his work to create a mural of Black protest. But this ingenious encoded language has not yet been discussed in literature on both New Deal art and the Harlem Renaissance.

When Jonathan Harris unpacked the censorship of murals during the WPA in *Federal Art and National Culture: The Politics of Identity in New Deal America*, he offered the case study of Clifford Whyte's three-panel murals at Coit Tower in San Francisco in 1934, briefly alluding to the "censorship controversy" over Whyte's panel titled *Communism*. Whyte painted the panel with a hammer and sickle and the slogan "workers of the world unite" to offer viewers of the artwork "another alternative which exists in the current scene" of American life—only these elements of the mural were never seen by the public.[69] Facing intense backlash, the mural made headline news in the *San Francisco Chronicle* on July 5 in an article titled "Is This Red Propaganda? Murals on Coit Shaft Hint Plot for Red Cause."[70] Whyte was forced to erase the Communist iconography from his mural series before it was unveiled to the public on October 12, 1934. It's interesting and perhaps very telling that while Whyte faced scrutiny over the "inflammatory" imagery of his artwork, Douglas was able to navigate this fraught terrain in the same artistic era by developing an encoded revolutionary language in his Black protest murals without drawing the ire of his white patrons.

But while Douglas created strong, celebratory, and emboldened murals of Black protest in the 1930s, he wasn't the only interior muralist to do this. Following the zenith of modernism, muralists adapted the mural form to also fit the needs of social realism in the late 1930s and 1940s, and as a result, murals were embraced by Black artists such as Charles White. Unbound by white patrons, white audience members, or the restrictions of being displayed at government-sponsored state fairs in the South, White used his canvas not to encode messages of rebellion beneath surface narratives but to depict overtly radical images that protested the racial and political landscape of the time. He created explicit languages of revolution in his murals by resurrecting radical Black memory and layering imagery inspired by the socialist murals emerging from Mexico. White, therefore, was also able to use his murals to openly challenge the threat of Fascism in Europe, the deepening condition of economic bondage for Black Americans, and the unbridled capitalism sweeping across the United States, but this time in very different ways.

Social realism in the United States emerged in the 1930s almost as an antithesis to the modernism of the Harlem Renaissance. It found a stronghold among African American artists and writers in the 1930s and 1940s in large part due to the hard times of the Depression, which inspired artists toward proletarian themes in their work. But it was also the revolutionary socialist murals coming out of Mexico—namely from Diego Rivera, José Clemente Orozco, and David Alfaro Siqueiros—that turned African Americans on to social realism. To Rivera, the suppression of culture and the subordination of the working class formed one of the main links between Mexican and African American oppressions. "The colonial rulers of Mexico, like those of the United States, have despised that ancient art tradition which existed there, but they failed to destroy [it] completely," he wrote. "With this art as background, I became the first revolutionary painter in Mexico. The paintings served to attract many young painters, painters who had not yet developed sufficient social consciousness. We formed a painters' union and began to cover walls of buildings in Mexico with revolutionary art."[71]

In Mexico, Los Tres Grandes—as Rivera, Orozco, and Siqueiros were known—were united by a radical process of creating artwork. They shared progressive and egalitarian points of view, creating images that opposed dictatorship, discrimination, racism, exploitation, the scorned, and the powerful, using what they believed was the most democratizing art medium to do so, as Orozco declared in 1929: "The highest, the most logical, the purest and strongest form of painting is the mural. In this form alone, it is one with the other arts—with all the others. It is, too, the most disinterested form, for it cannot be made a matter of private gain; it cannot be hidden away for the benefit of a certain privileged few. It is for the people. It is for ALL."[72] This belief led to a proliferation of expansive, radical murals in Mexico—murals with an emphasis on folkloric characters, historic epics, and the socially, racially, and politically dispossessed.

Following the cultural revolution launched in Mexico in 1921, the secretary of education, José Vasconcelos, echoed Orozco's sentiments, believing the state should not sponsor artwork meant for the homes of the wealthy but should instead fund public murals enjoyed by the masses.[73] These murals would speak to and for the workers of Mexico by reflecting class structures, revolution, and oppression, and it was these themes that provided a blueprint for African American artists to create social realist murals of their own in the United States. "I used to go down to Radio City when Rivera was painting the one they destroyed [*Man at the Crossroads*]," muralist Charles Alston admitted, "and between his broken English and my broken French we managed to communicate and I was very much influenced by his mural work."[74]

Charles White also spoke of his time spent in Mexico in 1947 studying at the Taller de Gráfica Popular and working with Los Tres Grandes and artist Leopoldo Méndez: "I saw artists working to create an art about and for the people. . . . That had the strongest influence on my whole approach. It clarified the direction in which I wanted to move. No artist can isolate himself in a studio separate from the people. . . . [C]ontact with the people must become part of an artist's everyday life."[75]

Social realism gave White the freedom to create explicit, radical artworks. As a movement, it focused on the harsh realities of working-class life, the laborers, the impoverished workers, and those toiling in the fields every day invoking the memory of a slavery supposedly abolished. It was about social issues depicted in a real way, and it was a movement facilitated by the growth of the American Communist Party in the 1930s amid the enthusiasm for leftist politics and culture. Less concerned with experimentation and metaphorical representation, it gravitated toward proletarian and underclass themes, with social realists of the 1930s and 1940s defining the artist as "an agent of democratic consciousness raising and social change."[76] Followers of the movement, then, shared a profound belief that cultural work could "leverage transformations in the social and political sphere on behalf of America's poor and working class."[77] Social realism was both a product of and a response to the entrenchment of European Fascism and the growth of leftist, Communist ideologies among both Black and white Americans—and to artists such as Charles White, it provided a perfect visual movement through which to overtly protest the oppressive conditions rippling across the nation.[78]

Missing the crest of the Harlem Renaissance and coming of age as an artist in Chicago in the late 1930s during the Chicago Renaissance, White created a body of work that extends across every artistic medium.[79] White is heralded as one of the greatest Black artists in history, and his work spans graphic prints to cartoons and watercolors to murals. Born in Chicago in 1918 to Mississippi-born domestic worker Ethelene Gary and railroad din-ing car waiter Charly White, White spent his formative childhood years discovering his artistic passions against the backdrop of the Great Depression. Before he was old enough to pursue his own employment, White was taken to work with his mother, and he watched her scrub, cook, wash, and sew for wealthy white families for nominal pay. This experience nurtured his radical consciousness and spurred his participation in Communist Party activities. White's strong political and social conscience found an outlet in his artwork from an early age. Using Black life as his muse, he created an extensive repertoire of murals and paintings that gave dignity, meaning, and truth to Black subjects while simultaneously lacing such artwork—especially in his earlier works before and during World War II—with his own feelings about Communism, U.S. race relations, and the growing threat of Fascism in Europe.

In 1937, at the age of nineteen, White joined the FAP under the WPA, where he was soon infatuated with mural painting, quickly transferring from the easel to the mural unit and becoming one of the first African Americans in that unit. But during his tenure at the WPA, White spent more time actually fighting discrimination than he did painting: "My first lesson on the [Illinois Art Project] . . . dealt not so much with the paint as with the role of unions in fighting for the rights of working people."[80] When a significant number of Black artists faced discrimination (Chicago Renaissance artist Archibald Motley was one of them), a union was formed that picketed the project for unfair racial practices. During his time at the mural unit, he also worked with prominent leftist muralists Edward Millman, Edgar Britton, and Mitchell Siporin, all of whom traveled to Mexico in 1938 to work with Rivera, Orozco, and Siqueiros. These WPA muralists, along with Morris Topchevsky and Si Gordon, later introduced White to the readings of Engels, Lenin, and Marx, and it was during these years that White's political consciousness flourished.

Although he never joined the CPUSA, White felt moved to become politically active.[81] "It was the most natural thing in the world," he told Peter Clothier in a 1979 interview, "or should I put it the other way, it was most unnatural not to be involved politically."[82] In 1938 White took part in an exhibition titled An Exhibition in Defense of Peace and Democracy, which was held in Chicago to generate funds for victims of Fascism in Spain and China. He also became involved in the local chapter of the American League Against War and Fascism, as well as producing illustrations for leftist publications, before serving as a contributing editor for *New Masses* from 1946. "I am interested in the social, even propaganda angle in painting," he said in a 1940 interview with Willard Motley. "I do know that I want to paint murals of Negro history," White continued. "I had no other tools to fight with . . . so the only way I had to fight was with my brushes."[83]

In 1943 a politicized Charles White turned to the mural form to protest the world around him. Far removed from the coded message of protest displayed in *Into Bondage* just seven years earlier, White created an outwardly radical Black mural at a Black college in Virginia. Drawn to the impactful size of the mural because it allowed him to deal with reality and truth on a large scale, White used a twelve-by-seventeen-foot wall at Hampton Institute to paint a mural that explicitly contested World War II, Black unemployment, unbridled capitalism, and Jim Crow. Unlike Douglas, White had the artistic freedom to articulate explicit historic and contemporaneous rebellion not only through the style of social realism but also because of the mural's location and sponsorship. In 1942 White was awarded $2,000 through a Rosenwald Fellowship, a private grant program that supported Black artists and writers between 1928 and 1948. In White's proposal to the foundation, he outlined his project in three parts. First, he would tour the U.S. South, sketching the lives of Black farmers and workers; second, he would travel to Mexico to refine the mural skills gained during his tenure at the WPA, undergoing formal instruction at the Escuela Nacional de Pintura y Escultura in Mexico City; and third, he would culminate the project by creating a large fresco mural at an HBCU depicting the contribution of African Americans in the United States. White's proposal was accepted, but his plans to study in Mexico were thwarted the night before his intended departure when his local draft board refused to allow him an exit permit. The board's refusal is believed to be related to White's alleged authorship of a 1936 pamphlet about racism and oppression; the pamphlet was used by the CPUSA to recruit young people to the party.[84] Instead, White was relocated to the Schomburg Center for Research in Black Culture in Harlem—his pilgrimage to Mexico would have to wait until 1947.

For the painting division of the WPA "there were no holds barred," Black artist Charles Alston admitted, but "there wasn't the same freedom in the Mural projects. There were these stop signs and 'you can't do this and you can't do that,'" he continued.[85] This meant that HBCUs became common sites for Black murals, standing at the "forefront of the preservation of African American history and culture."[86] In the public domain and reaching large audiences, murals at Black colleges faced less scrutiny and sanitizing from conservative politicians and bureaucrats; instead, these spaces granted artists such as White independent and unhampered institutional support to explore radical content. As part of his Rosenwald Fellowship, White selected Hampton Institute in Virginia, a state weighted with painful memories, to paint *Contribution of the Negro to Democracy in America*. It was during his time in Virginia that White was forced to the back of a bus at gunpoint. "These two years in the South were one of the deeply shaking and educative experiences of my life," he later said. "I was in the real home of my people, where the vast majority had lived and worked from the days when they were brutally bought in the slave ships."[87] Being close to his ancestors in the South, White "began to understand the beauty of my people's speech." He noted "their poetry, their folklore, their dance and their music, as well as their staunchness, morality and courage. Here was the source of the Negro people's contribution to American culture, and of the far vaster contribution they could make to the world in the future."[88] Attuned to the powerful space of the Hampton Institute, White painted *Contribution* for the empowerment of Black viewers. Like Douglas, he used socialist imagery and Black memory to challenge U.S. racism and global Fascism, but unlike Douglas, he layered his mural with revolutionary historical allegory to recuperate marginalized heroes of Black history obscured by the distortions of a white school curriculum.

At the age of fourteen, White had absorbed Black history, literature, and culture when he read Alain Locke's *The New Negro*. At that moment, the weight of an obfuscated Black history enveloped him, causing him to recalibrate his position in the world as a young Black teenager. "The point of my awareness of blackness," he explained, "was the discovery of black history."[89] He found books that unveiled a host of hidden names such as Nat Turner, Crispus Attucks, Frederick Douglass, Harriet Tubman, Denmark Vesey, and Sojourner Truth. For the first time, White "became aware that Negroes had a history in America."[90] But this newfound knowledge clashed with White's high school history curriculum: the assigned textbook included only one line devoted to Black history, that Crispus Attucks was the first man to die in the American Revolutionary War. White asked his teachers why the names of Douglass, Turner, Tubman, and Truth were omitted from his textbook, only to be told that "the histories from which we were taught . . . were written by competent people, and whatever [was] not mentioned, was simply not important enough to mention."[91] So when White created *Contribution* in 1943, he used his mural to remedy the near blackout of African American history in the mainstream.

Contribution fills the twelve-by-seventeen-foot wall with multiple narratives of Black radicalism and monumental heroism. Displaying the ubiquitously erased contributions of enslaved figures, exploited workers, and anonymous soldiers, White's mural reads as a history book replete with the memories of antislavery freedom fighters Douglass, Turner, Tubman, Vesey, Peter Still, and Peter Salem and cultural icons such as Lead Belly, Marian Anderson, and Paul Robeson. Twenty-eight Black heroes are organized around the cold industrial machine that occupies the central position in the mural, their figures entwining and spilling into each other. Transcending chronological boundaries, White's mural brings multiple historical narratives from the 1830s to 1943 into view within a framework of unity to underscore the "definite tie-up between all that has happened to the Negro in the past and the whole thinking and acting of the Negro now."[92] He collapsed the structured linearity and chronology of time and instead placed Black history and memory in a continuum whereby every underrepresented narrative feeds into and enhances the next—the story of Crispus Attucks informs the narrative of Nat Turner, which gives weight to the life of George Washington Carver, and so forth.

Unlike Douglas, White wasn't bound by the constraints of government patronage; instead, he used his public wall to amass a radical Black army that ideologically and visually fought against the suffocating choke hold of Fascism, Jim Crow, and economic bondage in 1943. One of the most prolific revolutionary freedom fighters we see in *Contribution* is Nat Turner, situated in the top left-hand side of the mural. A radical figure of Black history seldom covered in history lessons, Turner was enslaved on a Southampton County plantation in Virginia, where he became a preacher after feeling the word of God. A liberatory hero of Black freedom and resistance, he was "inspired by a series of heavenly visions to lead his people in a great battle to destroy slavery," and on August 21, 1831, these visions were enacted.[93] His heroic rebellion in Southampton County left around eighty people dead, many of them white Southerners. But in response, white Southerners murdered hundreds of Black people, and Turner was eventually hanged, transforming him from a revolutionary freedom fighter for justice and liberty into a monumental and folkloric martyr of Black history. Turner's memory has frequently been (re)negotiated throughout history, but his identity as an enslaved man and a man who radically threatened the core values and institutional supremacist structures of the antebellum South means his revolutionary and complex life is still largely undiscovered. So by granting Turner a prime position on the mural, White immortalized him into the annals of Black history and by doing so used his likeness as a symbolic revolutionary touchstone that layers *Contribution* with overt memories of self-emancipation and liberation.

Dressed in clean white-and-cream attire with ragged and ripped sleeves, the strong, physically imposing body of Turner wields his broad arms aloft to brandish a fiery torch. The billowing smoke from the glowing golden flames curls above his head and envelops the wings of an armed guardian angel prepared to take up battle alongside Turner. The large blade of her downward-facing sword is ready to sweep below and slash the chains looped around the necks of the three unknown figures, but she waits patiently for Turner's signal. As he looks down upon the three manacled bodies of the anonymous enslaved figures indirectly attached to the industrial machine, the revolutionary martyr points to the guardian angel to release the choking shackles. Before she undertakes this militant act, she warns Turner of his impending danger by pointing toward four bayonets angled straight at him. Mirroring the memory of Turner being hunted during his rebellion, the bayonets unsurprisingly extend from the only white figure in the artwork: a Tory colonist in the bottom left-hand corner of the mural. Representing the paradoxes of American freedom expressed in the Declaration of Independence, he attempts to destroy a bill of the 1775 Provincial Congress that reads: PROVINCIAL CONGRESS. IV. Resolved, THAT THIS CONGRESS . . . WILL NEITHER IMPORT FOR . . . OR PURCHASE ANY SLAVE . . . ED FROM AFRICA OR ELSEWHERE . . . SIGN 1775.

Glowing a golden yellow color, the parchment stands upright, creating a wall between the white and Black figures of the mural. Beyond the parchment, Crispus Attucks falls in front of soldier Peter Salem and enslaved revolutionary Denmark Vesey, who sits astride a horse. The powerful image of Vesey gripping the barrel of a gun appears beneath the unyielding likeness of Frederick Douglass, who bisects the mural through a deliberate point toward George Washington Carver; the Fifty-Fourth Massachusetts Regiment neatly nestled under Douglass's arm. An army of Black heroes also surrounds Carver. Harriet Tubman stands behind him guiding figures in the distance toward the Underground Railroad, while Booker T. Washington, founder of the Tuskegee Institute, singer Marian Anderson, Paul Robeson, and Lead Belly all frame the renowned scientist and inventor.

Working under the remit of social realism, White used muted colors to facilitate his message of protest, one that could be achieved through Communism, he suggests. With much of the mural following a distinct color palette of dark browns, blacks, blues, and grays, White abstained from using red, a color commonly associated with Communism, until he reached the far right-hand side of the wall. Positioned at the front and center of *Contribution* is a self-portrait. White kneels barefoot on the floor, with Robeson and Ferdinand Smith (both prominent Communist labor activists) to his right. Resting upon White's knee is a blueprint, whose plans we do not see, but Robeson and Smith gesture in its direction, breaking the fourth wall and attempting to tell the audience something. Perhaps these plans are a way out of the economic bondage plaguing Black communities; perhaps they are plans to overthrow the stifling grips of capitalism, white supremacy, and Fascism; perhaps these are revolutionary plans waiting to be enacted through the ideology of Communism.

Beyond the threshold of White's likeness, the mural is tinged by large traces of red: Tubman's shawl, Smith's collar, Lead Belly's shirt and guitar, and a red flag in the top right-hand corner. To balance the inward-facing, radically posed Nat Turner, White painted Peter Still, a man who escaped his enslavement, in the top right. Still waves a flag with the incendiary and revolutionary statement "I will die before I submit to the yoke" to assert the authority and agency of enslaved men and women as he raises his other hand in a signal of onward marching. The flag, painted in a rich, bright red, with the wording in a golden yellow, is an homage to the Soviet proletarian hammer-and-sickle flag. As White's likeness draws central focus in the mural, he holds a blueprint potentially supporting the ideology of Communism—something the figure of Frederick Douglass also acknowledges as he points in the direction of the red wave of color in the mural.

To continue the didactic narrative that shows how the weight of oppression can be met with Communism, White imprinted iconography from the Mexican socialist murals of Diego Rivera. In the center of *Contribution* stands a "colossal being"—a looming instrument of capitalism resurrected from Rivera's *Pan American Unity* mural, painted at San Francisco Junior College in 1940 and depicted in the popular magazines *Time* and *Life*.[94] The mural is anchored in its center by this imposing piece of machinery and symbol of northern industry, while a pantheon of socialist heroes ideologically counteracts its presence. Rivera assembled an overlapping array of artists, scientists, prolific individuals, and laborers around the giant machine, and he confined the threats of Fascism to a smaller panel of the mural toward the bottom right-hand side. He invoked Hitler's presence through his literal likeness next to Benito Mussolini and Joseph Stalin, as well as through an homage to Charlie Chaplin's film The Great Dictator (1940), in which Chaplin parodies the life of Hitler through the egomaniacal character of Adenoid Hynkel. The mural is decorated with swastikas, American flags, a portrait of Heinrich Himmler, and scenes of war as Rivera highlighted the growing threat of Fascism and its effect throughout the world. As a determined Marxist, Rivera painted peasants as modern heroes, and much like White's work during the 1930s and 1940s, Rivera's work consistently addressed issues of labor and oppression. By relying heavily on the template of Rivera's mural, therefore, White imprinted Contribution with the weight and ideological memory of Pan American Unity to strengthen his own radical language of leftist resistance and to bring into sharp focus the importance of using Communism as an armor against capitalism and Fascism.

White also used the image of Rivera's colossal being to further unite historic slavery and economic bondage. In similar fashion to Rivera's pantheon of socialist heroes, the catalog of Black leaders making up Contribution is revealing. White resurrected the memories of Turner, Vesey, Still, Douglass, Salem, Tubman, and Attucks not only to teach an overlooked Black history but also to "articulate social commentary of contemporary relevance" and underscore the oppressive similarities between historic slavery of the nineteenth century and economic bondage in a 1940s capitalist society.[95] A pair of oversized hands belong to a struggling Black worker who grips tightly to Rivera's symbol of industrialization. These angular hands cling desperately to this emblem of capitalism, turning his knuckles white with desperation to ensure that his job—represented by the industrial machinery—remains firmly in his grasp and not in the hands of a white worker. He grits his teeth and winces at the difficulty of maintaining his job in a factory where African Americans are the last to be hired and the first to be fired. "They cut down low [on people] to keep from laying off, cut down to three days a week or no days a week," African American industrial worker Bill Young recalled of the Inland Steel Company in Indiana in the 1940s.[96]

Without the memory of Rivera's *Pan American Unity*, White's mural becomes a simpler commemoration of radical Black history, but the industrial machine sits in perfect harmony with Black history to deepen the connections between historic slavery, contemporary neoslavery, and the fight against economic bondage. White gave further ballast to the allegorical parallels between historic slavery and economic bondage by drawing on the image of Frederick Douglass and the symbolism of chains. Douglass, featured below the industrial worker, acts as a guiding source of inspiration. One of the largest figures in the mural, he immediately captures the attention of viewers through his stoic yet concentrated gaze and crown of gray hair as he stands proudly with outstretched arms, almost Christ-like. A giant of Black history, Douglass is positioned with open arms to invite his brothers and sisters into his revolutionary world and follow in his footsteps to overturn economic bondage. Although White reclaimed Douglass's memory by inserting him into a Black public space, he also used the memory of the famed abolitionist to offer a solution to discriminatory employment practices by visually depicting an act of dissidence. Douglass's straightened right hand stretches across the industrial image and reaches for the hanging shackle around the wrist of the unknown figure. The sharp, unswerving shape of Douglass's arm in tandem with his determined stare tells the viewer how he is trying to relinquish the shackles from the grasp of disparate employment practices and industrial capitalism in the 1940s.

The final allegorical layer of the mural is White's resurrection of the Fifty-Fourth Massachusetts Regiment, an African American regiment of Union soldiers during the Civil War. The mural, painted at the height of World War II, made it almost impossible for viewers to look upon the soldiers without thinking of the participation of Black soldiers in the fight against European Fascism.[97] In fighting Nazi Germany, Allied troops opposed an openly racist enemy, but Black Americans fighting in segregated units for justice on the world stage were not afforded the same equality when they returned home.

Lacing *Contribution* with references to World War II, White visualized one of his fears: "Hitler and fascism threatened us with renewed slavery and extermination of any opportunity for continued cultural advancement and social progress."[98] Subtle homages to the Double V campaign, combined with Rivera's influence, Peter Still's red flag in the top right-hand corner, and the dark red palette informing the mural's color scheme all gesture toward a solution to the growing threat of Fascism, domestic economic bondage, and unbridled capitalism. Joining the activism of people such as Paul Robeson, Claude McKay, and Margaret Burroughs, who sought to extend the popular front era demand for "anti-fascist self-scrutiny on the American home front into the World War II era," White believed that militant activism and ideological and intellectual revolution were a way to achieve radical democratic social change.[99] "Paint is the only weapon I have with which to fight what I resent," White declared, and by understanding the full potential of his twelve-by-seventeen-foot public-facing wall, he was able to openly protest the injustice of the world around him.[100]

In 1943 White painted a mural that highlighted its full protest power. While Douglas's modernist murals show how Black muralism had the capability to evade artistic lily-whitism and still operate as a potent symbol of Black protest, *Contribution* shows the full protest potential of Black murals by overtly depicting socialist, radical, empowering, and subversive iconography at a time when artwork such as Whyte's Coit Tower murals was being censored. Looking at White's mural in dialogue with Douglas's *Into Bondage* gets to the heart of how Black muralists working from the 1930s to the 1950s were able to push the conceptual boundaries of muralism for the first time. Using the public walls of government buildings, state fairs, and HBCUs, Douglas, White, Alston, Woodruff, Biggers, Scott, Hayes, and Seabrooke ushered in a new moment of Black muralism by creating public art that celebrated Blackness. For the first time, audiences saw the liberatory acts of Black freedom fighters, heroes of Black history, and Black daily life reflected back to them.

The 1940s and 1950s saw a dramatic shift in the art world in both content and patronage. The onset of World War II brought about an end to New Deal mural painting sponsorship as the WPA/FAP ended in 1943, although private sponsorship for Black murals at HBCUs continued into the 1950s, as we see with the *Art of the Negro* series (1950–51) by Hale Woodruff and the murals of John Biggers. But in the 1940s official interest in art programs stopped. With a war effort to fund and the fear of Communism gripping the United States—giving rise to the era of McCarthyism and the creation of the House Un-American Activities Committee (HUAC)—supporting public art was a low priority for Congress, especially an art that heroized Black radicalism and lambasted the American government.

This lack of support didn't cause Black mural art to disappear, though.

As a radical movement, it evolved once more in the 1960s at the height of Black Power—only this time, it appeared in the streets. Black muralism grew from an interior patron-sponsored tool of Black protest in the post-depression era into a transformational, inspirational, and demanding form of art in the streets of de facto segregated Black America. Although they had evolved in form, content, and location, street murals of the Black Power movement continued the artistic development of unbridled, revolutionary public images of Blackness, and they extended the symbiotic relationship between politics and mural art created by Douglas, White, Woodruff, Biggers, Scott, Hayes, and Seabrooke into the 1960s.

CHAPTER 2

"The WALL Is for Black People"

The Evolution of a Movement

We are constantly forced to see ourselves through white eyes.
—*Larry Neal, Black Arts Movement writer, poet, and critic*

Women have been the centers of the black family. It [is] very important
that a woman's image be seen. . . . [W]omen have an important role to
play in our society. —*Carolyn Lawrence, artist and member of AfriCOBRA*

So give me a Wall of Respect. Look into my eyes and see my life-style.
My/our culture. My culture—unceasing brutality from foreign troops
in blue; my culture—pain and frustration and degradation. And with
your brush raise my consciousness to a higher level. Give me an outdoor
gallery that will bring me outdoors where the struggle outta be—soar
me to new realization—to the wall of respect. —*Anonymous in the Greater
Milwaukee Star, 1970*

"Everyone's chest started to swell" as they gazed upon "[this] thing of
beauty," read an article in the *Greater Milwaukee Star* in 1969.[1] When a class of
Black students from Milwaukee's Parkman Junior High School visited Chicago on February 17 that year, little did they anticipate a cultural awakening.
After touring a Black-owned museum where Miss Megwa of Biafra told stories of overlooked Black history in such inspirational detail that "you could
have heard dust drop," the children headed to East 43rd Street and South
Langley Avenue in Chicago's South Side.[2] As they gazed at the colorful wall
of a TV and radio repair shop, the Black students were taken aback. In front
of them was a pantheon of Black heroes. In the streets of Chicago, in an area
overlooked and purposefully segregated to the south of the city, the students
witnessed something unprecedented. They saw themselves—their history,
their culture, and their heroes woven into the streets of Black America for
the first time, celebrating Blackness and demanding acknowledgment. Mal-

colm X, Amiri Baraka, Nat Turner, Ossie Davis, W. E. B. Du Bois, Gwendolyn Brooks, Stokely Carmichael, Marcus Garvey, and Nina Simone wallpapered the building in front of them under the title the Wall of Respect.

In the summer of 1967, when Bill Walker and the Organization of Black American Culture (OBAC) painted the Wall of Respect in Chicago's South Side, they created something groundbreaking. Reclaiming a building's wall in a de facto segregated area of the city, the Wall of Respect was a monument for the Black community, offering the first illustration of what Black street murals were and what they could be. These murals would be unapologetic images of Blackness. They would be painted directly into Black communities, interactive, vulnerable to the elements, and open to critique and vandalism from residents. Before 1967 "Black neighborhoods did not even have any Black faces appearing on billboards to sell liquor or cigarettes to the community," but here, physically layered into the street at 43rd and Langley, were uncensored images of Black pride and Black excellence.[3] You couldn't walk by Johnny Ray's Radio Repair Service without getting lost in the Black faces painted onto its facade, beautifying the neighborhood. For the first time in the Black community, residents were given "a chance to understand that your heroes belonged to you [and] that your art belonged to you."[4] Commemorating Black life in a run-down area of Chicago's South Side, the wall was more than a wall. It was a site of imagination and a gatekeeper into an individual and collective transformation. It was a mirror of Blackness reflecting the past and present, and it offered a glimmering pathway into a future full of pride. As a tangible work of public art in the streets, the wall altered the physical, emotional, and spiritual landscape of the neighborhood. During its existence, poets recited, dancers performed, musicians jammed, and activists such as Stokely Carmichael lectured on the cool, pale concrete in front of it, sanctifying the land.

Pinpointing the arrival of the Black mural movement in the streets in 1967 and cascading both forward and back from this moment in time, this chapter explains the important context leading up to the emergence of murals in the streets. Laying the important contextual groundwork for the following two chapters, this chapter delves into the intricate relational, spatial, visual, and interactional characteristics of the nation's first Black street mural, the Wall of Respect, before highlighting the growth of the mural movement on the national stage. In many ways this chapter stands, quite simply, as an introduction to Black community murals, offering a new explanation for their emergence and beginning to answer some broad and fundamental questions (that continue to be answered in chapters 3 and 4) about their unprecedented role in Black neighborhoods against the backdrop of Black Power. Why did Black murals emerge in the streets? How did these early murals alter the physical, mental, spiritual, and emotional landscape of Black communities across the country? And why were they such important works of art in the fight for cultural and racial self-definition during the crusade for Black Power?

As a direct continuation of the preceding interior mural movement, Black street murals were born out of the interwoven relationship between the deepening residential segregation of the 1950s and 1960s and the budding movement for Black self-awareness, expression, and confrontational politics that made up the pillars of Black Power. By collapsing the distance between interior murals of the Harlem Renaissance and New Deal era and street murals during the age of Black Power, we can see how this celebratory, empowering, and unique Black mural tradition arcs across the twentieth century not as disparate artistic moments in time but instead as one continuous and evolving movement in the fight for Black emotional, physical, intellectual, and spiritual liberation.

The *Wall of Respect* was a watershed moment in Black muralism and an evolution of the Black mural movement from previous decades.[5] While the radical interior murals of the Harlem Renaissance and New Deal era flourished in the 1930s and early 1940s, the dissolution of the WPA in 1943, the decrease in politically and socially conscious art with the arrival of abstract expressionism, and the deepening hunt for "anti-American" sentiment across all cultural forms due to the rise of McCarthyism saw a small but significant decline in Black interior mural art. One of the most prolific artists working from the late 1940s to the arrival of street murals in 1967 was John Biggers. While the murals of Aaron Douglas, Charles White, Georgette Seabrooke, Charles Alston, William Edouard Scott, Vertis Hayes, and Hale Woodruff began to taper off (though Woodruff would go on to create the *Art of the Negro* series at Clark Atlanta University in 1950–51), Biggers remained dedicated to creating murals across the country. He produced magnificent, large-scale works such as *Baptism* (1948), *Day of the Harvest* (1949), and *Night of the Poor* (1949) at Penn State University (his alma mater); *Harvesters and Gleaners* (1952) in Houston, Texas; *History of Negro Education in Morris County, Texas* (1955) at George Washington Carver High School in Naples, Texas; and *Web of Life*

(1960) at Houston's Texas Southern University. But as Biggers busily extended interior murals deep into the 1950s and early 1960s, the foundational blocks for an imminent community mural movement in the streets of Black America were also being laid.

As is often suggested in scholarship, documentaries, and classrooms, the 1960s was the most turbulent and explosive decade of the twentieth century. It was a decade that saw the growing civil rights, women's, and gay liberation movements; a deepening involvement in the Vietnam War and its mounting resistance at home; the multiple assassinations of political and movement leaders; racial rebellions across the North paradoxically happening in tandem with the Summer of Love; the emergence of a subversive counterculture concerned with peace, free love, and mind expansion; intensifying declarations of Black Power; and the increasingly influential Third World Liberation Front, which united oppressed peoples across race, class, gender, and sexual orientation. In the Black cultural world, birthed from this intermingled web of events, ideologies, and beliefs was a cocktail of new music, poetry, dance, film, literature, artwork, and plays and a new grassroots community mural movement that was frequently overlooked but that was so important in the broader movements toward Black agency, liberation, and self-determination.

Although street murals as part of this cultural mélange emerged in the 1960s, they were not created in a vacuum confined to the decade, nor did they surface as a separate and isolated movement from their interior predecessors of the prewar and postwar periods. The *Wall of Respect*—and the subsequent community mural movement—arose from a cauldron of events. While so many factors are at play, creating a complex tapestry to untangle and understand, perhaps two of the most potent forces leading to how and why Black community murals materialized in this period are the convergence of deepening residential and institutional segregation in the urban North during the 1950s and early 1960s and the growing movement toward assertive Black self-determination and liberation during the era of Black Power.

The Black Power movement of the 1960s was not monolithic. It was not simply a movement concerned with radical politics. And it was not, as previously vilified by the mainstream, the civil rights movement's "evil twin" practiced only by gun-toting Black Panthers.[6] It was a movement comprised of underground newspapers, small publishing houses, independent schools, community museums, arts collectives, study groups dedicated to learning about the Black diaspora and Pan-Africanism, university-based Black and African studies departments, radical organizations, and art, poetry, literature, plays, and music all declaring that Black is beautiful. Contrary to common misconceptions, it was a movement felt across the country, from the Black sharecroppers in Lowndes County, Alabama, to the militants of Harlem and Chicago, to the female antipoverty workers of Baltimore and Durham, and to the radical trade unionists of Detroit.[7] It was also a movement—as the incredible work of Rhonda Y. Williams, Kimberly Springer, and Ashley D. Farmer show us—that cannot be fully understood without an examination of the role of Black women. "In the age of rights, antipoverty, and power campaigns," as Williams so powerfully shows, "black women in community-based and often women-centered organizations harnessed and engendered Black Power through their speech and iconography and as participants of tenant councils, welfare rights and groups, and a black female religious order."[8]

Also contrary to popular belief, although the term "Black Power" was declared by Stokely Carmichael and Willie Ricks during James Meredith's March Against Fear in Mississippi in 1966, the two activists actually gave a preexisting movement a "spectacular brand name."[9] Thanks to the groundbreaking work of activist-scholars such as Peniel E. Joseph, we can see early iterations of Black Power radicalism and militancy forming during the Great Depression and postwar era to the mid-1960s and beyond. What Carmichael and Ricks gave name to then was a shifting ideological movement in the mid-1960s that gave birth not only to the formation of radical organizations such as the Black Panther Party for Self-Defense, the Organization Us, and the Lowndes County Freedom Organization but also to a new Black aesthetic and Black consciousness that rejected white and European standards of beauty and promoted Black self-love. So when the *Wall of Respect* was painted in a run-down area of Chicago's South Side, a perfect storm of events and ideologies had been unfolding, leading to the wall's creation in 1967 and the more than fifteen hundred Black murals painted across the country in the immediate aftermath.[10]

A MILLION IN CONFINEMENT

"It was said that you could not expose segregation in the north because it was subtle. It was everything but subtle. It was dynamic, it was real, blatant, violent."[11] In 1966 Jesse Jackson shone a light on the overt and widespread nature of Northern segregation during a news interview about the Chicago Freedom Movement. In 1965 Dr. Martin Luther King Jr. and the Southern Christian Leadership Conference (SCLC) migrated their attentions away from the South and instead concentrated on de facto segregation and housing problems in the North, which went on to become one of their most ambitious civil rights campaigns. Wanting to show how nonviolent direct action could bring about social change outside of the South, the SCLC formed alliances with the Coordinating Council of Community Organizations (CCCO) and the American Friends Service Committee (AFSC) to create the Chicago Freedom Movement. "Now is the time to get rid of the slums and ghettos in Chicago, now is the time to make justice a reality all over this nation," declared King.[12] Focusing their attention on creating access to open housing across the city, King and the SCLC tried to reverse the decades-long entrenchment of residential segregation that controlled and confined Black populations across the country.

In the 1940s, 1950s, and 1960s residential segregation across the North was changing. Racially explicit laws, regulations, and government practices prohibited freedom of movement for African Americans in cities such as Chicago, Boston, St. Louis, Detroit, and San Francisco, perpetually reinforcing separate Black communities surrounded by white suburbs—or, as King so hauntingly described it, "white nooses around the Black necks of the city."[13] Racially restrictive covenants were drawn up that legally forbade white real estate agents from selling homes to African American families. In Chicago, for example, by 1943 around 175 neighborhood associations enforced deeds that barred sales and rentals to Black residents.[14] And working hand in glove with restrictive covenants was another legal practice known as redlining, a practice that further hardened the racial boundaries imposed upon residents of color.

Redlining, first practiced in 1934 by the Federal Housing Administration (FHA), was based on newly drawn residential security maps created by the Home Owners' Loan Corporation (HOLC), which color-coded areas of a city based on the identities (a dog whistle for "racial background") of neighborhood occupants as a way to decide which of them could receive mortgages and loans. Green, classed as "best," was assigned to areas of the city where the most "desirable" people lived, in HOLC's view, that is, wealthy businessmen. It's important to note as well that an area couldn't be coded as green unless racially restrictive covenants were already in place. Blue was classed as "still desirable," that is, areas where "good people like white-collar families" lived. Yellow was assigned to pockets of the city that were "definitely declining," which really meant an "area with working class families." And red, meaning "hazardous," was reserved for areas of the city that housed "detrimental influences, hazardous, like foreign-born and low-class whites and most significantly" African Americans.[15]

Racially restrictive covenants and redlining were in many ways the Jim Crow of the North.[16] With African Americans denied access to certain areas across cities, severe housing shortages plagued communities of color. To exacerbate these housing pains, urban renewal projects were introduced throughout cities to "fight urban 'blight,'" which was a racially coded dog whistle for communities of color with poor, dilapidated housing that cities wanted to clear.[17] Across the North, these "renewal projects" bulldozed their way through Black neighborhoods, creating concrete ribbons of tarmac and tram lines that fractured communities.

In the years following the Second World War, to deal with the mass migration of African Americans to the North in what is known as the Great Migration, the federal government promised better housing for Black residents in cities across the region.[18] But this promise was met in the form of large-scale public housing that sought to further control and contain Black populations. By the late 1950s and early 1960s, housing projects had become almost exclusively segregated along racial lines, and many of those built for African American families took the form of high-rise blocks, further removing and isolating Black residents from the rest of the city and creating what Arnold Hirsch describes as "the vertical ghetto."[19] In Chicago, for example, whose Black population skyrocketed in the postwar period from 4 percent of the city's total population in 1920 to 30 percent in 1966, housing projects such as the Robert Taylor Homes and Cabrini-Green were built in an attempt to control the booming populations that were already legally restricted from moving to white suburban neighborhoods.[20] Built upward instead of outward, the Robert Taylor projects comprised twenty-eight units of sixteen floors that were grouped in a U-shape and encircled by cages of mesh wire, with the Dan Ryan Expressway hemming residents in to the west and Lake Michigan blocking them to the east.[21]

Public housing represented white-designed spaces of confinement. African Americans were removed more than ever from mainstream society, being "packed into high-rise ghettos where community life was impossible, [and] where access to jobs and social services was more difficult," Richard Rothstein argues in his seminal book *The Color of Law: A Forgotten History of How Our Government Segregated America*.[22] In a "lily-white" residential area south of Detroit, for example, an entire chemical plant industry had no African American employees because the industry only hired local workers.[23] Similarly, in San Francisco's Bayview–Hunters Point, the conditions of the barracks-style housing used by Black residents were often unbearable. With limited access to stores, transportation, and public and emergency services, many public housing projects such as Sunnydale and West Point were completely isolated within pockets of the city.[24] What happens then, as George Lipsitz describes in *How Racism Takes Place*, is that "the racial imagination . . . relegates people of different races to different spaces, produc[ing] grossly unequal access to education, employment, transportation and shelter" and imposing upon Black residents "a racial tax."[25]

Routinely relocated, regarded as peripheral, and frequently cleared, African American communities are seldom afforded the luxury of space.[26] Black communities constantly faced the threat of urban renewal, and when not displaced, these communities were habitually maintained by boundaries and barriers controlling the parameters of where residents could and could not live. "What we are looking at here," Hirsch writes of the creation of Chicago's South Side, "is the construction of the ball park within which the urban game is played. And there is no question that the architects, in this instance, were whites."[27] Statements like these beg us to ask big questions: What happens when people live in environments built to contain them? What happens to the physical landscapes of the community? And what are the emotional impacts upon the residents who live in these confined neighborhoods?

Speaking to the racialized confinement of barrios throughout the United States, Raúl Homero Villa has documented how "*barrio* residents have consciously and unconsciously enacted resistive tactics or defensive mechanisms to secure and preserve the integrity of their cultural place-identity within and against the often-hostile space regulation of dominant urbanism."[28] In other words, marginalized communities create ways to culturally assert their right to segregated and purposefully designated neighborhoods. This speaks to Lipsitz's suggestion that "people who do not control physical places often construct discursive spaces as sites of agency, affiliation and imagination."[29] Here, Lipsitz and Villa both point to the reactions of oppressed, marginalized, and segregated communities of color and the ways in which these communities create "spatial imaginar[ies]" through a host of cultural expressions to contest, combat, and even reclaim such forms of segregation.[30]

In the late 1960s one of the ways in which racially segregated Black communities constructed these sites of agency, affiliation, and imagination was through murals. Murals became a way for Black communities to reclaim public walls physically, culturally, emotionally, and spiritually in their designated neighborhoods, to create spaces of imagination and Black pride. When Black sociologist Kenneth Clark told the world in 1965 that "the dark ghetto's invisible walls have been erected by the white society, by those who had power, both to confine those who have no power and to perpetuate powerlessness," Black muralists such as Boston's Gary Rickson made these invisible walls seen.[31] In 1969 in Roxbury, Boston, Rickson made visible a wall on the side of the community's YMCA that he knew many people would see. "Thousands come into the city and thousands leave on a daily basis, so I put the murals where the traffic is," he said.[32] In a Black enclave in Boston, Rickson reclaimed a public wall to transport residents into a surreal, mystical, and prehistoric world under the title *Africa Is the Beginning*.

Nighttime recedes as the dawning of a new day—and a new era—emerges across the mural. An engulfing deep red platform symbolizing the earth dominates a third of the expansive wall, with a small, glowing pyramid perched atop casting an elongated, pointed shadow across the rich, earthy ground. Bisecting at a diagonal angle is a deliberate fork of lightning disconnecting the quiet night sky of the past from the serene dawning of the future. The front facade of the pyramid faces toward the parting bolt of lightning. The structure straddles both past and future worlds because to Rickson, the pyramid symbolized the first civilization, one rooted in Black culture.[33] In his book *Freedom Dreams*, Robin D. G. Kelley beautifully conceptualizes that most radical art "is not protest art, but works that take us to another place, that envision a different way of seeing, perhaps a different way of feeling," and murals of the 1960s and 1970s, as Rickson demonstrates here, offered a window into a new perspective in the streets of Black America, a different way of seeing that celebrated Black culture and Black heritage.[34]

When murals lined the walls of Black communities in the late 1960s, their creation of celebratory Black images in streets around the country formed an important thread in the assertive quest for Black self-expression, liberation, and determination encompassed under the term "Black Power." A new Black consciousness and aesthetic were growing in society, and they were concerned with Black space, Black culture, Black history, and Black beauty. In Black communities all over the nation, many residents were living and breathing this new Black consciousness. It was an immaterial hum that one could simply "feel in the air," Larry Neal, prolific poet, essayist, and cultural theorist of the Black Arts Movement (BAM), has suggested.[35]

The term "Black consciousness" emerged from the "short-term" gains of the civil rights movement, Neal argued. To him, Black leadership focused too intensely on integration, failing to deal with "the issues of blacks controlling the institutions." This meant that "the organizations which claimed to represent us were not even finally controlled by us, the control was rooted in the white liberal establishment whose interests could not, ultimately, coincide with ours," he felt.[36] The days of demanding seats at lunch counters were long gone, replaced instead by the assertive demand for the land upon which the counters were built. "We don't have enough living space; but in our communities, that which is not needed can be found in abundance," poet, author, educator, and founder of Chicago's Third World Press Haki Madhubuti suggested in 1968. "We have to start asking ourselves, why is this so? The answers are obvious—we are still being controlled from the outside. Our minds should be thinking about the power of ownership at the community level. . . . We must move towards true community control and ownership."[37]

Shifting away from the mainstream integrationist platform of the 1950s civil rights movement, this new Black consciousness and aesthetic of the 1960s uncompromisingly, unapologetically, and unquestioningly celebrated and demanded the acknowledgment of Blackness. "When we speak of aesthetic," Neal posited, "we . . . mean the destruction of the white thing. We mean the destruction of white ways of looking at the world."[38] Sometimes this meant promoting Black separatism, at other times it meant celebrating Black cultural nationalism, but what it always meant was to reject the supremacist standards of culture, history, and beauty ubiquitous throughout the United States.

"Our history and our culture were completely destroyed when we were forcibly brought to America in chains. And now it is important for us to know that our history did not begin with slavery's scars," Malcolm X declared in 1963.[39] "Our culture and our history are as old as man himself and yet we know almost nothing of it," he warned. "We must recapture our heritage and our identity if we are ever to liberate ourselves from the bonds of white supremacy."[40] In the 1960s a Black cultural awakening was emerging—an awakening that could be achieved by recuperating Black histories and identities erased by dominant white optics. Learning and unconditionally celebrating Black history across the diaspora would enable Black Americans "to be comfortable in the knowledge of themselves" so that they no longer attacked the "lips, skin, hair, legs . . . and self that we had been trained to hate," Neal suggested.[41] Growing numbers of people "snapp[ed] off the shackles of imitation and [wore] their skin, their hair, and their features 'natural' and with pride."[42] As Hoyt Fuller, editor of *Negro Digest / Black World*, revealed, after centuries of being told, "in a million different ways, that [Black people] were not beautiful, that whiteness of skin, straightness of hair, and aquilineness of features constituted the only measures of beauty, black people have revolted."[43]

It was clear in the mid-1960s that a new Black aesthetic was necessary and that it needed to correspond with the reality of Black life in the United States. The BAM answered this call through the poetry, music, paintings, and essays of individuals such as James T. Stewart, Sun Ra, Sonia Sanchez, Ron Welburn, Marvin E. Jackmon, Dindga McCannon, Ben Jones, Carolyn Lawrence, Jeff Donaldson, Larry Neal, Floyd Barbour, Kay Brown, Ademola Olugebefola, John Coltrane, Sonny Rollins, Dudley Randall, Gwendolyn Brooks, Phil Cohran, Marvin X, and Haki Madhubuti. Created "for the people, by the people and from the people," music, drama, dance, literature, and poetry all shifted focus in the late 1960s to encompass assertive celebrations of a Black experience in the United States.[44]

This pronounced shift was also felt in the depths of the art world. "For many of us who exhibited works of art in the 1950s, the turbulent years of the 1960s came as both a shock and a relief," artist, scholar, and curator David Driskell wrote. "We were shocked to see how different our art was from that which had recently burst upon the scene flaming with Black rhetoric and revolutionary advocacy; the kind set on registering change focused on social issues that centered primarily on race."[45] American art at the time was dominated by a Western aesthetic, but Black artists were ready to push back. White artistic paradigms failed to align with a Black experience in the

United States, and white control over American art ignited Black artists to challenge an art world that elevated white European paintings as the zenith of artistic talent.

At the vanguard of this movement were street murals. The decade's new Black consciousness was about recapturing Black heritage and identity, and it was about no longer wanting a seat at the lunch counter but the land upon which the restaurant was built. The 1960s new Black aesthetic was about overthrowing supremacist ideas of art and beauty in the United States, espousing proclamations of "Black is beautiful," and creating artwork that highlighted the magnificence of Blackness. Murals in the streets were a successful embodiment of this. If people who don't control physical places often "construct discursive spaces as sites of agency, affiliation and imagination," then Black street murals of the 1960s were a way for artists to transform segregated streets into spaces of community control.[46] From 1967 murals offered a way to reclaim "the dark ghetto's invisible walls" in segregated Black communities and to fill them with depictions of Black pride. Activists were tired of Black liberation being rooted in "the white liberal establishment," so it was time to celebrate Black history and culture. Murals were a way to create pockets of unyielding, uncompromising, and adoring Black pride in the heart of America.[47]

THE WALL CAME FROM SOMEWHERE, AND THAT SOMEWHERE WAS BLACK CHICAGO

By the summer of 1967, at 43rd and Langley in Chicago's South Side, the stage was set for a group of muralists to transform a wall into a space of Black pride and imagination. From conversations in Hoyt Fuller's living room between himself, poet and writer Conrad Kent Williams, and activist and theorist Abdul Alkalimat, the Organization of Black American Culture (OBAC)—pronounced *o-ba-see*—was formed.[48] As an organization concerned with celebrating Blackness, the group wanted to use art as a way to "make ourselves more beautiful to each other," wrote Alkalimat, "more beautiful to ourselves, more beautiful to each other, more beautiful to everybody, because somebody who knows they are beautiful *Is* [sic] beautiful."[49]

On June 14, 1967, members of the Visual Arts Workshop of OBAC held their first meeting with Black artists. The meeting was a chance for the group to brainstorm ways to create artwork that fed the movement for Black liberation and to figure out how their work could be viewed by the masses—

this was important, considering Black artists were often rejected from mainstream art galleries (discussed further in chapter 4). During the meeting, artists decided on a collective project where they could "become agents of Black liberation" by promoting positive self-esteem and community values in their artwork.[50] Present at the meeting, under the invitation of friend and photographer Billy Abernathy, was artist Bill Walker. Having worked in Memphis creating interior murals across the city in the mid-1950s, Walker arrived in Chicago in the 1960s and began working with artist Mitchell Caton, turning him on to the power of mural painting as well.

During this period, Walker began to formulate the idea of doing large collaborative murals.[51] Driving through different neighborhoods in the South Side and meeting local residents, he was struck by the amount of street walls defaced with gang inscriptions and scrawled graffiti, especially around 43rd and Langley, a contested gang territory between the Blackstone Rangers and the Black Disciples. At the OBAC meeting, Walker told the group he was in discussion with community members to paint a wall at 43rd and Langley, which the Visual Arts Workshop loved. From the heart of the South Side, deep in the Black community in one of the most racially segregated cities in the nation, one of the most important local expressions of the country's Black consciousness would emerge.

Nestled into the streets of 43rd and Langley—an area of high crime and drug use but with a vibrant and energetic spirit—the wall was where it needed to be, in the "blues and funky scene . . . later renamed Muddy Waters Drive."[52] All that was left to do was decide what it would depict, and "heroes of Black history" was the final consensus. Shortly after the workshop meeting, Walker strolled the streets, "[getting] to know those people, and those families in and around the communities" and requesting their permission to paint a mural. The mural was going to belong to the community, after all, so community input was paramount.[53] Local residents knew Walker, "they respected him and they trusted him," and Walker built upon this relationship by asking residents and members of local street gangs whom they wanted to see immortalized on a wall in their neighborhood.[54]

"The men and women depicted were carefully chosen, debated and vetted to be a representation of how we saw and understood heroism for Black people," Alkalimat suggested.[55] Given the rise of Black Power in the mid-1960s and the flourishing BAM on the national stage, individuals were chosen that spoke to the contemporaneous shift from the integrationist Southern movement for civil rights to a more radical, Black nationalist ideology. After conferring with locals, the artists selected figures from the past and present who everyone believed "charted their own course" through life and "did not compromise their humanity."[56] "Ruby Dee—celebrates the sensitivity of Black womanhood," "Ossie Davis—victorious and glorious," "Nat Turner—made a meaningful protest," "Claudia McNeil—evokes the eternal struggle of Black motherhood," "Nina Simone—Mississippi goddess," and "Stokely—the power dimension," so the selection of Black heroes read on OBAC's original plans.[57]

On these typed-out plans, however, we see the crossed-out names of Ronald Fair and Floyd McKissick, hinting at how OBAC and Walker were in constant discussion and debate over which likenesses and memories would live harmoniously on the wall in the community. James Brown, James Baldwin, Thelonious Monk, Malcolm X, Cecily Tyson, Claudia McNeil, Stokely Carmichael, H. Rap Brown, Elijah Muhammad, Nat Turner, Gwendolyn Brooks, and Muhammad Ali spoke to the principles of the community, making the cut to be painted onto the wall. But "we didn't put the Supremes up, or Whitney Young from the Urban League," Jeff Donaldson admitted.[58] Local residents and gang members even flatly rejected the presence of Martin Luther King Jr. on their shrine to Blackness because "the people in the neighbourhood didn't believe in nonviolence," Donaldson suggested.[59]

With a rough selection of figures chosen for the wall, Sylvia Abernathy, a member of the Visual Arts Workshop, submitted a structured design for the mural that harmonized with the architectural composition of the building. The wall was broken down into seven sections, each having a theme, color scheme, painter, and photographer. Bill Walker was assigned "Religion," with photographs taken by Robert Abbott "Bobby" Sengstacke; Norman Parish was given "Statesmen," with photographs by Roy Lewis; the "Sports" section saw Myrna Weaver on painting; Jeff Donaldson painted the "Jazz" section, with Bill Abernathy on photography; Roy Lewis took photographs for the "Theater" section, while Barbara Jones-Hogu did the painting; and Edward Christmas painted "Literature," complete with Amiri Baraka's poem "S.O.S.," while Darryl Cowherd took photographs.

Split into these seven sections through use of color and architectural structure, the mural showed revolutionary leaders lined up along the top left-hand section of the mural, painted by Norman Parish. In photographs of the mural, we see the faces of H. Rap Brown, Marcus Garvey, Adam Clayton Powell Jr., and Stokely Carmichael looked upon by the larger, somewhat looming presence of Malcolm X, who dominates the wall. These five statesmen live as separate, individual portraits but remain connected to one another through the colored background—the earthy swatches of color reach from Malcolm X toward Garvey in the shape of an abstracted orange branch. Although temporally and ideologically distinct, these heroes live in visual harmony on the wall. Directly and indirectly, OBAC's focus on racial memory across time spoke to BAM writer Julian Mayfield's 1972 essay in *The Black Aesthetic* and his discussion of Black consciousness: "For those who must create, there is a Black Aesthetic which cannot be stolen from us. It is our racial memory, and the unshakable knowledge of who we are, where we have been, and springing from this, where we are going."[60] Mayfield's words come to life on the wall as the neutral colors of the "Statesmen" background dance around the likenesses of Malcolm X and Garvey, H. Rap Brown and Adam Clayton Powell Jr. akin to branches on the family tree of Black history, connecting the figures in a continuum of twentieth-century Black liberation.

Toward the center of the mural, we see the boarded-up bay window displaying African American athletes such as Muhammad Ali and Wilt Chamberlain partition the revolutionaries from the musicians, who are laid out in portrait-like fashion on the right side of the wall. The faces of Louis Armstrong, Charlie Parker, Sonny Rollins, Lester Young, Nina Simone, and Ornette Coleman sit directly above the "Theatre" section and the second largest portrait on the wall, actress Claudia McNeil, painted by Barbara Jones-Hogu. The young McNeil counterbalances Malcolm X, and the two figures face away from each other, guarding and protecting different sides of the mural. With the large portrait of McNeil placed in such a prime position, the wall stood as a fundamental reminder of the roles played by Black women in the movement toward Black liberation both culturally and ideologically. Women "are a force," women "are the foundation," Jones-Hogu believed, and she showed us this by painting McNeil as a focal point on the mural at eye level with audiences on the street: a gatekeeper, a force, a foundation.[61]

In 1968 the wall underwent a second, unplanned phase. Because of the growing mood of Black nationalism and Black Power in the urban North, Bill Walker "wanted to have [the wall] as a newspaper or a magazine" that "changed from week to week, month to month" to ensure it would always be a true ideological and cultural reflection of current life for local residents.[62] Eugene Wade, known to many as Eda, was an artist and close friend of Walker, and he was instructed by Walker to repaint Norman Parish's "Statesmen" section without the original artist's permission, sparking controversy that eventually led to the demise of the OBAC Visual Arts Workshop and later to the formation of AfriCOBRA.[63] The panel was whitewashed by local resident Herbert Colbert under Walker's instructions. "When that section was whitewashed, and I painted over there, Bill and I's names were absolute mud," Eda recounted during a 2017 interview.[64] But while this second phase of the mural disturbed the waters of OBAC, it maintained the wall's presence as an emblem of Black consciousness in the South Side community, reflecting "what was current [in] the movement and the mood." To Eda and Walker, the late 1960s "was calling for something . . . a little more dramatic" to be put on the wall—"the Black Power symbol, the Blackness in terms of the color, more Blackness, more militan[cy]," Eda suggested.[65] Further assassinations throughout the decade, deepening involvement in the Vietnam War, the turbulent Democratic National Convention in Chicago, and the strengthening Illinois Black Panther Party under the inspirational leadership of twenty-one-year-old Fred Hampton needed to be acknowledged.

In the updated "Statesmen" section, Eda still included the faces of Malcolm X, Stokely Carmichael, and H. Rap Brown on the wall but deviated from Parish's initial design by positioning the three men alongside prominent female activist and lawyer Florynce "Flo" Kennedy.[66] Focusing more intensely on the composition of this panel, in contrast to Parish, Eda placed the figures in a cohesive narrative to convey a more overt message of Black Power. Brown and Malcolm X face Carmichael and Kennedy, only to be vertically bisected by an authoritative clenched fist piercing the space between them. Painted midlecture, Malcolm X and Carmichael look animated, the pulse of Black nationalism coursing through their bodies as they preach the tenets of loving oneself in an imaginary street sermon. Eda textured the backdrop, an all-Black background symbolically claiming the wall as a space of "Blackness," around Kennedy, Brown, and Carmichael with flecked white lines around the raised, clenched fist to depict the vibrations of Black Power rumbling throughout the neighborhood.

These Black heroes painted on the *Wall of Respect* were more than just two-dimensional drawings on a blank wall. They were symbols of Black pride, keys to unlocking a door into self-love, and a way of recalibrating one's sense of self. "That imagery in the *Wall of Respect* might have been the first-time people had really seen something positive," artist Michael D. Harris said, "something like this, what it looks like . . . success looks like. That can be very powerful in ways that we don't even understand."[67] The wall provided spliced moments of Black history, moments that viewers could mentally cycle through, reimagining voices, images, songs, and speeches from the figures on the wall. They hear Nina Simone's powerful voice. They see Claudia McNeil in *A Raisin in the Sun*. They imagine James Baldwin's words from *The Fire Next Time*. And they remember Muhammad Ali's knockout of Henry Cooper in 1963. The images painted on the wall create a flipbook in the viewer's mind where these resurrected memories meet on the contours of history to be woven together in a visual quilt of Black pride and a dedication to Black respect.

As prolific activist-scholar Margo Natalie Crawford conceptualizes, when viewing the paintings upon the mural, the phrase "black light"— birthed from the BAM—comes to mind. The somewhat oxymoronic term "black light" was a recurrent metaphor used during the movement for Black liberation, and it found traction among poets, authors, photographers, artists, and performers of the 1960s and 1970s. "Black light" challenged the racist connotations that aligned "whiteness" with "light," "purity," and "enlightenment." "The optic itself has been tainted by the racist privileging of whiteness," notes Crawford, and in response, Black novelists, poets, artists, and photographers of the 1960s employed the idea of "black light" as a way to oppose the supremacist meanings of whiteness.[68] Cultural theorists, artists, poets, and photographers of the BAM created art that idolized and "accentuate[d] all the features that antiblack racism has vilified."[69]

In his 1970 poem, "Judy-One," for example, Haki Madhubuti subverts the image and idea of dark skin absorbing light while being photographed:

> her smile is like
> clear light
> bouncing off
> the darkness of the
> mediterranean at nighttime.[70]

Here, Madhubuti reconstructs the process of photography by transforming the young girl's image into a bountiful projector of light. No longer an ab-

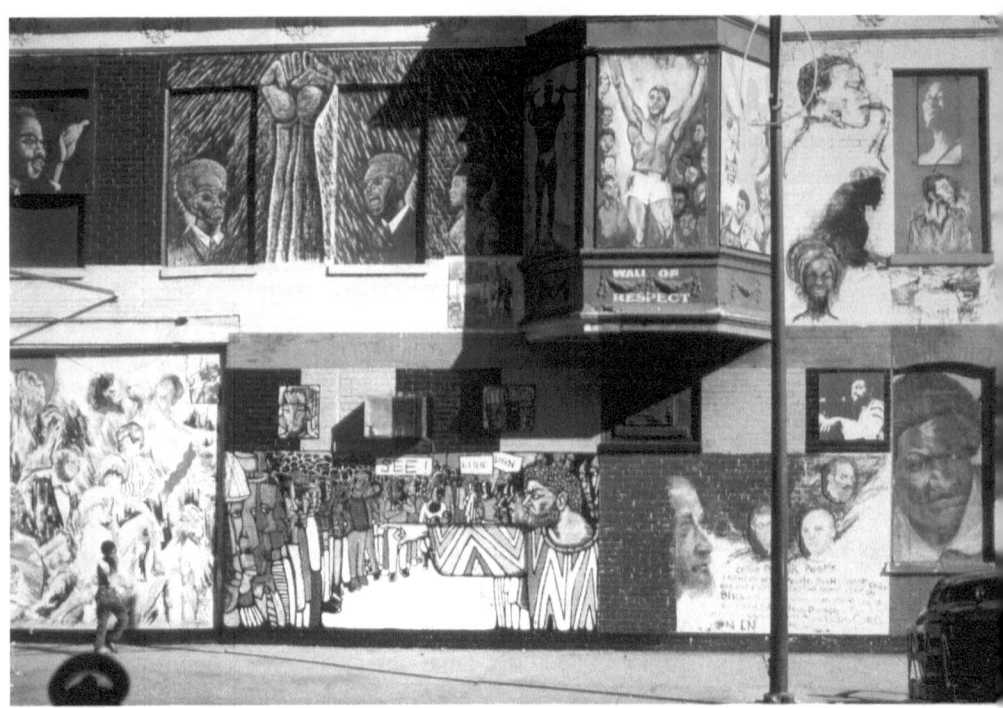

Wall of Respect (new panel) (1968), 43rd and Langley, Chicago, Ill. Original wall painted by William Walker, the Organization of Black American Culture (OBAC), new panel created by Eugene "Eda" Wade. Photograph by Georg Stahl. Courtesy of the Georg Stahl Mural Collection, University of Chicago Visual Resources Center Luna Collection.

sorbent instrument of the white gaze, the girl is instead a reflection of true Blackness, and in much the same way, the *Wall of Respect* engages in this process.

In traditional artistic palettes of white Western art, "white" and "light" influenced "the entire palette . . . creating a predominance of infinite, pastel colors and light," but the *Wall of Respect* undermined this process to make Blackness seen.[71] Walker and the OBAC artists literally made the color black visible by relegating whiteness to the background in half of the mural and painting portraits on top. The faces of carefully selected Black heroes were painted either in gray scale—to align with the black-and-white photography pasted on the mural—or in rich, deep brown celebratory tones to move the color black from the background to the fore. Black as a color therefore served as a central light—a black light, a light of illumination—when muralists used its dominance to paint the faces of Black heroes with little accentuation of white light, celebrating and lionizing the "Afrikan velvet skin."[72]

But the conception of "black light" wasn't just about an aesthetic awakening and the alteration of an artistic palette to be seen physically. It was about culturally, spiritually, commemoratively, and historically making the invisible visible as well. It was about invalidating the tainted optics of white supremacy in all its permutations and lifting Blackness—Black history, memory, culture, spirituality—from the background and placing it center stage, an ideological and intellectual foregrounding of Blackness that would lead to an expansion and a reconfiguration of oneself. "We know who we are," Larry Neal writes, "and we are not invisible, at least not to each other. We are not Kafkaesque creatures stumbling through a white light of confusion and absurdity."[73] Neal speaks to the duality of "black light" here both as a visual awakening through the literal illumination of the physical Black self and as an ideological awakening that occurs through an immersion in and understanding of Black history. The *Wall of Respect* engages in this duality of "black light" when it not only celebrates the "Afrikan velvet skin" of the Black heroes it visualizes but also sheds light on the Black history, memory, and culture that remain absent from America's historical, commemorative, and mainstream landscape.

One of the reasons the *Wall of Respect* was so intent on visualizing figures of Black history, Eda suggests, was because "we did have our own sheroes and heroes that made a contribution [but] that may not be included in a textbook because of whatever political or social reason."[74] The wall offered a way to see, a way to feel, and a way to understand Blackness. "It was the beginning of a message to the community that . . . our self-worth is not defined by the powers that be," artist Howard Mallory admitted; it was defined instead by those in charge of their own image.[75] So the wall became a way to show the Black community at 43rd and Langley who they were and where they had been throughout history, or as Mallory so beautifully put it, "our offering to the planet."[76]

As the first Black community mural in the streets, the wall was groundbreaking. It was complex, interactive, and transformational. "The WALL is for black people," Useni Eugene Perkins wrote in his 1968 poem "Black Culture."

> It is too black to decorate the
> galleries of Baroque museums,
> or adorn the Victorian mansions

of clamorous belly aristocrats,
who refuse to appreciate
the sacredness of blackness.[77]

The wall highlighted a proud Black community in Chicago's South Side, it created a space for viewers to expand their imaginations, and it became a popular site for locals and tourists to congregate and visit in the thousands.

"I really don't know why people got so excited over it," Eda admitted. "Although I was part of painting it, I'm still trying to figure it out."[78] But regardless of Eda's attempts to understand the widespread significance of the wall, "people fe[lt] better when they walk[ed] by there," recounted Donaldson.[79] "The effects on the neighborhood were palpable," and it is in these interactions with local residents that we can see more clearly the powerful role of the wall in the Black community and how it captivated the street and those in its orbit.[80] "I saw a young man sitting [outside] and I was in the television shop, and I walked out of the television shop," Bill Walker once recalled. "He was sitting in front of the wall. So I said, 'How are you doing, brother?' [and] he said, 'I'm getting my strength.'"[81] To the anonymous man on the street at 43rd and Langley, the *Wall of Respect* created a space of personal empowerment, a space for the contemplation of his Black identity, and a space for him to see his history, see himself, and to be given strength. In the 1960s "Black faces were not prominent in the mainstream. We were not in the newspaper or on television," said Abdul Alkalimat.[82] So by portraying the faces of Black individuals such as Du Bois, Garvey, and Robeson alongside the many contemporary figures of Kennedy, Ali, Simone, Coltrane, McNeil, Brown, Carmichael, and Baldwin, the wall was able to "rescue a sense of pride" for residents.[83]

But the wall was not only a sight to see, it was also a site to experience. "I saw women weep because of pride," Walker recalled.[84] During the mural's creation, residents of the neighborhood around 43rd and Langley met each other and interacted with the muralists, gazing, questioning, and passing judgment on the images being created. "What is that ugly thing?" a woman asked Jeff Donaldson of his portrait of Nina Simone. "I got to look at that ugly mothafucka you just painted every day?" Taking on board this resident's brutally honest critique of his painting, Donaldson repainted his portrait of the singer, which was met with a more agreeable assessment.[85] Donaldson recalled that around twenty-five to one hundred people would come by each day and ask questions of him and the other artists, and around three hundred people would visit the site on the weekends to try and understand this unprecedented scene of Black women and men in their neighborhood.[86] "People had a great attachment to that Wall," said Walker. "I suppose maybe it was because they didn't have anything," and in many ways, this made the wall a collective project with them and for them.[87] Once it was finished, children in the neighborhood would even offer to explain the mural to visitors— for a small fee, of course.

The OBAC artists and Walker thought the mural needed twenty-four-hour surveillance to ensure it wouldn't be vandalized or defaced. But "the people watched the wall, the people in the community," Madhubuti suggested.[88] Shortly after its creation, the warring gangs of the Black Disciples and the Blackstone Rangers informally declared 43rd and Langley a "neutral ground" for gang activity. "The Black Disciples, who was basically in that area, . . . decided that they'd protect it," Eda said. "They saw that it was important in terms of what we were trying to do, and what the community was responding to."[89] Understanding the power of the mural in their own streets, Chicago's gangs took it upon themselves to become protectors of the wall, so they policed it day and night to deter vandals and prevent the paints and scaffolding from being stolen. During the mural's four-year life cycle not a single act of vandalism befell the wall, which lived as a symbol of Black pride in the community until its untimely end.[90]

Shortly after the mural was dedicated in August 1967, visitors came from far and wide to see the nation's first Black street mural. "Even before we finished, there were people lined up down the street and around the corner, because this was the biggest tourist attraction to African Americans who were coming to Chicago, some to visit family, family reunions. And every day, it was just lines of traffic," photographer Bobby Sengstacke recalled.[91] Milling about the wall was a "panoply of artists, poets, actors, musicians, activists, journalists, community residents of all ages, local visitors and tourists from afar."[92] But also present at the wall on a regular basis were undercover police officers and FBI agents surveying the OBAC artists and their work. The FBI had launched the Counterintelligence Program (COINTELPRO) in 1956, and its purpose was to "infiltrate, disrupt and destabilize 'subversive,' 'radical,' and 'un-American' organizations."[93]

Threatened by both the images of Black pride on the wall and the positive, empowering, and inquisitive effect the mural was having on the community, the Red Squad, an intelligence-gathering unit of the Chicago Police Department, opened investigation files on both the wall and OBAC members.[94] "I'm kind of curious that a move toward self-determination and self-control is considered revolutionary," AfriCOBRA member Michael D. Harris said. "Usually, revolutionary means you're trying to take over something else. But when you start trying to take over yourself, that begins to be defined as revolutionary?"[95] To sow seeds of dissension between OBAC and local gangs, workshop members received fraudulent letters and anonymous phone calls accusing them of being traitors and spies from whom they assumed was the FBI. Jeff Donaldson remembered receiving an anonymous threatening letter warning him of his imminent demise the next time he mounted his scaffolding to continue painting the wall.[96] "I did not realize the power of art until I saw people with guns down there thinking that we were going to start a revolution by having this wall," Barbara Jones-Hogu mentioned.[97] To be viewed as a threat, the wall "didn't have to have 'revolution' written in letters, but it clearly had self-determination and a new sense of self that was made in visual form," she continued, and that was enough to concern the police.[98]

The threat of urban renewal plans throughout this area—as part of the Model Cities economic development program put forth by the U.S. Department of Housing and Urban Development—meant the police no longer needed to worry about this "revolutionary" work of public art in the heart of the Black Belt, though.[99] Protests against the proposed urban renewal rumbled throughout the neighborhood, reaching boiling point on August 14. By the summer of 1969, the *Wall of Respect* and the *Wall of Truth*, which was painted in 1969 by Walker and Eda on the opposite wall (see chapter 4), had become priceless monuments in the community. Local residents turned out to protect their shrines to Black pride. Demonstrations stretched over a two-week period, attracting a 150-car parade and over a thousand protesters, including civic leaders, government officials, and the Black Panthers. "The wall must stand 'even if it means open warfare with the pig power structure,'" Illinois Panther Willie Calvin declared.[100] The protests were a success, and on August 28, 1969, Third Ward Alderman Ralph Metcalfe drew cheers when he announced that plans for demolition had stalled.

While the *Wall of Respect* lived without threat in the South Side community for two more years, it became weather-beaten and dilapidated, and then in 1971 a fire suspected to have been caused by arson gutted and charred

Johnny Ray's building, damaging many of the panels. Members of the local community mourned the loss of their monument to Blackness, and people immediately began removing panels from both the *Wall of Respect* and the *Wall of Truth*.[101] Various stories emerged that speculated about the cause of the building's and the wall's demise, but artists, activists, and the Black community had their own theory. The suspicious circumstances surrounding the fire, the constant presence of the FBI throughout the wall's creation, and white America's discomfort with images of Black pride left no doubt in the minds of the Black community. "They did not want images of black consciousness!" musician Phil Cohran declared. "I *know* that's what it was."[102]

While this mural in the heart of Chicago's Black Belt was lost to the supremacist forces that felt threatened by its existence, its memory and legacy endured throughout the nation, sparking a cultural and artistic movement that would continue throughout the following decades, as we begin to see below. Lining the streets in major cities, predominantly across the North and along the West Coast, were Black murals depicting prideful, heroic, powerful, sometimes bleak, but oftentimes celebratory narratives of Black life and Black history in America and across the diaspora. The *Wall of Respect* may have been physically erased in 1971, but by 1968 the mural had already created a template for artists to transform walls of their own communities into sites of imagination, celebration, and pride across the country.

MEMENTOS OF THE BLACK POWER MOVEMENT

"Built so Blacks can see their (Blackness) tower . . . Towering untouchably / Over timid stares of the 'enemy'" is how poet Eugene Redmond described a wall on the west side of St. Louis.[103] In 1968, after seeing an *Ebony* magazine article about Chicago's *Wall of Respect*, LeRoy White and six other artists painted a mural at the intersection of North Leffingwell Avenue and Franklin Avenue, funding the project with their own money. "UP YOU MIGHTY RACE" read the words on a wall surrounded by the portraits of Marcus Garvey, Amiri Baraka, Dick Gregory, Malcolm X, Elijah Muhammad, James Baldwin, Harriet Tubman, Frederick Douglass, W. E. B. Du Bois, Martin Luther King Jr., H. Rap Brown, Muhammad Ali, and Stokely Carmichael. Simplistic in style, the mural was set against a black background with individual portraits arranged to the left-hand side of Garvey's assertive declaration to Black America. Much like its Chicago counterpart, the wall became a meeting point for the community, drawing political figures, artists, and performers into its space and playing host to a series of concerts, rallies, street theater, and speeches about local issues and Black history. According to the leader of the St. Louis organization Zulu 1200s, such events at the wall inspired a "black awareness and black consciousness of black history" throughout the community.[104] Although the wall was later defaced with white paint before the whole building was eventually razed, the *Wall of Respect (Up You Mighty Race)* displayed for a short while potent visualizations of Black pride on the streets of St. Louis, creating, much like its Chicago counterpart, sites of imagination and celebration for a local Black community.[105]

That same year but over a thousand miles away in the community of Roxbury in Boston, more murals were being painted into the streets of Black neighborhoods. Both *Segregation B.C.* and *Stokely and Rap: Freedom and Self-Defense* were created by Gary Rickson and Dana Chandler and sponsored by funding from the Summerthing program, a project created by the Mayor's Office of Arts and Culture that, following the long, hot summer rebellions of 1967, sought to inaugurate community programs to help diffuse racial tensions.[106] Painted on the facade of the three-story Exodus Building in Roxbury—an alternative school for Black residents of the area—the first mural, *Segregation B.C.*, was a call to arms that spoke to the growing militancy of the 1960s.

"ARM YOURSELF OR HARM YOURSELF," read a statement upon the wall in bold black letters nestled in between two windows on the second floor. To the left-hand side of the statement, as we see in photographs of the mural, stands two men, one in a green suit with a gun slung over his back and holding what looks to be a globe displaying only the continent of Africa and the other in a bright blue suit standing behind him. With a protective and encouraging stance, they both lay their hands upon the shoulders of a child and their friend or sibling, who stands next to the Black liberation flag. "Black art is not a decoration," Chandler said. "It's a revolutionary force."[107] In front of this generational scene hatches an egg from which an arm bursts forth, holding a gun pointing directly toward the statement to take up arms. "I'm not trying to be aesthetically pleasing, I'm trying to be relevant," Chandler spoke of his art. "It's more important to me that my paintings say something to black young people and black older people in terms of their existence in this country. . . . I consider myself to be a political reporter in terms of my art."[108]

When he visited the Boston Museum of Fine Arts as a child, Chandler noticed the absence of Black artists across the gallery. "Whites do not know that there are brilliant Black artists. Blacks never receive the education in the Black arts to know that we exist at all, let alone are brilliant," he told *Mind-blower* magazine.[109] Inspired to create murals because of the lack of Black art in the Boston Museum of Fine Arts, Chandler worked to create a Black museum in the community instead: "I was determined that there was going to be African American art in the community, so if they weren't going to put it up in the museum, then we were going to put it up on the walls."[110]

Shortly after creating the powerful mural on the Exodus Building, Rickson and Chandler turned to a five-story building at a major intersection close to downtown to continue creating their street gallery. After transforming an abandoned lot into a playground, the South End Neighborhood Action Program enlisted the help of three MIT graduate students and local children to design the apparatus and basketball court. Chandler and Rickson were asked to paint a wall to the rear of the playground titled *Stokely and Rap: Freedom and Self-Defense*, and the children added their own art to a lower segment of the mural.[111] Split into three separate sections, Rickson's portion of the mural covered the top half of the wall. In the mural, a large weeping eye looks out across the rooftops of the city as vertical and horizontal lines of black, red, and beige bisect the frame. Toward the bottom of Rickson's panel a gallows with a white man hanging from it stands on a platform. A multicolored teardrop from the weeping eye is ready to drip onto this anonymous figure. Underneath Rickson's signature is Chandler's panel of the mural. "The purpose of my mural is the representation of Black people in action with historical perspective," Chandler said.[112] Motivated to paint the reality of Black life in the community, he was "moved to start painting relevant things after [he] saw [his] friends being beat up and brutalized."[113] Stokely Carmichael and H. Rap Brown flank the left- and right-hand sides of the frame. Carmichael projects psychedelic beams of energy from his hands to break the chains shackling two anonymous Black men. Coming to Carmichael's aid is Student Nonviolent Coordinating Committee (SNCC) leader H. Rap Brown, who hurls a gasoline bomb in the air in self-defense.

Assertive and direct in both their content and challenge to the entrenched and pervasive systems of white supremacy across the nation, the murals of Rickson and Chandler were significant and groundbreaking in the Black community in Boston. Chandler carried this theme into his mural-making of the 1970s when he created *Knowledge Is Power, Stay in School* (1972) and *The*

Black Worker (1973) in the Roxbury area. Laced with the colors of the Black liberation flag and heroes and martyrs from the contemporaneous present—Martin Luther King Jr., Malcolm X, and Medgar Evers—the first mural stood at Ziegler and Warren Streets in Roxbury as a message to Black male teenagers to learn Black history. "I was directing much of the mural to African American males because even at that point in 1973—and long before 1973—I knew that we were an endangered species," Chandler said. He believed that the power of education and knowledge would help young Black men develop "the kind of resources necessary to lead our people to true freedom in the United States."[114] But as Chandler acknowledged, "Education doesn't necessarily mean the kind you get just from the Eurocentric school system, which still today is highly extant in African American communities. But the process that begins and then leads you to do some research about our people and our own history so that you will have a fine understanding that our people are the beginning of all humanity. All cultures came out of the wellspring of our African forefathers and mothers."[115] Having no access to mainstream art galleries, Chandler turned the walls of his community into a gallery. "I believe that Black art should reflect the needs of the community and be an integral part of the day-to-day existence of our people," he expressed, and the effects of his murals were palpable.[116] "It makes me feel proud to be black," local resident Jim Clark stated about Chandler's murals in an article in the *New England News Clip*.[117] In the late 1960s and early 1970s, as a prolific and deeply talented artist, Chandler took to the walls of his community to create a series of murals that reflected the pride of Black life, the importance of education, and the power of Black people across the world.

The mural movement also migrated south to the state of Alabama in 1969 when students at Miles College in Fairfield, outside of Birmingham, painted their own *Wall of Respect*. The mural was constructed by students Columbus and Harvey Keepler and was conceived by Jeff Donaldson, who was working as an instructor in the Summer Institute at Miles College. The mural was "the first wall of its type to be constructed on a college campus," and following a collaborative process similar to that of its namesake, artists worked with staff and students to decide which figures would make the cut to be painted on the wall.[118] Wanting to tell the story of African Americans who have contributed to the creative process in America, the artists selected Muhammad Ali, Willie Mays, Duke Ellington, Aretha Franklin, Marcus Garvey,

Malcolm X, LeRoi Jones, Frederick Douglass, Elijah Muhammad, James Baldwin, Mary McLeod Bethune, James Brown, Martin Luther King Jr., and Lucius Hosley Pitts Sr., the president of Miles College. "The persons who created the wall did so because they seek to improve the image of black America and to give [them their] proper place in working toward the realization of the American dream," read an article in the college newspaper, *The Milean*. "The Wall represents an effort to show Negro heroes as we see them and feel they should be portrayed."[119] Not only, therefore, did murals become landmarks in the streets of segregated Black communities across the country, creating spaces of imagination and pride for local residents, but they also continued the tradition inaugurated by individuals such as Aaron Douglas, Hale Woodruff, and Charles White, using Black colleges as spaces to showcase empowering images of Blackness to the next generation.

"PAINT A WINDOW, PAINT A DOOR, BUT PAINT A BLACK WOMEN'S MURAL"

Existing for a short while on a storage shed at West Chestnut and North Orleans Streets in Chicago's Cabrini-Green was a mural celebrating Black women.[120] The mural was painted in 1970 by seventeen-year-old Vanita Green. It held the portraits and names of influential Black women such as Aunt Jemima, Betty Shabazz, Nina Simone, Angela Davis, Harriet Tubman, Kathleen Cleaver, Cleopatra, Mary McLeod Bethune, and Coretta Scott King, as well as some fictional Black women. Green was inspired by Bill Walker and his expansive mural *Peace and Salvation*, painted in the same neighborhood in the same year, but she couldn't help but notice how Walker's peacemakers were all men.[121] Grabbing her paintbrushes, she created a space for Black women in "the narrative of community building," making a lasting comment about the power, beauty, and contribution of Black women in the movements for liberation happening across history.[122]

    Black Women eloquently, beautifully, and deliberately decorated the urban landscape of Chicago's Cabrini-Green, but unfortunately not for long. Shortly after Green's mural was finished, white paint was thrown directly onto the faces of the Black women, prompting Green to retitle the mural *Racism*. In 1970, at the time of the wall's vandalism, *Black Women* was one of the only murals in the whole of Chicago to be defaced. The motivation of the anonymous vandal is, of course, unknown, but their choice of mural—one that celebrated the life and beauty of Black women—speaks to the undeni-

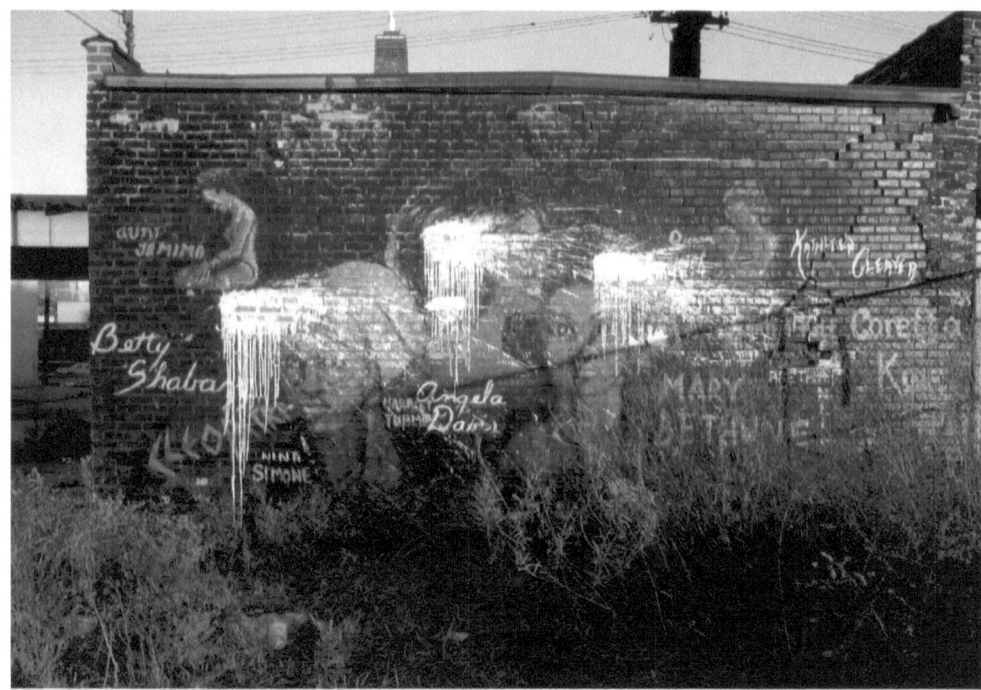

Black Women (Racism) (1970), 861 N. Orleans, Chestnut and Orleans, Chicago, Ill.
Painted by Vanita Green. Photograph by Georg Stahl. Courtesy of the Georg Stahl Mural
Collection, University of Chicago Visual Resources Center Luna Collection.

able power of the subject matter. Recounting the incident to muralist and
documentarian Eva Cockcroft shortly after the wall's defacement, Green
stated, "It says more the way it is. Before it was just a bunch of pretty pictures. Now, people have to stop and think, why would anyone do that to a
painting?"[123]

Green's contribution stood in 1970 as one of the first community murals
in the country created by a Black woman. While the Black mural movement
was inherently male-centric and populated by a predominance of male artists—much like the preconceived notions of Black Power more broadly—
Black women were an integral part of it, breathing life into an artistic movement that was beginning to take hold across the country. Throughout the
1960s and 1970s, Black women mobilized across the nation, giving a voice
to inequality across both race and gender lines.[124] Embedded into the movements for Black liberation, they stood sometimes as Black feminists, sometimes as Black nationalists, and sometimes without wanting to be confined
to a label. Black women created artwork that "challenged popular mascu-

linist perceptions of Black Power," and they asserted the "centrality of black women to the era's political projects."[125] Yet because these women neither "jibed with the popular and simplistic media-cultivated image of armed black men, nor joined nationally known freedom organizations or militant groups," Rhonda Y. Williams explains, "their economic and political activism has remained relatively invisible."[126] But throughout the 1960s and 1970s, Black women were pivotal in the community mural movement, creating stunning and inspiring works of art that spoke to the broader themes of Black freedom, focused specifically on celebrating Black womanhood in all its possible forms, and showed the pivotal role of Black women in the fight for liberation.

In 1975, in the heart of Chicago's South Side, an artists' coalition known as the Black Women's Mural Group was established to create murals detailing Black female empowerment. Headed up by Justine DeVan and with the help of South Side artists such as Dorothy Higgenson, Ruth Poinsett, and Annie Pierce, the group worked to create its first project, a Black women's mural, somewhere in the South Side. After meeting with Nathan Kirkwood, president of the 79th Street Business Association, the women sought permission to paint a laundromat (part of the association) on East 79th Street. After being given immediate verbal permission from Kirkwood, the army of women washed, sealed, and primed the wall given to them by the association president. Quickly but perhaps unsurprisingly, however, problems began to emerge for the mural group. According to the association, the group was never given official consent to paint the wall (even though Kirkwood reassured the group of his verbal commitment), meaning the women had to organize further meetings to ask for permission yet again. At these meetings, the association outlined new concerns and stipulations for the project. Association members felt that a mural on their building would interfere with the work and message they wanted to promote. Instead, they offered the women a wall on the side of their building, this time with the caveat that the association could paint over the mural at any point. "We could not paint a mural under those circumstances," said DeVan, declining the association's offer. The association counteroffered two interior walls instead, only this time in the building's basement.[127] She declined again.

The project was postponed until the summer of 1976, when the plans for the women's mural were yet again called into question. This time the issues extended beyond the logistics and location of the mural. Now the theme of

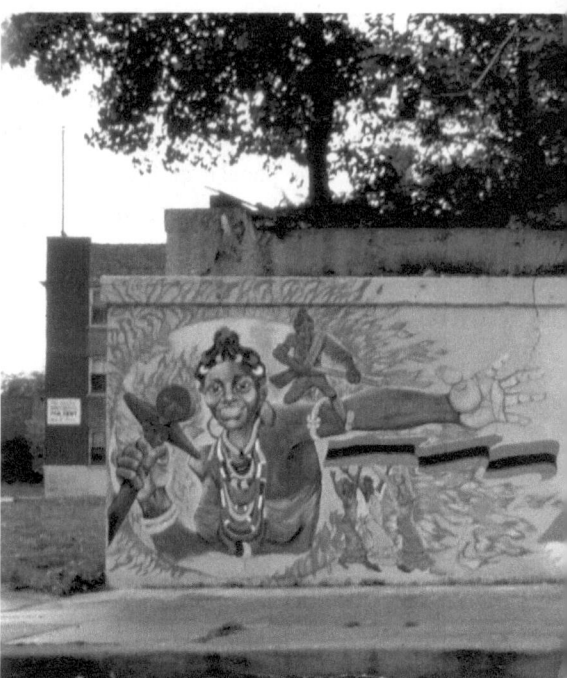

Black Women Emerging (1977), 4120 South Cottage Grove Avenue, Chicago, Ill. Painted by Justine DeVan and assisted by Midas Wilson, James Harrel, Larry Simms, and other community members. Photograph by Georg Stahl. Courtesy of the Georg Stahl Mural Collection, University of Chicago Visual Resources Center Luna Collection.

"Black womanhood" was up for debate, which led to the artists writing a rationale and justification for their thematic choice. "1) international year of the woman, 2) Times of Feminine Consciousness, 3) Bicentennial Preparation, 4) identity role expansion for women to view themselves in different working relationships (civic, social, painting a mural), 5) few walls about Black women done *by women* (most done by men)," DeVan wrote in a report on the mural-making process.[128] Outlining the sexist barriers blockading the mural's creation, DeVan continued:

> Most businesses, contacts, realtors negotiated with were men who sometimes listened, responded, often times did not respond at all to our communications and . . . most apparently lacked interest and confidence that "we" a group of *women, could* do such a project . . . paint a mural. . . . [T]he above is further supported by the fact that we often had to bring slides and photos of our work . . . when many, most men artists, ask a building owner, receive a verbal agreement immediately, work sight unseen.[129]

The constant hostility from businesses, coupled with blatant acts of sexism, discouraged many women on the project, some of whom eventually withdrew from the group. Others, however, became even more tenacious

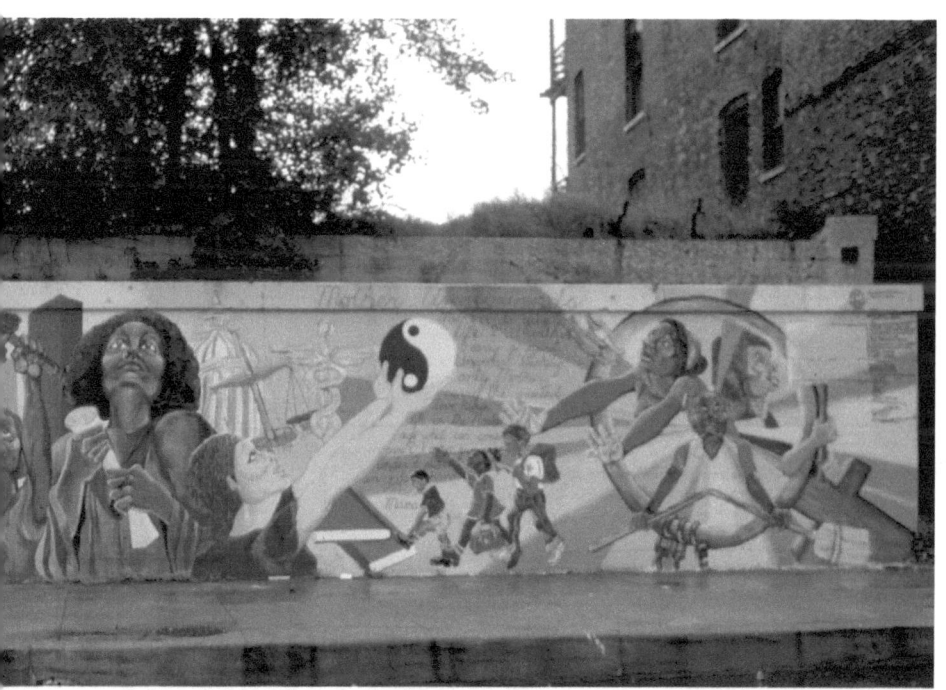

in the face of injustice, seeking out further ways to get exposure for their quest. "The J. Johnson Publishing Company promised to do a photo spread for us on the women's wall when completed," DeVan said, and Margaret Burroughs of the DuSable Museum of African American History promised to paint on the wall when the project was under way.[130] While extensive planning clearly went ahead for the mural, it seems unlikely that the wall was actually painted in 1976, and if it was, no images of it exist.

A year later, however, Justine DeVan created a mural on East 41st Street and South Cottage Grove Avenue titled *Black Women Emerging* (also known as *Emerging Black Women*) that was part of a bicentennial mural project conceived by the Black Women's Mural Group.[131] The aim for this mural was to "motivate young Black women, to give them a framework for identification and a timeline for viewing progress of Black women," the artist said.[132] Black womanhood was not homogeneous, and DeVan wanted her mural to reflect this back to a "community where there are lots of households headed by Black women."[133] Across the brightly colored mural, women of all ages burst forth from the wall, alive with power and energy. To the left-hand side, African tribal women, dancers, and warriors are birthed from the flames of a glowing golden sun. A symbol of diasporic history, these women depict the beginning of Black female womanhood, and across the mural stands

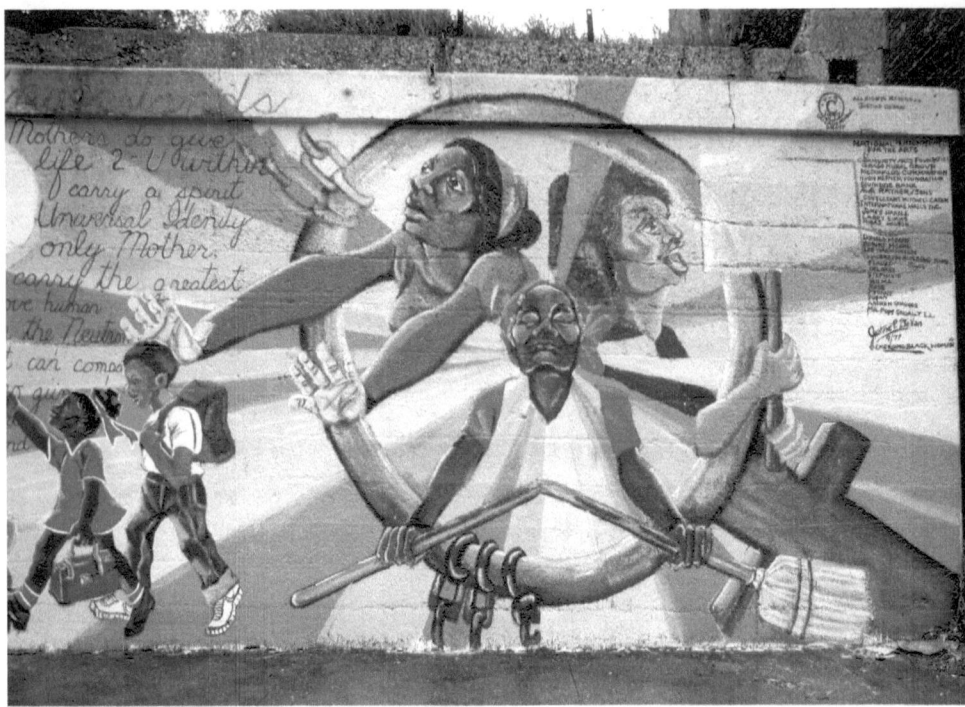

Black Women Emerging (detail) (1977), 4120 South Cottage Grove Avenue, Chicago, Ill. Painted by Justine DeVan and assisted by Midas Wilson, James Harrel, Larry Simms, and other community members. Photograph by Georg Stahl. Courtesy of the Georg Stahl Mural Collection, University of Chicago Visual Resources Center Luna Collection.

their ancestral sisters in the United States, physically connected to their past through a ribbon of material painted in the colors of the Pan-African flag. In the center of the mural stands three women, one holding a gavel, one a diploma, and one the symbol for a doctor. Surrounding them are a collection of books that bleed into the final frame. A metal ring tries to encase three young women but they break free of it, one wielding a protest placard, another snapping a broom, and the third stretching along the wall to reach her children. Black women have choices, Black women have autonomy over their own body and their own life, and Black women are powerful, reads the mural.

"Painting the mural in this community gave the little girls, children and adults a chance to see a Black female artist at work . . . far removed from an art studio . . . working with and for them in their community," DeVan recalled.[134] When she conceived of this mural, she wanted it to be an all-female endeavor to help promote Black female empowerment and self-love and to perhaps introduce young girls to the possibility of becoming artists. To help inspire the next generation, DeVan recruited many young girls to assist throughout the process. "My first volunteers in the neighborhood were Walgreen Building girls ages 8 years to 12 years," but that didn't stop women of all ages coming by to offer help, DeVan remembered. "A 67-year-old woman with a cane passed frequently nodding her approval as the priming progressed—then lent her hand at priming. The second adult female volunteer was Marie who lived in the projects. [And] a mother of fourteen children . . . sent her teenage daughters daily at the end of the day to gather up the paint and carry it to the storage area."[135] Men also helped out on the project, DeVan remembered, and it didn't take long for the mural to become "very much a part of the community."[136] After months of painting and repainting following vandalism (and some initial but quickly remedied hostility when the mural was unknowingly painted on a faded wall dedicated to fallen members of the Blackstone Rangers), *Black Women Emerging* was finally dedicated on September 3, 1977, to a proud community.

Black women, while sometimes overlooked or perhaps diminished in the movements for Black liberation during the 1960s and 1970s, stood uncompromisingly in the face of injustice, working to fight against not just the ills of racism but also the scourge of sexism and misogyny. Black women throughout this period of Black radicalism therefore developed "distinct but overlapping bodies of literature and artwork dedicated to diversifying public perceptions on black womanhood" and empowering Black women across the country.[137] While the names of muralists such as Vanita Green and Justine DeVan appear less frequently in print than those of their male counterparts, in large part due to the lack of information about them, they stood as invaluable artists of the community mural movement, working to not only reclaim and beautify Black neighborhoods but also herald the magnificence of Black women throughout history.[138]

Not all famous battles of the mid-twentieth-century civil rights movement took place "in stores at lunch counters, on trains and buses, and in schools."[139] Some battles took place on the sides of buildings in Black communities, and in 1967, born out of the cauldron of the radical movement for Black Power and amid the context of a deeply entrenched residential and institutional segregation, an artistic movement emerged that was dedicated to

Black liberation in the streets. In 1965 Kenneth Clark wrote how the walls of Black communities were boundaries and barriers imposed by white America, but by 1967 muralists had disrupted this process by using walls to invite community engagement.

In 1967, when the *Wall of Respect* was painted, it was groundbreaking not only because it was the first African American street mural in the United States but also because it strengthened the relationship between residents and their local physical landscape, and among residents with each other—something that became commonplace in the Black community mural movement. "The *Wall of Respect* was just phenomenal," Masequa Myers, executive director of the South Side Community Art Center suggested. "It was uplifting when you saw pictures and displays" of your Black heroes, and it was "uplifting on the fact that it was bringing people together."[140] The wall celebrated Black life and showed the neighborhood what it meant to be beautiful. Painted on a wall in an impoverished neighborhood and filling that wall with a pantheon of Black heroes, the mural showed Black communities, for the first time through public art, who they were and where they had been. Providing a tangible space for the celebration of Blackness where "new identities would arise," OBAC and Bill Walker fused "social content and historical foundation" together in an outdoor environment to create an unprecedented template for an unprecedented cultural form so successful that it rippled throughout every major city across the country.

In the 1960s the movement for Black freedom was "more than sit-ins at lunch counters, voter registration campaigns, and freedom rides; it was about self-transformation, changing the way we think, live, love, and handle pain," Robin D. G. Kelley writes, and community murals were an integral piece of this journey toward Black liberation at the grassroots level.[141] Resurrecting Black memory and retelling Black narratives from a Black perspective, murals were part of the cultural awakening of the Black Power movement. These murals not only beautified neighborhoods and covered up graffiti scrawled on the sides of buildings but also demanded the acknowledgment of Black life, asserted Black dominance over a segregated Black space, signified the presence of a proud Black community, and told stories of Black heroes. They created sites of imagination and inspiration where residents could gain their emotional, spiritual, and mental strength, and they provided a sanctified landscape where performers could mount the concrete at the mural's threshold and become an extension of the mural itself. These murals were an unmatched cultural form living in the heart of Black communities twenty-four hours a day, seven days a week, and "you could see [the murals] any hour, day or night, and people did."[142] These murals existed unapologetically and uncensored in Black neighborhoods, radiating truth, love, and life to all who walked by. But as the 1960s yielded moments of violent and rebellious protest, these murals had another role to play. As the decade strode on, the years became marked by racial rebellions across the nation. Murals evolved across the country into ritualistic talismans healing the wounded, fractured landscapes in the aftermath of these rebellions and inspiring ritualistic community performances.

CHAPTER 3

"All Worship the Wall"

Healing, Performance, and Ritual

Murals are public-access stained glass windows. They sanctify the community like the Stations of the Cross sanctify the church.
—*Nelson Stevens, artist*

It was not listed on any official travel brochures as a must-see attraction, but it was a stop that many Black people made while visiting Chicago. My grandfather first showed me the wall; it was in the neighborhood where he grew up. It was a symbol of pride pointed to as a ray of hope by residents of the South Side like my grandfather. Whenever I visited the Wall, there were always other African-American visitors there as well, coming to a modern-day shrine. —*Seitu Jones discussing the Wall of Respect*

The concept of Black Power had reached me and I would walk around stenciling a black fist with the words "Black Power" over it. We had not completely focused on the meaning of the term, but we knew it was correct and ours! —*Amiri Baraka, speaking of his time in Newark following the 1967 rebellion*

"EARTH IS NOT OUR HOME. EARTH IS THE PREPARER PLACE WHERE KING, MALCOLM, JESUS, JOHN BROWN, LINCOLN, GHANDI [sic], MOHAMMAD, BUDDA & THEM DIED 4 LOVE. WE MUST DIE 4 LOVE ALONE WER [sic] EARTH IS NOT OUR HOME," reads a line upon a wall in Chicago's South Side. "(OUR FATHER WHICH ART IN HEAVEN) PREPARETH A PLACE 4 US—HERE NOW WE MUST BE FRUITFUL & MULTIPLY, HAVE DOMINION OVER THE EARTH & . . ." continues the poem on the mural *Home*.

When local muralist, poet, musician, and reverend C. Siddha Sila Webber painted a unique and colorful Afrofuturistic poem on a wall as part of a mural in Chicago's South Side, he didn't necessarily expect it to have a long shelf life. But the mural has remained unscathed, albeit adapted and

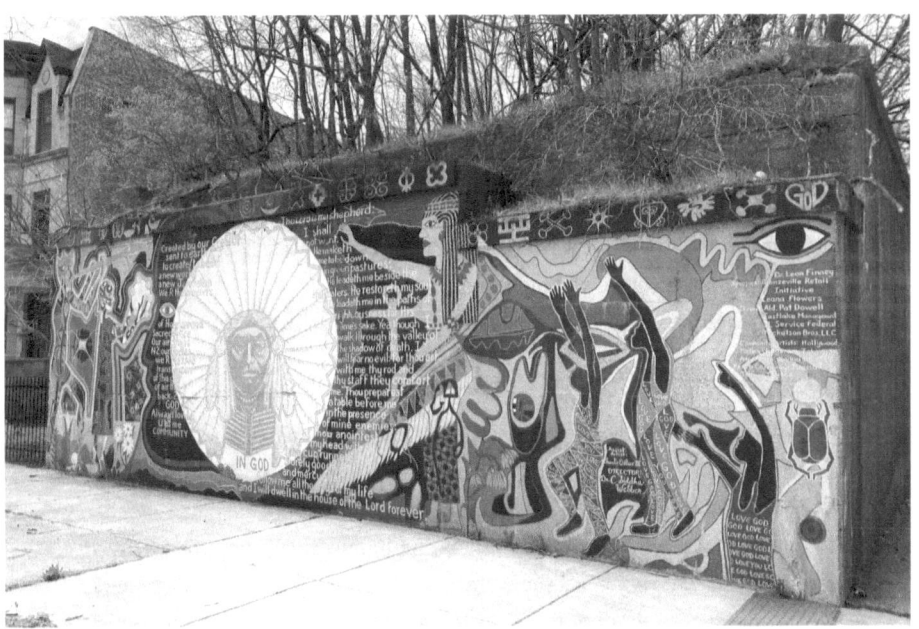

Earth Is Not Our Home (1981), restored in 2015, Dr. Martin Luther King Jr. Drive and 40th Street, Chicago, Ill. Painted by C. Siddha Sila Webber. Photograph taken by the author.

restored, since 1981.[1] Nubian figures, religious symbols, and saintly musicians flank the poem, and positioned to the left-hand side of the mural and enveloped by psychedelic layers of glorious bright color—purples, blues, greens, yellows, oranges, reds, and whites—are geometric patterns of energy radiating out into the street, ready to play host in the hearts and minds of passersby. Directly in the center of the artwork stands a shining golden coin with the large likeness of a Native American figure wearing a beautiful headdress that haloes his face. Painted faintly as an image, the portrait looks like an ancient imprint stamped deeply into the concrete, and to the left-hand side of the stoic figure reads a second inscription to counterbalance the poem, this time Psalm 23, which begins, "The Lord is my shepherd." "He restoreth my soul: he leadeth me in the paths of righteousness for his name's sake. Yea, though I walk through the valley of the shadow of death, I will fear no evil: for thou art with me," the white block writing tells the neighborhood.

In 1981, when Webber began painting the Afrofuturistic mural on Martin Luther King Jr. Boulevard, he didn't anticipate quite how strongly and in some instances literally the epitaph "he restoreth my soul" would resonate with locals. Psalm 23 usually serves as a declaration of one's faith to God, recited from the Bible as a collective or individual statement that, in return for such love and trust, sees the restoration and even completion of one's soul. But on a South Side street in the warm summer months of 1981, the painting became infused with such significance and sanctity that it began to restore the souls of those who engaged with the mural, healing and energizing through its creation and presence.

Early one Saturday morning, during the formative stages of painting, Webber was approached by a local sex worker who struggled with drug addiction.[2] Feeling a strong kinship with the muralist and his goal of wanting to create a space of "hope and pride and beauty" in the neighborhood, the young woman asked Webber if she could paint with him.[3] "She wanted to contribute something to her community, the area she worked in," Webber suggested, and after a brief discussion, he handed her a paintbrush.[4] Unfazed by the Chicago heat, the woman worked relentlessly for four hours, "mak[ing] a contribution, in her heart" and in the neighborhood in which she lived, imbuing Home with a ritualistic act of personal salvation.[5]

Weighted with spiritual and religious significance, Home also spontaneously energized Martin Luther King Jr. Boulevard. The mural inspired sanctifying acts of individual and collective engagement. People intentionally walked by the mural at all times of the day, Webber said, and "sometimes they'd been out all night. And then they would stumble and see the words. And then they would look up and start reading the prayer. . . . Then after they'd read the prayer, they would get hope and embellishment in what they read," he added.[6] Standing or sinking to their knees with their eyes fixed on the gravitational poem, restorative psalm, and vibrating colors, passersby staged their own acts of personal ritual by praying at the mural's threshold. When they "started praying . . . it would send them on their way, under that energy with the colors, the ideas, whatever it was."[7]

In many ways, Home can be viewed as a ritualistic talisman in the South Side of Chicago, offering a space for the repenting of one's sins and, in the case of the young woman, a healing of one's soul.[8] But in many ways as well, Home stands as a small but significant example of the sacred power community murals can have, giving us a new way to understand and interpret the creatively engaging, enigmatic, and varied roles murals played—and still play—in the movement for Black liberation. With the movement being about "self-transformation, changing the way we think, live, love and handle pain," murals became foundations from which Black communities could grow emotionally, spiritually, and sometimes physically when offering tangible sites for speeches and sermons. Lining the pavements during the marches, rallies, protests, and picket lines toward Black liberation that wove through the Black streets of the South, Black neighborhoods of the North, and Black enclaves of the East and West were community murals. We've seen how murals were born from the cauldron of geographic confinement, supremacist housing, and city-planning policies in the postdepression era and from the growing movements for Black beauty, self-awareness, and consciousness in the quest for Black Power. And we've also seen more broadly how these murals offered spaces for the collective and individual understanding of one's identity. Murals did many things concurrently in the 1960s and 1970s, and this chapter and the following one delve more deeply and specifically into the various ways these murals lived among the people during the radical and revolutionary era of Black Power, showing us how murals inspired community interaction and how they energized the streets in unique ways.

Webber's mural *Home* helps us recognize the unprecedented relationship murals have with ritual. Through it we see how murals can be created in a catharsis of healing, as shown by the young woman who contributed to *Home* to heal a wounded part of her soul. We also see through Webber's mural that artists, oftentimes unknowingly, created murals that would invite acts of ritual such as praying at their sites. Murals invigorate the streets and those who encounter them, and in this chapter, we see how some murals were given such power by both artist and residents that they became sacred works of art. Some murals, such as the *Wall of Respect* (1967), by Bill Walker and the OBAC artists, and *Rip-Off / Universal Alley* (1970–74), by Mitchell Caton and Webber, held such significance that they often inspired performances and ceremonies, enveloping the streets with celebratory enactments of Black love, pride, and respect. Other murals were created to try and heal fractured physical, social, and racial landscapes, and Bill Walker and Eugene "Eda" Wade's 1968 Detroit murals, *Wall of Dignity, Wall of Pride*, and the *Harriet Tubman Memorial Wall (Let My People Go)*, demonstrate these healing properties, especially in the aftermath of rebellions. At the height of the Black Power movement, in a nation vibrating from the heart of Black communities with a fervor that tirelessly strove for self-determination and liberation, then, was a Black artistic movement that energized the streets of America with sacred and healing celebrations of Blackness.

In the summer of 1970, on the side of Olivet Baptist Church in Chicago's Near North Side neighborhood, muralist Eugene Wade, known as Eda, painted an impressive mural depicting the ancestral legacies of Black people in the United States titled the *Wall of Meditation*. "This mural is meant to contain the history, the frustration, the hopes and the violence of the black revolution," wrote the *Chicago Tribune*.[9] Seeking to elevate the local Black community's consciousness, Eda painted a mural that drew upon empowering and self-affirming diasporic and national Black history. On the left-hand side of the large mural we see Egyptian pharaoh figures and an ankh symbol. Mirroring their position to the right-hand side is a member of the Black Panther Party in full regalia, an enslaved figure trying to break his chains, and a Black Panther symbol above his head. In the center of the frame are the likenesses of Martin Luther King Jr. and Malcolm X, and below them are three outstretched, muscular arms and an anonymous figure with their head bowed in meditation and contemplation. "I was combining the relationship of Africa with the African American struggle and putting those things in between there," Eda said. "At the bottom I got a figure that is bowing down and praying. It's part of the struggle that we've gone through with enslavement," he continued.[10] Eda set these heroes and figures against an almost vibrating purple backdrop alive with yellow, orange, and red lines conveying movement, perhaps the movement through time.

The mural contributed "to the morale and mental health of the black community," and when Eda finished the wall in the summer of 1970, it was dedicated to the community at the Olivet Community Center's Health Happening.[11] The health festival, which focused on both physical and mental health, highlighted the importance of preventative medicines; showed informative videos on alcohol and drug abuse; had educational experts on hand to answer questions; and even had mobile units from the Tuberculosis Institute available for locals. Endurance tests and "mini-Olympics" were held for the children, and scientists with microscopes set up stations for school kids to look at close-up images of cells and organisms. Hundreds of nearby residents flocked to the community center to take part in the festival, and wrapped into the day's events was a dedication for Eda's wall. Sidney Yates, a Democratic member of the House of Representatives, and Oscar Brown Jr., a Black Arts Movement poet, musician, and civil rights activist, turned out for

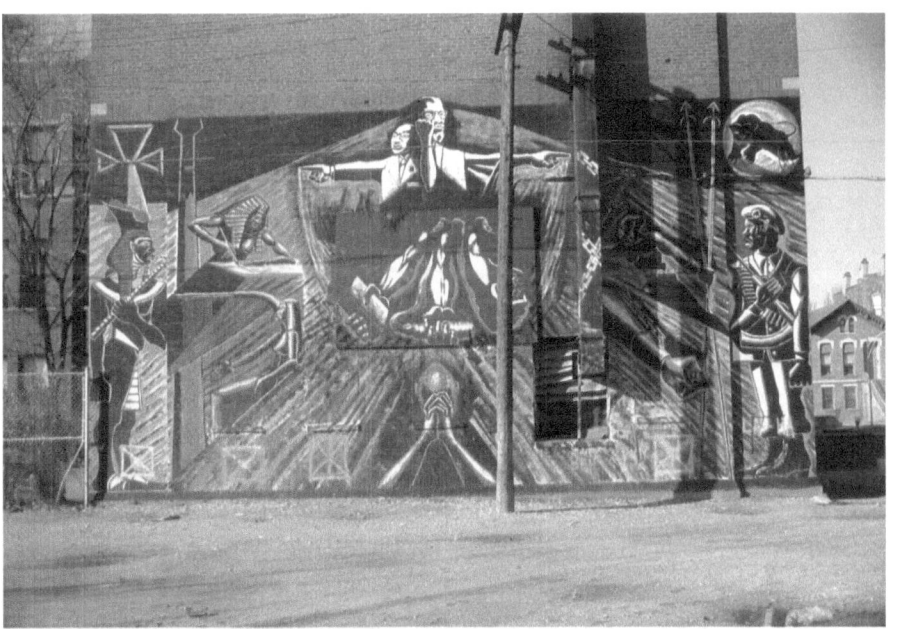

Wall of Meditation (1970), 141 N. Cleveland Avenue, Olivet Community Center, Chicago, Ill. Painted by Eugene "Eda" Wade. Photograph by Georg Stahl. Courtesy of the Georg Stahl Mural Collection, University of Chicago Visual Resources Center Luna Collection.

the ceremony, speaking to members of the neighborhood, reading poetry, and playing music. The wall and its respective dedication ceremony were so successful that they gathered people together from all walks of life, brought "relevant art . . . into the community, out of the galleries," and contributed to "the mental health of everyone concerned."[12]

Typically after murals are finished, muralists and their corresponding communities host dedication ceremonies to make sure a mural is handed over to the local residents and carefully embedded into the neighborhood as a symbol of pride in the hope that this will ensure its longevity. Performances during dedications are always significant and meaningful and in many ways become ceremonial rituals. In the 1960s and 1970s poetry by famous poets and local community members was read, traditional African dance was performed, prewritten and spontaneous music jams took place, and street parties evolved with food from locals. Such ceremonies could last from a few hours to a few days and occasionally intrigued celebrities such as Nina Simone, Aretha Franklin, Muhammad Ali, Gwendolyn Brooks, and Haki Madhubuti, who would turn up to add even more weight to the sanctity and significance of the mural.

As we've seen throughout this book so far, murals were not and still are not a static cultural form. They are uniquely dynamic and inspire all shades of physical, emotional, spiritual, communal, and personal interactions, solidifying the relationship between community members, their physical neighborhoods, and the mural itself. When residents performed at these sacred walls, they collapsed and to a larger degree erased the boundary between art and community, becoming in many ways extensions of the murals themselves. As Alan Barnett writes in his seminal mural anthology, *Community Murals: The People's Art*, "Community murals are uniquely a performance art."[13] And nowhere is this more perfectly demonstrated than in the dedication ceremony for the nation's first Black community mural, the *Wall of Respect*.

As we saw in chapter 2, the *Wall of Respect* was unique, and in 1967, when OBAC photographer Robert Abbott "Bobby" Sengstacke was preserving this artistic moment of history, he captured candid moments of intrigue and excitement among the locals that demonstrated just how unprecedented this mural was. Awe, admiration, and wonder dance across the faces of a group of young men at 43rd and Langley who look toward the mural, just out of camera range. At this moment of capture, two of the seven men spot Sengstacke and his camera. Their gaze meets the lens and they smile casually, their body language relaxed as they hold cigarettes, papers, and a blazer. Behind the two smiling onlookers are two more men standing in the doorway of a run-down building. In a completely honest moment, they pay no attention to Sengstacke and his camera, instead fixing their eyes on the mural, immersed in the uniqueness of this artistic moment. In an overlooked area of the South Side that experienced high crime rates and deepening levels of poverty, the sight of an artist's collective working to cover a wall with "sheroes and heroes" of Black history was a sight to behold.[14]

Also in 1967, around the time of the mural's completion, Sengstacke and Bob Crawford photographed two similar moments from children taking in their new street gallery. Sengstacke's black-and-white picture shows two young girls peering out of their window in the apartment block opposite the wall. They gaze at the mural serenely. We can see more of the young girl in the left-hand side of the frame. She sits on the windowsill, her body in profile but her head facing forward—whatever she had been doing by sitting on the ledge is no longer interesting to her. Instead, she contemplates the captivating wall by casting a long gaze over her left shoulder. The view she takes in is new and exciting, and as she enjoys what she sees, a smile creeps over her face and dimples her young skin. Her sister or perhaps a friend moves forward to the window to gaze at the same enchanting spot. The two young girls become immersed in the mural's creation, unable to tear their eyes away.

Bob Crawford's photograph was taken during the same summer, but this time from a worm's-eye angle. Standing or crouching next to a building, he photographed a young boy sitting on a rooftop staring at the wall. The boy's legs hang from the edge of the building, and his face holds an intense gaze. Perhaps the boy climbed onto the roof to get a new perspective of the mural, or perhaps he just wanted a clear view of the wall without the obstruction of the masses of onlookers who swarmed around the mural throughout the summer of 1967. Either way, the photographs of Sengstacke and Crawford convey just how potent and significant the *Wall of Respect* was to the residents—both old and young—who lived around 43rd and Langley. Since neighborhood residents were often excited, intrigued, and in some instances mystified by the mural, it seemed only natural that the mural, the first of its kind, should be given a proper community ceremony.

On August 27, 1967, the *Wall of Respect* was dedicated. The atmosphere was festive and vibrant with performances that electrified the streets with celebrations of Blackness. Lerone Bennett gave a speech in front of the mural, Lester Bowie and Roscoe Mitchell played a duet on the saxophone and trumpet, and Gwendolyn Brooks and Haki Madhubuti (formerly Don L. Lee) performed poetry that described not only the elevated mood of Black consciousness instilled by the wall but also the sacred relevance of "the mighty black wall" to the community.[15]

"All, worship the Wall," Brooks declared in preacher-like fashion to her audience in the heart of the South Side. Performing her dedicatory poem at the mural's very site, Brooks metapoetically recounted the ritual ceremony happening in that moment when she read:

> It is the Hour of tribe and of vibration,
> the day-long Hour. It is the Hour
> of ringing, rouse, of ferment-festival.[16]

Acknowledging the buildup of the commemoration to Blackness, Brooks stepped onto the small wooden stage for the "day-long Hour . . . of ferment-festival" as one of the performers. She discussed the transformational power of the wall, underlining the exact process summarized by George Lipsitz, that "people who do not control physical places often construct discursive spaces as sites of agency, affiliation and imagination."[17] The dedication was electric with artists, musicians, poets, and community residents celebrating Blackness in the heart of the South Side, and "women in wool hair chant[ing] their poetry," Brooks told the audience.

> Phil Cohran gives us messages and music
> made of developed bone and polished and honed
> cult.[18]

Brooks commented on the spontaneous and electrifying performances happening on the hot tarmac around her at the wall. She carried the listener through a Black space vibrating with snapshots of the decade's new Black consciousness bursting from the images of Black heroes, where "boy-men on roofs fist out 'Black Power!'" alongside the "hundreds of faces, red-brown, brown, black, ivory . . . / ready to rile the high-flung ground."[19] Since the *Wall of Respect* was created by, existed in, and belonged to the Black community at 43rd and Langley, Brooks continued, "No child has defiled / the Heroes of this Wall."

> So "All Worship the Wall," she echoed again.
> I mount the rattling wood. Walter
> says, "She is good." Says "She
> our Sister is." In front of me
> hundreds of faces, red-brown, brown, black, ivory,
> yield me hot trust, their yea and their
> > Announcement
> that they are ready to rile the high-flung ground.
> Behind me. Paint.[20]

In saying this, Brooks collapsed the boundary between her performance and her poem by narrating the experience of dedicating the mural in real time. "I mount the rattling wood," she told the audience. The wood, vibrating with the excitement and anticipation of the onlookers, ignited not only the physical space but also Brooks's emotional state—"she is good." Her commentary here underscores the pivotal role of the wall in the landscape of Chicago's South Side, as well as a new form of ritual shown by the "hundreds of faces" gathering at the site to hear her dedication and the exclamations of "Black Power!" by those who viewed the wall.

Echoing Brooks's acknowledgment of the mural's unprecedented sanctity, Haki Madhubuti's poem "The Wall" also formed part of the mural's dedication festival. Speaking to the energizing power of both the live community ritual and the mural itself, Madhubuti outlined the pilgrimage-like journey for Chicago residents who came to visit the gallery of Black heroes. Viewers arrived

> from south shore &
> hyde park coming to check out
> a black creation.[21]

This is the "mighty black wall" that "whi-te people can't stand," because "black beauty hurts them" he declared. "Picasso ain't got shit on us," he said of the moving feelings of Black consciousness and Black aesthetic springing forth from the mural and finding host in the South Side audience:

> send him back to art school
> we got black artists
> who paint black art
> the mighty black wall.[22]

Although the dedication ceremony may only have been scheduled for one day, an unofficial festival ensued for the entire following month.[23] Jazz musicians jammed, actors performed, and poets continued to recite their poetry. Those performing at the wall became part of its narrative, enveloped in its meaning and purpose. "Milling about the Wall was a panoply of artists, poets, actors, musicians, activists, journalists, community residents of all ages" who were now "part of the history of the Wall as object and performance," OBAC member Abdul Alkalimat recollected.[24] The mural "radically changed the immediate space around it," he continued. "It turned the street into a public forum for poetry, music, theatre, and political rallies."[25] Alkalimat acknowledged here how murals were and still are powerful enough to inspire and invite acts of ritual at their sites through performance and ceremony. And by describing this community engagement as "an ongoing event" that went beyond the parameters of the wall's dedication, Alkalimat captured the murals' ability not only to invigorate the physical space on the

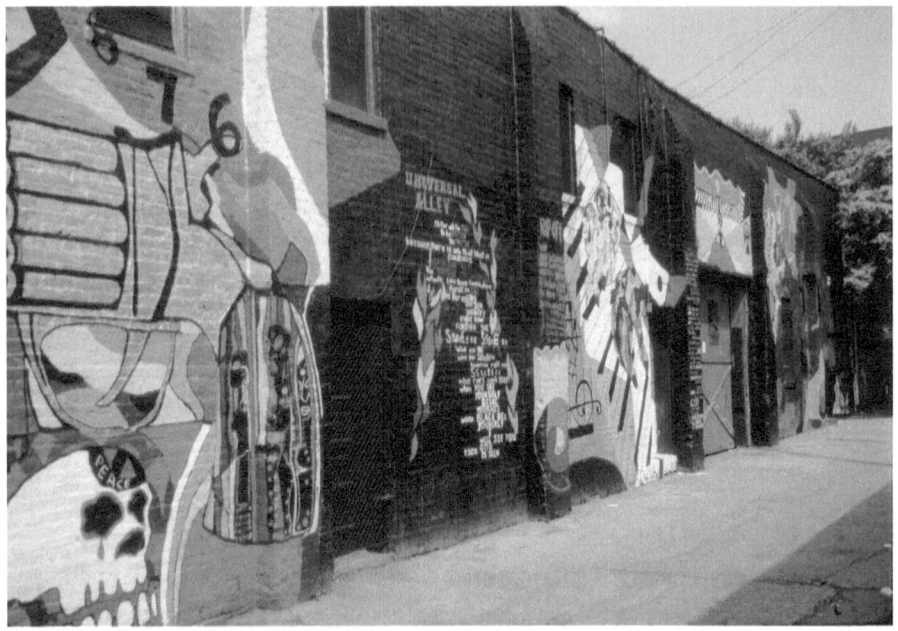

Rip-Off / Universal Alley (1970–74), 50th Street between Champlain and St. Lawrence, Chicago, Ill. Painted by Mitchell Caton and C. Siddha Sila Webber. Photograph by Georg Stahl. Courtesy of the Georg Stahl Mural Collection, University of Chicago Visual Resources Center Luna Collection.

streets but also inspire community interaction and performances on a daily, weekly, and monthly basis.[26]

Shortly after the creation of the *Wall of Respect* and seven blocks south, at 50th Street in a small alley between Champlain and St. Lawrence, muralist Mitchell Caton began painting a vibrant mural titled *Rip-Off* that, with the help of C. Siddha Sila Webber, would continue to grow and evolve throughout the decade into *Rip-Off / Universal Alley*.[27] Since the late 1950s, the alley between Champlain and St. Lawrence had been a popular spot where locals would shoot dice and play records every Sunday. Arthur "Pops" Simpson and his friend Little Chuck spun the records of Count Basie, Charlie Parker, Ella Fitzgerald, and Duke Ellington, and before long, local musicians such as Sonny Stitt and Jimmy Ellis would come by and play a set. Wondering how to give an artistic makeover to this small but animated urban corridor in the heart of the South Side, the artists decided to create, in their words, a "change in the environment," a "safe-zone" where they could "give art to the people, making art relevant to the people," raising "the level of consciousness [and] community participation."[28]

For the mural to work and, perhaps more importantly, to survive any potential defacement, local residents needed to feel connected to the wall both physically and emotionally. Acting as a self-described "social-liaison," Webber often talked with kids and grownups around the area who would pass by and ask questions.[29] Generating a buzz around 50th Street, the muralists got to work, and the alley soon became a prominent and interactional gathering place in the community awash with untrained volunteer artists, visitors, assistants helping to erect scaffolding, young children desperate to paint, and jazz artists raising money for art supplies.[30]

"This is a very unique environment, much like a clan," Caton remembered of the local community. "The kind of spirit being shown by this group of people showed guts and initiative," so the wall's imagery would need to reflect this, the artists felt.[31] To get a sense of the local culture and character, Caton took Webber to meet local musician Jimmy Ellis. "When I got there, maybe 50 to 100 people were standing around inside an alley, with the big garage door, and there would be maybe 5 . . . DJs . . . in this garage spinning records," Webber recalled. The street was alive with music and an indefinable spirit, so whatever the artists were going to paint along the walls of the concrete corridor needed to capture and echo this feeling.[32]

The monumental mural, measuring around one hundred by fifteen feet, mirrored the spontaneous music at 50th Street and Champlain. Reflecting the impulsive and free-flowing music vibrating throughout the corners, doorways, and garages up and down the alley, Caton and Webber depicted vivid musicians playing pianos, trumpets, and saxophones in the *Universal Alley* section of the wall. In extant photographs of the mural we see these shapes organically entwine along the length of the walls as visual resurrections of the melodies invigorating this South Side haven. Interested in the organic motions of everyday life, Caton found rhythm and beauty in the mundane: "Early in my life as an artist, I had the idea of finding a technical approach that would enable me to capture what especially interested me in the city, the threading traffic, its lights, the river of humanity charted flowing through and around itself."[33] Drawing upon his interest in the musical rhythms and natural cadences of urban landscapes, Caton painted expansive scenes of music reverberating from one instrument, represented by an abundance of geometric shapes, that embraced the musical notes from another as they framed the garage doors from which the real live music poured out. Enigmatic and alive with the energy of an artistic jazz session, musical notes and multicolored hands painted in a cubist-like style wove up and down the mural to envelop a poem by Webber titled "Universal Alley."

Wanting to create an environment that elevated the collective spirituality of the people, Webber wrote a prayer-like poem for the wall that spoke to Black identity, self-awareness, and self-love.

UNIVERSAL ALLEY
is for all to SEE
to be RAISED
to TRUTH
because there is only that

that is CONSCIOUS
LORD—GOD—ALLAH
the SUPREME CONSCIOUSNESS
infinite time space forms, done
for all to SEE
as far as life
can See
infinity
right now
forever see
SSSSsEEEEESSsssEEEE
what eyes can't SssEEE
when you SEE
yourself
BEING
Yourself
when BLACK BES you
'I'
will SEE you then
GOD
Is SEEN

Paralleling the electric rhythms of the visual jazz session, Webber's poem perfectly complements the vibrating aesthetic cadences of the painted wall. But as the poem and painted musicians lived harmoniously side by side, as we see in surviving photographs of the wall, they are offset by a macabre message. Created by Caton at the threshold of the alley, two figures stand with their backs to the viewer and pressed up against the wall, representing the Rip-Off part of the mural. Their arms are raised in surrender, and their legs are spread as the barrel of a silver pistol passes through their torsos and out the other side, smoking, as a psychedelic cloud fills the air around them. "Caton looked on much of the system [the American government] as a rip-off," said Webber, so when Fred Hampton was murdered by the Chicago Police Department and the FBI in 1969, Caton vented his frustrations on the wall through the image of the pistol and surrendering men.[34]

As a "warning sign" against violence but also as a celebration of Black creativity, then, the mural and Webber's poem created an energetic and visual vibration that changed the dispossessed streets around St. Lawrence and Champlain, home to gang violence, high murder rates, and drugs, into a "safe-zone [for] people" where hordes of local residents gathered weekly to perform music and have jam sessions, music battles, and street parties.[35] The colorful mural became "a magnet to pull people" in to the wall, animating the alley with locals who gathered weekly for community performances. Before the mural was painted, around fifty people played music and threw dice, but after Rip-Off / Universal Alley was finished, these weekly gatherings skyrocketed to between two and five thousand people every Sunday.

"The set was beautiful, all ages of people were dancing, having fun," Caton remembered.[36] And after the mural's first week, people came back "en masse, to be lined up all the way back to the mural," recalled Webber. "So now the people just came to stand in front of the mural, and then it would pervade all the way down the alley. And it was a very spiritual activity. People would come together, thousands, and just enjoy the spirit of being a community. And being with each other. There was maybe 2,000 people in an alley—it was a place where people could be hip."[37]

To the left-hand side of the mural, at the entrance to the alley, a colorful sign was pinned up that read: "CLUB CAPER / BATTLE JAZZ / GUEST DISC JOCKEYS." The promise of an almost weekly ritual of jazz battles, guest disc jockeys, and an electric atmosphere drew mass crowds as "people would come together [in the] thousands, and just enjoy the spirit of being a community," Webber said.

One guy would play a tune, say Dexter Gordon, and the next guy would play a tune, trying to beat that tune, sound better, he would play maybe a Sonny Stitt. And then the next guy would play maybe a Charlie Parker. . . . And then maybe once a month, live musicians would come by and join in that set. . . . So people would be dancing in the garage, some kids would come by, they'd dance with the grown-ups, they'd learn some steps. People would get up and do their own dance. And maybe some cats would get up and improvise to the music. Then, when the live set would happen, live musicians would come. Sometimes they'd be joining in like a jam session. . . . [T]here were guys that would sing, singers, both male and female singers would sing to the band. And some guys had improvisational instruments, something like karaoke—pantomiming an instrument.[38]

When local residents descended upon the alley at 2:00 every Sunday afternoon to create music and recite poetry at the wall, what they performed, in many ways, was a collective ritual and celebration in their community, one that even existed beyond the life cycle of the mural. Although the weekly gatherings no longer take place in the small urban corridor at 50th Street and Champlain, until his death in 2016, Webber organized a new location for a yearly summer series known as the Universal Alley Jazz Jam, which now takes place weekly (at least up until 2021) in July and August in front of another mural at East 71st Street and South Constance Avenue in Chicago's South Side. Although Webber passed away in 2016, the summer Jazz Jam series continues in the image of the weekly rituals at Rip-Off / Universal Alley: people play music, speak poetry, and dance, celebrating the community and invigorating the neighborhood.

Buried in the heart of Black America and nestled into the corners, alleys, and streets of Black communities during the movement for Black Power lived these vibrant murals—an enigmatic, engaging, and unique form of public art. These murals became sacred in communities and in many instances inspired what could be perceived as acts of ritual. The walls encouraged ceremonial dedications, and their presence in Black neighborhoods frequently sparked daily, weekly, and sometimes monthly performances from residents and visitors. These murals told tales of Blackness, they reclaimed streets in Black neighborhoods, they celebrated Black identity, and, as we can see through the Wall of Respect, Rip-Off / Universal Alley, and countless other murals across the country, they energized the streets in unprecedented ways that inspired communal and individual celebrations of Blackness through performance. But murals also had, and still have, another almost ritualistic power in communities across the nation, and that is the power to heal.

A HEALING FUNCTION BETWEEN THE RACES

"Don't worry about a long, hot summer. We're going to have a cool, calm, constructive summer," said New York Police Commissioner Michael J. Murphy at a dinner party in 1964.[39] But on July 16 that year, two weeks after President Johnson's signing of the Civil Rights Act, Murphy's confidence looked misplaced when fifteen-year-old James Powell was killed by Lieutenant Thomas Gilligan in the Upper East Side neighborhood of Yorkville. Powell, a Black student from the Bronx, was attending a summer remedial reading program at the Robert F. Wagner Middle School on 76th Street and 2nd Avenue when he and his friends were sprayed with a hose by building superintendent Patrick Lynch for lounging on his apartment stoop. After throwing a bottle in retaliation, Powell and his friends were leaving the building when he was struck by Gilligan's three fatal shots.[40] Gilligan was rushed from the scene, and confrontations broke out between police officers and students. Although the night of July 16 passed without much disturbance, a powder keg had been mounted in Harlem and Bedford-Stuyvesant waiting to be lit. The following day, word of the incident echoed around the city's boroughs, swiftly followed by demands for indictments and Gilligan's dismissal. For six nights, peaking on July 18, around four thousand New Yorkers took to the streets to express their disgust with the systemic racial injustice plaguing their city.[41] Ending on July 22, the rebellion resulted in more than 100 injuries, 450 arrests, and around $1 million in property damage. It "was worse than anything I ever saw in Mississippi," Congress of Racial Equality (CORE) field secretary Louis Smith recalled.[42]

The 1964 rebellion in Harlem cast a much-needed spotlight on Black life in the North. With the nation's attention focused predominantly on the movement for Black freedom in the South throughout the 1950s and early 1960s, after 1964 people paid more attention to the assertive demands coming from Black neighborhoods across the North and along the West Coast.[43] As we saw in the previous chapter, Black life in the urban North was equally harassed by segregationist housing policies; racialized confinement; a lack of economic, social, and physical mobility; growing unemployment; and a system designed to ensure that African Americans occupied the lowest rungs of society. Tensions reached the boiling point in the 1960s, and the Harlem revolt sounded the arrival of what would become a fiery era marked by racial rebellions across the country, concentrated most concretely in the North. Between 1963–64 and 1972 the nation witnessed over 750 rebellions with upward of 525 cities affected, nearly all of which had a Black population of over fifty thousand.[44] Watts in Los Angeles burned for six days in 1965 and witnessed the deployment of sixteen thousand National Guardsmen, over a thousand people injured, and four thousand arrested.[45] But news of Watts was quickly replaced by the 1966 rebellions in Cleveland, San Francisco, and Chicago, and when 1967 rolled around, the volatile revolts truly erupted as a match was dropped in the tinderbox of the urban North.[46]

Under the moniker of the "long, hot summer," from April to July of 1967 cities such as New Brunswick, Omaha, Louisville, Boston, Cincinnati, Philadelphia, Dayton, Buffalo, and Minneapolis exploded in flames of frustration and discontentment, and in July the decade of revolts reached its zenith. Between July 12 and 16 Newark, New Jersey, experienced extensive property damage after Black cab driver John William Smith was brutally beaten by Newark police officers. Newspaper headlines were dominated by mass protests and violent clashes with the police that led to twenty-seven deaths and eleven hundred injuries, only to be usurped one week later with coverage of an even larger rebellion in the Midwest. Detroit was one of the costliest race rebellions in modern U.S. history: forty-three fatalities, thirty of which were caused by law enforcement; around twelve hundred people injured; two thousand fires; $40 million worth of damage; over seven thousand arrests; and the deployment of the U.S. Army and the National Guard.[47] On July 23, in the early hours of the morning, people in an after-hours club were celebrating the return of two Black Vietnam soldiers. Detroit police raided the club, arresting and escorting everyone from the building when a crowd of over two hundred people started to gather in the streets. As the night slowly crept into the next morning, violence and looting broke out on Twelfth Street.[48] The rebellion raged for five days, leaving parts of the city in ruins.

Detroit was scarred both physically and socially, and the aftermath of the rebellion proved to be a pivotal moment in the city's history, confirming racial fears for both African Americans and whites. To the white residents of Detroit, the rebellion reinforced racist perceptions of its Black population, which accelerated white flight throughout the 1970s. To the city's Black residents, the rebellion legitimized their belief that government institutions weren't concerned with their well-being.[49] Exacerbating racial and class divides throughout the city, by 1970 the population of 1.2 million white residents from ten years earlier had shrunk to 816,000. Twelfth Street and its neighboring blocks are still haunted by the skeletons of buildings and boarded-up windows.[50]

To try and make sense of these violent rebellions happening across the nation, President Lyndon B. Johnson established the Kerner Commission, headed by chairman Otto Kerner and vice chairman John V. Lindsay, in July 1967 to answer three basic questions: What happened, why did it happen, and what can be done to prevent it from happening again? In 1968 the answers were released in the *Report of the National Advisory Commission on Civil Disorders*. Concluding that "our nation is moving toward two societies, one black, one white—separate and unequal," the report went on to suggest that "what white Americans have never fully understood—but what the Negro can never forget—is that white society is deeply implicated in the ghetto. White institutions created it, white institutions maintain it, and white society condones it."[51] It seemed that Kerner, Lindsay, and their advisory team had landed on the same conclusion Kenneth Clark had published in his 1965 study *Dark Ghetto: Dilemmas of Social Power*—that "the dark ghetto's invisible walls have been erected by the white society, by those who had power, both to confine those who have *no* power and to perpetuate powerlessness."[52] Cities throughout the nation were designed by those in power—white Americans—and what the country saw in the mid-1960s was Black America responding.

In an attempt to quell the unrest coming from the Black grass roots across the country, the government funneled funds into Black businesses and community organizations in cities such as Detroit, and Black community murals were folded, albeit indirectly, into these acts of regeneration.[53] In Detroit in 1968 three Black pride murals—*Wall of Dignity, Wall of Pride*, and the *Harriet Tubman Memorial Wall (Let My People Go)*—were painted in scarred areas of the city.[54] These murals were "more about healing than confronting," writer Jeff Huebner suggests, and they offered radical declarations on the rights of the people to "define their own history and culture, to assert their own power and identity, and to improve their own environment."[55]

In 1968 the East Side Voice of Independent Detroit (ESVID) was one of the local Black organizations to receive government funding. The group was headed up by community activist Frank Ditto, a thirty-nine-year-old community organizer who was profiled by *Time* magazine as "the burly, brood-ing [man] who prowls the streets in a dashiki, arous[ing] fear or hatred in many whites."[56] Ditto moved to Detroit shortly after the rebellion to establish ESVID, which was an organization focused on Black pride projects such as citizen patrols, police monitoring, street clean-ups, political study groups, a free employment agency, and a weekly newspaper called *The Ghetto Speaks*.[57] But after returning from a trip to Chicago in 1967, Ditto was transformed.[58] He had a new idea for a Black pride project after seeing the *Wall of Respect*, a mural that not only celebrated Blackness in the heart of Black America but also in many ways reclaimed the streets. "I was so fascinated each time I saw that. There was such a sense of pride and dignity and history. . . . I couldn't get it out of my mind," Ditto said of the wall. "I admired Eugene and Bill's work in Chicago. [So] we decided we wanted to put up some murals in De-troit."[59] After being invited to Detroit, Eda remembered how "Ditto . . . set about healing and empowering the community. . . . 'You guys got a *Wall of Respect*, well, I want a *Wall of Dignity*,' Ditto would say."[60] In Detroit's Black community on the East Side of the city, then, in an attempt to reclaim, re-store, and rejuvenate the burned-out, scarred streets, Ditto deemed a mural the perfect antidote to begin the long, slow process of healing the fractured physical and emotional landscape of Detroit.

On the corner of Mack Avenue and Lillibridge Street stood an abandoned ice-skating rink and wrestling gym—an ideal site for a mural, thought Ditto. This area of Detroit wasn't a particularly "blighted or depressed area," Eda remembered, especially not in comparison to 43rd and Langley in Chi-cago, which was apparently "100% black, and poor, and destitute . . . an en-tity in itself."[61] But the map of civil disturbance from July 1967 shows how the blocks surrounding the abandoned wrestling gym were razed during the rebellions and in dire need of repair.[62] Broken bricks, peeling paint, dere-lict buildings, and burned-out houses lined the streets of the city's East Side, telling stories of pain, rage, and frustration. To remedy this narrative and after raising $2,000, ESVID, Walker, and Eda looked to "create a mural that would 'project an expression of unity.'" The mural would show to the neigh-borhood "the Black man's [sic] contributions to America and world history and culture," and after recruiting other Black artists such as Edward Christ-mas and Al Saladin, Walker and Eda planned the visual content of their cu-rative mural.[63]

Listening to the mood of the city following Detroit's recent violent con-

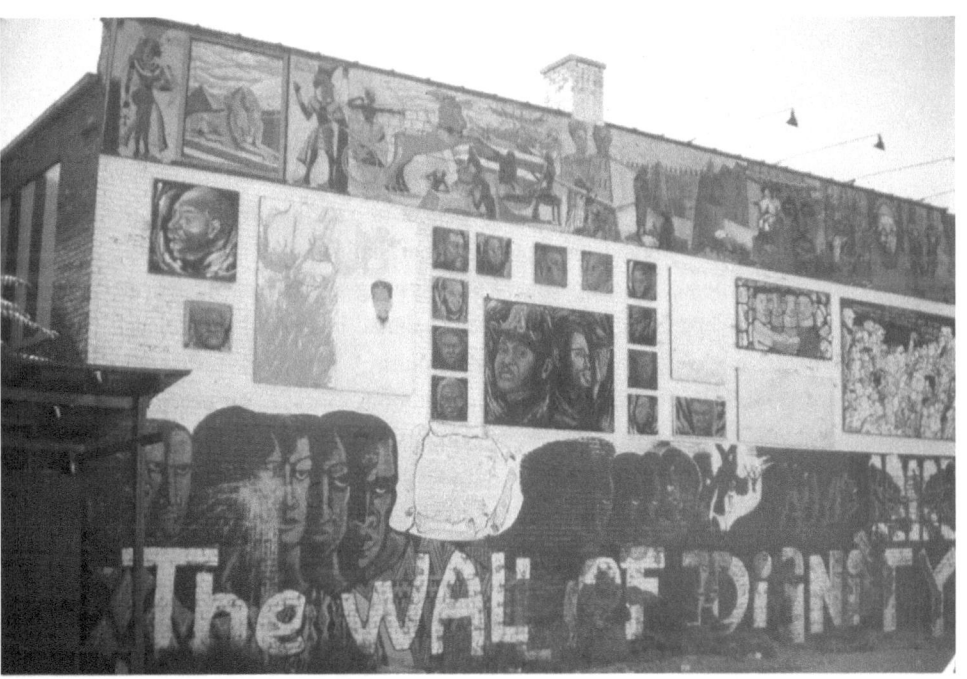

Wall of Dignity (1968), Mack Avenue and Lillibridge, Detroit, Mich. Painted by William Walker, Eugene "Eda" Wade, Edward Christmas, Al Saladin Redmond, Eliot Hunter, and others. Photograph by Georg Stahl. Courtesy of the Georg Stahl Mural Collection, University of Chicago Visual Resources Center Luna Collection.

frontations, Walker and Eda focused on creating a composition that would showcase the diasporic existence of Black people. "As a Black artist, I tried to find how I could contribute to the elevation of Black people, and as I began to search and find ways, I began to discover that one of the best ways I could utilize my talent to elevate Black people was to paint the past history of our people," Eda told *Colored People's Time* host Tony Brown. "The reason for this is that I find that in the so-called American history book, we've had a great deal of Black history omitted on purpose, and if we do a little searching, we find that you had a conspiracy of whites both in the North and South to both omit Black history on purpose. So I tried to bridge this gap to let them know who they are, and maybe this is to let them gain a sense of understanding themselves, a sense of pride and dignity."[64]

Walker and Eda split the wall into three horizontal sections: ancient African empires across the top, enslavement and emancipation at the bottom, and African American heroes in the center. "Many Black groups in Detroit prefer to look to their African past rather than to their history of slavery in

America," news anchor Marlene Sanders suggested, speaking directly to Eda's "need to paint . . . the contribution of Blacks in terms of world history and what they did, especially in reference to Africa."[65] On the mural's top panel, Eda used a bright, earthy palette to paint diasporic, ancestral imagery onto the urban landscape. His panel challenged a violent narrative etched into the surface of the streets, and his imagery was used to physically brighten the boarded-up neighborhood, haunted by looting and damage. "We were just trying to beautify the community," he said. "We wanted an outdoor gallery put directly in the neighborhoods, where it was needed the most, where people could somehow get a sense of pride."[66]

As viewers gaze upon the left-hand side of the frieze, they are met with a scene rooted in the ancient empire of Nubia—present-day Egypt. In images of the mural, we see pyramids, the Great Sphinx of Giza, pharaohs, and warriors in chariots ornament the wall as if lining the inside of a museum, illuminating ancient African history. The strong, dark figures cast silhouettes upon the frieze when they stand in powerful poses, tension coursing through their bodies as they assert their ownership upon the land. Moving across the top panel, the viewer is transported southwest of Nubia and into Benin City—now present-day Nigeria. Refined faces of Benin and Ife casters envelop the right-hand side of the mural, shrouded in darker, earthy tones, while the central section of the top panel conveys a scene of everyday life in a bountiful ancient African empire. Huts and brick walls frame the view as a ship floats on a glistening blue sea. Here, local people work in unity.

The narrative is calm, peaceful, and uncomplicated—a prideful glimpse into an ancestral past on the African continent and a moment of serenity in contrast to the physical location of the mural. "The idealized naturalism of these figures is of great beauty, certainly one of the achievements of human culture," Alan Barnett wrote of Eda's panel. "Eda clearly wanted to impress this on the people of the Detroit ghetto," Barnett continued.[67] Elevating the stature of such beautiful figures, Eda reclaimed colors commonly associated with fire by using oranges, earthy reds, and pale blues to brighten the bruised corner of Mack and Lillibridge. No longer did these colors resemble anger, violence, and pain. Their original meaning was replaced; instead, they immortalized an African ancestral narrative in the streets of Detroit.

Considering the rebellious confrontations a year earlier that led to the death of forty-three people, Walker and Eda "recognized what had happened in Detroit" and "didn't put any guns up there [on the mural]."[68] In-

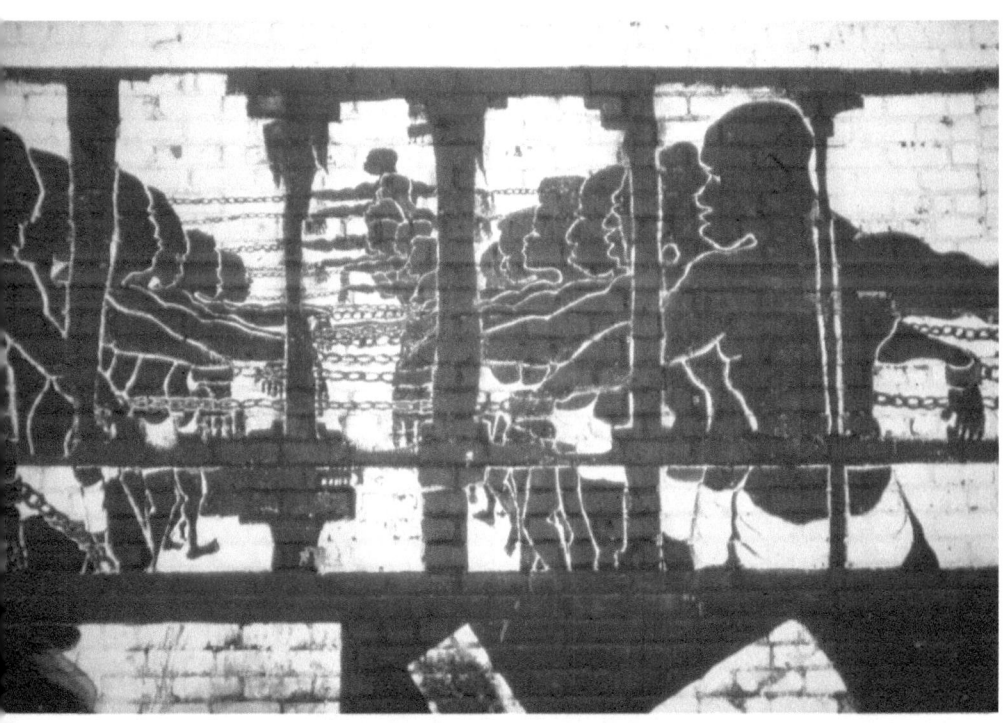

Wall of Dignity (detail) (1968), Mack Avenue and Lillibridge, Detroit, Mich. Painted by William Walker, Eugene "Eda" Wade, Edward Christmas, Al Saladin Redmond, Eliot Hunter, and others. Photograph by Georg Stahl. Courtesy of the Georg Stahl Mural Collection, University of Chicago Visual Resources Center Luna Collection.

stead, the artists used African American heroes "to show [people] talking to each other, showing what needed to be done" to repair the wounds of the rebellion.[69] The ancestral faces of individuals such as Marcus Garvey, Malcolm X, Martin Luther King Jr., Stokely Carmichael, Mary McLeod Bethune, Harriet Tubman, and Sojourner Truth stare out onto the street, arranged as a pantheon of heroes. Walker, Eda, and their team of muralists painted figures whose memories and likenesses would "inspire our Black youth today to match and even excel the accomplishments of the great Black personages depicted there."[70] Below them, surrounding the large white words and title of the mural, "THE WALL OF DIGNITY," are vignettes of enslavement and emancipation. In the bottom right-hand corner of the mural is a small scene in which rows of enslaved men and women stand with outstretched arms, shackled to one another. Moving across to the center of the mural, these figures are no longer imprisoned; instead, they raise their arms in acts of liberation, having broken free from the chains binding their wrists. Painted directly onto the brick and adding gravitas to the enslaved figures above is a hauntingly powerful poem, "Slave Ship," written from the perspective of African people stolen from their bountiful motherland and transported to America via the Middle Passage:

I AM A PRiNCE, SPeaK WiTh RespecT
I ShaLL NoT be Chained To YouR
BLoodY deck
TO LivE IN This FiLTh and STeNch?
OOOOAAEE. A Poor soul has died oN this bench
This MEANiNg does burst The drums OF my EARS
A PRinNcE To EAT The FOOD OfJACKALS!!
MY ARMS, MY LEG Bleed From YOUR ShAcKLES
YOU MUST LOOK TO MY WOMAN
WHAT hAS been done TO ONE SO SWeeT, SO MiLD?
AAAHHH! WiThiN HER WAS My CHiLD
STRANGE TONGUEd-goLden HAiRED MAN
I WILL NOT TO JOURNEY TO YOUR LAND.
LEAVE ME . . . LEAVE ME BE . . .
CAST MY CARCASS iNTO The seA
THE SEA..BLACK
BLACK LIKE ME

These three vignettes lived harmoniously on the wall together, informing each other's narrative as they moved from the idealized lands of ancient Africa, to the harrowing journey of the Middle Passage and the powerful acts of self-emancipation, and finally to the ancestral heroes on American soil striving for the liberation of Black people in the New World.

"One may wonder why there are no white people portrayed on the wall," read an article in ESVID's weekly magazine. "There IS no dire need for white people to grasp a more prideful Image of themselves; but for the Black man today, Our Wall of Dignity fulfils that need."[71] The healing wall stood as a symbol, celebration, and statement of Blackness, telling the community: "HERE WE ARE: WE HAVE BEEN JAILED, ROBBED AND BEATEN. WE HAVE BEEN PERSECUTED, MURDERED AND KIDNAPPED, BECAUSE WE ARE BLACK. WE STAND FOR BLACKNESS. WE ALL, EACH OF US, IN OUR OWN WAY, HAVE STRUGGLED TO BE FREE! WE ARE PROUD OF THIS BLACKNESS; WE LEAVE THIS LEGACY FOR OUR PEOPLE."[72]

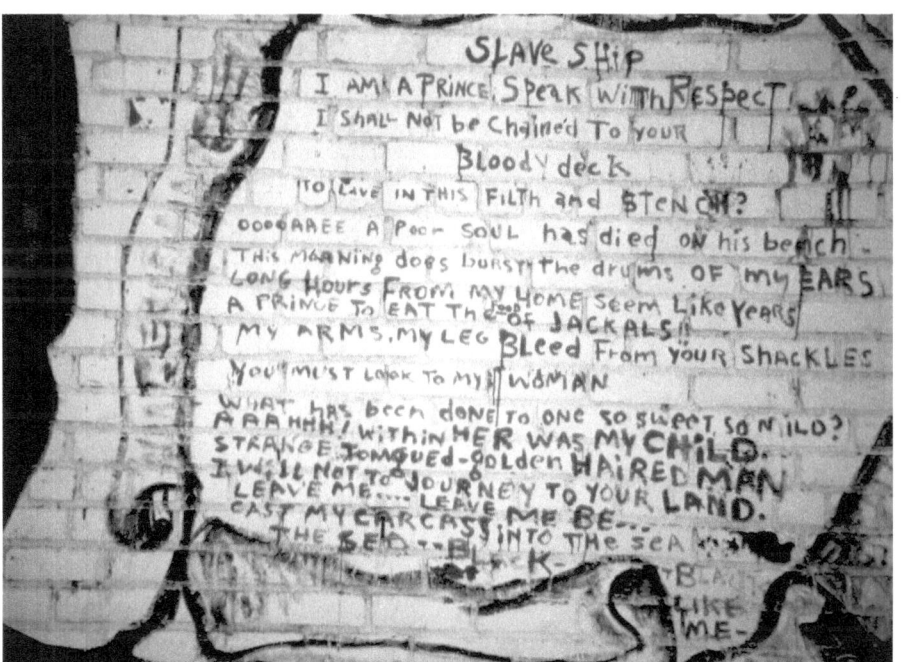

Wall of Dignity (detail) (1968), Mack Avenue and Lillibridge, Detroit, Mich. Painted by William Walker, Eugene "Eda" Wade, Edward Christmas, Al Saladin Redmond, Eliot Hunter, and others. Photograph by Georg Stahl. Courtesy of the Georg Stahl Mural Collection, University of Chicago Visual Resources Center Luna Collection.

To the members of ESVID and local residents, the *Wall of Dignity* was a bandage that began to heal not just the physical space in the community but also the emotional trauma caused by the rebellion and years of oppression. "The *Wall of Dignity* means race consciousness and pride of accomplishment," one resident spoke of the mural, and "every time I walk by the wall, I get a fierce hot feeling in my chest."[73] The wall became a declarative and restorative statement that told Black people living in the heart of the community, "You have something to be proud of; you have something beautiful"—your history, your ancestors, and therefore yourself.[74]

"The purpose of a wall is to separate," ESVID wrote, reminding the world of Clark's and the Kerner Commission's findings—that white America was deeply implicated in the creation of separate Black neighborhoods—"but through the artistry and commitment of Black artists Bill Walker, Edaw, A. Saladin Redmand, E. Christmas and A. Williams of Chicago, Illinois, THIS particular wall has inverted the purpose from that of division to one of UNITY!"[75] Although some of the buildings and streets surrounding Mack

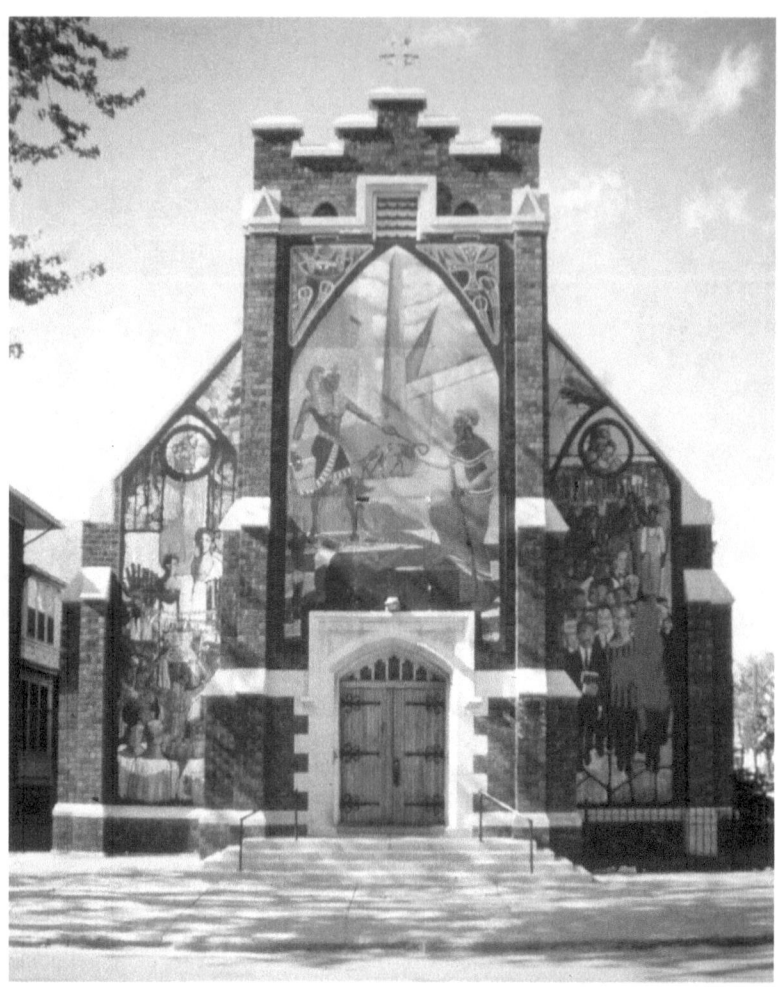

Harriet Tubman Memorial Wall (Let My People Go) (1968), St. Bernard's Catholic Church, Mack Avenue and Lillibridge, Detroit, Mich. Painted by William Walker and Eugene "Eda" Wade. Photograph by Georg Stahl. Courtesy of the Georg Stahl Mural Collection, University of Chicago Visual Resources Center Luna Collection.

and Lillibridge had been razed to the ground, the *Wall of Dignity* stood in the neighborhood "as a monument to Blackness" in the middle of a ruined area, "lift[ing] people's spirits and ha[ving] a positive effect" by offering an oasis of calm and pride to the citizens of Detroit.[76] "Here are Black people!" the wall said to local residents. "They are beautiful, they are brilliant, they have made an impact on the world!"[77]

In the fall of 1968, a few months after completing the *Wall of Dignity*, Walker and Eda created another mural at Mack and Lillibridge, this time on the front of St. Bernard's Catholic Church. While the *Wall of Dignity* focused on healing the emotional trauma of the city's Black population as well as the physical streets in the East Side, when the artists painted the *Harriet Tubman Memorial Wall (Let My People Go)*, or "the biblical wall," as it informally became known, they wanted to create a public work of art that would also serve as "a healing function between the races" because "the need for respect and understanding between nations and races [had become] more and more essential" following the racial rebellions of the long, hot summer.[78] "Unless we unite all men, we will be drowned in ignorance and unleash the forces of hate," and since St. Bernard's Catholic Church was attended by an integrated congregation, the artists wanted to tear down the divide between races by creating a mural that equated all forms of human suffering, regardless of background.[79] Father Thomas Kerwin, pastor of St. Bernard's Church, and Allen J. McNeeley, director of St. Bernard's community school, proposed the idea of a healing wall that compared the struggle of the Israelites in the book of Exodus to the suffering of a Black experience.[80] "Someone recently said that we are living in the darkness of the lies that have been taught about black people," Walker lamented, so "I hope these paintings will help to deliver the message of respect and understanding."[81] For Walker and Eda, the biblical wall would be a place to understand the lineage of Black history told through an accessible narrative that would appeal to both Black and white viewers, and it would be a place of learning for the white churchgoers.

The mural was made up of three large panels geometrically in unison with the physical structure of the church. The two side panels—offering a history of enslavement on the right-hand side and an exodus out of bondage on the left led by Martin Luther King Jr. and Malcolm X—complement the main religious narrative on the front of the building. To teach of Black suffering, the left-hand image shows a host of figures at various stages of enslavement. Solemn individuals stare toward the viewer, half their body in shadow as manacles shackling inert dark wrists are pulled tautly across their frames. The image was painted in a faux woodcut style, with dark vertical lines vibrating down the long, thin panel, with the wavy lines connoting the idea of tears and trembling bodies.[82] Moving up the image toward the top left-hand corner, two figures are behind bars, tugging at the wrought iron to demand their freedom, while at the bottom of the panel a small group of people dressed in white clothing stare longingly upward.

Their gaze reaches beyond the imprisoned figures to instead rest upon a thick-rimmed circle encasing the profiles of five anonymous men. To create a mural that served as "a healing function between races," Walker depicted everyone from a rainbow of racial backgrounds.[83]

Reading the mural in the same way as a history book, the viewer's eyes are next met by the largest panel of the mural: a central panel that equates the movement for Black freedom with the Israelites' liberation from bondage in Egypt. "There was so much similarity between the fight of the Israelites for freedom and that of black Americans that we used it as a base for teaching history" in the community school, McNeeley admitted.[84] The story "seemed to have so much relevance for all of society," and given the mural's aim to foster unity and understanding in a city decimated by racial rebellions, he and Father Kerwin wanted to use these parallels to "project that lesson to the community."[85] The background of the panel looms large and imposingly in a style similar to that of Aaron Douglas's murals *The Founding of Chicago* (1933) and *Aspiration* (1936). In the distance, three figures are bent double pulling large rocks, and in the foreground stands a young Black pharaoh and an older Black Moses. "History tells us that Moses came from Kush, and Kush is no more than Ethiopia today where people were Black and brown," Eda has said. "And I portray[ed] Moses as being a Black brother with the beard with nappy, kinky hair. Now history also tells us that the Egyptians were Black and brown people. What I attempted to show in these paintings was the conflict Moses had with the pharaoh, let me go, and of course pharaoh is hard of heart and refuses to."[86]

In this panel, Eda subverted the narrative of the Israelites by replacing them with African Americans. Depicting them working together toward liberation, he provided a template of racial unity for the community to use. Moses, a visibly older man, steps onto a platform to reach the same physical level as the young leader, and the hierarchy of age is debunked. If both men agreed to work together, freedom would be achieved.

Presenting a narrative of compassion and reconciliation, the mural achieved the visual, thematic, and emotional goals of Kerwin and McNeeley's vision. Walker and Eda's wall created a space with a potent, interactive message for churchgoers and local residents: "Let all who study the segments of the memorial wall ask themselves who is the Pharaoh today and who will carry God's command to . . . . let His (Black,

Brown, White and Yellow) people go free of oppression, political exploitation, poverty, fear, unemployment, ignorance, apathy, wars and hate."[87]

In the mural's dedication booklet, released in 1968, McNeeley asked viewers to engage with the figures upon the healing wall. Who will carry God's command of racial unity? Who will ensure that racial injustice and suffering are quashed? And who will work together to fight for liberation, regardless of racial background? As viewers pondered these questions, the pharaoh and Moses in the mural became malleable, interchangeable figures, taking the form of any interracial leader the viewer wished so long as that leader strives toward the unification of races. At the feet of the powerful young pharaoh, two smaller shirtless figures in loincloths visually represent the stages of emancipation. One leans forward onto a platform, hands and feet shackled together and head bowed. Lying upon the plinth, he is next in line for his freedom—a freedom that looks like the figure standing behind him. This figure raises both arms, creating fists of solidarity directly above his head. His body coursing with the power of liberty, he brandishes his unmanacled wrists proudly for the entire world to see. He is a free man and a visualization of what could be achieved through the collective work of those in the community.

As the viewer's eyes drift once more from the central panel to the right-hand side of the mural, they are met with another hopeful sight. Following the path of the gaze flowing throughout the mural—upward from the left-hand panel, forward in the central panel, and downward in the final panel—a couple hold their baby as they look down at the crowd of unified marchers led by Malcolm X, Martin Luther King Jr., and an erased Elijah Muhammad.[88] The host of leaders represent a new exodus out of bondage, out of segregation, and out of inequality as they march directly toward the viewer. They stand upon a red-tiled floor that echoes the appearance of a stained-glass window, placing King, Malcolm X, and their followers as saints to the community. Toward the top of the mural, again making sure the theme of racial unity spans the entirety of the church, three hands of different races extend open-palmed in search of a liberated world that perhaps they would one day find in Detroit.

Not all the Detroit murals lived harmoniously in the community, however. Shortly after finishing the Wall of Dignity, Eda and Walker were joined by local artists LeRoy Foster, Kwasi Asante (formerly Robin Harper), Bennie White Jr. Ethiopia Israel (formerly Bennie White), Henri Umbaji King (formerly Henry King), Jon Onye Lockard (formerly Jon Lockard), James Malone, Arthur Roland, and Nana Akpan (formerly Gerald Simmons) to paint the *Wall of Pride*. Venturing farther this time onto Twelfth Street and Virginia Park, near the epicenter of the rebellion, the group of artists created a mural that was described in the *Detroit American* as looking "almost out of place in the rundown neighborhood surrounding it."[89] In the heart of a Black community and created only nine blocks from where the 1967 rebellion began, the *Wall of Pride*, painted on the side of the Grace Episcopal Church, expressed "hope in an area which gives the appearance of having lost all hope—an area of cluttered vacant lots and rows of decaying buildings."[90] Walker, Eda, and the artists used their contacts from ESVID to approach Reverend Marshall Hunt and Reverend Arther Williams to create a restorative wall in the heart of the city's scars.

Just like the artists who created the *Wall of Dignity*, the *Wall of Pride* artists painted scenes of ancient African history across the top of the church, and below it they depicted raised fists of Black Power and heroes of Black history—Amiri Baraka, Malcolm X, James Baldwin, Muhammad Ali, H. Rap Brown, W. E. B. Du Bois, Jomo Kenyatta, Sojourner Truth, Nat Turner, Martin Luther King Jr., and Reverend Albert Cleage Jr. The wall elevated feelings of pride—as promised by the title—and, much like the *Wall of Dignity*, it provided a space for some emotional healing, as well as an injection of color into an otherwise aching street. To the community, the wall became "their wall," and on Sundays, suburban folk would pilgrimage to the mural to catch a glimpse of the "black personalities who represent the diverse elements in the black community."[91] The wall "says to the people on the streets something which they do not hear inside the church. It speaks of beauty where there is bleakness," said Reverend Hunt, but "we took a definite risk" in doing it, he continued, referring to the ideological and racial makeup of the church's congregation.[92] With over half the congregation made up of middle-class African American families from the north side of the city, around 20 percent from the local neighborhood, and the rest white congregants, the muralists found themselves caught in the middle of a tense clash between conservative civil rights politics and progressive Black Power beliefs.[93]

To certain members of the congregation, the portraits of radical figures were unholy and the fists of Black Power unnecessary, but the main image that stoked the fires of controversy was Lockard's portrait of Albert

Cleage Jr. Leader of the Black Christian nationalist movement and founder of the Pan-African Orthodox Church, Cleage renamed his Central Congregational Church the Shrine of the Black Madonna, where he realigned the figures of Jesus and Mary as Black leaders. Rejecting what he classed as "slave Christianity," Cleage sought to make the church "relevant to the Black Revolution."[94] During Lockard's rendering of Cleage, conservative congregants complained to the church, objecting to his Black nationalist politics and demanding that the painting stop. "They wanted me to remove it," Lockard said, "and I just refused."[95] Speaking to the desired healing purpose of the wall, Walker defended Lockard in a church meeting by rebutting, "The image was not meant to antagonize. . . . [I]t was meant to help people understand each other."[96] Reverend Hunt also stepped in to defend the mural by proclaiming that "although you may disapprove or even dislike some of the people on the wall, you cannot deny that they are part of the black experience. To have failed to include them would have been less than honest for these are the people who have meaning in this community."[97] Walker, Lockard, and Hunt's defense fell on deaf ears, however, and Cleage's portrait was forced to be whitewashed.

On September 9, 1968, the *Wall of Pride* was unveiled. The wall was "the sort of thing many churches must do if they are to relate to their community," Walker told a local newspaper.[98] While the arguments caused by Cleage's portrait may have partially thwarted the mural's purpose to create understanding among church congregants, what remained an undeniably positive force from the wall's creation was the sight of young Black men working together on scaffolding to paint an outdoor mural that celebrated Black heroes of history. Slowing down traffic along Twelfth Street and drawing many onlookers, the creation of the *Wall of Pride* was unprecedented in Detroit. "Things in [the city] were not good at all," Bill Walker recalled, so "we worked toward painting about love, unity, and understanding as best we could. People understood—they had a desire to get along," and the sight of twelve Black artists working toward a collective goal represented that.[99]

When Walker and Eda painted the *Wall of Dignity*, the *Wall of Pride*, and the *Harriet Tubman Memorial Wall (Let My People Go)* in Detroit—a city marked by looting, burning, and rebellions—they began repairing the physical, racial, and emotional wounds of the city. Community activists and artists working to paint colorful images of Black life and history on the front of churches and buildings gave the streets of Detroit a new narrative, one that looked different from the destruction and violence that took place just a year earlier.[100] These collective acts of painting, along with the visual content of the murals, were potent enough that they not only energized the blocks by creating healing celebrations of Blackness but also began to shift Detroit's narrative of violence and anger to one of pride, reconciliation, and unity.

"It was a hell of a time, man," Walker said of painting in Detroit. "The spirit of the people, especially young people, was tremendous, they were all trying to do something—they were all trying to do the right thing. That's all I can say. I was privileged to be part of it," he continued.[101] When Walker and Eda took to Detroit to create "renegade grassroots" murals among a community of people so willing to alter the national image of their city, little did they realize they would push the conceptual boundaries of Black muralism by creating reconciliatory and healing murals. These monuments to Blackness told the residents of Detroit that "they are beautiful, they are brilliant," and "they have made an impact on the world."[102] So in 1968, when newspaper headlines echoed around the city claiming that "Detroit's Wall of Pride Gives City Big Lift" and "Power, Pride and Self-Help, Aiding Black Movement," it began to look, even ever so slightly, as if the city of Detroit was beginning to mend.

In 1967, when a Black community mural was painted into a Chicago street, artists and local residents were unaware of just how powerful this work of art would be. Little did they know as well of the artistic movement about to be born across the country in cities such as Detroit, St. Louis, Boston, San Francisco, Oakland, Philadelphia, and New York. When people think of the crusade for Black Power, they rarely think of this mural movement beating from the heart of the people, but in tandem with marches, protests, the growing power of radical organizations, and deepening quests for Black self-love were curative walls lining the streets of Black neighborhoods. In many ways, these murals became rituals, invigorating and sanctifying the streets by inspiring daily, weekly, and monthly performances and dedication ceremonies at the wall, couching the streets in celebrations of Blackness. And when racial rebellions erupted in cities across the country, murals responded to try and heal the racial, emotional, and physical landscapes.

Murals were important individual and collective tools in the fight for Black liberation, and as these painted walls emerged throughout the 1960s and 1970s in cities across the country, they became even more inventive and complex in their content and interactive form. The assertive demands for education and storytelling from a Black perspective that made up the bedrock of Black Power led to an expansion of iconography on walls. It was no longer just pantheons of historic and contemporary heroes, which still prevailed during this period. Murals began to depict full-scale narrative scenes and compositions of Black history and life in the United States, and nowhere was this more perfectly demonstrated than in the murals of Bill Walker and Eda Wade in Chicago and Dewey Crumpler in San Francisco.

CHAPTER 4

"Africa Had No History, and Neither Did I"

Public Learning in the Black Community

Keeping in mind he who controls the image controls the action.
—*Haki Madhubuti, poet*

Take me into the museum and show me myself, show me my people,
show me soul America. If you cannot show me myself, if you cannot teach
my people what they need to know—and they need to know the truth, and
they need to know that nothing is more important than human life—
then why shouldn't I attack the temples of America and blow them up?
—*June Jordan, poet, essayist, teacher, activist*

I am a father with a daughter who is seventeen-years-old, a son who is
sixteen, and another daughter who is eleven. A part of my obligation to
my children is that I construct for them some heroic figure that confers
upon them a sense of their importance denied them by our racist board of
education. —*Ossie Davis, actor and activist in conversation with James Baldwin*

In 1965 James Baldwin stood in front of William F. Buckley Jr. and a sea of
Cambridge University students at the Cambridge Union Society and told
them, "When I was growing up, I was taught in American history books
that Africa had no history and neither did I. . . . I was a savage about whom
the less said the better."[1] In 1968, when actor Ossie Davis discussed William
Styron's controversial novel, *The Confessions of Nat Turner* (1967), with James
Baldwin, he also spoke to the invisibility of Black America in school textbooks and public history, criticizing the embedded structural racism that
elevated whiteness and attempted to erase Blackness in America's public
imagination. This attempted eradication of Black history and culture infiltrated every facet of mainstream American life in the 1960s, with public
and educational spaces such as school curricula, presses, museums, and art
galleries demonstrating some level of racial bias. Some curators and artists

at museums and art galleries had the power to decide which new talent to invite into the inner circle. "For the average person—the average artist—there was no way to enter [the art gallery] unless they got, literally what the slaves got: a note from the master to come in," Black artist Benny Andrews recounted.[2]

Before 1967 there were less than a dozen museum exhibitions featuring the works of African American artists, and on rare occasions when the work of Black artists was shown, it was in typically segregated contexts.[3] When Black history and culture were included in white mainstream galleries and museums, which happened only rarely, they sat uncomfortably in places such as the Metropolitan Museum of Art, the Boston Museum of Fine Arts, and the Smithsonian Institution, all of which represented "grand paeans to European culture, with neo-classic architecture and extensive collections of objects categorized as either 'high culture' or 'primitive.'"[4] And when these institutions attempted to diversify their collections, they failed, sparking some of the most controversial exhibitions in U.S. history.[5]

In 1968 the Whitney Museum of American Art in New York held a show titled The 1930s: Painting and Sculpture in America, curated by William Agee. The 1930s saw the tail end of the Harlem Renaissance and the exponential growth of the WPA, leaving the country awash with works by incredible Black artists such as Archibald Motley Jr., Loïs Mailou Jones, Aaron Douglas, Charles White, Charles Alston, Hale Woodruff, Jacob Lawrence, Elizabeth Catlett, William H. Johnson, Palmer Hayden, Horace Pippin, Sargent Claude Johnson, and Augusta Savage. But none of these artists were included in the exhibition, and while the show displayed over a hundred works of art by eighty artists, not a single Black artist appeared on the walls of the Whitney. Responding to the exhibition, artists Faith Ringgold, Benny Andrews, and Henri Ghent, among others, picketed the museum before mounting a counterexhibition at the Studio Museum in Harlem that same year titled Invisible Americans: Black Artists of the 1930s. This exhibition showcased around fifty works of art from twenty artists, including Alston, Douglas, Hayden, Lawrence, Savage, Richmond Barthé, Romare Bearden, and Joseph Delaney.

A year later, in 1969, the Met shone another light on the representational inequality of art galleries when it participated in an exhibition that—while attempting to rebuff the appearance of a white elitist institution—would become a controversial exhibition failure. Titled Harlem on My Mind: Cultural Capital of Black America, 1900–1968 and cocurated by Thomas Hoving, the

Met's director, and Allon Schoener, the visual arts director of the New York State Council on the Arts, the exhibition attempted to explore the cultural history of Harlem's Black community, given the Met's proximity to Harlem. Although the exhibition was littered with problems, there was one staggering flaw: It failed to engage with and consult members of the Black community of Harlem. Overlooking the role of African American art, regardless of the extensive catalog of Harlem Renaissance artists and artworks, the exhibition instead favored photographic reproductions of life in the community. In an attempt to be innovative and experimental, the white curators tried to create immersive photographic walls by using the work of Black photographer James Van Der Zee, but instead, this gave the appearance of a documentary study.

In Black communities across the country during the 1960s and 1970s, in response to pervasive whitewashing and misrepresentations of Black history and culture, a quest for self-determined Black knowledge and learning was under way. Against the backdrop of the Black Power movement and guided by the principles of Black control, nationhood, power, liberation, and education emerged the demand for Black studies departments across the country in tandem with a groundswell of Black community museums, art galleries, and newspapers—all reclaiming and retelling national memories and stories from a Black perspective.[6] And alongside these demands for Black studies programs and Black-owned, Black-run institutions of learning in the hearts of Black communities stood murals. As unofficial museums, history books, and newspapers that told stories of Black life by Black artists for Black residents in Black communities, many of these murals responded to and challenged the omnipresent role of white supremacy throughout mainstream institutions, with some even offering direct challenges to specific galleries and museums themselves.

In 1971, in response to the Met's and the Whitney's offensive and lackluster attempts to showcase Black art in mainstream institutions, the Studio Museum in Harlem mounted a retaliatory exhibition. Destabilizing the process of visiting museums and underscoring the inaccessibility of elitist institutions, Studio Museum director Edward Spriggs organized a series of murals to be painted across the Harlem community, taking the museum literally into the streets to bring Black art into the lives of Harlem residents, especially those who weren't regular museumgoers.[7] Known aptly as Studio in the Streets, the six-part mural series displayed the works of Curtis Bryan,

Babatunde Folayemi, Dindga McCannon, Ted Pontiflet, Vincent Wilson, and WPA veteran artist Joseph Delaney.[8] Watching the interactions between Delaney and passersby during the annual summer Washington Square Outdoor Art Exhibit, Spriggs wanted to replicate this same call-and-response relationship between artists and the local community of Harlem. He aimed to "expose the Harlem community to some bold artistic images and the ideas underlying them, within the context of the broader national Black Arts Movement. He wanted residents to interact with the art and the artists," Studio in the Streets coordinator Evelyn Crawford said.[9]

For a two-week period in the summer of 1971, the six artists created two extensive murals—one at Fifth Avenue and West 128th Street and another at Seventh Avenue and West 126th Street. "We were given complete freedom regarding what we would paint," Ted Pontiflet recalled. "None of us were interested in participating in a free-for-all," so instead the artists worked closely to create cohesion and continuity between their styles and visual narratives.[10] As a result, they turned the Studio Museum inside out to show colorful and prideful images of the Black diaspora; honest, unhampered Black depictions of Ghanaian fertility symbols; possible connections between Egyptians and the Maasai people of Kenya; images of Black Christ figures; narratives of Black life in Harlem; and images of Black pride. "It was important to re-examine history, to encourage people to do their own research and come up with their own conclusions," Folayemi said of the didactic purpose of his murals and the Studio in the Streets murals more broadly. He wanted to revisit the symbols "people take for granted and offer images that reinforce their pride."[11] Having studied the work of Los Tres Grandes— Diego Rivera, José Clemente Orozco, and David Alfaro Siqueiros—and having worked in Chicago, Folayemi also knew of Bill Walker. "These artists influenced me," he said, "their social conscience and the need to bring art to the people, the idea of working on the street in the public sphere."[12] In 1971 Edward Spriggs, along with Bryan, Folayemi, McCannon, Pontiflet, Wilson, and Delaney, conceived of an idea that manipulated the physical boundaries of a Black community museum and reconceptualized how murals had the power to become not just street counterparts to community museums but also part of a visual movement to contest the white co-option of Black history.

The ubiquitous assaults on Black history and knowledge by the mainstream had been part of the fabric of the United States for centuries, and in the 1960s and 1970s during the movement for Black Power, Black communities responded loudly, visually, and colorfully. Paralleling the rise of community Black presses in cities such as Harlem, Detroit, Boston, and San Francisco and Black studies curricula across the country were their unofficial counterparts in the streets. Building upon the complex, interactive, and self-transformational roles of murals discussed in chapters 2 and 3, this chapter shows how didactic and educative murals, incorporated into the movement for Black freedom in the 1960s and 1970s, sought to provide strength, knowledge, and learning, to promote truth, and to radiate Black pride to Black communities across the country. Focusing on the *Wall of Truth* (1969–70) in Chicago, by Bill Walker and Eugene "Eda" Wade, and *Education Is Truth* (1971), *Multi-Ethnic Heritage Mural: Black, Asian, Native/Latin American* (1974), and *The Fire Next Time I* (1977), by Dewey Crumpler, we see how the walls of Black communities throughout the 1960s and 1970s became unofficial newspapers, museums, and history books, seeking to teach local residents about Black history and life so frequently overlooked. During a movement that believed "the black artist must construct models to correspond to his own reality," many muralists turned community walls into sites of Black history and learning, constructing art about the realities of Black life and showing that Africa did have a history and that it needed to be learned.[13]

TELLING IT LIKE IT WAS

On a corner of 43rd and Langley in Chicago, opposite the *Wall of Respect*, a small stencil of Fred Hampton appeared in December 1969 on a mural titled the *Wall of Truth*. Although the mural was created in the summer of 1969, it was by no means a finished product. Bill Walker and Eugene Wade, known as Eda, created the mural to become "a newspaper magazine to paint out what was happening during this particular time period."[14] So when Chicago Black Panther leader Fred Hampton was killed by the FBI on December 4, 1969, the *Wall of Truth* reported it to the Black community of Chicago. The mural became a bastion of current and historic information when week to week and month to month the muralists "changed the scenery and the event—or whatever we had painted—to bring it up to current events."[15] Throughout the mural's two-year life cycle, panels portraying brutal acts of racial terror and lynching, families in poverty, the Vietnam War, drug addiction, and heroes of Black history turned a wall of Chicago's South Side into a community newspaper depicting local and national headlines frequently reported in the Black press but so commonly omitted from their mainstream white counterparts.

In 1827 the Black press was inaugurated by New York's *Freedom Journal*, telling for the first time stories of a Black experience in the United States—those purposefully excluded from white newspapers. Capitalizing upon the success and popularity of the country's first Black journal, in 1905 Robert Abbott (whose great-nephew, Robert Abbott Sengstacke, went on to photograph the *Wall of Respect* and *Truth*) established the *Chicago Defender*. Five years later, after the success of the newspaper in Chicago, the *Defender* was disseminated throughout the South, significantly increasing its readership. Outselling every newspaper in the country, by 1920 the *Defender* had a circulation of one hundred thousand copies a week. Using its position as a prominent vessel of Black news, the *Defender* was one of the few newspapers in the country to openly display the racial terrors of lynching and mob violence plaguing the South. With over four thousand African Americans lynched between 1882 and 1919, Abbott employed the *Defender* as a weapon to spread awareness about the evils of lynching infecting the country.[16]

During World War II, when the newspaper was used to mobilize support for the Double V campaign, circulation for the paper increased to two million a week, but the rise of "integrated" newspapers over a decade later in the early 1960s saw a decline in the circulation of Black newspapers more broadly.[17] In 1965, when news of the Watts rebellion in California ricocheted throughout the country, white newsrooms suddenly needed reporters to go undercover for news stories on the long, hot summer. Looking for writers and photographers who could inconspicuously report from Black neighborhoods, white newspapers "raided the vast talent pool they long had ignored": the newsrooms of Black publications.[18] Black papers lost the monopoly on Black news, with a wealth of Black readers steadily turning to the newly integrated news of the white press. But while Black Americans may have been physically present at these "newly integrated" presses, they still had little to no influence over the mass media's production and distribution of images. True integration would have seen an equal circulation of stories detailing the entire spectrum of Black life, but instead the press played up "the newer class blacks, the successful doctors and lawyers, the NAACP and the Urban Leagues," leaving narratives of Black Power, liberation, and self-determination, along with the more somber stories about drug epidemics, rates of poverty, and racial inequality, on the cutting room floor.[19]

"We did not get any respect, we did not get any recognition in the 1960s," poet Eugene Perkins declared. "During that period people thought we were angry black people. There were no reviews—the white press did not acknowledge us at all. . . . We wanted to change society. We were revolutionaries! We wanted to lift the consciousness of our people, and challenge white supremacy."[20]

This lack of parity in the so-called move toward journalistic integration, the glaring omissions of Black life in mainstream news, and the growing ideology of Black separatism in the mid-1960s gave rise to a new strain of independent, community-based publications that resisted integration and reported the Black news never to reach the mainstream press rooms.

So when the intellectual, ideological, and emotional landscapes of Black neighborhoods were being shaped by Black community newspapers and journals such as *Muhammad Speaks*, the *Black Panther*, the *Detroit Chronicle*, *Freedomways*, the *Chicago Defender*, and the *Milwaukee Star*, for example, Black murals joined them in their quest to report Black news for Black people by Black people.[21] With the decade's growing Black consciousness focused on recapturing Black heritage and shaping new, prideful Black identities, murals such as the *Wall of Truth* lived in Black communities to celebrate, respect, and educate about Black life. Using a public wall, Walker and Eda asserted their own control over the distribution of Black news, creating a space in Chicago's South Side for residents to have access to Black news directly in the streets twenty-four hours a day, seven days a week.

When the *Wall of Truth* was created in the summer of 1969, it remains unclear if Walker—who conceived of the idea of a community newspaper when planning the *Wall of Respect*—was directly influenced by the turbulent climate of the Black press during the 1960s. But when Eda was asked if the mural had become a way to relay Black news constantly ignored by mainstream publications, he answered: "I think so. I think that was Bill's concept. He wanted people to know what was going on, and to show what was happening. 'Here, you can read this, we are painting it out for you, we are telling you the things that are happening,' and so you're absolutely right . . . yes."[22]

As an artist for the people, Walker paid close attention to his audience, which, as Margaret Burroughs has suggested, "is the masses, the plain people, the disenfranchised people of the streets. He is not interested in what the bourgeoisie or the academics think of his work. His work is of the people and for the people."[23] Sharing an audience and address with the *Wall of Re-*

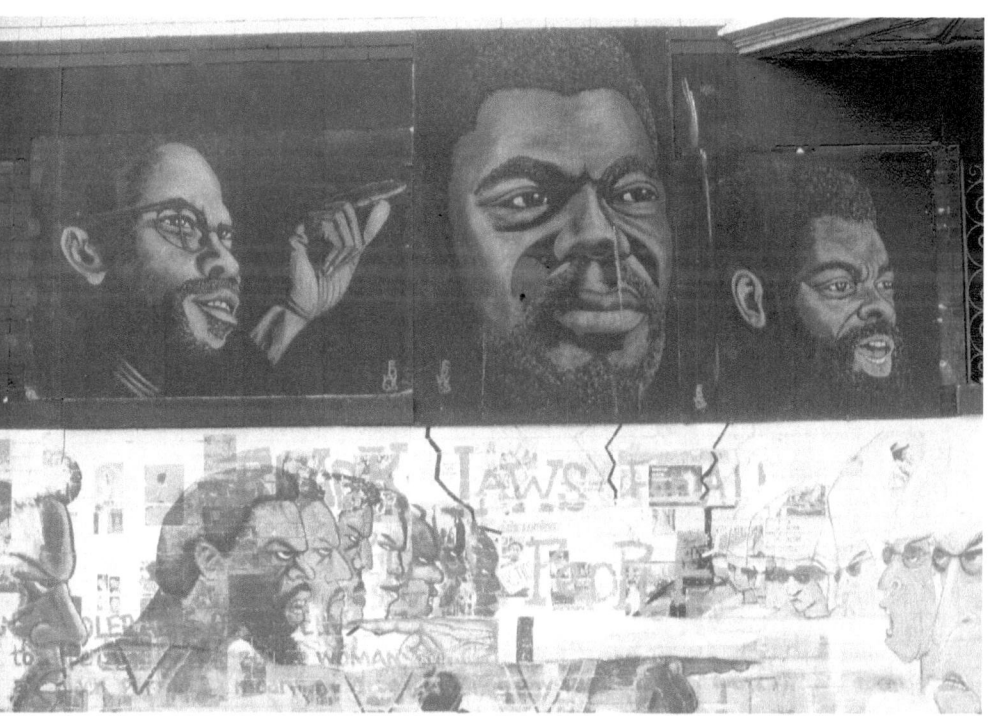

Panel of *Wall of Truth* (1969), 43rd and Langley, Chicago, Ill. Painted by William Walker and Eugene "Eda" Wade, with participants Eddie Harris, Louis Boyd, and others. Photograph by Georg Stahl. Courtesy of the Georg Stahl Mural Collection, University of Chicago Visual Resources Center Luna Collection.

spect meant the *Wall of Truth* reported news to an overlooked Black community that was, in Eda's words, "one hundred percent Black and poor—destitute . . . with gangs, with prostitution, with drugs," and where deaths by shootings, police brutality, and overdoses were tragically common.[24]

But a shared audience and address did not mean the murals shared a purpose. As an artist for the people, Walker wanted to create something new that spoke to the residents at 43rd and Langley in a different way. Both murals demanded the acknowledgment of Black life, curating sites of imagination and interaction for locals, but while the *Wall of Respect* offered a timeless message of Black pride by commemorating and eulogizing Black role models, leaders, and liberators, the *Wall of Truth* wove topical scenes of poverty, brutality, and racism, based on the headlines of the day, into the community's landscape to inform and to report.[25]

"Published" on a regular but often ad hoc basis, the *Wall of Truth* illustrated honest, prideful, and sometimes tragic news stories. It told the stories of people; the stories of experience, "hunger, things of that sort; the reality of hatred, the reality of things that we felt the community should deal with," Walker said.[26] So when headlines such as "Black Jobless Rate Still Unchanged," "Periled by Drug Epidemic," and "Drugs Strangle Ghetto" ran in the *Chicago Defender*, the *Chicago Metro News*, and the *Milwaukee Star*, Walker and Eda visually translated these stories and published them on the community's walls.[27] Making sure to report on local news around 43rd and Langley, "Bill was painting what he saw and what he knew. . . . [T]here were people in the neighborhood that didn't have food, there were mothers that didn't have food enough to feed their children. . . . [T]his is what we saw," Eda recounted.[28] In the image of the harsh, honest realities surrounding them, Walker and Eda used an expansive wall in Chicago's South Side as their printing press, telling the stories of a pregnant single mother, a starving orphaned boy, and a young girl, forced into prostitution on one of the largest panels of the mural.

To replicate the layout of a newspaper page, multiple small vignettes tessellated around three larger news stories that occupied most of the "page," while posters filled the empty spaces around them. Working in unison with the physical structure of the derelict building, Walker—the painter of this section—artistically removed the building's fourth wall by painting a cross section of its interior to give the community an honest insight into the run-down tenement. The wall that usually veiled the realities of daily life at 43rd and Langley from the rest of the community was "torn down" to report a triptych of real-life narratives.

The first story gives viewers a glimpse into the life of a young girl forced into prostitution, Eda explained. In it, a father grasps a pimp's shoulders—shoulders that we, the audience, cannot see—as his body fades into the background of the empty room, emerging from the darkness. The shadowed figure of the pimp in a white hat and dark clothing reaches forward and grips the young girl; his hands, large at almost half the size of her body, begin to envelop her, drawing her into him so she can no longer escape. A broken expression contours her father's face, and he sheds a single tear from his right eye as he stares down at her, fighting the inconceivable truth about what her future holds. The walls are dark, dank, and worn, and the floor is empty, without a single possession in sight, rendering the bare apartment bereft of warmth. The two men in the story look down at the young girl, but she stares directly out of her window, meeting the eyes of the viewer.

An expression of resignation arcs across her face; her young exterior has been hardened by her childhood in poverty, and she no longer looks upon the world with a playful innocence or even a wonderful childish naivete. Instead, she is a victim of the cold and harsh reality of child prostitution. This narrative is unforgivingly bleak, but Walker gave a few strokes of optimism to the panel as a small solace. Although the adults' bodies fade into the background of the empty and foreboding tenement room, leaving them incomplete figures shrouded by poverty, he outlined the edges of the young girl's brown dress in lighter tones to accentuate her strong presence in the room and to indicate that, just perhaps, she would not become captive to the desolation behind her.

"The reason we named it the *Wall of Truth* was because we dealt with subject matter relating to what was happening in the community," Bill Walker told Victor Sorell in an interview in 1991.[29] As the residents at 43rd and Langley "read" this news story and felt it resonate in their own community, they were met with an equally harrowing sight in the next panel. A young child sits on the floor with his back against the wall and his hands clasped together as if praying for food to appear in the empty plate between his legs. Around ten feet tall, the panel tells the story of an emaciated young boy staring lifelessly at a fixed point in the distance while a rat runs past his feet. Starvation and malaise wash over his body as he sits in a bare room with nothing but an empty plate and spoon in sight. The door remains ajar as he waits for a parent to return, or maybe he just wishes for it, hands knitted tightly together at his chest, pleading for company as well as food. With more of a focus on color in this panel, Walker used pastel shades of red, green, and black to consciously or maybe unconsciously draw subtle attention to the flag of Black liberation. Although life appears bleak for the young boy as he rests his back against a stained wall, the small allusions to this flag, coupled with the cascade of light enveloping him from above, tinge the apartment scene with a hint of promise. While the boy's face remains buried in the shadows, the pool of light bathing his feet steadily makes its way up his torso to illuminate his face and, much as it did for the young girl in the first panel, ensure that his body isn't imprisoned by the poverty surrounding him.

Outlining this vignette is a thick white border reminiscent of that on a Polaroid photograph. Whether intentional or not, by invoking the method of storytelling through photography, this panel reminds us of the evocative photography of Gordon Parks, specifically, his series for *Life* magazine on the Fontenelle family during Thanksgiving in 1967. Being sent into "the field" by *Life*, Parks and his two white colleagues, Gerald Moore and Jack Newfield, were told to document the living conditions of Black families in poor communities in the North. Moore and Newfield photographed Chicago's West Side and Bedford-Stuyvesant in Brooklyn, while Parks focused solely on the Fontenelle family in Harlem.[30] After spending time with and photographing Bessie Fontenelle, her abusive husband, Norman Sr., and their nine children in a small tenement in Harlem, Parks started his article for *Life* with an impassioned plea to the nation:

> We are not so far apart as it might seem. There is something about both of us that goes deeper than blood or black and white. It is our common search for a better life, a better world. I march now over the same ground you once marched. I fight for the same things you still fight for. My children's needs are the same as your children's. I too am America. America is me. It gave me the only life I know—so I must share in its survival. Look at me. Listen to me. Try to understand my struggle against your racism. There is yet a chance for us to live in peace beneath these restless skies.[31]

When Parks wrote these beautifully poetic words in 1967 about his experience with the Fontenelle family, he could easily have been talking about life at 43rd and Langley. Buried in the photographs of the large, impoverished family are the same stories in Chicago or Detroit or Roxbury or St. Louis. When a tear forms in the corner of five-year-old Ellen Fontenelle's eye and tracks her cheek, it could easily be the tears of the boy in Walker's vignette or the young girl forced into prostitution. In much the same way that Gordon Parks used his photography to report a story, convey a message, and tell a harrowing truth, Walker and Eda used the *Wall of Truth* as a vessel of communication to portray the realities of life in an impoverished Black community in 1969 Chicago.

Moving across the mural to the final and smallest room in the tenement, Walker revealed a pregnant mother surrounded by her three embracing children. A strong and resilient woman—a woman like Bessie Fontenelle—sits in profile view in the room and stares down at her children, who could be read as both comforting her and pleading with her. Much like her neighbors' apartments, the room she's living in is completely bare, and the walls are blank and stained. Nothing fills the space but a table and chair. The mother forgoes food as she lays three empty plates out for her children in anticipation of their next meal; a glass of water will suffice for her. As he did in the other two images, Walker left a fragment of hope for viewers about the woman's future by highlighting her pregnant stomach with the lightest color in the room. The young girl in room number one is outlined by a bright light, the starving boy in room number two is bathed in a warm spotlight, and the mother and her children are also outlined with bright colors. They refuse to fade into the backdrop of obscurity and poverty attempting to envelop the community, hinting at hope for the next generation.

Although the Wall of Truth is somewhat chaotic and haphazard to look at (it reads as a series of constantly growing panels, making it difficult to know where the one-hundred-foot mural starts and ends), its sections become unified when they are read as a community newspaper in the streets. Much like the reporters that work for printed newspapers, the artists didn't just focus on local news for their publication. In 1970 Arkansas-born muralist Eddie Harris added a national story to a long, thin section of the mural. Venturing geographically farther afield with his content, Harris depicted a story about the brutality and pervasiveness of Southern lynchings. Having spent his childhood picking cotton in Arkansas, he was moved to tell a story of racial violence in the South to a Black community in the North. Although antilynching activism and the Great Migration saw national lynching rates decline from the 1930s, with 1952 being recorded as the first full year without a lynching, the physical act of terror still haunted the nation.[32] With Black Americans in the North facing acts of police brutality, like the drugging and shooting of Fred Hampton, and Black families across the South witnessing the 1955 lynching of Chicago-born Emmett Till in Mississippi, Harris's panel made sure the horrors of Southern racism were not disconnected from Northern acts of violence but instead joined in a geographical continuum that drew attention to the ubiquitous national reach of racial terror against all Black Americans.[33]

"This wall . . . was more about poor people trying to survive [and] how black people were treated," Harris said of the Wall of Truth, and in his panel he conveyed just how brutally Black people were treated.[34] A strong, darkwooded tree flanks the right-hand side of the image, and a thick branch extends across the panel with three Black men hanging lifelessly from it. Their bodies dominate the center of the image while the laughing, drinking depictions of four young white men are positioned above and below them, their skin marked and putrid, rotting with the infections of evil. Two men sit upon the extended branch facing each other with their legs entwined as their icy-blue hands, drained of humanity, grip bottles to drink from—clearly in acts of celebration. A second pair of men stand at the base of the tree joining in their celebration as they look up to the bodies swinging in the wind above them. One of the men brandishes a cross with the initials K.K.K. at the base of the panel, and as he stares up at the body of the central Black figure, a smile etches into his face as he proudly holds his symbol of racism aloft. With the lynched bodies painted in the center of the panel, the African American men are entombed within the frame and trapped by the inescapable actions of racism. The tree creates an impenetrable border to the right-hand side of the picture, and the physical presence of the four white men barricades the top and bottom of the image, while chains, a scythe, and a wooden pair of hands ornament the left-hand side of the mural.

But much like the official Black press, the news reported on the wall was not all unrelentingly bleak. Walker and Eda used a large portion of the mural to tell empowering and commemorative stories that reported Black history in similar fashion to the *Wall of Respect*. A panel at the heart of the mural functioned almost as a visual obituary, depicting heroes of Black history interspersed with current leaders. Eda constructed a grid-like design that showcased the portraits of Marcus Garvey, Mary McLeod Bethune, W. E. B. Du Bois, Martin Luther King Jr., Frederick Douglass, and a modern portrayal of Harriet Tubman wielding a rifle, wearing an afro, a modern dress, and hoop earrings. Alongside the visual commemoration of these historic heroes, we also see the likenesses of Fannie Lou Hamer and Stokely Carmichael, both popular activists still working during the creation of the mural. By supplementing the bleak but realistic panels of life at 43rd and Langley with a panel of Black pride, the wall counterbalanced current issues in the community with a history of Black resistance, a Black resistance that was felt most strongly in the imposing presence of the revolutionary Nat Turner.

At around ten feet tall, the shirtless portrait of Turner brandishes a bloodstained sword that has maybe just taken the life of the man who shackled Turner's wrists and stole his liberty. In a powerful act of self-emancipation, Turner swipes the sword through the chains binding his freedom and breaks himself free, sending a fragment of the manacles flying into the distance. The sword is gripped firmly as the viewer imagines the muscles on Turner's right arm twitching with the prospect of revolution. The handle of a shotgun is braced at his hip as he wields it upward in military fashion, pressing the cold steel into his cheek. Eda cleverly manipulated the use of color here by highlighting Turner's torso with accents of red to depict where the light contours his skin. Choosing red as the primary contrasting color, Eda conveyed the aftermath of a bloody and violent confrontation upon Turner's body. The inflections of red upon his torso, as well as spattered red across the background, look like smudged, blood-ridden handprints grasping for mercy at the feet of the self-emancipator. Unshackled and liberated, the giant Turner wears a hardened expression on his face, eyes fixed and focused on his newfound freedom. Although the image remains largely static, metaphorically representing the quiet after the storm, the dynamism of the swinging chains haunts the panel to the point where the viewer can almost imagine the sound of slashed and clinking metal.

"We were trying to bring about more awareness, just creating the continuation of a more militant mood in terms of what was happening and taking place in the community," Eda has suggested. "We wanted to make people aware of what had happened in terms of the struggle."[35] Carving out a space where residents could reflect on the past alongside the news of the day, the artists collapsed the temporal boundaries of Black history. Invoking the resilient and inspirational memories of heroes such as Douglass, Bethune, and Turner, Eda drew a direct line between historical strength and fortitude and contemporary resilience, granting residents the strength to face their modern-day battles against the entrenched forces of racism and white supremacy.

With a panel of harrowing news stories and an obituary-like pantheon of heroes, the Wall of Truth stood in Chicago's South Side as a groundbreaking work of art and an unprecedented and didactic counterpart to the Black press. But the artists' visual community newspaper not only broke artistic boundaries for its originality. It also transcended the boundaries of the printed press, becoming, in some respects, more powerful than a newspaper by doing things a newspaper simply couldn't. The ephemerality of the press renders yesterday's newspapers obsolete almost immediately, readily discarded into the trash. But the Wall of Truth avoided this issue of redundancy altogether. The mural was less about erasure and more about addition. As a "changing daily bulletin board, a sort-of proto visual rap—the 'CNN of the streets,' oral folklore made visible, an early form of citizen journalism," the largest panel of the mural became a nucleus of information, constantly being updated in accordance with the news.[36] Because of the *Wall of Truth*, news stories were not discarded or thrown away; instead, the mural became a palimpsest of Black news with stories—both historic and contemporary—constantly layered on top of each other.

Articles and photographs from the *Chicago Sun-Times*, *Ebony*, *Jet*, the *Chicago Defender*, and the civil rights movement photography book, *The Movement*, by Loraine Hansberry, were physically pasted onto the wall for local residents to read. By layering these articles instead of discarding them, this panel of the mural was able to collectively visualize the diverse news stories from the Black press in one united space, elevating them to new heights by keeping them constantly in the public consciousness and in conversation with one another. "As artists we felt that we had the right to paint what was going on . . . the African liberation, the whole movement in terms of freedom and equality," Eda said.[37] And as a result, the twelve-foot-long section at the heart of the mural became a bricolage of articles and images dealing with the contemporary racial subjects of civil rights, Black Power, the Black diaspora, police brutality, and "Black is beautiful." When Fred Hampton was assassinated on December 4, 1969, his stencil was layered over the newspaper cuttings. When rallies were held to protest racial poverty in Black communities, posters were pasted onto the section, and when the growing presence of the Panthers intensified nationwide, images of radical revolutionaries appeared on the panel. If the panels reporting on the starving families were the inside stories of the newspaper and the historic faces were the obituary, then this section of the wall was the front page, constantly updating residents with the latest breaking news.

Unlike the other panels on the mural, this noticeboard of information had no overarching narrative. Instead, pages of the *Chicago Defender*, *Ebony*, and *Jet* were cut out and pasted onto the panel to create a bricolage of national news stories about Black liberation, radicalism, and politics. As a nucleus of information, this section inspired a unique call-and-response dynamic with locals. As a space where people could congregate, this panel was significantly different from the others on the mural not only because of the frequency with which it changed but also because it provided a space for news stories that required physical action from residents. As a community noticeboard, this panel gave key dates and times on when and where community protests and rallies would be held, and it displayed uniting cries to "Fight against *Poverty*" (emphasis original) in attempts to inspire

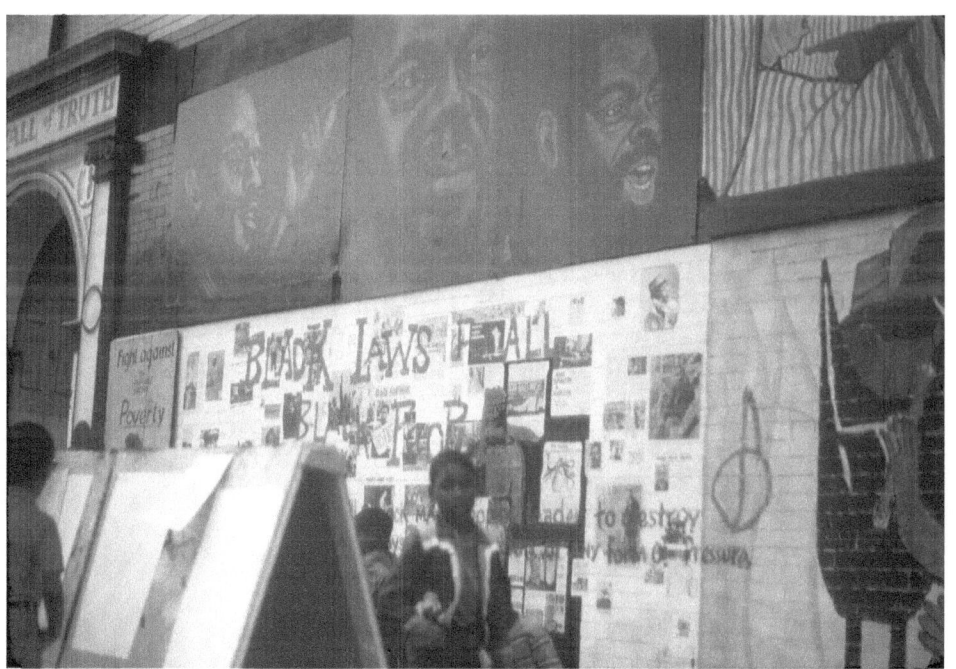

Panel of *Wall of Truth* (1969), 43rd and Langley, Chicago, III. Painted by William Walker and Eugene "Eda" Wade, with participants Eddie Harris, Louis Boyd, and others. Photograph by Georg Stahl. Courtesy of the Georg Stahl Mural Collection, University of Chicago Visual Resources Center Luna Collection.

community action. This panel became an interactive noticeboard that challenged community members to combat the harrowing conditions of their neighborhood. Walker even stretched the parameters of community murals further by inviting children and teenagers to contribute to the wall. "If somebody came by and said they were an artist, then Bill would get them a paintbrush to see what they could do," said Eda.[38] In fact, a number of artists (some of which were children), like Ziff Sistrunk, Louis Boyd, Will Hancock, Eddie Harris, Jim Malone, and Doug Williams, are seldom credited or recognized for their work on the wall, Jeff Huebner suggests.[39]

One of the most potent news stories painted upon the *Wall of Truth* was created in 1970. Reeling in the aftermath of Fred Hampton's assassination in 1969, Eda was, in his words, "really telling it like it was" when he painted a visual news story about police brutality.[40] Going beyond the minimalist, commemorative stencil of Hampton's preaching figure spray-painted onto the mural as a quick homage to the slain leader, Eda's painting depicted the contorted body of a young man lying face down on the sidewalk. Gunshots

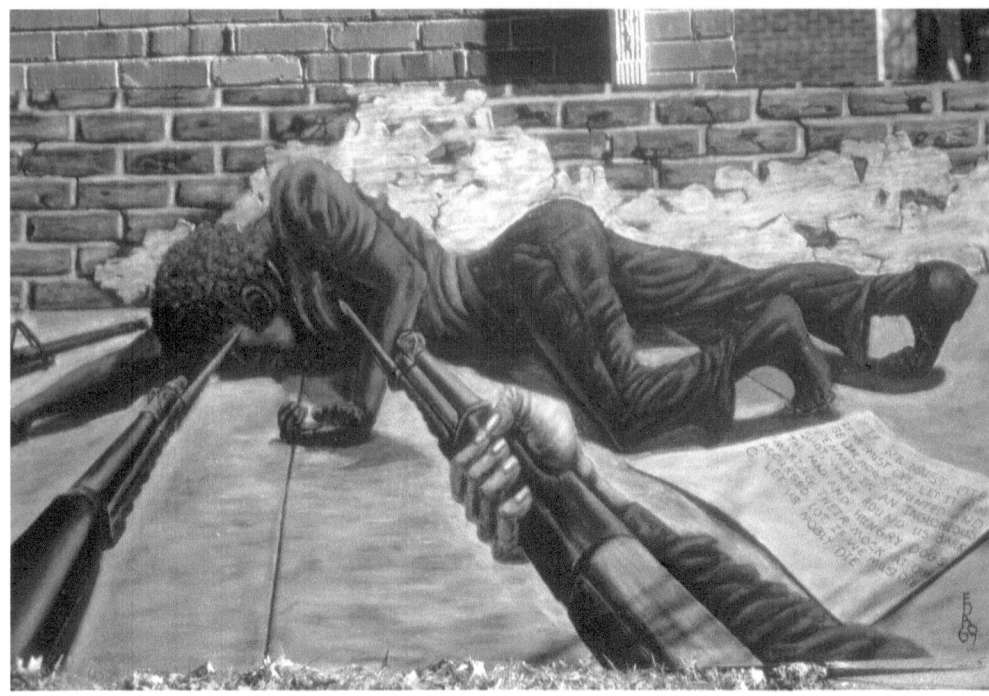

Panel of *Wall of Truth* (1969), 43rd and Langley, Chicago, Ill. Painted by Eugene "Eda" Wade. Photograph by Georg Stahl. Courtesy of the Georg Stahl Mural Collection, University of Chicago Visual Resources Center Luna Collection.

pierce his shoulder and chest as his downturned head inertly rests upon the cold, pale concrete. A small pool of blood spills from his face and escapes toward his unnaturally upturned hand. Clearly, the man was unarmed; his only weapon is the pen with which he wrote Claude McKay's 1919 lynching poem, "If We Must Die," whose presence also brings a deeper awareness to the historical continuum and geographical pervasiveness of lynching in Harris's panel. The final line of the poem, "Pressed to the wall, dying, but fighting back!" is omitted from the handwritten version; instead, the twisted lynched figure invoking Hampton's memory becomes the physical enactment of these words.[41] Pressed against the muted colors of the brick wall, the left side of his body conveys signs of struggle—no shoe and sock on the foot, a raised leg, and a twisted arm—with the right side of his body attempting to "fight back." Tension courses from his outstretched hand to his dressed foot as the lines from the poem drift away from him in the wind.

The dying man's body is enveloped by a concrete halo, also perforated by the bullets of the assassinators, both of whom stand in the foreground wielding guns in similar fashion to the National Guard in Southern cities such as Little Rock, Selma, and Birmingham and more recently in the Northern cities of Detroit, Watts, Newark, and New York City during the long, hot summer rebellions. This is not their first killing. Uniformly gripping the gun, an icy-blue hand is devoid of circulation, much like the unhuman skin of the white lynchers in Harris's panel. The wielder of the second gun remains anonymous, however. When asked if this panel was a reference to Hampton, Eda replied, "Absolutely yes!" before lamenting how Hampton was betrayed. Here, Eda was referring to William O'Neal, who, in return for a monthly stipend and the dropping of charges for car theft and impersonating a federal officer, infiltrated the Chicago Black Panther Party to provide counterintelligence to the Chicago Police Department (CPD). The CPD was acting under the orders of J. Edgar Hoover's Counterintelligence Program (COINTELPRO). Shortly after infiltrating the Chicago Panther rank and file, O'Neal became Hampton's bodyguard, and throughout his time undercover with the Panthers, he supplied information and the floor plans of a Panther apartment at 2337 W. Monroe Street to the CPD. These floor plans were invaluable, and the police, acting under orders from Edward Hanrahan (Cook County state's attorney), raided the apartment in the early hours of December 4, 1969, killing Fred Hampton in his bed and Mark Clark in a chair. For working on the case, O'Neal was rewarded a bonus by the FBI.[42] By omitting the second pair of hands gripping the gun on Eda's panel, then, the muralist offers a powerful warning about trust and loyalty to the viewers of the mural in Chicago's South Side.

When Walker and Eda crafted an unprecedented newspaper in the streets of Chicago, they weren't creating it because of the shortcomings of the Black press. By building an interactive site of communication—a space that asserted the presence of Black life and demanded the acknowledgment of a Black experience—the muralists created the Wall of Truth to report Black news stories in an easily accessible way that didn't rely heavily on reading. "When you have a language on a wall, it is only readable by those who are literate," Walker suggested, "so one wants to try and be as universal as possible with a public wall."[43] As Black Panther Minister of Culture Emory Douglas explained, "The masses of Black people aren't readers, but activists."[44] Here Douglas isn't necessarily suggesting that swaths of the Black community were illiterate but that they instead weren't avid readers. So when wanting to feed a message to the community, Douglas focused closely on building an accessible image-text relationship in his artwork for the *Black Panther*. In every issue of the organization's magazine, he supplemented the written component of the newspaper with a visual poster on the back page to be ripped out and pasted onto the walls of the community. Douglas and Panther supporters used the community as their gallery when "these extraordinary works of art were not displayed on pristine gallery walls, but [were] wheat-pasted on abandoned buildings in ghettos." They were put up everywhere—from "storefront windows, fences, doorways, telephone poles and booths" to "buses, alleyways, gas stations, barbershops, beauty parlors, Laundromats and liquor stores."[45] Just like murals, his posters were works of art for the community that translated messages into a visual medium to reach all audiences. As Sorell points out, murals have a discursive function to "communicate very direct messages . . . because they illustrate, if you will, a lost or silenced history."[46] So by frontloading a visual language, murals such as the *Wall of Truth* spoke not only to readers of the community but also to those who considered themselves as nonreaders, making not just lost and silenced history more accessible but an overlooked Black news more readily available too.

The visual language printed upon the *Wall of Truth* was both potent and affective, so potent, in fact, that the *Chicago Sun-Times* regarded Eda's lynched figure "as powerful as Orozco's 'Christ Destroying His Own Cross' at Dartmouth University."[47] The strength of the mural's visual language, in tandem with its unique purpose to convey accessible information in the streets of one of America's most impoverished neighborhoods, made it a target for white America. The creation of the *Wall of Respect* meant that 43rd and Langley became a hotbed of FBI surveillance and police occupation, as well as a target for Housing and Urban Development's Model Cities economic renewal program. So on August 14, 1969, in front of two hundred people, Walker sent a message to the white racist power structures. He nailed a handwritten plaque to the side of the *Wall of Truth* that read: "WE THE PEOPLE OF THIS COMMUNITY CLAIM THIS BLDG iN Order TO Preserve What is OURS." To the neighborhood at 43rd and Langley, the mural was more than a work of art. It was a monument. By 1969 Walker and Eda had successfully transformed the wall into a Black printing press, a pictorial language, a vessel of communication, and a touchstone of Black pride. It was a manifestation of Black life by Black people for Black people. But in 1971, when the *Wall of Respect* was burned during a suspected arson attack (as discussed in chapter 2), people began removing panels from both it and the Wall of Truth, leaving the walls empty and dilapidated. The Chicago Daily Defender reports that the building remained intact until 1972.[48] After asking for permission from Walker, a collection of panels from both walls were gathered up by Rosa C. Moore and later put on display at Malcolm X College in Chicago.[49]

Although the physical existence of the Wall of Truth was short-lived, its legacy wasn't. It turned the walls of 43rd and Langley into an unofficial vessel of Black news—subversive and occasionally more powerful than its official counterpart. The mural became "a newspaper [that] people [came] and read from week to week," Walker said.[50] Curating a unique interaction for Black murals, Walker and Eda were able to subvert the biased politics of white publications: If white mainstream newspapers relegated a Black experience to the margins, then Walker and Eda put the margins at center stage and created a space to reclaim such news on the walls of the community.

Formed from the perspective of Black voices, murals provided honest, informative, and empowering pictorial languages, but they didn't just live on the streets of Chicago. Shortly after the Wall of Truth sprang up in the South Side, muralists across the country painted visual languages into the streets of their own hometowns to counter biased mainstream narratives and assert their presence in largely segregated neighborhoods. And in the streets of Bayview–Hunters Point in San Francisco, a local muralist by the name of Dewey Crumpler transformed the walls of his Black community into Black history books, etching historical memories of heroes erased from school curricula onto the walls of his neighborhood.

BRINGING THE CAMPUS TO THE COMMUNITY

"Why did black people leave Africa?" Miss Martin asked a group of young African American schoolchildren as they toured the Anacostia Community Museum in Washington, D.C. According to a 1973 article in the Washington Sunday Star, it was "because they were afraid of animals," the schoolchildren replied.[51] Museum assistant director Zora B. Martin recalled how a group of schoolchildren were unaware of their history when touring one of the capital's museums. "Black people didn't want to leave their homes. White people came to Africa, separated the families, and put them into boats. When black people were brought to America, they called them by a different name. Do you know what that was?" Miss Martin followed up by asking. "White people?" a child replied. "No," Miss Martin said. "They called them slaves."[52]

Although this is an example of a single case study in Washington, D.C., in the 1970s, the story of Miss Martin and her group of schoolchildren reported in the *Washington Sunday Star* reflected a universal erasure of Black history from textbooks and curricula throughout schools and colleges nationwide. These institutional arenas of knowledge and learning were full of biased narratives reflecting a white-only history that relegated Black historical experiences and even existences to the sidelines. "All the history books have been untruthful . . . not with lies—but by what [they] excluded from the material," museum director John Kinard argued.[53] In the 1960s, with the powerful quests for Black self-determination, liberation, and nationalism reverberating throughout the country, there was a pronounced nationwide push to bring Black history out from the shadows and place it firmly onto the pages of syllabi, undergraduate courses, and history books.

"The subordination of black people is perpetuated by the educational system, which either refuses to educate or deliberately and systematically mis-educates Black children," James Turner, director of the Black Studies Center at Cornell University, wrote in *Ebony* in 1969.[54] The psychological and emotional effects of this miseducation were felt deep in the psyche. "By the time I reached sophomore year I was emotionally exhausted with the material I had to master in classes," recounted an anonymous woman in the same *Ebony* article. "I was taught to worship Western civilization, and I could hardly believe that racial repression was also a fact of history. Balancing inconsistencies and omissions of knowledge is too much for a black student to take alone. When the movement hit Radcliffe—it was a matter of clutching for a straw to save my very soul."[55]

In response to the pervasive, deliberate, and systemic miseducation of Black students, universities and high schools across the country began effecting change at a grassroots level in the 1960s. Between 1967 and the early 1970s, demands for Black studies departments and curricula increased as students at both predominantly white institutions such as Columbia University, Cornell, and Yale and at HBCUs such as Howard University protested and staged sit-ins.[56] But while protests rippled across the country from coast to coast, the epicenter of Black student activism came from San Francisco State University (SFSU), home to the largest college strike in U.S. history.[57]

From November 1968 until March 1969, students at SFSU went on strike, citing a list of fifteen demands. The strikes ceased when multiple arrests were made and when a handful of these demands were met, including the creation of the Black Studies Department, headed up by Dr. Nathan Hare, the Ethnic Studies Department, and more Black students enrolled in the university.[58] Although the strike ended prematurely, student activism on the campus of San Francisco State was an instrumental catalyst in the national movement toward creating Black spaces for learning Black history. It sparked a domino effect throughout the country, with over 125 universities and high schools striking for Black studies departments and degrees.

"For half of a century, black people have programmatically and systematically been miseducated by the most political institution of this country—the institution of education," Dr. Nathan Hare argued during a press conference for the Black Student Union (BSU).[59] So finally, as James Turner wrote in Ebony, a "quest for new values and definitions that are meaningful and appropriate for black people . . . which will give substance and significance to their lives" was being pursued at a university level.[60] But while the creation of Black studies curricula nationwide was undeniably successful—and one of the lasting legacies of the Black Power movement, as Peniel E. Joseph argues—the implementation of these Black studies curricula was not without limitations.[61]

In 1967 Amiri Baraka migrated across the country to witness firsthand the flourishing radicalism of West Coast Black Power. Taking up a visiting professor position at SFSU, he headed up a BSU project about Black communications. At a meeting with the Associated Students organization on whether his project should continue receiving financial support, Baraka told a packed meeting room about the role a college campus should serve in the community: "It is my contention that a university has no real moral basis for existence unless it is there to refine experience in the communities at large. The university is supposed to refine that experience, it's supposed to analyze that experience, and show it to the light of reason so that each man [people] may benefit by it. You all know for instance that Black people, the majority of them, cannot go to college."[62]

Hitting upon the inaccessibility of the university experience both physically and intellectually, Baraka's sentiments were echoed two years later in 1969, when David Hilliard, chief of staff for the Black Panther Party, gave a speech to the BSU. Picking up on Baraka's discussion of the disconnect between campus and community in San Francisco, Hilliard declared: "I think the one thing we have to hold clear in our minds is that the campus only occupies the teachers and the students 7 or 8 hours a day; and after that they're back into the community. . . . [S]o if we have problems, we have to bring the community into campus. We have to stop isolating ourselves from the community."[63] Although Hilliard spoke about waging a revolution against the more abstract struggle of structural racism in California, by pointing to the separation of the Black community and the predominantly white campus he raised important questions about not only the inaccessibility of learning Black history and culture at the institutional level but also the effects of this upon the local Black community. This in turn begs the following questions: How do those in the community unable to go to university because of systemic racism learn Black history? And how do students going to schools where curricula fail learn Black history?

Looking at the relationship between Black communities and the university, Baraka and Hilliard pointed to the importance of bringing the community to campus to create a stronger movement toward the ideological liberation of Black Americans. But while the relationship between campus and community is mutually exclusive, the idea of bringing the campus *to the community* was not acknowledged. But Black history did find its way into the neighborhoods of Bayview–Hunters Point in San Francisco, and this happened through the murals of local artist Dewey Crumpler.[64]

Much like Chicago's South Side, Bayview–Hunters Point was home to around a 95 percent Black population and was a similar space of de facto segregation. Housing projects, increased poverty levels, and vast unemployment rates were rife across the neighborhoods, but coupled with its physical isolation, the population also felt emotionally secluded from the rest of the city when newspapers such as the *San Francisco Chronicle* sensationalized the area as a hotbed of juvenile delinquency and gang warfare.[65] In much the same way that murals such as the *Wall of Respect*, the *Wall of Truth*, *Segregation B.C.*, and *Knowledge Is Power, Stay in School* stood in Black communities across the North as monuments of Black pride, power, and consciousness, Crumpler's murals lived as magnificent and unapologetic celebrations of Black life and history on the walls of Black neighborhoods, asserting the presence of proud Black communities just forty minutes from SFSU. "I was interested in communicating," Crumpler said in 2017, and through his series of murals around Bayview–Hunters Point, the artist was able to bring learning into the community by creating a visual language that transformed the streets of Bayview into artistic Black history books.[66]

To suggest that Crumpler's murals operated as vessels of communication is not to suggest that murals are a more successful form of education than Black studies departments, nor does it debunk the importance of Black studies curricula and the work done by those striving for their implementation. But these examples of Crumpler's murals, which go beyond the restrictions of Black studies departments, show the pure power, pervasiveness, and beauty of Black murals in the fight for Black liberation in the 1960s and 1970s. Finding solutions to the limitations of college curricula expressed by Baraka and Hilliard, Crumpler brought the information from the campuses to the communities by putting it directly into the streets of his hometown. "Every mural I've ever painted was a form of education," he said.[67] "What led me to make murals was my need to record African American history. For me . . . murals became a way to writing novels, writing the history that had not been written," he suggested, and his murals *Education Is Truth* (1971), *Multi-Ethnic Heritage: Black, Asian, Native/Latin American* (1974), and *The Fire Next Time I* (1977) were painted to erase the images perpetuated by a white supremacist history.[68]

"Part of a problem with American history is that it is based in much part, on inaccurate information or misleading information," Crumpler said, so in 1971, when he painted *Education Is Truth*, his mural attempted to repair this reality.[69] As the mural flanked the street, viewers of the wall saw the pages of a central oversized book splay open. This book, the only book in the mural to open outward toward the viewer, displays the likenesses of Malcolm X and Dr. Martin Luther King Jr. They are the largest pages of the mural— perhaps because they are the most well-known figures and therefore offered the most accessible entry point into an overlooked Black history, or perhaps because the two men were recent martyrs to the movement for Black liberation, and Crumpler wanted to commemorate them. On either side of the central, outward-facing book, two smaller ones are being read. This time, we as the viewer see their front and back covers, decorated with the indelible likenesses of W. E. B. Du Bois, Harriet Tubman, and Muhammad Ali. Ordinarily an onlooker isn't privy to the words read by the reader, but in *Education Is Truth*, Crumpler manipulated this dynamic by opening the book outward for the community to read, maybe an indirect commentary on the need for colonized universities and curricula to tear down the impenetrable wall and become both truthful and accessible for all.

In the mural's foreground, a man and woman sit facing each other, relaxed, with books resting gently in their laps, smiling and reading. The silhouettes of four smaller figures give an almost metacommentary on the educational purpose of the mural. "The kinds of images that we saw—no images of African Americans outside of Amos 'n' Andy—saw African Americans in creative acts, except as subservient," Crumpler commented in relation to the widespread visual assassination of African Americans, so "I began . . . making works that could inspire and speak to African American audiences."[70] The mural was made to teach Black history, and the silhouettes of a young family mirrored the function of the mural back to the neighborhood, underscoring the intergenerational power of education—a mother introduces her children to their ancestors. They gaze in wonder upon the open pages, which are illuminated by a warm orange glow that literally sheds light on an erased history.

In 1974, a few years after creating *Education Is Truth*, Crumpler completed another educational mural titled *Multi-Ethnic Heritage: Black, Asian, Native/Latin American*, at the George Washington High School (GWHS) in San Francisco. Although the idea for this mural emerged in 1966, both the mural and Crumpler faced many logistical obstacles, which meant the mural wasn't actually completed until eight years later. In 1966, already decorating the hallways of GWHS, were controversial murals by Communist artist Victor Arnautoff.[71] In these murals, titled *Life of Washington* (1936), Arnautoff depicts graphic images of a dead Native American figure and many enslaved men and women. The student wing of the Black Panther Party at GWHS saw these images as demeaning, racist, and abhorrent and thought they should immediately be removed. "They [the students] didn't quite understand what he was doing," Crumpler said of the tension between the students and the murals. "They saw the slaves in the murals and so they reacted violently—carving into the murals and throwing black ink on them."[72] In order to reach an agreement that would see a stop to the defacement of Arnautoff's murals, the students demanded that prideful artwork of a powerful, rich Black experience in the United States be painted and that they be painted by Crumpler. While the school district went along with the students, "some members of the Art Commission said I was too young and inexperienced in painting murals," Crumpler recalled, so "when they held up the process, I went all over the country" to get experience.[73]

Traveling first to Detroit, Chicago, and New York in 1968 at the age of twenty, Crumpler visited Bill Walker and Eda to get a sense of their process and philosophy behind mural-making. Although he appreciated the forms and purpose of the *Wall of Respect* and the *Wall of Truth* for the Black community in the South Side, "aesthetically, I had no interest in that," he admitted.[74] "Then when I went to see Walker's mural," he continued, most likely *Peace and Salvation, Wall of Understanding* (1970) in Cabrini-Green, and "it was much more interesting and much more constructed in a way that made sense."[75] But it wasn't until he followed in the footsteps of Harlem Renaissance and WPA giants such as Hale Woodruff, John Wilson, Charles White, and Aaron Douglas by visiting Mexico that Crumpler began to understand what he wanted to achieve from mural painting. "[David Alfaro] Siqueiros for me was the greatest painter and the greatest muralist I ever saw. That was what I wanted to do in mural painting," he said of the large, consuming compositions of the Mexican artist.[76] Studying with both Pablo O'Higgins and Siqueiros, Crumpler learned how to reconfigure space, environment, and composition in his own public art in ways that conveyed strong and timely educational narratives.

Returning from Mexico and having satisfied the GWHS art commission's request to gain more mural experience, Crumpler held meetings with the students council and student Black Panther Party to decide what the new murals needed to look like. "I and several students in the Black Panther Party felt the mural should be [thematically] broader, even though none of the students from other communities participated in forcing this issue." As a result, the proposed murals would focus not only on a Black experience but also on an Asian, Native, and Latinx American experience.[77] With forty to fifty people engaged in these artistic meetings, Crumpler asked students and teachers which figures of Black, Asian, Native, and Latinx American history they wanted to see on the wall to make sure it was a collaborative process.

Painted at the end of a long corridor and flanked by the two panels on Asian, Native, and Latinx American history stands—still to this day— Crumpler's mural depicting the lineage of Black life in the United States and the diaspora. Bordering the edges of this mural is a large, thick bronze chain woven throughout the other two panels and meeting in this frame, entombing the figures of Blackness within its boundary. While the likenesses of Black heroes and African symbols look trapped for a brief moment, the muscular bodies of two shirtless Black men extend their powerful arms down the chain, gripping it tightly in their hands—muscles twitching with the metaphorical weight of Black strength throughout history as they snap the chain in two, breaking it toward the viewer. From the clean break emerges the fiery figure of a pregnant woman, her body curved and contoured with the anticipation of a new Black life. A young child with outstretched arms and an afro looks down upon the scenes of Blackness below—the stoic image of a young Frederick Douglass, a proud Nubian pharaoh, an embracing Black couple, and on the periphery of the broken chain but separated from those couched inside its metal border stands John Brown.

Although many of the Black figures were selected by students at the school, Crumpler created something unprecedented to accompany this mural to make sure it was as informative as possible. He wrote a key to the symbolism of each element of the painting "to let everybody know who all the people were in the mural, what the fire meant, what this meant, what that meant," he said. "When you looked at the mural you could go in the office, and they would give you the key, and you could go and take it and read it and then take it back to the office."[78] And this was a common occurrence: "The principal, who I'd gotten to be friends with . . . was saying, 'Well, the kids always come up and ask this and ask that,' and he said, 'Well, it would be good to make a key, you know, write something,' and I said, 'Sure, I'll draw out a thing and I'll give it to you and you can Xerox it.'"[79]

Although *Multi-Ethnic Heritage: Black, Asian, Native/Latin American* was actually an interior mural as opposed to one that lived directly in the streets of the Black community, even in the hallways of a high school in San Francisco, Crumpler was able to foster an unprecedented learning relationship between students and mural through a unique call-and-response dynamic that inspired individuals to conduct their own personal research on historical figures. The mural didn't need to live in the streets to have an edifying impact on the local community—it just required a story that needed to be told and an audience ready to learn.

Much like the visual newspapers of Walker and Eda, the murals of Crumpler possessed palimpsest qualities. While the *Wall of Truth* became a bricolage of local and national Black news pasted upon the wall, Crumpler's murals became transdisciplinary tapestries woven into the fabric of San Francisco. His murals went beyond inserting the likenesses of Black historical figures into the urban environment. In tandem with the pantheons of painted heroes, multiple moments of diasporic history and culture were braided together to create an intricate vessel of knowledge that drew

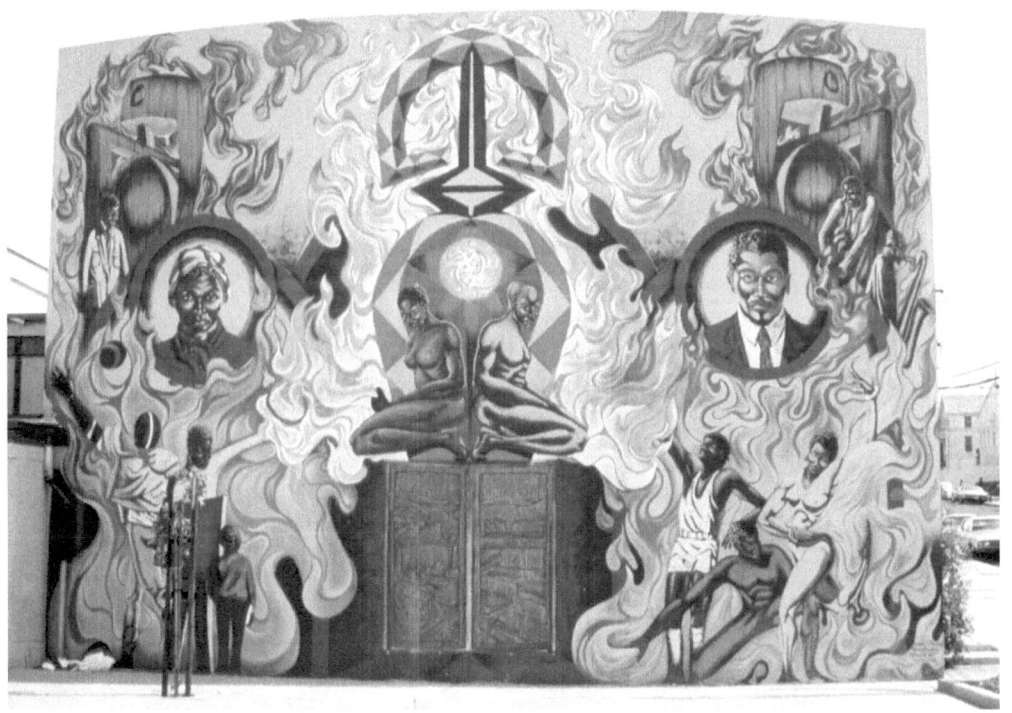

The Fire Next Time I (1977), Joseph Lee Recreation Center, Newcomb Ave, San Francisco, Calif. Painted by Dewey Crumpler. Image courtesy of Dewey Crumpler.

from the disciplines of art, literature, music, spirituals, and ancestral history. With the visual painted mural as the foundation of his palimpsest, Crumpler threaded layers of information into his murals, like *The Fire Next Time I* (1977), to share Black history and culture—both diasporic and national—with the community.

Painted on the walls of the Joseph Lee Recreation Center in San Francisco, *The Fire Next Time I* depicts three key aspects of Black life in the United States: education, religion, and culture. Echoing the compositional structure of Mexican muralism from artists such as Siqueiros, José Clemente Orozco, and Diego Rivera, Crumpler covered the entirety of the wall with engulfing orange flames, because "once I'd come back from Mexico and I understood how I wanted to use that fire as a theme, then I understood how to start constructing the actual forms and the mural."[80] Students, dancers, and athletes span the bottom of the frame, while the portraits of Harriet Tubman and Paul Robeson look upon them as focal points from above. "I was interested in education and that education for Black people was essential. Black people did not see themselves in any way other than the negative portrayals that were so constant in the 1960s," Crumpler said in a 2018 interview:

> The kind of buffoonish characters, the way Blacks were always, if they were ever in movies or television, they were shown as subservient. You know, it's the typical argument. It's rather boring and cliché to hear now, but at that time it was absolutely assaulting, and part of my reason for ever wanting to be an artist was to attack those kinds of images with images of clarity, or at least images that would provoke African Americans to ask questions about what that thing was—or at least to make pictures about history. So that was my interest in mural painting.[81]

Crumpler used the visual language on his murals to spark questions in the minds of the viewer, wanting to, in his words, "provoke African Americans to ask questions about what that thing was." He sought to include specifically unfamiliar imagery or content that would inspire his audiences to probe his work by asking the questions "What is that?" or "Why did he do that?"[82] If viewers wanted to learn Black history, they would have to actively partake in this educational process. In the hope that viewers would ask such questions and perhaps invite questions too, Crumpler again provided a key next to his street murals, hoping to satisfy any queries from the community. "I had a key to the symbolism of everything I painted," he admitted, and by doing this, he sought to provide just enough information for curious onlookers to research the historic figures of his mural in libraries and textbooks.[83]

During the painting of his history section of *The Fire Next Time I*, Crumpler had a visit from a member of the local community. A young man approached him and asked who the portraits were of. "Harriet Tubman and Paul Robeson," Crumpler said, to which the young man replied, "They don't live here man, you should put up a couple of locals like Richard and Edwina. They're a stone couple."[84] Seizing the moment to pass on knowledge of Black history and underscore the purpose of his murals, Crumpler recounted the following conversation:

> CRUMPLER: Well, these people are of the community.
> RESIDENT: I don't know any of them.
> CRUMPLER: That's the point. You have to get to know some of these

people, and the way to do that is go to that library across the street and look some of these people up.

RESIDENT: Who is that right up there?

CRUMPLER: That's Harriet Tubman.

RESIDENT: Does she live in the community?

CRUMPLER: Now see, that's why you have to go across the street, because Harriet Tubman is the reason you live in this community. If it wasn't for Harriet Tubman, you wouldn't be in this community.[85]

Several weeks later, after researching Tubman, the young man returned to the wall and admitted to Crumpler that he was right—that Black people "needed to know more about important leaders so they could have somebody to respect . . . and besides, Richard and Edwina had broken up."[86] The power of this story so perfectly encapsulates the interactive potency of Crumpler's murals not only as touchstones of community Black consciousness and pride but uniquely as visual entry points into an overlooked Black history. Crumpler curated a space of learning in the streets of Bayview–Hunters Point that gave a young man access to his history in an intriguing and inviting way that catalyzed his desire to read beyond Tubman and research other important leaders too.

But *The Fire Next Time I* wasn't only enlightening through its historical figures. The specifically chosen title was also layered with references to literature and spirituals. When asked if the phrase *The Fire Next Time* was a direct reference to James Baldwin's 1963 seminal book of the same name, Crumpler explained that the mural's title was actually borrowed from the spiritual "Mary Don't You Weep": "God gave Noah the rainbow sign. / No more water, the fire next time." As an early nineteenth-century spiritual, "Mary Don't You Weep" contains coded messages of hope and resistance sung by formerly enslaved people. It tells the biblical story of Mary of Bethany and her pleas to Jesus to raise her brother Lazarus from the dead, and it compares the resurrection of Lazarus to the deliverance of enslaved people from Egypt, paralleling resurrection with freedom.[87] While Crumpler believed that older generations of African Americans would understand this original biblical meaning, he admitted to using the lyric as an educational entry point into the work of James Baldwin. For anybody who looked up the title, "James Baldwin would come up first—that's the introduction to Baldwin. I was very clear on the use of Baldwin," Crumpler suggested.[88]

Addressed to Baldwin's nephew James, *The Fire Next Time* is made up of two powerfully emotional letters, "My Dungeon Shook" and "Down at the Cross—Letter from a Region of My Mind." "This innocent country set you down in a ghetto in which, in fact, it intended that you should perish," Baldwin laments. "You can only be destroyed by believing that you really are what the white world calls *nigger*. I tell you this because I love you, and please don't you ever forget it."[89] Written on the one hundredth anniversary of the Emancipation Proclamation, Baldwin's first letter weighs heavy with the history of Black pain and suffering. His mental fatigue, countered with his resilience and fortitude, seeps from the pages and into the minds of the reader and, of course, his nephew James. "Know whence you came, there is really no limit to where you can go," Baldwin tells him. "You come from sturdy, peasant stock, men who picked cotton and dammed rivers and built railroads, and, in the teeth of the most terrifying odds, achieved an unassailable and monumental dignity."[90]

Baldwin's second letter is couched less in the memories of Black history and more in the harsh realities of Black life in a crowded city such as Chicago. "My friends . . . began to care less about the way they looked, the way they dressed, the things they did," he writes. "Presently, one found them in twos and threes and fours, in a hallway, sharing a jug of wine or a bottle of whiskey, talking, cursing, fighting, sometimes weeping: lost, and unable to say what it was that oppressed them, except that they knew it was 'the man'—the white man."[91] His symphonic writing navigates through the power, purpose, and positions of race and religion in 1960s America, recounting his own relationship with Christianity and attending to the growing popularity of Islam in Harlem. In much the same way that Crumpler's keys of information gave viewers an entry point into overlooked figures of Black history, his malleable use of the title *The Fire Next Time I* constructed a didactic call-and-response relationship that would introduce locals to Baldwin or perhaps just remind them of not only ancestral spirituals but also a profound and influential piece of writing on Black life in America.

The final layer woven into Crumpler's mural deals with diasporic memory. African cultural symbols and symbolism are etched into the artwork because it "felt absolutely necessary to connect to Africa," Crumpler said. "African Americans pretty well understood that Africa was a part of their thing completely," so he wanted to ensure that diasporic imagery was seamlessly interwoven with African American history to underscore the ancestral lineage of Black life in America.[92] During the creation of *The Fire Next Time I*, Crumpler collected African art and studied Yoruba cosmology, which found its way into his murals through African textiles, artifacts such as masks and doors, and mythical creatures such as the Senufo bird. By using diasporic symbolism, Crumpler wanted to create an educational space that elevated his viewer's understanding of not only Black history but also ancient African history. While the portraits of Robeson and Tubman sit proudly as frontispieces on the side of the gym, a blanket of fire envelops them, framing two nude figures painted in front of a patterned backdrop. The two central nude figures are perched upon a magical, ancient-looking door, facing away from each other with their heads angled down toward the fire. The presence of the fire and the unclothed figures incited anger and outrage from members of a local church, but the concerns over the propriety of the mural were soon allayed when Crumpler explained their purpose and symbolism. The two central nude figures symbolized duality, which was important in Dogon and Yoruba culture, and the flames, while invoking the memory of the recent turmoil of the long, hot summer—which had struck Bayview–Hunters Point in 1966—took on a purifying meaning, much like in the book of Revelation, as opposed to destructive forces, Crumpler explained. After hearing these descriptions, the church members were satisfied, and having learned something new, they permitted him to continue his work without their interruption.[93]

More than paintings in the streets and in schools, Crumpler's murals stood (and still stand) in Black communities as part of the deepening quest for self-determined Black power, knowledge, and transformation in the 1960s and 1970s and even into the 1980s. His murals stood at the vanguard of communal learning, offering the residents of Bayview–Hunters Point a truthful snapshot into a history hidden by the mainstream. Embedded into the broader movement for Black liberation, Crumpler and his murals stood in the Black community as artwork *of* the people and *for* the people, giving voice and image back to Black stories constantly assaulted by structural supremacist dominance.

For years, decades, and centuries, the permeation of white supremacy in every mainstream institution across the country attempted to erase Black history, life, and culture from the surface of America, but in the radical

1960s, the tide was turning. Black Power, Black pride, Black love, Black nationalism, Black culture, and Black is Beautiful rang out across the nation, truthfully showing Black America as it really was. Alongside the call to learn Black history and control Black news in this new era of Black consciousness came a swell of murals that used historic and ancestral memory and narratives of Black life to transform community walls into places of learning. These walls of knowledge destabilized the biases of white institutional spaces, honestly and truthfully telling of a history so frequently erased from America's mainstream. But as the late 1970s saw these fiery flames of radical, revolutionary Black Power flicker to a faint glow, it looked as if a new moment in the movement for Black liberation was on the horizon. With the nation looking down the barrel of decades of neoconservatism and austerity, the pursuit for Black liberation in the 1980s, 1990s, and 2000s was about to face new forms of racial, emotional, and physical injustice in ways never felt before. And standing there alongside the powerful and unyielding marches, protests, and renewed battles for civil and human rights—just as they have been since the 1930s—were Black murals, ready again to take up the fight in any way they could.

CHAPTER 5

"I Wanted the Wall to Scream"

Black Community Murals in a Post–Civil Rights America

We've dressed the city with our names. —SKEME, graffiti bomber, 1983

The ghettos and barrios of our cities are more abandoned and more endangered than 30 years ago. Jobs have gone, drugs and guns have spread,
hope is down, violence is up. —Jesse Jackson, 1993 March on Washington

This was our gallery, this was our museum. You could take pictures of
graffiti, you could take pictures of street art and put them in a gallery
but it immediately loses its context so there is an opportunity for us to
really let people see what it's like when we paint in these environments,
when we paint in these spaces. —Brandan Odums, talking about ExhibitBE,
painted in abandoned building after Hurricane Katrina

"We are still picking up the pieces of the eighties today," former crack cocaine user Felecia Pullen said in 2021. "Why?" she asks. "Because the responses were not designed to help the people that were in trouble."[1] The
years following the legal, ideological, and revolutionary strides of the
civil rights and Black Power movements were marked by three decades
of unshakable austerity, a tightening chokehold of neoconservatism,
record-breaking numbers of Americans dropping below the poverty line
(especially in communities of color), a drug epidemic, and a reckoning with
the largest racial rebellion in U.S. history. In 1982, following the presidential landslide victory for actor and former governor of California Ronald
Reagan two years earlier, his administration eliminated half a million
people from welfare rolls, one million from food stamps, and 2.6 million
children from lunch programs.[2] The Reagan and George H. W. Bush administrations constructed a systemically racist framework within the U.S. legal
system that criminalized drug users and targeted communities of color—
especially Black and Latinx communities—through the introduction of

"mandatory minimum" sentencing, and by the late 1980s and early 1990s, the federal antidrug budget had increased to $12 billion, six times greater than when Reagan assumed office.[3] These decades of deepening conservatism also birthed the restructuring and militarizing of police forces from "beat cops" to police units with high-power weaponry, armed vehicles, and new surveillance tactics, which subsequently played a part in the exponential growth of the prison-industrial complex that swelled prison populations from 513,900 in 1980, to 1,179,200 in 1990, to 2,015,300 in 2000.[4]

With this era of Republican rule—followed by Bill Clinton's conservative Democratic reign from 1992 to 2000—the movement for Black liberation fought on, and embedded into it, as always, were Black community murals. Lining the walls of Black neighborhoods from border to border and coast to coast, these murals stood proudly, as they did in the 1960s and 1970s, in the heart of the Black community, inspiring, transforming, healing, and educating. With a rich and fertile foundation to build upon from the previous two decades, the mural tradition wasn't doing anything unprecedented or overtly unique. The clocks didn't chime midnight on January 1, 1980, and usher in a new moment in the movement. Instead, post–civil rights murals continued in the vein of their artistic ancestors: They just evolved and grew, adding greater complexity to the extant tradition. These murals remained a steadfast and omnipresent feature of Black America, responding to the turbulent climates of the decades and offering a visual antidote to the rising tides of conservatism and white supremacy. But this period of growing conservatism was also a period of reconciliation. It was a time when leaders, activists, and community members waded through the wins and losses of the civil rights and Black Power movements, figuring out, yet again, how to survive and push for accountability in an America that criminalizes, confines, and exterminates the lives and livelihoods of people of color—only this time, not just through the tried-and-true methods of violence and de facto / de jure segregation but also through drugs, new legal sentencing, and new policing. So just as murals of the previous generations did, those in the 1980s, 1990s, and early 2000s stood in the Black community, demanding acknowledgment of Black neighborhoods, reclaiming Black space, celebrating Blackness, and empowering those still purposefully overlooked but simultaneously harassed by the systemically oppressive power structures.

Weaving through the years marked by Reagan, Bush Sr., Clinton, and Bush Jr. administrations, this chapter takes us from Los Angeles to New

York via Chicago and New Orleans, showing how murals from artists such as Bill Walker, Brett Cook, Noni Olabisi, and Brandan Odums remained embedded into the movement for Black liberation. It details how changes to funding and mural sponsorship from the National Endowment for the Arts (NEA) and the Comprehensive Employment and Training Act (CETA), as well as new social, racial, and economic events, added greater complexity to the mural movement. The years were punctuated by events such as the War on Drugs, the Gulf War, Hurricane Katrina, 9/11, the Iraq War, the war in Afghanistan, and the Rodney King beating and subsequent rebellions. These decades also saw a steep increase in the election of Black politicians, multiple marches and protests, a steady uptick of lynchings, an almost tripling of the Ku Klux Klan's national membership, significant legal battles over affirmative action, and mass levels of unemployment and homelessness across the country.

Covering three decades in one chapter is no easy task, let alone when these decades span a multiplicity of social, racial, political, and global changes, as well as multiple artistic movements. It's worth noting that this period of Black community mural-making in the 1980s and 1990s concurrently unfolded alongside a graffiti movement. Graffiti and its signature spray-paint materials became wrapped up in the public art scene of the decades, responding, in many ways as murals do, to the austerity of corporate power structures. In the 1970s a graffiti movement and a "style wars" emerged across the country before becoming ubiquitous in the 1980s. Surfacing in Philadelphia in 1965 but reaching New York City in 1968, graffiti was a movement about power and takeover. "You started on your street, then you went to the buses. You take over your neighborhood, then you take over all [the] city," said artist Luke "SPAR ONE" Felisberto. With a very different process and mentality to community murals, graffiti was an individual endeavor and not one rooted in the ethos of by the people and for the people. It was about saying names "loud all across buildings, bus stops, and subway station walls uptown." It was about a singular identity and a personal goal.[5] "It's a matter of bombing and knowing that I can do it," explained graffiti bomber SKEME. "Every time I get on the train, you know, I can always see my name. . . . Yeah, I was there. . . . For me it's not for nobody else to see. I don't care about nobody else in it or the fact that they can read it or not. It's for me and other graffiti writers."[6] Graffiti, then, was a way to gain status among other artists. Your name was your currency, and you "created value by making your mark in the niches" or painting it everywhere.[7] In the 1980s graffiti evolved into more than getting your name up in many places. It was about innovating and expanding to see how you could create the most intricate and unusual forms, shapes, letters, backgrounds, and characters possible, and these aesthetic influences began to stylistically infiltrate community murals during the era and beyond.

Given the anthology of events and artistic styles of the 1980s, 1990s, and 2000s, then, the pages that follow focus more intimately on recording, appreciating, and discussing a geographically diverse selection of murals that are both murals of consolidation (documenting current events in the same vein as their artistic forebears) and murals of diversification (engaging in new aesthetic approaches and social practices).[8] In 1984 muralist Bill Walker told Margaret Burroughs that he was "trying through [his] art to make a statement about the times in which [he] lives," and this testimonial rings true for many muralists throughout the era.[9]

PAINTING TOO MANY SWEET THINGS NOW

Funding is a necessity when creating a mural, whether the money has been raised by the local community or the artists themselves or perhaps comes from governmental or nonprofit sponsorship. Painting materials, scaffolding rentals, and the artists' and crews' time cost money. In the late 1970s, with the dawning of a neoconservative reign heaving into view on the horizon, funding for community murals began to dry up and change in nature. When the mural movement was facing its greatest period of expansion, it simultaneously confronted funding and potential censorship pressures.[10] Since 1970 across the country, the NEA had been one of the major sources of public funds for murals, but in 1973 the slow but pronounced tapering off of NEA funds rolled on through the early years of the Reagan administration, thwarting plans for further community murals.[11] "The principal explanation," according to mural documentarian Alan Barnett, "must be the decline of riots and militancy in the inner city together with the recession that began in 1974."[12] It was the long, hot summer that supposedly catalyzed the government into taking fiscal action for community projects in the first place, he said. So while some government employees were passionate about the power of community arts developments, the main motivation for funneling money into Black neighborhoods (which artists such as Dana Chandler in Boston and Dewey Crumpler in Bayview–Hunters Point were both recipients of) was to quell the potential of further racial rebellions. As the demonstrations of the mid- to late 1960s flamed out in the 1970s, so too did NEA funding for community arts programs.[13]

In search of alternative funds, muralists turned to the CETA, which in many ways was modeled on the WPA of the 1930s and 1940s in that it provided training and grants for artists to create public art, but the number of artists funded by CETA dwindled in comparison to those funded by the WPA. Under CETA, artist salaries reached around $700 a month, but much like the NEA money, which was administered by the Department of Labor, those salaries began to decrease in the late 1970s before being eliminated entirely in 1981.[14]

"Access to culture began to seem like a natural right," Chicago muralist and cofounder of the Chicago Public Art Group (CPAG) John Pitman Weber said of the mural funding. "But in this new regime of tax cuts and recession, it wasn't realistic to think the private sector would pick up the funding slack for murals of quality, content, character and critique."[15] It's this latter point mentioned by Weber here that became a point of contention for artists during this period and even stretching back into the mid-1970s. Muralists such as Mitchell Caton had a growing concern over how problematic and sanitized government sponsorship was becoming. Wanting the funding to come from deep in the community, he told the *Chicago Daily Defender*: "I wish the businessmen and the clergy on the South Side would come together in terms of getting matching funds from the government in order to make the mural movement more meaningful."[16] Nationally during the 1980s and through the end of the twentieth century, there was a swell of support from private and government funding for both street and interior murals, as well as for school mural programs. In Philadelphia, for example, Mayor Wilson Goode established outreach programs such as the Philadelphia Anti-Graffiti Network and the Mural Arts Project.[17] But these sources of money often came with caveats. "Nothing about violence, nothing critical, nothing politically left" was the message written between the lines.[18] In many ways, murals had become "almost completely institutionalized," said artist and mural documentarian Tim Drescher. "Organizations, not artists, controlled imagery, and critical politics was shunned in favor of affirmation."[19]

It looked like the community mural movement was reliving the stifling grip of patronage and censorship felt by Black interior muralists of the 1930s and 1940s. When Aaron Douglas openly apologized for his sanitized final panel in his *Aspects of Negro Life* (1934) series, discussed in chapter 1, he lambasted himself in the *New York Amsterdam News* for not creating a fifth panel that spoke to Black liberation through the unity of Black and white workers in the class struggle, worried that the entire series would be rejected by the Public Works of Art Project (PWAP). "Under our present system . . . the artist must paint what his employer wants," he said in 1934. "If he is to keep his own self-respect, however, he must try to maintain a certain honesty and present the picture as he sees it."[20] Fifty years later, in 1982, this concern and warning from the Harlem Renaissance artist rang out in the words of Bill Walker: "Artists are painting too many sweet things now. They have to realize that they've got to quit relying on government money if they really want to say something. . . . [I]t is a test period of whether artists can hold onto their principles and weather the storm."[21] Fearful of the effects government sponsorship would have on the message and visual content of murals in the 1980s and 1990s, Walker warned artists not to muzzle their own artistic message. They should simply speak to the issues they feel passionately about, not compromising their beliefs to do so. And in 1982 one of the issues Walker felt passionately about conveying through his artwork was the stifling sweep of conservatism.

Nestled into the backstreets of 55th Place and S. Indiana Avenue in Chicago's South Side stood one of Walker's angriest murals, *Reaganomics*, on the side of G & S Liquor Store, owned by friend Tommie Lee Norwood.[22] "I was mindful of Mr. Reagan and his policies and his presidency in relation to the lack of sensitivity be they black or white. . . . [I]f they were poor, they were left out," said Walker.[23] Wanting to send a message about the evils of the Reagan administration to the blocks around 55th and Indiana, Walker painted the president's likeness onto the wall, presenting him as a jack-in-the-box caricature in the center of an empty blue frame, his arms aloft in a cactus shape. With Reagan's oversized head painted in intricate detail, Walker captured every contour and fold of Reagan's creased face, showing how it wrinkles and cracks under the weight of his unnatural and malicious smile. Playing on the jack-in-the-box analogy, Walker painted the president's skin a pale, almost-white shade with purple tinges at the outlines as his cheeks become flushed with a bright red and his lips run a deep purple, almost plum-like color. His body, drawn in a basic two-dimensional style, seems almost incongruous to the detailing of his face, and the skin on his neck becomes bunched and folded to fit into his tight white shirt and black tie. Walker painted Reagan's body in a much more geometric style. His left hand holds up a picture of a baby with the word "Reagan" underneath, and with his right hand he makes the universal symbol for "OK," which ironically, since around 2017, has been reappropriated as a symbol of white power and white supremacy—something that saw a pronounced increase under the Reagan administration.[24]

Just above Reagan's box, under a headline that reads "1st DISTRICT SAYS FIGHT BACK," stands a list of itemized statistics on budget cuts in community social services, such as "FARM SUBSIDIES AGAINST INCREASE 75%," "BUSINESS SUBSIDIES INCREASE AGAINST INCREASE 75%," and "JOB PROGRAM CUT AGAINST CUT 95%." Here, Walker is drawing upon some of the harrowing facts and figures reported during Reagan's first year in office. By 1981 the number of poor Americans had increased by 2.2 million. The following year, the real median income for all Black families had declined by 5.2 percent, and according to *The New York Times*, much of the progress made in the 1960s and 1970s to battle poverty among poor Americans had basically been wiped out in a single year under Reagan.[25] Walker alluded to this poverty in his mural through a woman holding an empty plate in his direction, spilling into his frame—she is a victim of these budget cuts, she is living below the poverty line, and she is trying to attract Reagan's attention but, sadly, to no avail. To her left stands Walker's 1980 mural titled *Peace, Peace*, a mural that urged Black unity and offered a plea to warring street gangs to stop shooting each other.[26]

Walker's disdain of Reagan wasn't only evident in his 1982 mural, however. In the previous year, Walker had already painted a mural of Reagan, also confusingly titled *Reaganomics* or *Reagan's Ax Cuts Aid to Millions*, on another of Norwood's properties at E. 47th Place and S. Champlain Avenue. This mural, at around seventy-five feet long, was comprised of a hodgepodge of anti-Reagan imagery.[27] "All this misery, this suffering and pain that existed within the community," Walker told Victor Sorell in an interview, "and the helplessness, the lack of leadership, the inability to address the real problems of drugs. . . . I wanted to do something about it, and the only way that I knew how to do that was to go about it visually and make visual statements."[28] Monsters, skulls, military weapons, desiccated corpses, community leaders, local children, and a composite of Reagan as a zombie-like Klansman made up the mural. Speaking to the angry and confrontational imagery on Walker's mural, Norwood "got kind of nervous about what people would think" of it.[29] But he need not have worried—the mural remained largely intact until it was whitewashed in 2005, standing in the neighborhood, etching, and in many ways preserving in the streets this pronounced era of neoconservatism that right-wing governments were simultaneously ignoring and, by doing so, driving further into poverty.

Under Reagan's eight-year reign and Bush Sr.'s four-year rule, "inequality as a political concept was defended as absolutely essential to continued economic growth and productivity."[30] The 1980s and 1990s were dominated by a new era of corporate wealth, in which the richest 1 percent of American families had nearly as much wealth as the bottom 95 percent combined. Between 1980 and 1993, just before Clinton assumed office, the average CEO salary increased by 514 percent, making that salary 157 times bigger than that of the average factory worker.[31] FHA allocation budgets were slashed from $30 billion in 1981 to $8 billion in 1986, curtailing housing for the working poor, the unemployed, and any household receiving support from the program Aid to Families with Dependent Children. This led to a doubling of the number of homeless Americans in the country by 1988, bringing the total to just shy of three million.[32]

In the 1980s and 1990s Black communities in the United States experienced "two distinct crises which threatened to pull apart its social fabric," the first being the rise of right-wing policies that slashed welfare budgets, caused a swell of mass unemployment disproportionately affecting Black communities, and led to dramatic increases in homelessness across the country. The second crisis, however, was "far more devastating to the spirit and cultural consciousness" of African Americans, Manning Marable suggests: "the ordeal of the African American family, neighborhood, cultural and social institutions caught in the vice of violence, crime, social destruction and drugs."[33]

The 1980s saw an influx of cocaine coming into the United States from drug cartels in Central and South America. Between 1982 and 1984 the amount of cocaine entering the United States increased by 50 percent, spurring the Reagan administration to wage a "war on drugs."[34] While cocaine infiltrated the country at an alarming rate, its ripple effect throughout Black communities across the nation, in concert with the government's ineffectual, racist, and draconian responses to stamping out drug activity, left poverty and devastation in its wake. The majority of cocaine consumers were middle-class white Americans, but new government policies and sentencing failed to reflect this. In 1999 the U.S. Commission on Civil Rights found that African Americans constituted only 14 percent of illegal drug users nationally, yet they made up 35 percent of all drug arrests, 55 percent of all drug convictions, and 75 percent of all prison admissions for drug offenses.[35] Instead, the consequences for drug dependency and addiction among the wealthy and elite social classes were through rehabilitation. It appeared, therefore, that this "paternalistic social infrastructure" of care and compassion was virtually nonexistent for the majority of Black, Latinx, and lower-income people wrestling with crack addiction.[36]

The narrative around drug addiction was manipulated and redefined not as an illness rippling throughout low-income communities and communities of color requiring help and aid but instead as an individual choice and a personal failure.[37] Ignoring the clarion call for increased spending on drug treatment, rehabilitation, prevention, and research, the Reagan administration did the opposite, directing funds instead toward law enforcement.[38] Addiction was criminalized, and the 1980s, 1990s, and 2000s would be punctuated by a series of strict and unjust laws and bills that targeted the poor and communities of color. In 1986 the Anti–Drug Abuse Act was signed by Reagan. This legislation introduced mandatory minimum sentencing, which was already problematic as it took control away from judges, requiring them to issue long-term prison sentences without the possibility of early parole. But one of the most infamous aspects of the Anti–Drug Abuse Act was the hundred-to-one crack cocaine ratio. Powder cocaine was typically used by the wealthy and social elite, whereas crack cocaine was smokable and inexpensive to obtain at around five dollars per rock, making it used more broadly in lower-income communities.[39] Under the 1986 act, crack cocaine was much more heavily criminalized: A person possessing just five grams faced the same mandatory sentencing of five (the minimum) to forty years as someone possessing five hundred grams of powder cocaine.[40] In 1988 this law was extended to anyone in possession of any amount of crack cocaine, signaling, if at all possible, an even more pronounced shift from the Reagan administration to criminalize drug users, especially those poor and of color. Powder cocaine doesn't harm others, was the prevailing logic, but crack leads to delinquent and harmful behavior.[41]

"Rising levels of abuse, addiction, and drug-related violence should have been a sign that something was wrong with America," James Forman Jr., son of civil rights and Black Power activist James Forman, said. "It should have led the nation to focus on the myriad of ways in which 350 years of white supremacy had produced persistent Black suffering and disadvantage."[42] But instead it led to deepening poverty, unemployment, and a prison-industrial complex across the country. Two years after Clinton assumed office, the Violent Crime Control and Law Enforcement Act (colloquially known as the Clinton Crime Bill) was signed into law on September 13, 1994, ironically and uncomfortably marking the twenty-third anniversary of the violent suppression of the Attica Prison uprising of 1971. The crime bill was the largest in U.S. history. At 356 pages long, it was extensive, providing for one hundred thousand new police officers, $9.7 billion in funding for prisons, the expansion of the death penalty to around sixty offenses, and the three strikes rule.[43] The moral panic produced by Clinton's law-and-order policies and rhetoric served "as a proxy for more explicit calls to suppress Black movements and ultimately to criminalize indiscriminately broad swathes of the Black population," argues prison activist Angela Y. Davis, and it led to an unprecedented expansion of the penal system in both the prison population and the building of new correctional facilities.[44] In 1989, 23 percent of all Black males in the United States were, on any given day, either in jail, on parole, awaiting trial, or on probation. In California, between 1981 and 2001, for example, twenty-one new prisons were built to accommodate its 160,000-person penal population. Similarly, during the same period, New York state constructed thirty-eight new facilities.[45] Although the legal battles for desegregation and voting rights had been won through the passing of the Civil Rights and Voting Rights Acts of 1964 and 1965, respectively, by the mid-1990s it looked as if racial injustices in the United States were reaching a new nadir.

On the surface, the 1980s and 1990s seemed to be making strides in the right direction. During the movements for civil rights and Black Power, demands were made for "a Black face in a high place," which meant the movement for Black liberation should include African Americans in positions of authority and power. One of the yardsticks for measuring racial progress was the percentage of African Americans represented in political, professional, and managerial positions of influence. In the twenty-five years since the Civil Rights Act, Black elected officials increased from one hundred to nearly seven hundred; the number of African Americans enrolled in colleges and universities increased fourfold; the size of the Black middle class began to swell; and Black mayors were finally winning races in major cities—Harold Washington in Chicago, David Dinkins in New York, Andrew Young in Atlanta, Kurt Schmoke in Baltimore. Jesse Jackson even received millions of votes as a Democratic presidential candidate in both 1984 and 1988.[46] And by 1995 forty African Americans sat in Congress, and over eight thousand had been elected to government positions. But this model of "symbolic representation clearly broke down in the 1980s" when elected African Americans pursued policies that went directly against the interests of Black working-class communities and instead catered to a capitalist vision that increased sales taxes on the public and reduced taxes on corporations.[47]

Also throughout the era, racial violence prevailed, lynchings increased, and proracist demonstrations took place at Smith College, Brown University, Arizona State University, the University of Michigan, and the University of Wisconsin to push back on affirmative action programs for minority faculty and students.[48] The movement for Black liberation needed to take even larger strides than anticipated, it seemed, and just as they had done in the previous decades, murals lined the walls of Black communities to become part of the movement—inspiring, transforming, healing, and educating in any way they could. These murals wallpapered the streets, rebuking the structural and systemic racism that shackled communities of color through homelessness, unemployment, drug addiction, and incarceration. They functioned, just as they did in the era of Black Power, to elevate Blackness in the nation's commemorative landscape and visualize the beauty, power, and excellence of Black life at a time when white standards of beauty still prevailed throughout society on billboards, in the media, and on television. And they lived, again uncompromisingly, in the streets and on buildings to reclaim a Blackness that was trying to be extinguished, whether through omissions and sidelining in cultural institutions, police brutality and violence such as the beating of Rodney King, or the destruction and disappearance of Black communities in New Orleans following Hurricane Katrina.

When Walker feared the sanitization of Black public art in the 1980s and 1990s, he may not have fully accounted for the power of noninflammatory imagery. While he called for a direct challenge to the neoconservative system, worried that artists would paint "too many sweet things," other artists of the period responded to the entrenched systemic racism of the country in their own ways, not always through direct and provocative imagery such as *Reaganomics* but also through images of community love, self-celebration, Black history, and Black pride.

In 1996 artist Brett Cook was approached by a group of high school students who were curating a show in New York City, and they asked him if he wanted to contribute something. After contemplating this offer and having it sweetened by the promise of being given a wall to work on, Cook agreed. Granted an exterior wall adjacent to the school, the Satellite Academy, Cook immediately knew what sort of murals he would paint. "I'm going to do pictures of you," he told the students, pictures that would become part of the community, given that images of people of color were so seldom elevated in society.[49] Integral to Cook's process and ethos as an artist was to create public art that was inclusive, educational, and transformational—but not confrontational. "Part of my interest in putting it out is . . . I was trying to put it in places where people would see it and with the idealism that this would transform the way they saw the world and make them see it different," he said.[50]

Taking a somewhat deviated approach to Walker's mural that contested the neoconservative government, Cook focused more on community love and strength. "Telling people that stuff's messed up, people already know that stuff's messed up, they don't need me to tell them—and that's not changing that it's messed up. That's just giving it more energy," he believed.[51] Instead, Cook wanted to create something new and innovative that embedded the people's voices into his work. "In the history of western art, the model seldom has a voice to speak, except usually through the filter of the artist," he feels, but "part of the radicality of my work" is that "I'm just gonna use this [art] as a vehicle for your voice. You already have one, but what does it mean to magnify it specifically to the place where you're going to be installed?"[52]

In a 2014 lecture given at the Arts Research Center at the University of California, Berkeley, Cook commented on the soullessness of certain public art installations and the importance of location. Citing the example of Piet Mondrian's cow sculptures near the Brooklyn library, he went on to say:

> Not a lot of French people in this neighborhood, so Mondrian doesn't really make sense—and there's no cows in Brooklyn! This artwork exists because the public art fund has the resources to put it wherever they want it. This is not something the community asked for necessarily. . . . [T]his is totally the reason why people think art doesn't matter, because in this

case it doesn't. It doesn't speak to the people in that community, it doesn't come from their interests or their needs, it doesn't reflect their image, it doesn't embody any kind of liberation or issues or ideas that they have in that place.[53]

So in 1996, when Cook began working on the wall next to Satellite Academy, he focused his attention on portraits of locals, painting their likenesses directly into the communities in which they lived, layering their voices over the top, and making sure his murals spoke to and served the local neighborhood. "If you could tell the world one thing, what would you say?" Cook asked the students.[54]

See What We Can See, measuring fifteen by fifty feet, stood at the corner of Eldridge and Stanton Streets in New York's Lower East Side. It depicted the beautiful, glowing portraits of six students of color, based upon individual photographs taken by Cook. The portraits were organized almost like a yearbook, with the smiling likenesses positioned next to each other with a quote above or below. Painted in hyperrealistic detail, each face is perfectly shadowed by the natural midday light. "I knew the wall got really direct sun, so I lit them with these heavy cast shadows, then made a composition so it looks like they're standing in the sun with their quotes," said Cook.[55] Reading along the wall are each model's statement in response to Cook's question, "If you could tell the world one thing, what would you say?" "To represent," reads the first testimony above a teenage boy whose cap and hood shade his eyes but leave the rest of his features bathed in sunlight. "Don't compare me to another," reads the next statement below a boy who stares out directly into the eyes of the viewer. "I learn / I go to school," reads the middle statement above a smiling portrait of a teenage girl who comfortably and calmly looks forward. The next portrait has no words, just the stoic, half-smiling likeness of a young boy wearing a hat who stares intensely toward Cook's camera lens. The final two portraits are young girls. The first is a joyful portrait of an African American teenager caught midlaugh. Her electric and vivacious depiction, alive with motion, seems almost contradictory to her testimony: "I'm quiet. I don't really say nuttin'." The final statement reads, "I just to myself [sic] what people think about me is whatever," and it sits above the smiling, confident portrait of a young girl with black hair wearing a bandana and a red zip-up hoodie.

Through Cook's work, local residents become magnified and embedded into their own communities, and this is where his work really derives its power: through decentering himself as the artist and elevating his local subjects in the hope that doing so empowers people in their own communities as they go about their lives. Cook created these murals in New York City at a time when neighborhoods were fractured by cocaine and heroin and when the shockwaves of Reagan's and Bush Sr.'s presidencies were still being felt. "My work is about neighborhood beautification and giving people a voice. . . . [M]y goal is to empower people and have them see that they are great for who they are," because "there aren't a lot of images of people of color alive, happy, talking about things they care about."[56] Propelled by the belief that "representation in public space would cause radical change," Cook created the change he wished to see in the world.[57] "I am trying to be an artist, an educator, an activist, a writer, a person who speaks out about things, an advocate of social change," he says of his role. And these impulses feed into all his public artworks when he creates something unique for local communities that doesn't directly challenge political institutions but that radically showcases Black, Asian, and Latinx vibrancy, beauty, and happiness in the streets.[58]

A few years later, in 1998 and 1999, Cook undertook two more projects in New York City, only this time up in Harlem. The first, titled *Specialness* (1998), was removed from any institutional affiliation, the artist has said, describing it as a "self-catalyzed" project.[59] To celebrate young people from the community, Cook met with children from businesses he'd gone to and older students from the now-closed Hale House, a charity that cared for homeless infants and toddlers. "I asked them six questions about being special—what was special about them, something special that they do, some things about who they were, etcetera," he said of his process. "From those six questions I had them pick out their four favorites and write them on four pieces of paper. On those four pieces of paper I helped them do a collage that represented whatever their statement was. From those four collages I picked one of the statements and put that text on an image of them and mounted that in the neighborhood where they lived."[60]

The project ran throughout neighborhoods across Harlem, and on one of the large billboardesque panels of wood, Cook painted a young girl. On the left-hand side of the panel, which was split into a diptych, the girl appears crouched on a bench with a colorfully painted park scene behind her. She wears a denim jacket and jeans and calmly looks out to the viewer.

In the right-hand frame, Cook zooms in further to her likeness to paint a close-up headshot in tighter detail. This time the viewer can make out the rabbit on her jacket and the slight curve of her smile as she sits in front of a multicolored, blooming sunflower. Layered on top of the portraits is her statement, "My personality makes me special," and underneath are her four collages on individual pieces of paper. "*Specialness* addressed a lot of the same issues that my other works in the past have done in terms of empowering these people in their community . . . giving people a voice," Cook told Jim Prigoff in 1999.[61] And much like *See What We Can See*, *Specialness* did something unique in the streets of America to respond to the oppressive social, racial, and political climate. Cook used people from the community as the centerpieces of his work to make sure he elevated those in the community who were so constantly overlooked and visually, emotionally, and mentally oppressed.

Cook's second uptown project, *Expressions of Harlem* (1999), was created after he completed an exhibition at the Studio Museum. "I realized that the institution, even though it was in the center of Harlem, was really alienated from the community. I wanted to do something that built a bridge," he commented on the inaccessibility of galleries for communities.[62] The museum felt distinctly separate from the residents of Harlem, so, much like Curtis Bryan, Babatunde Folayemi, Dindga McCannon, Ted Pontiflet, Vincent Wilson, and Joseph Delaney, who created *Studio in the Streets* (1971), discussed in chapter 4, Cook sought to turn the institution "inside out" for the local residents. Meeting people from a nursing home and schools and random residents from across the neighborhoods, Cook focused on seventeen people who had never been to the Studio Museum before. He mounted their images inside the museum with audio and visual media and uniquely complemented them by erecting seven giant likenesses with their own quotes throughout the streets of Harlem in public sites and without gaining permission.[63] These street murals were so powerful, he believed, because they reflected "multicultural blackness at a time when Gap advertisements that towered above 125th street only featured white models. . . . [I]t was radical portraying multi-ethnic, multi-aged people from Harlem talking about things they cared about."[64]

In the 1990s Cook was doing something new and invigorating in the community mural movement. Artists of the 1960s and 1970s were undeniably crafting something unique and unprecedented in the streets, something that used images of Black history, Black love, Black pride, and sometimes Black pain to create and embolden relationships between community and art. But what these murals rarely did (apart from later iterations of the *Wall of Respect*), and what Cook did in the 1990s, was use the likenesses of community residents for his murals to make sure "the people become monuments."[65] Unlike *Reaganomics* of the 1980s, Cook refrained from using inflammatory imagery to challenge the structural racism across the country and instead immortalized the likenesses of community members in the streets in which they lived, allowing them and their friends and family to walk by their images every day and see their faces embedded into the local landscape. By doing this, Cook didn't actively pass comment on the effects of neoconservatism in poor and Black communities across the nation; instead, he elevated the faces and voices of those purposefully left out of the mainstream by white power structures. He removed all agency and airtime from those in institutional positions of power and in their place bestowed power on those in the community. They became monuments in their neighborhoods. They became immortalized. They became what was important. Detaching himself from the work and elevating everyday people, Cook purposefully left his work unsigned—the only words on his murals are those spoken by the subjects, because, as he believes, public art must speak and directly reflect the community in which it lives.

Being of and for the community, as Cook believes public art should be, his street installations are just that: They become celebrations of the immediate community. His murals give local residents a foothold in their own physical space by layering their likenesses into their own landscape, celebrating themselves and giving agency through the power of their own image and voice. Cook ensures that the murals he creates speak specifically for the communities in which they live, and this organic mural-making practice is mirrored across the country. Standing as a cultural centerpiece in grassroots movements toward the liberation of Black America in the 1980s, 1990s, and 2000s, murals continue to reflect to communities—in whatever way they can—the social, political, and/or racial mood of the time, adapting with the climate. And in 1992 one mural in particular spoke directly to the streets of Los Angeles following the volatile rebellions in the wake of the Rodney King trial.

In the early hours of March 3, 1991, Rodney King was driving down the I-210 in Los Angeles while under the influence. His drive quickly turned into a high-speed chase throughout the city when he was followed by multiple police officers. King was finally stopped and ordered out of the car; he was then kicked, tasered, and struck at least fifty-six times with a baton for around fifteen minutes by the surrounding officers. He suffered multiple broken bones, a concussion, a pulverized eye socket, broken teeth, a concaved cheek bone that required reconstructive surgery, and permanent brain damage. In 1991 police brutality was not an uncommon occurrence—the ACLU was reporting at least fifty-five calls of police violence each week—but to have video evidence of such an incident in 1991 was unprecedented. Upon seeing the violence in the street opposite his house, resident George Holliday pulled out his video camera and started recording footage that showed King laid out, unthreatening and almost inert, on the ground and towered over by more than a dozen police officers, some of whom were repeatedly beating him with their weapons as he writhed around in pain. The footage quickly became ubiquitous across the nation, played on news outlets, with photographic stills lining the front covers of newspapers. "This is an aberration, something that should never have happened," Los Angeles Police Department Chief of Police Daryl Gates said. "We had in place all of the procedures that would keep it from happening. Those procedures fell down because of human error."[66]

But many residents of Los Angeles, especially those in communities of color harassed by the police on a regular basis, knew this not to be true. "Human error" did not lead to the beating of Rodney King. As the nation watched the grainy footage of an unarmed Black man being beaten on the ground by police officers, it was hard for witnesses to view the attack as anything other than racially motivated, and this was further supported by the subsequent police indictments (or lack thereof) and acquittals. Following the incident, four of the police officers—Stanley Koon, Ted Briseno, Timothy Wind, and Laurence Powell—were put on trial for assaults with a deadly weapon, excessive use of force, bodily injury, and false reports. Shortly after the trial began, it was coincidentally moved to the distant and lily-white suburb of Ventura County, where the racial makeup of the jury consisted of nine white, one Latinx, one Asian, and one biracial juror.[67] At 3:00 p.m. on April 29, 1992, the four officers were acquitted of assault charges, and three of the four were acquitted of using excessive force. A few hours later, unrest began to unfold throughout the city that raged for six days.

"For generations, California has been known for its San Andreas Fault, the geological fracture beneath the earth's crust," reflects Marable.

> The periodic eruptions along the fault line have been responsible for mas-sive destruction and hundreds of deaths. Yet, far more devastating than the San Andreas Fault is America's "race/class fault line," the jagged di-vision of color and income, education and privilege which slashes across the soul of this nation. In California, the race/class fault line rudely sepa-rates the posh affluence of Hollywood and Beverly Hills from the crime, fear, and hunger of south-central Los Angeles. That same race and class division runs down Detroit's Eight Mile Road, separating the poor, un-employed, and homeless from comfortable suburban white enclaves. It sets apart Harlem and Bedford-Stuyvesant from the multi-million-dollar estates in Connecticut's posh suburbs. The Los Angeles race uprisings can be understood only from the vantage point of the race/class fault line, because the violence unleashed by Rodney King's court case was just a tremor along that division.[68]

As Marable acknowledges here, the uprisings in Los Angeles were not a response to an isolated event of police brutality. The rebellions responded, in the same vein as the long, hot summer, discussed in chapter 3, to the entrenched institutional and supremacist structures that prop up a racial and class hierarchy in the United States, pushing poor and communities of color farther to the sidelines. When the Watts uprising rippled across Los Angeles in 1965, also ignited by police brutality but erupting due to lack of housing, jobs, health care, and education in the city for Black people, the McCone Commission sought to answer questions about the rebellion: Can it happen again? How will it happen again? What can we do to prevent it? "So serious and explosive is the situation . . . that unless it is checked, the August riots may be only a curtain raiser to what could blow up one day in the fu-ture," CBS News reported in 1965.[69] And blow up it did. Between April 29 and May 6, 1992, in the aftermath of the Rodney King verdict, more than 10,000 National Guardsmen and 2,000 federal troops were deployed, 58 people died, 2,383 were injured, 11,000 were arrested, and property damage exceeded $1 billion, usurping the 1967 Detroit race rebellion as the costliest in U.S. history.[70]

In 1992 muralist Noni Olabisi took to the streets at 54th Street and Western Avenue in south-central Los Angeles, in the heart of where the uprising took place, to paint a mural that captured the anguish, frustration, and "impatience of the black community over the persistence of police brutality and injustice."[71] The mural was sponsored by the city's Social and Public Art Resource Center (SPARC)—an organization headed up by muralist and social activist Judy Baca—but when Olabisi received confirmation that she had won funding to complete a mural (which coincidentally was her first), she was initially unsure what to paint for the south-central neighborhood. After watching footage of people responding to the acquittal of the four officers on trial for King's violent arrest, Olabisi saw the hurt and anger within the Black population.

"Do you know what that means, Noni," said one of her colleagues from the Good Fred Beauty and Barber Salon, upon which the mural was to be painted. "That means open season on Black people."[72] Drawing upon the history of her ancestors and from different social justice movements across the world, such as the movement against apartheid in South Africa, Olabisi felt inspired to paint a mural that reflected the "very chaotic" shots on the news of people rebelling throughout the city. "I thought, 'Oh my God, there it is,' and something burst inside me," she recounted after seeing the uprisings and ensuing violence on her block.[73] "There was . . . an incident that happened where there was a patron" outside the barbershop. "I didn't see the beginning, and I don't know why she had a knife, but she had a knife in her hand, and she was surrounded by nine police officers, and they drop-kicked her right in front of that wall, they . . . tied her . . . like a hog . . . and drop-kicked her right on that cement," Olabisi remembered. "When I saw that, I said I wanted the wall to scream." And that's exactly what she did.[74]

Titled *Freedom Won't Wait*, the mural stands in south-central Los Angeles as a point of convergence for visualizations of Black pain and suffering throughout history and across the diaspora. Olabisi presents, in intimate and honest detail, a series of close-up emotional faces painted in black and white and upon a red backdrop, screaming out in pain. In the top right-hand corner of the mural, we see a charred, burning cityscape—Watts from 1965 and present-day Los Angeles. The buildings are shrouded in plumes of smoke that engulf their presence in the city. The flames of anger and

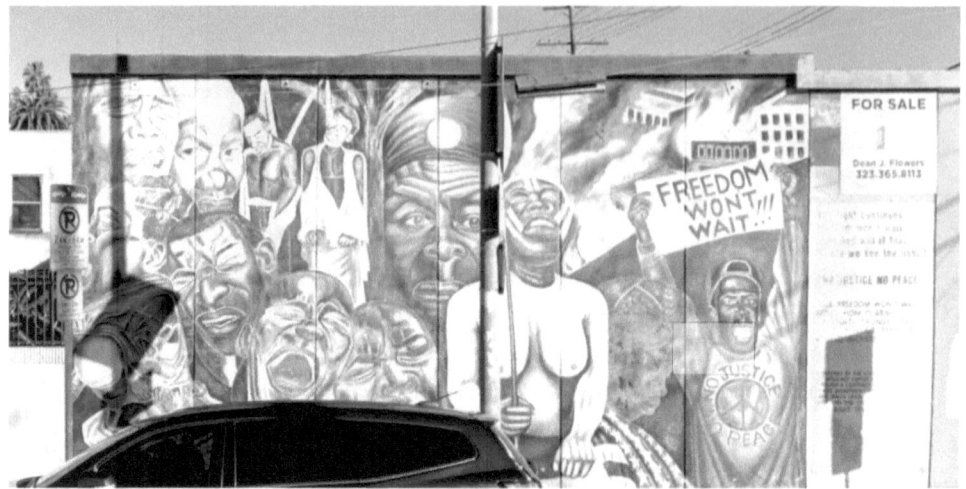

Freedom Won't Wait (1992), 1815 W. 54th Street, Los Angeles, Calif. Painted by Noni Olabisi. Image taken from Google Maps, 2024.

injustice consuming the corner of the mural bisect the frame to reach the central figure, who immediately grabs the attention of the viewer. A tribal woman from Africa stands in traditional dress and markings, holding her spear upright as she angles her head to the sky with an expression of pain and sadness etched into the contours of her face. Enveloping her are stories of Black suffering. To her left, in the bottom left-hand corner of the frame, stands the retold story of Rodney King's violent arrest and the violent arrests of countless others across the nation. His prostrate body strains against the full weight of a police officer who kneels on King's back while pressing his hand into the back of King's neck.

Surrounding this vignette are multiple floating heads, each crying out in more agony than the next as they trace the lineage of Black pain throughout history. Clasped around three necks are shackles, fracturing and breaking open from the pressure of such emotion, and tracks of tears mark the anguished faces as they wince and scream out for a justice that never arrives. Above these floating heads and the three more to their left hang two lynched men, their shirts ripped open to display their bare skin as they swing, now lifelessly, from a branch just out of shot. Embedded into the center of the frame between the African woman and the lynched figures lives the likeness of Harriet Tubman. As the central figure in the mural, she remains the only one to make eye contact with passersby. Her gaze penetratingly stares out onto the street, capturing attention and inspiring the audience's contemplation across the mural. Upon her headscarf is the undeniable focal point—a large yellow dot, something typical in all Olabisi's work. It's a "representation of the Sun within as well as without," she has said. "It is the giver of life. . . . [I]t's also my way of honoring, paying homage and my gratitude for life that connects us all as one."[75] By placing the yellow dot upon Tubman's forehead, Olabisi gives a nod to Tubman's strength and heroism, of course, but also to the strength and power of those across the mural who live their lives tirelessly striving for a liberation that buckles but never breaks under the weight of oppression. Just as the sun is the giver of life to all in the mural, it is also a giver of strength—a strength of spirit that drives people to demand justice and, just as the figures in the bottom right-hand side of the mural demonstrate, tell the world that "freedom won't wait."

"The mural becomes a community," Olabisi said, "where I'm listening to what they're saying and what they are going through. One of my friends said, 'it's not freedom *can't* wait,' because that's what I originally wanted to name it, but it's 'freedom *won't* wait.' I listen to what people say and then I incorporate it . . . then put the emotions that were going on in the community," she continued.[76] As a result, two young protesters stand in the corner of the frame, with one wielding a handwritten sign displaying the statement "FREEDOM WON'T WAIT!!!" His face, angry and mid yell, stands as a direct response to the ancestral pain and suffering we bear witness to next to him. To mirror his sign held aloft, upon his jumper read the words "No Justice, No Peace," a statement that rings out across the streets of the nation in the age of Black Lives Matter. The second protester stands just to the left of him. A young girl, much less animated, has her head bowed to look at the impotent star-spangled banner draped around her neck that fails to represent the freedom, liberty, and equality supposedly embodied under the nation's flag. And to complement the activism of these two young protesters, Olabisi painted a declaration of protest onto the side of the wall under a Pan-African flag:

The fight continues
freedom won't wait
how long will it take
before we see the light?

"NO JUSTICE NO PEACE"

The mural still lives, albeit slightly faded, at 1815 W. 54th Street in south-central Los Angeles, still belonging to and resonating with the community it serves. "The people's response to it" when it was painted in 1992 "was like a release or relief," Olabisi reflected ten years later. "What's on the mural is things they would like to say right, and don't say, and so it becomes one voice."[77]

Olabisi's mural—just as the murals of Cook, Walker, and countless others did in the 1980s and 1990s—became a pivotal artistic expression in the movement for Black liberation that lives in the heart of the community, at the epicenter of injustice, strife, and struggle. Her mural, like many murals that preceded it, forms a necessary part of the movement of liberation and freedom across the country, commanding acknowledgment and asserting a Black presence. Her mural screams. It shouts. It cries. And it demands. It's a collective voice, a unified one that reverberates not only across the city of Los Angeles but also across the country and the diaspora. The pain evoked throughout the mural is a mutual suffering that stands in the battleground of America's streets where Black bodies are brutalized and mental, emotional, and spiritual torture prevails. Olabisi's mural—much like those in the 1980s, 1990s, and 2000s—doesn't necessarily do anything new or unprecedented in the tradition of Black muralism. But it doesn't need to. It stands, just as the Wall of Dignity, the Wall of Truth, Rip-Off / Universal Alley, or The Fire Next Time I did, showing the nation the indomitable fight for Black liberation ignited decades ago that refuses to be extinguished still today. It shows the immovable presence of Blackness on the nation's landscape, and it shows, as murals always have done in the movement for Black liberation, "the unshakable knowledge of who we are, where we have been, and springing from this, where we are going."[78] Freedom Won't Wait commands a Black presence and claims a Black space, and this communal process is one that continues deep into the 2000s and one that we see perhaps most pronounced in New Orleans's Ninth Ward.

FROM THE STRUGGLE COMES BEAUTY

"One of the myths about New Orleans is that everyone who did leave had the opportunity to come back," muralist Brandan Odums says of the physical and emotional aftermath of Hurricane Katrina. "Something that I notice about blight is a connection to that idea. Every time you look at blight you might look at it as a problem for yourself . . . but it's connected to a

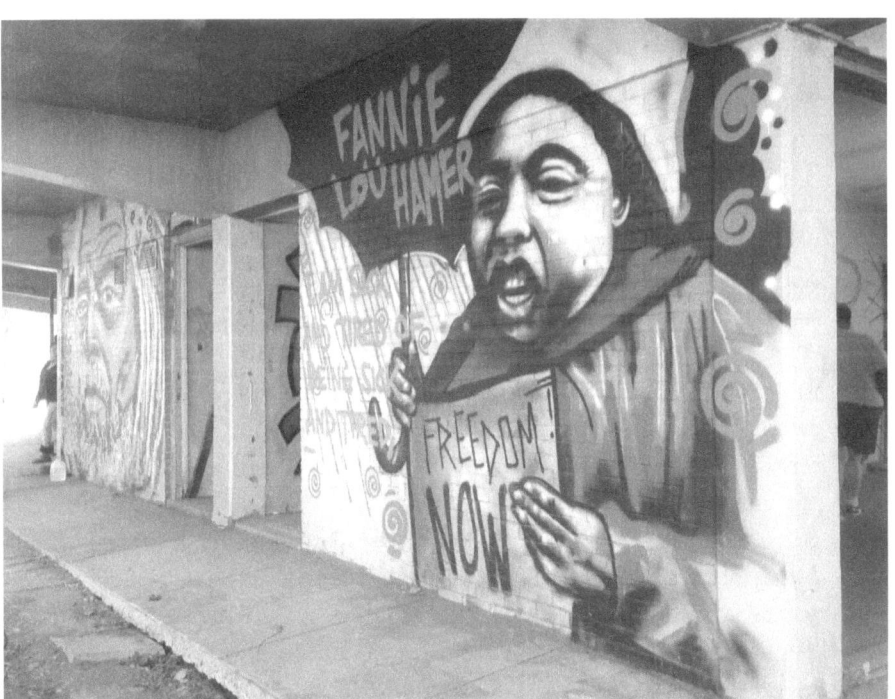

Panel of *ExhibitBE* (2014), DeGaulle Manor, Algiers, New Orleans, La. Painted by Brandan Odums. Image from Flikr, photograph taken by mags, CC BY-ND 2.0. No changes made to image.

story, it's connected to a community, it's connected to an individual."[79] Inspired by the beauty and courage that come from a collective and communal pain, Odums was drawn to areas of dereliction in his hometown to create powerful sites of public art in Black spaces destroyed by the hurricane. In 2005, when Hurricane Katrina stormed through the city, it left nothing but rubble in its wake. Black neighborhoods were hit the worst, suffering extreme losses when entire areas were razed to the ground. The Center for Social Inclusion reports that 44 percent of those harmed by broken levees were African American, nearly 70 percent of the poor people affected by the storm were African American, and in the city of New Orleans, communities of color made up around 80 percent of the population in flooded neighborhoods.[80]

"The awful spectre of black bodies floating in New Orleans, of hundreds of thousands being dispersed throughout the country and being denied constructive federal aid," says Marable, "underscored just how enduring the great racial and class divides are within the fabric and logic of American institutions of power."[81] Abandoned neighborhoods still wait to be rebuilt—a community that was once alive and full is now haunted by skeletal housing frames, boarded-up windows, and caved-in roofs. But "from the struggle comes beauty," believes Odums.[82] From the rubble and wreckage comes an opportunity to rebuild from the grassroots, to create something artistic, something meaningful, and something that reclaims these sites of trauma.

In 2014, when wandering around his community of Algiers in the Ninth Ward, Odums saw constant reminders of neglect. Windows were smashed, people's abandoned possessions were molding over, and lots that had been vacant for ten years had fallen into disrepair—including a 360-unit apartment complex ceremoniously named DeGaulle Manor. Residents of the "manor" were forcefully evicted following the hurricane, rendering the apartments lifeless and empty for almost eight years. But blight is connected to powerful stories, Odums insists, because "it's connected to a community," which in this instance was a displaced one. "Every time I see this space, it reminds me of these stories of individuals . . . who lived there, of family members," people who created lives in the building but that were forced out without notice. To resurrect the building and its once busy existence, Odums began to "paint where it ain't" by filling the walls with color, memories, and history. "I found myself in this space a lot," he said, "painting in a legal gray area but mostly with the understanding that artists are communicators. . . . I was trying to communicate something to the people that had to walk by that space every day . . . to create images that would boost their system's morale, inspire them. Hopefully they will see themselves reflected in the things that I was creating."[83]

After a few months of dipping in and out of the building to add sketches and paint to his designs, he was approached by the complex's new owner, who, to Odums's delight, gave him access and approval to paint the entire building. "A lightbulb went off," said Odums. "What if we temporarily transform the space and invite the public to come and experience it?"[84] Calling upon around thirty local artists and setting the deadline of November 1 for the one-off event (just fifteen days away), Odums got to work. Inspired by Paul Robeson's statement that "artists are the gatekeepers of truth" and Cornell West's philosophy that "the condition of truth is to allow suffering to speak," Odums and the other artists wanted to ensure that they told the story of DeGaulle Manor in a truthful way. "Speaking to the residents, speaking to formal community leaders in this space and asking questions . . . we use[d] that information" to inform the visual language used to transform the building.[85] The results saw the likenesses of H. Rap Brown, Harriet Tubman, Muhammad Ali, Fred Hampton, Amiri Baraka, Frederick Douglass, Marcus Garvey, Gordon Parks, Angela Davis, James Baldwin, Assata Shakur, Martin Luther King Jr., and Malcolm X line the walls, complemented by the contemporary figures of Radio Raheem from Spike Lee's 1989 classic film, *Do the Right Thing*, hip-hop legends Tupac Shakur, the Notorious B.I.G., and Mos Def, and tributes to victims of police brutality that read "SAY HER NAME" and "AM I NEXT?"

"We want people to come out and experience [this space] and see what happens, see if art does have the power to heal space," Odums suggested. So by November 1, 2014, after the artists worked around the clock to transform, heal, and reclaim DeGaulle Manor, the building was complete, and an audience was ready. ExhibitBE opened its doors to twenty-five hundred people. The popularity of the show was unexpected, but given the positive feedback and an agreement with the building owner to stay open for another three months, Odums managed to secure weekly openings of the show until January, closing finally on Martin Luther King Jr. Day in 2015 to ten thousand people, with performances from Erykah Badu and Dead Prez. Every weekend from November to January, around three thousand people descended upon DeGaulle Manor to give meaning and purpose back to a building in a community long ignored by the government. "It was a living space every weekend," said Odums. "People who used to live there would come in with stories and say, 'You know, my grandmother lived here. Can you add something about that?' and we said, 'Yeah.' 'So this happened here. Can you add something about that?' and we said, 'Yes.' . . . Every weekend we would try to find different ways to activate the community. We would have poetry readings, . . . DJ battles. We had a car show where we transformed the parking lot and brought the parking lot back to life."[86]

Thanks to ExhibitBE, DeGaulle Manor became a living, breathing space again. But perhaps one of the most moving and important relationships fostered between the murals and the community was the week-day school tours. Throughout the course of each week, over three thousand students toured the exhibition led by one of the artists. They heard stories of the space that many knew so well. "They would walk in certain rooms and say, 'I remember my cousin stayed here' or such and such. The teachers remembered former students that lived there," recalled Odums. Toward

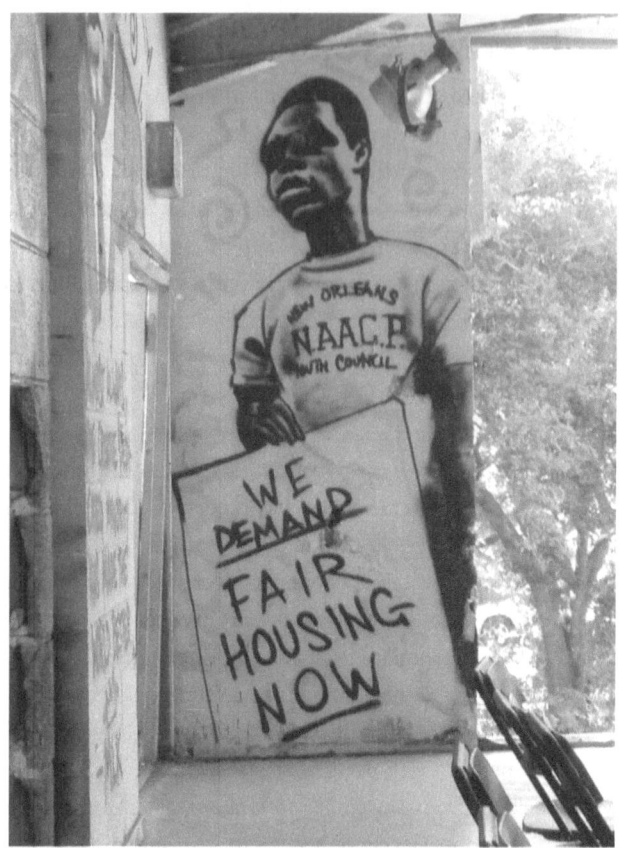

Panel of *ExhibitBE* (2014), DeGaulle Manor, Algiers, New Orleans, La. Painted by Brandan Odums. Image from Flikr, taken by mags, CC BY-ND 2.0. No changes made to image.

the end of each school tour, Odums would then hand the students art supplies and tell them, "You're going to leave your work here. . . . Leave your truth into this space, and now you're one of the artists here."[87] Listening to Odums, the students created. They drew chalk pictures on the floor, wrote their names into the space, and transformed old tires left in the lot. They became artists in collaboration, now embedded into the story of *ExhibitBE*.

At the center of Black life in New Orleans, *ExhibitBE* stood as a monument to Blackness in 2015, transforming a symbol of structural racism into an arena of community love, celebration, and Black empowerment. Around thirty artists used murals to bring a building back to life, and for three months, DeGaulle Manor became a place that no longer represented trauma and abandonment but that was instead reclaimed as a site of healing. "We were able to transform that space. . . . We would change the lives of people around that space," acknowledged Odums. "Obviously, we could have spent all that time trying to demand this space be demolished or demanding the space be built, fixed up, or a timeline to be produced . . . but instead . . . we made a decision to come in and create in [this]," because as Odums so rightly acknowledged, from the struggle comes beauty.[88]

When Bill Walker told Margaret Burroughs in 1984 that he was trying through his art "to make a statement about the times in which [he] live[d]," he was not painting alone. The 1980s, 1990s, and 2000s were marked by emotional, honest, and relevant public art that spoke to the conditions of Black America. The post–civil rights era was intricate and complicated with undulating political, racial, and social landscapes that simply cannot be captured in their entirety or even delved into beneath the surface in one chapter. But what we can uncover and what we do know is that the movement for Black liberation continues in the heart of Black America, deep in the community, in the streets of Black neighborhoods. This post–civil rights era was marked by four full presidential administrations; multiple wars, both international and home-grown; natural disasters; and the continuation of racial violence, segregation, white supremacy, and inequality. And in response to such turbulence, murals once again lined the walls of Black communities, just as they did in the previous decades, to remind America of an unshakeable, unyielding, proud, and resilient Black life and history woven into the fabric of the nation.

The murals of the 1980s, 1990s, and 2000s were bold. They artistically stood in the fight for Black liberation, continuing a legacy started long ago during the Harlem Renaissance. This chapter hasn't tried to categorize a new moment in Black muralism—partly because many murals in this post–civil rights era continue in the same vein as their artistic forebears. But it also hasn't tried to categorize this period, as it seems almost arbitrary to. The Black community mural tradition that arcs across the twentieth and twenty-first centuries, as this book shows, doesn't stretch across time as a series of disparate movements on a historical timeline; instead, it is a continuously evolving lineage of community art, and one that is still unfolding today. When Noni Olabisi painted the words "NO JUSTICE NO PEACE" onto *Freedom Won't Wait* in 1992, little did we anticipate that these words of history would echo throughout the streets today, just as the violent and racially motivated beating of Rodney King still does. Although they were painted more than three decades ago, Olabisi's words live on not only aurally in the streets today but visually too. In the age of Black Lives Matter, murals have evolved and adapted once more to become a prolific visual accompaniment to the unfolding movement—one that is still fighting for Black liberation, still trying to dismantle the skeleton of white supremacy holding up America, and still having to show the world that Black lives matter.

CHAPTER 6

A Space to Have a Voice

Murals and Black Lives Matter

"Black is beautiful" rang out in the sixties, "I am somebody" echoed in the seventies, and "Black lives matter" resonates in our day.
—*Michael Eric Dyson, author*

And you know now, if you did not before, that the police departments of your country have been endowed with the authority to destroy your body.
—*Ta-Nehisi Coates, author, journalist*

It is to the moving image, rather than still photography, that our communities now turned to capture the increasing precarity of Black life—that is, the precarious circumstances of black people and the increasing prevalence of premature Black Death. And it is through digital rather than analogue technologies that we now document, archive, and disseminate the mounting threats to black communities. But we are also using these technologies to catalogue our everyday lives, the beauty of our bodies, our naive and bold aspirations, and our hopes and dreams for changing our current reality. —*Tina M. Campt, author*

In the early hours of New Year's Day in 2009, Oscar Grant III and his friends boarded a train home to Oakland after seeing in the new year in San Francisco—but Grant never made it home that night. At 2:00 a.m., in response to an alleged fight aboard the Dublin–Pleasanton train, Bay Area Rapid Transit (BART) police officers intercepted Grant's train at Fruitvale Station. Officers Tony Pirone and Marysol Domenici were the first to arrive before being joined by five police officers, one of whom was Johannes Mehserle. From the moment BART officers gathered at the scene, "there was confusion, chaos and pandemonium on the platform for some thirteen minutes; most of this was captured by several video camera devices."[1] Pirone ordered Grant off the train, and, in what has been revealed in a newly disclosed report written by a law firm hired by BART, he forced Grant to the ground, used racial slurs while detaining him, and hit him in the face in an unprovoked attack. Pirone's actions started "a cascade of events that ultimately led to the shooting" of Grant. While Pirone pinned Grant down with his knee—an act that hauntingly rang out in the murder of George Floyd by officer Derek Chauvin in Minneapolis—Johannes Mehserle attempted to handcuff Grant but couldn't because of the downward pressure from Pirone trapping Grant's hands. Mehserle then stood up, unholstered his gun after telling Pirone to sit back, and fired a shot into Grant, who was face down on the concrete. In subsequent reports, Mehserle claimed to have accidentally discharged his firearm instead of his taser—an explanation that painfully resonates in the killing of Daunte Wright by Kimberly Potter in Minnesota in 2021. Oscar Grant III was pronounced dead approximately nine hours later at Alameda County Medical Center. He was twenty-two years old and a father to four-year-old Tatiana. Following court proceedings, Johannes Mehserle was found guilty of involuntary manslaughter and sentenced to two years in jail. He was released after eleven months. Tony Pirone faced no jail time.[2]

At the time of Grant's death, the phrase "Black Lives Matter" was still four years away, yet to gain traction after the 2013 acquittal of George Zimmerman following the killing of Trayvon Martin. But in 2009 the residents of Oakland took to the streets to demand justice for Grant's death and to show that his Black life mattered. What we also saw shortly after his death was a new moment emerging in Black public art, one that would go on to provide a visual accompaniment to the imminent Black Lives Matter movement. The ritual of sacred Black transformation, as Michael Eric Dyson suggests, that turns "bodies from flesh and blood into . . . metaphysical martyrs for justice" was just beginning, and one of the ways it happened was through murals.[3] Large colorful likenesses of Grant's face were painted into the streets of Oakland and San Francisco, resurrecting his memory and offering a new commemorative layer that spiritually embedded Grant into the landscape he called home. His memory became part of Oakland's environmental fabric: He accompanied people on their walk home, he was part of their shopping trips, and he lined part of their journey to Fruitvale Station, where his Black life was subjected to a modern-day lynching after being deemed too much of a threat.

In *Long Time Coming: Reckoning with Race in America* (2020), Dyson captures a communal Black experience pulsing across time and space in the age of Black Lives Matter, one that murals engage in today: "Our bodies carry memory—not just our own, but the memory of the group as well. We feel the history in our bones as much as we witness it with our eyes. The convulsions of racial distress on-screen twist in the pits of our stomachs. . . . Their death is our death. Their suffering is our own. Their scream for help is our scream for help. Their cries for relief are literally spoken with our tongue, as we mouth their last words."[4]

As bodies carry memory—a memory that continually floods the psyche and weighs on the shoulders throughout moments in history—public art seeks to carry the body, lifting it from the ubiquitous acts of dehumanizing death and pain and collectively elevating it in the streets for all to remember in the age of Black Lives Matter. Always smiling, Grant's likenesses look out onto the streets he knows so well, editing and renegotiating the extant memories in each neighborhood and inserting his own narrative into their stories. In doing so, his memory becomes one with the community, which was echoed in the 2010 *Trust Your Struggle* mural, which depicted Grant and his daughter, Tatiana, in a loving embrace surrounded by the names of individuals victim to the same fate: Amadou Diallo, Sean Bell, Anthony Baez, Casper Banjo, Sheila Detoy. Enveloping Grant and his daughter is the uniting slogan "WE ARE ALL OSCAR GRANT," echoing Dyson's words, "Their death is our death. Their suffering is our own." Through the mural, his memory becomes both of and for the community, entwined with and embedded into its collective consciousness.

Following Oscar Grant's death, murals have continuously sprung up throughout the last fifteen years, honoring the memories of those victims whose deaths became high-profile cases in the media.[5] When Trayvon Martin was killed by George Zimmerman in Sandford, Florida, in 2012, murals emerged quickly in his hometown and across the country. A similar mural pattern followed with the deaths of individuals such as Sandra Bland, Michael Brown, Tamir Rice, Alton Sterling, Philando Castile, Aiyana Stanley-Jones, Eric Garner, and Freddie Gray. But in 2020, with the locked-down eyes of the world watching and listening to the killings of Ahmaud Arbery, Breonna Taylor, and George Floyd, and reliving Elijah McClain's death in 2019, the presence of these commemorative murals increased exponentially, something that former president Barack Obama even acknowledged in a statement on social media following the indictment of Derek Chauvin: "For

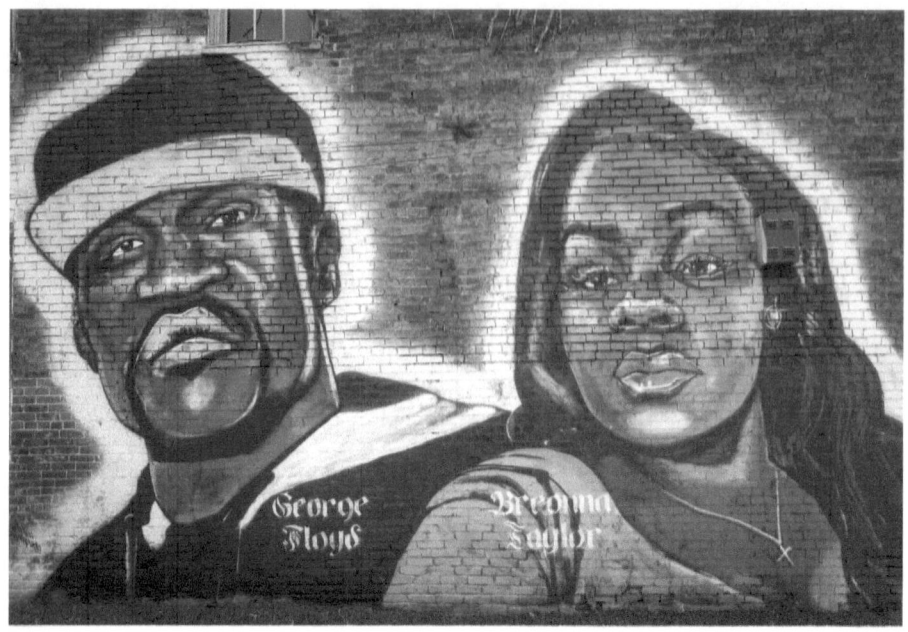

Breonna Taylor and George Floyd (2020), 543 S. Shelby Street, Louisville, Ky. Painted by Damon Thompson. Image from Flikr, taken by Don Sniegowski, CC BY-NC-SA 2.0. No changes made to image.

almost a year, George Floyd's death under the knee of a police officer has reverberated around the world—inspiring murals and marches."[6]

The traumatic assaults on Black life in 2020 shook the world. Housebound due to a global pandemic and perpetually consumed by the news reported on phones and computers, people struggled to comprehend these violent acts happening across the United States. We watched and read about twenty-five-year-old Ahmaud Arbery in Glynn County, Georgia, running for his life as he was hunted in the streets by a white father and son. We relived the harrowing final words of Elijah McClain as he tried to reason with the police officers slowly extinguishing his life: "I am an introvert, please respect the boundaries that I am speaking," we heard him cry. "I'm just different. That's all. I'm so sorry."[7] We read about the police officers who conducted a botched drug raid in Louisville, Kentucky, and killed the occupant, Breonna Taylor, breaking into her house as she lay sleeping in her bed next to her boyfriend. And for nine minutes and twenty-nine seconds the world watched the life slip from George Floyd's body as Derek Chauvin pressed his knee into Floyd's neck, the words "I can't breathe" struggling from the lips of another person of color being brutalized in the streets.

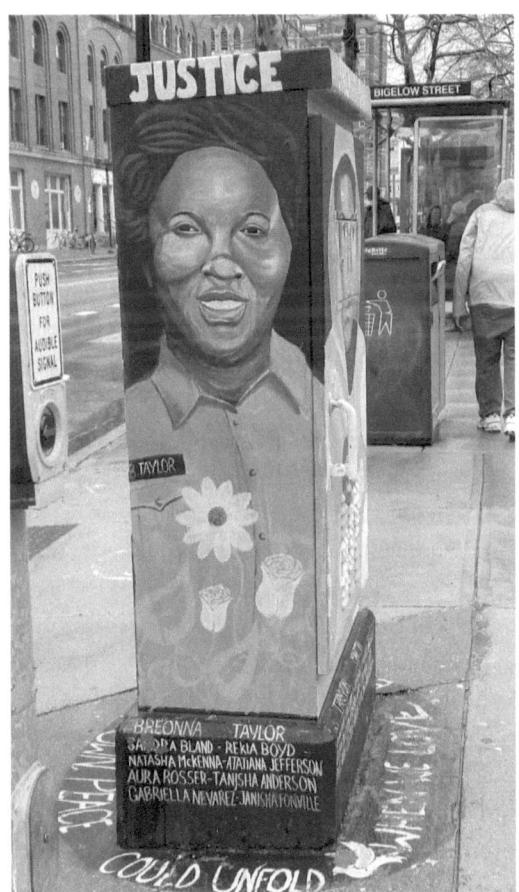

Untitled, date unknown. Inman Street and Massachusetts Avenue, Cambridge, Mass. Painted by unknown. Photograph taken by the author.

The year 2020 was a momentous milestone in the Black Lives Matter movement. The momentum garnered by protesters resulted in the largest movement in the country's history, with an estimated fifteen to twenty-six million people participating in demonstrations over Floyd's murder in the weeks following his death on May 25, 2020.[8] With over 4,700 demonstrations taking place, averaging 140 per day, people were increasingly waking up to the conclusions reached in 1967 by the Kerner Commission, that "our nation is moving toward two societies, one black, one white—separate and unequal."[9] In a June 2020 article published in *The New Yorker*, Jelani Cobb dissected the ideological, political, and spatial intricacies that he powerfully dubbed the "American Spring of Reckoning." "Consider a different idea," he asks the reader, "that the death of George Floyd did occur in another country: the traumatized version of America inhabited by black people."[10] Here Cobb acknowledges the horrific underbelly of America: a liminal space disregarded and overlooked by those in power, one of two societies, separated and unequal, where the weight of grief and poverty "still falls disproportionately on black shoulders."[11] When he discusses the deaths of police brutality victims, Cobb talks of a sentiment common among Black Americans, "that these people lived and died in black America, which is a different place from America at large—and that their deaths, most of which came at the hands of law enforcement, represent a broader reality, even though a significant number of white Americans were skeptical of its existence."[12]

But the intense climate of demonstrations happening throughout the country following Floyd's murder began to effect change, Cobb argues. Eyes were opening, minds were changing, and the fourteen successive days of protest opened people up to the possibility that George Floyd "died in America, not simply in its black corollary." So as protesters took to the streets in 2020 to draw attention to the fact that America's two societies—separate and unequal—existed in one country, artists picked up their brushes and joined them en masse. The words BLACK LIVES MATTER were painted onto the roads of every major city across the country, and the faces of Arbery, Taylor, Floyd, and McClain took over the streets from coast to coast and border to border, appearing alongside their already memorialized brothers and sisters such as Oscar Grant, Trayvon Martin, Tony Robinson, Philando Castile, Freddie Gray, and Sandra Bland.

In the Black mural tradition arcing across the twentieth and twenty-first centuries, we find ourselves today in a new moment that began in 2009 with the killing of Oscar Grant. His death inaugurated a potent visual accompaniment to what would become the Black Lives Matter movement four years later. But murals, while not uncommonly commemorative in the past, have a new role in today's social, political, and cultural context, as we will see in this chapter. The presence of these murals alone fits into a broader cultural movement happening currently in the battleground of America's streets, one that seeks to reclaim the streets from the commemorative stronghold of white supremacy entrenched through the presence of Confederate statues, flags, and street names. As part of a broader movement to alter the narratives and physical spaces of U.S. cities, Black Lives Matter murals play a fundamental role. They spring up immediately, oftentimes at the site of death, resurrecting and remembering those killed by the systems supposedly designed to protect them. The presence of these murals scattered throughout the United States renegotiates the meaning and memory of a street, marking sites and cities of death and transforming them into spaces for communal activism in the fight for Black lives.

Yet perhaps the most important role played by Black Lives Matter murals today is their rehumanizing purpose. Social media and the mainstream news as institutional forces are so powerful that they can render people powerless. A doctored photograph can be circulated online, a racist misrepresentation can be used repeatedly to add "validity" to a lie, and a video of a killing can be shared time and again until viewers become desensitized to the spectacle of death. From this sea of dehumanizing imagery, then, comes a powerful visual countermovement in the streets that begins to rehumanize the victims of police brutality. These murals are not just paintings, they are a way of asserting control over a narrative and a way of recuperating a life and positively commemorating a victim whose memory and visual afterlife get distilled into a soundbite, a manipulated photograph, or their final breaths of life.

These murals therefore are a fundamental but often overlooked element of the contemporary movement for Black lives. As a direct insertion into the contested streets of America, they become a tangible anchor and physical embodiment of the ideological, amorphous, and continuously growing protest movement. They visually resurrect the spiritual bodies of those who died at the hands of the police, rehumanizing their warped memories and offering rallying points and spaces for communal grassroots activism in cities across the country. And by consuming the streets of major U.S. cities, Black Lives Matter murals, whether intentionally or not, partake in the broader movement to overthrow and remove the entrenchment of white supremacy in America's commemorative and physical landscape.

BATTLEGROUNDS OF MEMORY

On June 2, 2020, in Richmond, Virginia, the infamous statue of Robert E. Lee on horseback was transformed. His memorial, cast in bronze and standing at around sixty feet tall, was stripped of its supremacist meaning and converted into a vessel that displayed powerful images of Black freedom fighters, abolitionists, heroes, and those who died from police brutality. As the glorified silhouette cut against the night sky, heavily charged with the memory and meaning of white supremacy, Lee's bronzed figure was renegotiated when the projections of Dr. Martin Luther King Jr., Black Union army soldiers, W. E. B. Du Bois, Harriet Tubman, and George Floyd lit up Monument Avenue. In an act of subversion of the Confederate general's memory, Lee's memorialized body instead became a display of centuries of "pain and resilience of Black lives through the figures who fought and died for justice."[13]

The Confederate statue debate, which commonly plays out on a local level, has a long and intricate history in the United States. But in 2015, following a massacre at the Mother Emanuel AME Church in Charleston, South Carolina, by white supremacist Dylann Roof, the debate was forcefully thrust into the national public consciousness.[14] Why do statues of Confederates line the streets? Why are streets named after such generals? And why are people forced to attend schools named after enslavers and white supremacists? As Karen Cox writes in her timely book, *No Common Ground: Confederate Monuments and the Ongoing Fight for Racial Justice*, such monuments to enslavers and Confederate soldiers were used by white Southerners to teach about "a mythological noble heritage completely stripped of the story of slavery," but what they actually "teach" is not history.[15] Such monuments stood and still stand as fixed weapons of racism on the nation's landscape, raised in the era of Jim Crow to intimidate and forcefully declare the "second-class status" of Black Southerners.[16] They stand as iconographical, visual, and commemorative declarations of white supremacy, cementing right-wing ideologies into the foundations of America.

"Public monuments are the most conservative of commemorative forms precisely because they are meant to last, unchanged, forever," Kirk Savage claims, adding that "while other things come and go, are lost and forgotten, the monument is supposed to remain a fixed point, stabilizing both the physical and cognitive landscape."[17] But in today's context, we know this not to be true. To distill the potency of these Confederate monuments and symbols of supremacy, activists and protesters have endeavored not only to debunk the racist connotations attached to such memorials but also to challenge the "fixed" and impervious status of the monuments themselves. Graffiti is an intervention into a physical space, and in the week following George Floyd's murder, protesters descended upon conservative monuments across the South to "change" and, perhaps more accurately, edit their meanings in the landscape.[18] In Richmond, graffiti was sprayed onto the United Daughters of the Confederacy headquarters. The statues of J. E. B. Stuart, Stonewall Jackson, and Robert E. Lee were all marked with paint. In

Charleston, South Carolina, the slogan "BLM" was sprayed onto the base of the Confederate Defenders of Charleston statue, and in the North Carolina state capitol in Raleigh, a Confederate monument was marked with a black "X." Since 2015, following the Charleston shooting, the Southern Poverty Law Center has estimated that at least 138 Confederate symbols have been removed from public spaces.[19] Although the quest to remove these state-sponsored symbols is not the first thing one thinks of when discussing Black Lives Matter, their removal forms part of a broader spatial reclamation and commemoration in the streets today, one that Black Lives Matter murals are a meaningful part of.

In the early hours of June 5, 2020, a significant mural project came together in Washington, D.C., in just under twenty-four hours. The golden words "BLACK LIVES MATTER" were painted onto 16th Street leading up to the White House at forty feet tall and the length of three and a half football fields.[20] The idea for the mural was conceived when D.C. mayor Muriel Bowser wanted to ensure that activists marching in the name of Black Lives Matter had a safe space in which to protest. Convening with eight local artists from the organization Murals DC, the Department of Public Works and the muralists worked throughout the night to install what would become a catalyzing mural on the street in front of Lafayette Square. The mural functioned as a demarcated space for protesters—one that felt officially sanctioned by the U.S. government—and stood, as The New Yorker acknowledged, as a refuge "beyond the reach of the military police squads that patrolled the surrounding blocks with dun-colored Humvees."[21] The mural itself, however, and the subsequent renaming of the area as Black Lives Matter Plaza, drew a variety of opinions, with late congressman and civil rights icon John Lewis declaring it "a powerful work of art," and criminal justice reform activist Mckayla Wilkes arguing, "It's not enough to have a pretty painting in the middle of the street, we need politics."[22]

Following D.C.'s lead, the words "BLACK LIVES MATTER" were painted onto roads in over seventy cities across the United States, each uniquely written, varying in style and decorative pattern, but also drawing both praise and criticism. "Are murals enough?" was a prevailing question. "Activists . . . are pushing for mayors and governors to move past symbolism and institute immediate policy changes," Politico reported of the murals. "What we're asking for is not . . . a symbolic recognition of how Black lives matter," Delilah Pierre, an organizer with the Tallahassee Community Action Committee,

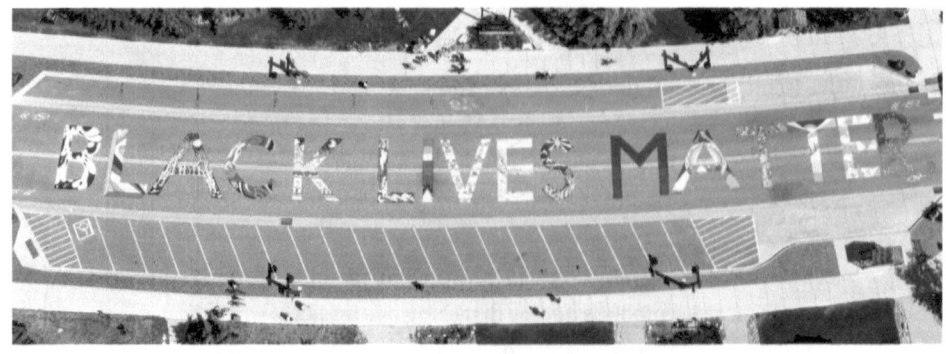

Black Lives Matter (2020). Plymouth Avenue, Minneapolis, Minn. Painted by Sean Phillips, Timi Bliss, Beverly Tipton Hammond, Kelly Brown, Peyton Scott Russell, Brittany Moore, Donna Ray, A. Drew Hammond, Christopher Aaron Deanes, Melodee Strong, Christopher E. Harrison, Reggie LeFlore, DeSean Hollie, Broderick Poole, Lissa Karpeh, and Kenneth Caldwell. Image from Flikr, taken by August Schwerdfeger, CC BY 2.0. No changes made to image.

stated. "We're asking for that to be something that's in practice. We're asking for real systemic change to the system that oppresses and marginalizes Black people."[23] To many activists across the country, the murals were inert gestures that detracted from the necessary pressure placed on municipal governments to tackle the brutalization of Black bodies by the police. "They don't stop the next murder of a Mr. Floyd, they don't improve K–12 in these neighborhoods . . . they don't do anything that would root out the systemic racism that's holding Black Americans behind," suggested Professor Dorothy A. Brown.[24]

But what these murals did, many argued, was bring awareness. "Art still has a special place in social movements, and the murals are not intended to be a substitute for policy changes," it was argued.[25] Instead, one of the most potent reactions from these large-scale ground murals is a reckoning with the power of protest itself. These murals remind us that "by marching these recent weeks, we are using our physical presence in public to communicate," making us more aware of the occupation of space during activism.[26] The roads on Plum Street between 7th and 8th Streets in Cincinnati, Ohio, for example, were inhabited by activism when each letter contained an individual narrative—a Black Power fist, a serene garden scene, and the statement "silence will not protect you." Similarly, outside the city council building in Salt Lake City, Utah, the letters on the mural contained the faces of individuals such as Breonna Taylor and Martin Luther King Jr. And when asked about the golden BLACK LIVES MATTER mural in the Greenwood

District of Tulsa, Oklahoma, local business owner Tori Tyson told *The New Yorker* that the mural was more than just a painting in the streets. "It brought young people, old people, Black kids, white kids, different people together, and they had a conversation," she said of the mural's affective and interactive role in the community. The mural curated a space of dialogue in the Black Wall Street district of the city, which a hundred years earlier, almost to the day, witnessed one of the most horrific race massacres in U.S. history. "To leave the mural there says that we recognize, as a city, that Black lives have not always mattered to the Tulsa government," Nehemiah Frank, editor in chief of the *Black Wall Street Times*, argued. "But today we're gonna change that narrative."[27]

Since 2009 Black Lives Matter murals have been changing dominant narratives in the streets across the United States. "It was beautiful," Michael Eric Dyson recalled of the summer of 2020, "because at the very moment that the Confederate flags and Confederate statues are being pulled down and even Columbus being pulled down, not only here, but across the world, then you got to replace it with something."[28] As Dyson acknowledged, there is an iconographical and ideological dialogue taking place in the streets today between the often forced removal of Confederate statues and the swift insertion of murals declaring the importance of Black lives. Symbols are necessary and iconography is critical in contextualizing and understanding historical memory in the streets, and Black Lives Matter murals are part of a movement today seeking to reframe the commemorative landscape that reflects the United States in a more truthful way. They function as an artistic embodiment of protest. When protesting, our physical presence communicates our message by being inserted directly into the environment. By creating murals, messages are similarly incorporated into a space, only this time painted directly into the landscape to imprint a meaning more indelibly and, we hope, with greater longevity once marches and protests subside or are curtailed by curfews.

"When it comes to activism, it [public art] allow[s] a space to have a voice, when for so long that voice has been suppressed and oppressed," U.S. muralist and teacher Melodee Strong said of the communal power of public art in 2020.[29] Black Lives Matter murals are ephemeral and vulnerable to defacement, yet their embedded presence in Black communities and their direct relationship to the unfolding protests in the streets turns them—whether intentionally or not—into sites of communal activism.[30]

Painted almost immediately after the latest acts of violence and brutality at the hands of the police or vigilantes, these murals are rallying points in the community. By embedding the faces of individuals such as Trayvon Martin, Michael Brown, Freddie Gray, Breonna Taylor, and Oscar Grant into the streets, muralists curate an emotionally charged space for congregation, protest, and commemoration.

In 2015, for example, an article published in *Popular Resistance* included a powerful photograph of a young woman standing in front of a Michael Brown mural at 1902 North Union Boulevard in St. Louis. The mural reimagines Brown. His likeness stares out into the streets, layered atop a colorful cloud and shining stars, and he is surrounded by the words "RIP," "STOP THE VIOLENCE," "MIKE BROWN" and "HANDS UP." The young woman, perhaps a local resident or perhaps an activist who traveled to the city to partake in Black Lives Matter protests, anonymizes herself. She turns away from the camera to face Michael Brown and, in an act of solidarity and respect, bows her head. This photograph is not about her. She raises her arms in surrender and mirrors the phrase "HANDS UP," which became popularized following the killing of Brown. The mural at 1902 North Union Boulevard was transformed into a site of community resistance as protesters traveled to the wall to pay their respects to Brown and to stage their own personal acts of demonstration.

Similarly, on April 25, 2015, six days after the killing of Freddie Gray, protesters marched through the streets of Baltimore demanding justice for his death. As the demonstrators filed to city hall, weaving throughout the city, they organized their route to walk directly past a mural of Trayvon Martin. Muralist Gaia painted Martin at around twelve feet tall, half in black and white and half in color. His face and shoulders remain in gray scale as his hands, painted in color, gently hold open the edges of his hoodie to fully show his face. During the march, protesters stopped by this likeness of Martin and stood for photos, holding placards and signs that read "Justice 4 Freddie Gray." Although the mural was erected in the streets of Baltimore prior to Gray's killing, it bridged the temporal and geographic distance between the two victims of police brutality whose memories became entwined over the circumstances of their deaths. Martin's image in the streets of Baltimore, as a checkpoint for a Black Lives Matter rally, adds gravitas to the demonstrations over the killing of Freddie Gray by offering a tangible exemplification of how Black men and women are repeatedly profiled, deemed a threat, and losing their lives at the hands of the police, and that nothing is being done to remedy this.

The streets of America are haunted by the memories of Black death, and the murals of today offer markers of this reality. But these murals not only curate spaces for community activism in the streets but also are often painted in the victim's hometown, occasionally marking physical sites of death. Places or sites of racist tragedy in American history "are difficult, if not impossible, to mark for memorialization," given their purposeful omissions in mainstream narratives, Manning Marable writes of official memorial-making on the American landscape. But Black Lives Matter murals ensure that this history and those being brutalized in the streets will not be forgotten.[31] "Place is not merely what was there, but also the interaction of what is there and what happened there," argues writer Ronald Lee Fleming.[32] Focusing on "what happened" at specific sites and suggesting that placemaking is about "giving memory a stake in the present," he gives us an understanding of memorial-making that unintentionally speaks to the immediacy of Black Lives Matter murals and the role they play being erected both in cities and at physical sites of death.[33] By marking sites of atrocity with the likenesses of police brutality victims, Black Lives Matter murals serve as honest, visual reminders of the broken racial justice system in the United States, and they demand acknowledgment of these violent acts. They sanctify the space where the lives of individuals such as Michael Brown, Freddie Gray, and Alton Sterling were taken, turning their sites of death into sites of memorial.

On July 5, 2016, Alton Sterling was shot dead at close range by two police officers responding to a 911 call. They apprehended the thirty-seven-year-old outside the Triple S Food Mart in Baton Rouge after he apparently threatened someone with a gun as he was selling CDs, although store owner Abdullah Muflahi was unaware of any incident that would have spurred such a call.[34] The officers, Blane Salamoni and Howie Lake II, were aggressive toward Sterling, they shouted profanities at him, and they repeatedly threatened to shoot him in the head before pinning him to the ground. While he was pinned to the ground, Sterling's gun became visible, and the officers then fired six fatal shots into his body. Like most cases of police brutality, the event was caught on video; and again, like most cases of police brutality, the police officers were not charged for their actions but were placed on administrative leave. In March 2018, however, new raw footage from police body cameras was released. When Sterling questioned why the officers were

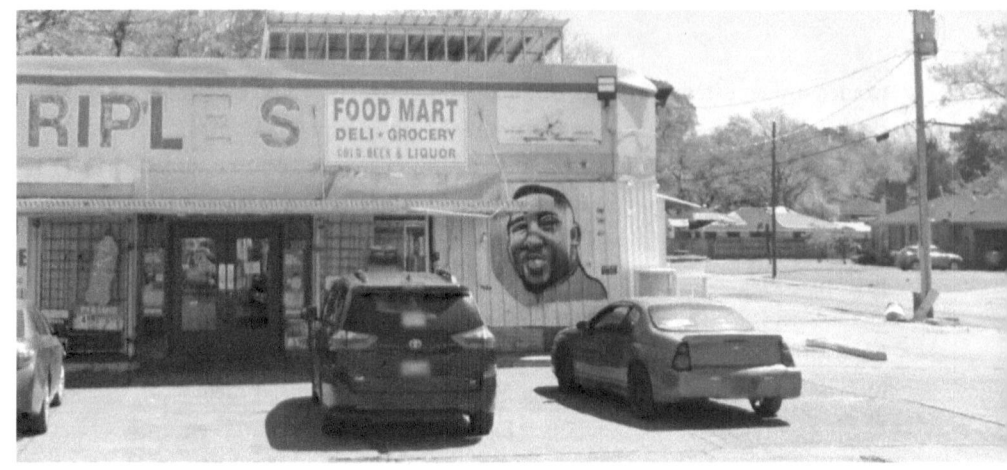

Alton Sterling (2016). Triple S Food Mart, 2112 N. Foster Drive, Baton Rouge, La. Painted by Jo Hines. Image from Google Maps, 2024.

detaining him, Salamoni shouted, "Don't fucking move or I'll shoot your fucking ass. Put your fucking hands on the car." This new footage led to Salamoni's termination.[35] "These actions were not minor deviations from policy," Chief Murphy Paul of the Baton Rouge Police Department said, "and they contributed to the outcome that resulted in the death of another human being."[36]

Shortly after Sterling's death, the Triple S Food Mart where he spent his final hour became an unofficial memorial. His portrait, painted onto the fifteen-foot corrugated iron wall by Jo Hines of the From the Walls Project, translated his memory into a metaphysical martyr for justice, immortalizing his smiling likeness against a golden halo at the site where his body was penetrated six times by the bullets of two members of the Baton Rouge Police Department. Protesters, friends, family, and locals frequently visited the store owned by Muflahi to both protest and pay their respects to Sterling, laying flowers, wreaths, photographs, and other commemorative trinkets. A short drive away from the food mart stood a second memorial for Sterling, this time painted by Langston Allston on Demcola's Furniture Warehouse, owned by Michael Gatz and Amy Strother. This memorial in the city of Sterling's death had a deeper call-and-response relationship with residents when it became a canvas of community emotions. "Enough is enough," reads a message painted onto the wall. Orbiting the outstretched stance of an unnamed Black man are personal messages of love, respect, and commemoration for Sterling. Statements such as "We won't forget," "Justice will be served," and "He never reached" envelop the central figure, couching him in a community embrace and reminding Sterling that he will never be forgotten. While the mural is a clear memorial to Sterling, the anonymous figure in the mural allows the wall to become a broader memorial to all Black men killed and brutalized in the streets at the hands of the police or vigilantes, something summed up by a short letter written just under his left arm:

Dear Black Men,

If you weren't so valuable or didn't
have the potential to be so powerful,
the world wouldn't be so hell bent on
EXTERMINATING
your very existence,

—Myeisha

Through their immediate creation at sites where Black men and women took their final breaths, murals become unofficial memorials at locations of atrocity, seeking to imprint memories into the landscape and to ensure that sites of racist tragedy are finally acknowledged and will not be forgotten. While we see this take place in Baton Rouge at the site of Alton Sterling's death, nowhere, perhaps, is it more strongly exemplified than the Baltimore murals dedicated to Freddie Gray.

On April 12, 2015, Freddie Gray was standing on a street in Baltimore's Gilmor Homes housing project in Sandtown-Winchester. Upon making eye contact with Lieutenant Brian W. Rice, Gray started to run. Rice began to chase Gray, calling for backup from Officer Edward Nero and Officer Garret E. Miller, who at the time were patrolling the area on bikes. After approximately one minute, Gray surrendered to Miller, who threatened him with a taser. Miller then moved Gray to the ground on his stomach and then put his legs into a leg lace before putting him into a police van without a seatbelt on. The van made multiple confirmed stops en route to the police station. At stop 2 Gray's legs were put into leg shackles out of sight of a growing crowd in the area. After this stop, Gray was placed on the floor of the van without a seatbelt and with his head facing the front of the wagon and his hands to the rear. Stop 3 was captured on a private camera, but the police haven't released the reasons for the stop. A fourth stop was made to check on Gray. At this stop, Officer Porter was called to the scene and heard Gray ask for help. A fifth stop took place to transport a second arrestee to the Western District Police Station. Upon arrival at the station, Gray was found unconscious, and paramedics were called.[37]

At every stop, officers failed to seatbelt Gray, and they denied medical assistance when it was requested, along with his inhaler. But as David A. Graham writes in The Atlantic, "It's not the leg [injury] or the asthma that killed him."[38] Medical experts have agreed that sometime in the twenty-five minutes between Gray's initial arrest and his arrival at the police station, he sustained a fatal neck and spinal injury consistent with the sorts of injuries typically caused by car accidents.[39] A week later, on April 19, Freddie Gray died. An autopsy revealed that his spine was severed and voice box crushed. When the police apprehended Gray, they found him carrying a legal switchblade, prompting questions about why the police chased, apprehended, and arrested Gray in the first place. With a similar response to the killings of Oscar Grant, Trayvon Martin, Michael Brown, Eric Garner, and Alton Sterling, protesters took to the streets to demand justice for Gray's death.

When NBC News interviewed Gray's godbrother, Brandon Ross, shortly after Gray's death, he told news reporters how Freddie Gray "wanted to be famous."[40] Recounting the life of Gray throughout the interview, Ross reflected on the first few months without his godbrother before admitting, "Well . . . he's famous now."[41] To commemorate Gray's life throughout Sandtown-Winchester and to turn sites of atrocity and violence into sites of memorial, a series of artists created murals that map the route of Gray's final hours in the community. Scattered across the neighborhood on North Avenue, Presbury Street, Mount Street, Baker Street, Leslie Street, and N. Calhoun Street, the murals serve as a pseudo–walking tour for Gray's life and death, beginning on North Avenue and Mount Street, where he started running from the police. Here, a mural titled Justice, painted by an artist under the moniker SORTA, depicts two peaceful activists from the Baltimore protests on the side of the King Grocery Mart, marching in honor of Gray.

Holding the American flag upside down in an act of subversion and protest, the two young men drain it of color, rendering it lifeless. What the flag supposedly represents—one nation under God, the protection of human rights, and life, liberty, and the pursuit of happiness—does not speak for the men and women of color who are killed in the streets by the forces designed to protect them. The two young men acknowledge this as they invoke

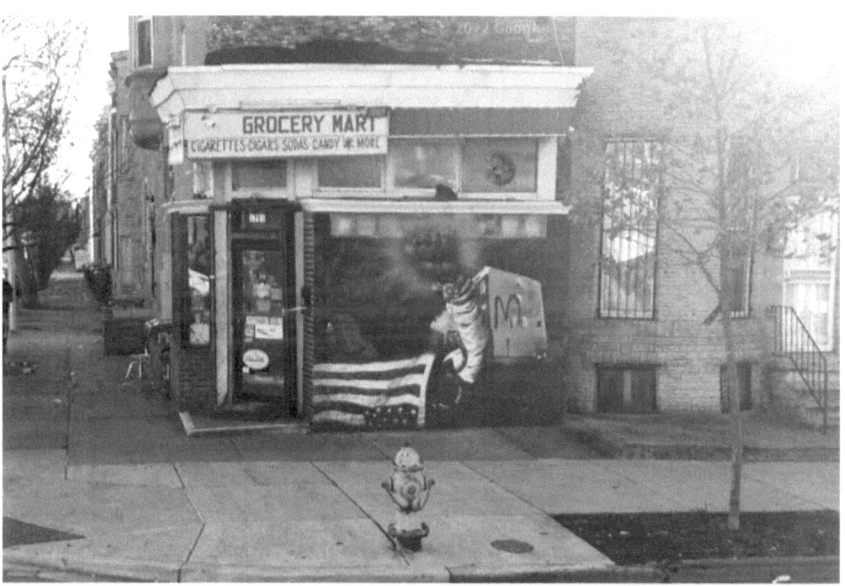

Justice (2015). King Grocery Mart, North Avenue and Mount Street, Baltimore, Md. Painted by SORTA. Image from Google Maps, 2024.

a physical symbol of protest made famous by their preceding activist brothers and sisters. A fist of Black Power punctures the air, almost breaking the fourth wall between mural and reality. Making contact with the oppressive climate enveloping the protesters, the fist releases an explosion of color. Red bleeding into orange bleeding into yellow shines upon the black-and-white mural, casting light upon the red, white, and blue of the protesters' caps. The impotent patriotism of the flag is instead usurped by the patriotism of the two peacefully marching men seeking justice for the death of Freddie Gray. Around the wrists of the puncturing fist hangs a pair of broken handcuffs—neoshackles of a contemporary society. Limply draped down the arm of the powerful protester, the open handcuffs symbolically suggest the inability to shackle his activism, or perhaps he himself has broken them in an empowering visual act of self-emancipation that can be traced back to Aaron Douglas's *Harriet Tubman (Spirits Rising)* (1930).

To push the contours of temporality, SORTA used the mural not only to honor the memory of Freddie Gray. Based on J. M. Giordano's photograph of peaceful protesters at the Western District Police Station following Gray's death, the muralist also offers a metacommentary that debunks the misrepresentative but sadly ubiquitous narratives of violence told by the media in the aftermath of the Baltimore protests. When Freddie Gray died on

April 19, peaceful protests filled the streets of Baltimore. But on April 27, when the protests turned violent, the media suddenly decided to cover the story. The period of rioting in the closing days of April saw media coverage on cable news spike by 162 percent in comparison to coverage of the peaceful protests in the week prior.[42] CNN was criticized for sensationalizing its coverage with dramatic interviews and looping negative imagery of flaming cars and clashes with police. Protestor Danielle Williams called out MSNBC's coverage to news anchor Thomas Roberts, making the valid and irrefutable claim that "when we were out here protesting all last week for six days straight peacefully, there were no news cameras. . . . So now that we've burned down buildings and set businesses on fire . . . all of a sudden everybody wants to hear us."[43]

During school closures in Baltimore, children swept the sidewalks, young African American boys handed out water bottles to police officers, crowds of peaceful protesters broke into spontaneous song, and individuals formed human barriers between the police and frustrated protesters to prevent violent clashes. But depictions of arson, looting, and violence prevailed throughout the media, perpetuating damaging misrepresentations. Speaking to the media bias covering the Baltimore riots, even former president Obama commented on how violence and looting across the city diverted media attention away from the peaceful protests:

> The violence that happened yesterday distracted [from the fact] that you had seen multiple days of peaceful protests that were focused on entirely legitimate concerns of these communities in Baltimore by clergy and community leaders. And they were thoughtful, and they were constructive—and frankly didn't get that much attention, and one burning building will be looped on television over, and over, and over again, and the thousands of demonstrators who did it the right way, I think, have been lost in the discussion.[44]

SORTA's mural speaks to this statement. It depicts on the streets of Baltimore the overwhelmingly peaceful protests that took place throughout the city. And whether consciously or not, SORTA cleverly used a sense of direction to tell Freddie Gray's story. The mural is painted at the spot where Gray saw the police, and the two painted protesters inwardly face toward Mount Street—the street Gray ran down in fear of the officers and where the artistic map of his final hour in Sandtown-Winchester continues.

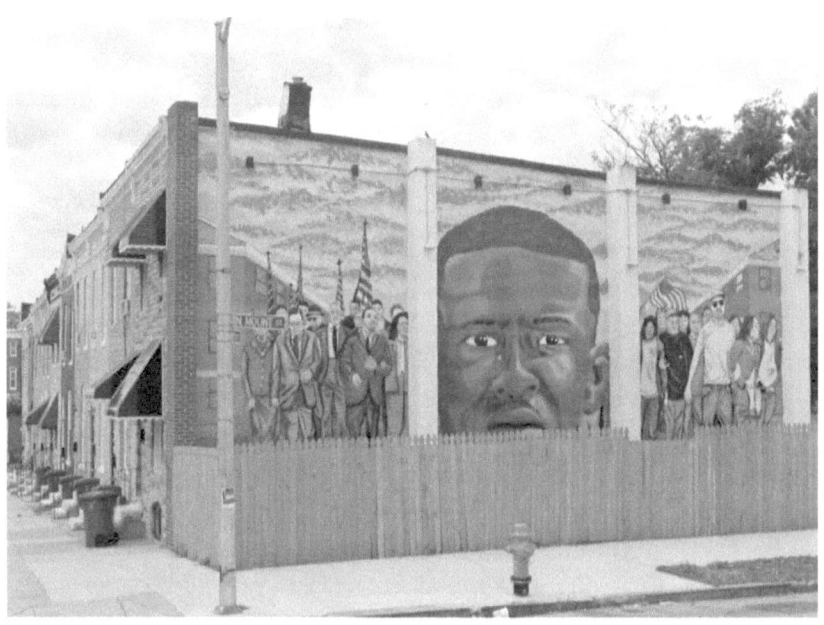

Freddie Gray (2015). Mount and Presbury Streets, Baltimore, Md. Painted by NETHER. Image from Google Maps, 2024.

Heading south on Mount Street to reach Presbury, the route carries on to the site where Gray was arrested. In a one-block radius from Mount Street and Presbury, four murals line the streets, honoring both the life of Gray and the strength of the community during the protests following his death. Standing at the intersection between Mount and Presbury, a mural painted by NETHER—with the input of Gray's godbrother, Ross—connects the history of Black protest in America in a visual continuum. Paying close attention to the architectural design of the building, NETHER compartmentalized the mural into three sections in accordance with three protruding white beams that vertically dissect the building into a triptych. On the left-hand section of the wall, Martin Luther King Jr. marches in Selma with a crowd of peaceful protesters dressed in suits and ties, and to the right-hand side, this historic moment is mirrored in the present when a group of young activists wearing jeans, sweatshirts, and sunglasses march in the name of Black Lives Matter. Both groups of protesters are painted in black and white, while their surroundings and raised American flags are in color, along with the likeness of Freddie Gray in the central frame. Gray is positioned in the foreground of the mural, somewhat detached from his surroundings in part due to his position in the frame and in part due to the demarcation of color. Removing the gray-scale figures from the mural for a moment leaves a hauntingly desolate image, one that reminds viewers that Gray, running through the streets of Baltimore fearing for his life, was alone.

The colorful American flags that remain in the reimagined frame—representing freedom, liberty, and equality—failed to protect Gray. He was racially profiled. He was deemed a threat. He was killed in a country that supposedly believes all people are created equal. But the flags positioned in the background away from Gray symbolize how this declaration doesn't extend to him. An expression with multiple possibilities curves the contours of his face—sadness, confusion, fear, calmness, and stoicism—allowing the viewer to interpret a full gamut of emotions. Painted in color, Gray's dark-brown skin is shadowed by the fiery light of the sky, perhaps to reflect Baltimore's mood or perhaps to give hope that a new day will come—one where police will always be held accountable for their actions but one that sadly we knew in 2015 had not yet dawned. The three white pillars slicing the mural into three sections look like bars, but by placing Gray in the central panel, the bars are subverted into frames instead, memorializing his likeness and immortalizing a moment of history in the streets of Sandtown-Winchester.

Standing directly at the intersection of North and Mount Street and looking south down the road with NETHER's mural in the right-hand peripheral vision, a second memorial to Gray textures a wall directly in view. A small headstone-like image is sprayed onto a brick wall reading: "Freddie Gray—8.16.89–4.19.15" at the actual site Gray was arrested. The small mural is an immediate response to the memory of his arrest, and the headstone depicts a blue cloud shadowed by a muted yellow shape that drips—almost blood-like—onto the ground. Perhaps the sun shines less brightly upon Baltimore after Freddie Gray's death as it begins to melt into the earth and drip away. A pair of bright white wings supports the dissolving clouds, and sitting in between them floats a melting halo. Frequently receiving visitors, the small commemorative mural painted by GHP stands proudly upon the wall ornamented by flowers, trinkets, and personal messages. No longer do the physical site of Gray's arrest on Presbury Street and his subsequent final moments in Sandtown-Winchester dissolve into obscurity. Instead, they become preserved upon the community's physical and emotional landscape, acting as a communal gathering point for Gray's friends and family.

Walking a few streets west to reach the intersection at Presbury and Ful-

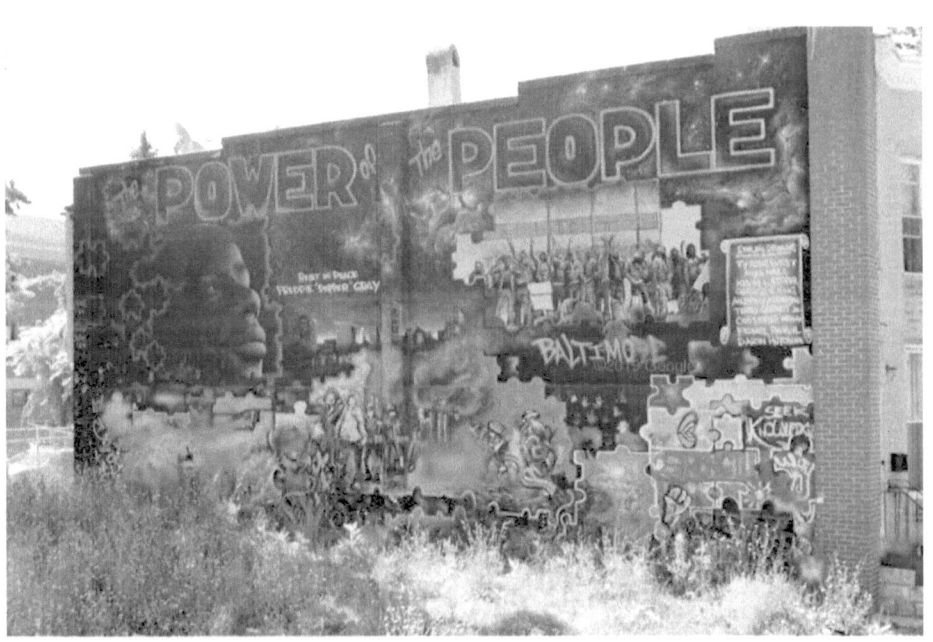

The Power of the People (2015). Presbury and Fulton Streets, Baltimore, Md. Painted by Beats, Rhymes, and Relief. Image from Google Maps, 2024.

ton is perhaps the most commemorative Freddie Gray mural. Painted by Beats, Rhymes, and Relief, the mural, in similar fashion to the others, transforms a space in Baltimore's Sandtown-Winchester area into a place of commemoration at a site near where Gray's violent arrest took place. The mural, much like others in the area, sanctifies the street by "giving memory a stake in the present" when it depicts the likeness of Gray painted in prophet-like fashion on the left-hand side of the mural from a worm's-eye angle.[45] Enveloping Gray's face are blue and orange puzzle pieces, but the puzzle remains incomplete as viewers try to understand why the police dehumanized and devalued Gray. The right side of Gray's face is illuminated by a warm yellow glow as he stares toward the sky, peacefully and serenely. Scenes of community protest decorate the remainder of the mural with a black-and-white narrative akin to the scenes on NETHER's street art a block away. A group of young adults assemble, raising fists of Black Power in solidarity with Gray and other victims of police brutality listed on the side of the mural: Tyrone West, Mya Hall, Kevin L. Cooper, George V. King, Anthony Anderson, Terry Garnett Jr., Christopher Brown, Fednel Rhinvil, and Darin Hutchins. In tandem with the fists of Black Power raised by individuals in contemporary clothing, the popular 1960s soundbite "Power to the People" is subverted to remove the radical undertones of the slogan, and above Gray's face reads the edited statement "The Power of the People." The all-encompassing, humanistic slogan unifies the masses in the name of Freddie Gray to underscore the potency of collective community action.

The final mural mapping the last moments of Gray's life in Sandtown-Winchester is at the intersection of Leslie and Baker Streets, the exact spot where the police made their stop to place Gray in leg irons. The mural, like those seen in chapter 3, promotes a message of communal healing in the wounded city of Baltimore. Countering the ubiquitous and misrepresentative news coverage of violence and looting in the city, the mural instead echoes Obama's acknowledgment of the "multiple days of peaceful protests" in Baltimore. Creating a meta street scene, the anonymous muralist depicts what appears to be a ceremonial "new beginning" in the neighborhood. A symbolic ribbon decorating a blue door is cut as anonymous Black and white individuals come together to shake hands. But as well as the handshake and ceremonial ribbon cutting, two peace candles are lit in the mural to perhaps commemorate Gray or to perhaps signify a new moment in the neighborhood, and an anonymous Black figure—possibly Freddie Gray—preaches to a diverse audience. In this utopian street scene, all community members unite under his name, again immortalizing his memory not just physically into the urban landscape but also socially to strengthen the community relationships in the city of Baltimore.

Murals have become an ingrained part of the Black Lives Matter movement, offering a visual accompaniment to the anguish, pain, fear, and hope being actualized in the streets through marches and demonstrations. Analyzing and understanding a movement as it happens in real time is difficult. What is undeniable, however, is the essential role Black Lives Matter murals play in the streets today by curating sites of community activism and reclaiming sites of death. Bodies carry memory, and Black Lives Matter murals carry the bodies and memories of those brutalized in the streets to ensure that cities and sites of racist tragedy are no longer difficult, if not impossible, to mark for memorialization. But while murals play this potent role in the Black Lives Matter movement, they also play another role. From border to border and coast to coast, murals stand in the streets today to rehumanize the victims of police brutality whose intimate deaths flood news feeds across the world, desensitizing us further to the spectacle of Black brutalization, and whose life and memory are subjected to racist critique and dehumanization in attempts to justify their deaths at the hands of the police and vigilantes.

BATTLEGROUNDS OF IMAGERY

"When my sons were in high schools and pictures of Philando Castile were on the front page of the *Times*, I wanted to burn all of the newspapers so they would not see the gun coming in the window, the blood on Castile's T-shirt, the terror in his partner's face, and the eyes of his witnessing baby girl," poet Elizabeth Alexander wrote for the Personal History section of *The New Yorker*. "But I was too late, too late generationally, because they were not looking in the newspaper; they were looking at their phones, where the image was a house of mirrors straight to Hell."[46] Images and videos of Black people being brutalized and killed in the streets line our newsfeeds on social media. Macabre, intimate moments of death are distilled into short clips to be shared time and again on Facebook, Twitter, and Instagram. Jelani Cobb cuts to the heart of this new, dystopian online moment surrounding Black death playing out on our phones by asking us, Do these videos do more to humanize or objectify the figures dying in the streets? "Yesterday, very few of us knew who George Floyd was, what he cared about, how he lived his life," Cobb wrote. "Today, we know him no better save for the grim way in which that life met its end."[47]

Videos, of course, have a purpose in showing the world the irrefutable evidence of what's been happening to people of color for centuries, and without these videos the progress of the Black Lives Matter movement today would look markedly different. But in a social media age, we constantly witness Black death. We've watched the videos of Eric Garner gasp for air as he choked out the words "I can't breathe." We've watched the harrowing video of Philando Castile take his last breaths of life in front of his young daughter. We've watched Walter Scott fearfully run for his life before being shot multiple times in the back. And we've heard Elijah McClain plead and attempt to reason with the police before they drugged him with ketamine. As a society, the surge of videos capturing these acts of atrocity makes us increasingly numb to the killings of people of color. "I suppose it was the fact that a video was even posted," Michael Eric Dyson wrote in an emotional letter to Elijah McClain. "It told me from the start that the outcome wasn't going to be good, that you wouldn't survive, that your death would be another death that would happen as if it hadn't happened at all."[48] Dyson is right. Whether due to the constant exposure of these videos or whether the weight of history collects inside us as we introspectively trace the lineage of brutality against Black people throughout time, we already know, before a video of a police encounter with a person of color automatically plays on our social media feed, that the outcome will inevitably be violent and that it could likely show a life being lost.

When news reporters in Virginia were shot and killed by a former co-worker on live television, national media outlets chose not to air the graphic footage, citing respect for the victims and their families. This same sense of humanity is not granted to victims of color, April Reign, a former attorney and now managing editor of Broadway Black, argues: "It's a dehumanization of Black people and we don't see that with any other race."[49] This fetishization and viralization of Black death is dehumanizing.[50] As Cobb quite rightly points out, we know the names of individuals such as Ma'Khia Bryant, Michael Brown, Freddie Gray, Akai Gurley, Tony Robinson, Tamir Rice, Sean Bell, and Amadou Diallo (although there are still so many names we do not know) because of the acts of violence that stole their lives. But the world is only privy to the details of their final hours of life. These intimate and harrowing last moments are continuously played throughout the media on a loop, but not only do these moments of death become omnipresent in society. "Death is too intimate a phenomenon to not be distorted by a mass audience," Cobb suggests, and as a result, these moments of violence get distilled into a soundbite, an image, or a video, dehumanizing victims not only for the constant loop of their death online but also through its transformation into a shareable, "retweetable" form. "When we reduce victims of police violence to symbols, we strip them of their humanity and fail to understand the gravity of the suffering they endured," Caelan Reeves writes in The Student Life magazine. "We become desensitized to Black pain. This issue may not be unique to social media, but it is exponentially worsened by it."[51] Some of the Black Lives Matter murals we see in the streets today, then, can stand as a direct response to this dehumanization and devaluation of Black life in the media and online. These murals use imagery and iconography that elevate individuals and ensure that their memory is not simply reduced to their brutalizing death.

In June 2020 Israel Solomon created For George Floyd at 342 Massachusetts Avenue in downtown Indianapolis. The mural formed just one of a twenty-two-part mural collective created by the Arts Council of Indianapolis in response to mass protests in the wake of George Floyd's death. Painting onto transportable plywood, Solomon created a mural of Floyd that sought to extricate his memory from the media vilification of his character and the ubiquitous photographs capturing the final moments of his life. Solomon made Floyd a person again, not just a hashtag and not just a video. "I put myself in Floyd's position, in his shoes," Solomon said. "What if that was a family member? What if that was a cousin? What if that was my dad? What if that was my brother? How would I feel?"[52] By asking these questions, Solomon created a mural that depicts George Floyd, a son, a father, a man. Burned into the nation's collective psyche is the image of Floyd's prostrate body laid out on the warm Minneapolis concrete, dying under the knee of Derek Chauvin. The world does not see the image of a forty-six-year-old man who grew up in Houston and was admired as a mentor in a public housing project, a man who turned to religion in his life, a man who was a talented basketball player, football player, and hip-hop artist, and a man who as a second-grader wrote that he dreamed of being a Supreme Court justice.[53] But through his mural, Solomon began to piece together George Floyd as a human being once more.

Created as a triptych, the eponymous mural depicts three portraits of Floyd atop a vibrant geometric background. The first portrait in the left-hand side of the frame shows an infant Floyd nestled in the arms of his mother's loving embrace. She looks toward the viewers—a large, glowing smile stretches across her face as her young son dreams peacefully upon her chest. This tender and loving moment between a mother and her son is painfully interrupted by the haunting memory of Floyd crying out for her in his final breaths of life, and here Solomon depicts for the viewer the safety and comfort Floyd was searching for in his last moments. In the center of the mural the viewer sees a likeness of Floyd not in his final hour and not crying out in pain, but reimagined in the streets of Indianapolis as the man he was, relaxed in a tracksuit jacket, baseball cap, and glasses. And to the right-hand side of the mural, Floyd is visually resurrected as Gianna's father. He stands proudly, as any father would, carrying his daughter nestled into his side. A large smile, just like that of his mother's, creases his face, and he stares out into the street in complete happiness. Gianna, looking comfortable in her father's embrace, points out toward viewers, almost as if to bring their attention to this loving moment between the two of them. Painting a visual timeline of some of the stages of Floyd's life, Solomon created a visual afterlife for Floyd that stands in direct contrast to the flood of dehumanizing imagery we saw surrounding him and his death. The mural reimagined Floyd to ensure that the public are exposed to imagery that honors his life rather than continuously visualizes his death. And on June 6, 2020, a similar act of rehumanization took place in the streets of Oakland, only this time seeking to resurrect the memory of a Black woman killed at the hands of the police.

The People's Conservatory created a community mural, painted the day after what would have been Breonna Taylor's twenty-seventh birthday, in the streets of Oakland at 15th and Broadway to honor her life. "We are doing a twenty-seven-hour mural. . . . [Y]ou can already see that we've got a bunch of our community here, painting, creating in solidarity. . . . [C]ome pick up a brush and add your voice," the organization said in a short video on their Instagram.[54] While the videos of Floyd's and Ahmaud Arbery's deaths went viral, subsequently followed up with arrests and indictments for their killers (which felt somewhat unprecedented already), Breonna Taylor's killing in March 2020 failed to receive the same recognition, maybe because her death wasn't captured on video or through photography, maybe because the news cycle at the time was dominated by the exponential growth of a deadly global pandemic, or maybe because she was a Black woman.

So frequently in the narrative of Black Lives Matter and the subsequent media reports on Black killings, Black women—as well as members of the LGBTQIA+ community—are omitted. The names of Trayvon Martin, Michael Brown, Tamir Rice, and George Floyd are household names, but what about Aiyana Stanley-Jones or Atatiana Jefferson? "Racism and sexism are overlapping, creating multiple levels of social injustice," Professor Kimberlé Crenshaw says of her groundbreaking concept of "intersectionality," where roads of oppression such as racism, sexism, ableism, transphobia, and homophobia meet and double/triple the social injustice experienced by such individuals. The consequences of not having intersectional politics when thinking about feminism and antiracism, she goes on to say—when feminism doesn't contest the logic of racism, and when racism refuses to take up questions of patriarchy—often end up reinforcing each other.[55]

When Crenshaw speaks at public meetings, she asks the audience to stand up until they hear an unfamiliar name. She then reads the names of Black men and boys killed by the police and whose deaths were followed by mass protests across the United States and sometimes across the world. Eric Garner, Freddie Gray, Tamir Rice, Alton Sterling, Walter Scott. The audience

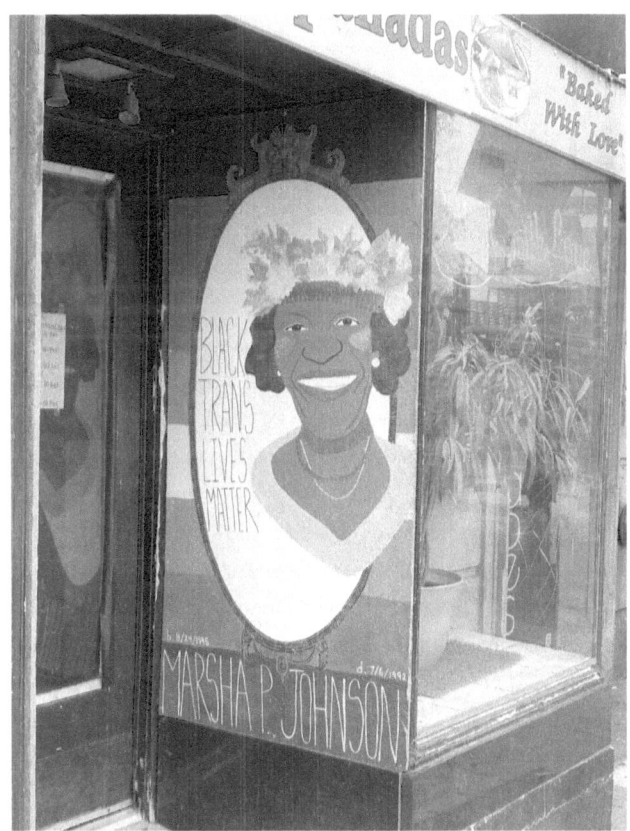

Marsha P. Johnson, date unknown. 1221 Connecticut Avenue, Washington, D.C. Painted by unknown. Photograph taken by the author.

remains standing. Natasha McKenna, Tanisha Anderson, Michelle Cusseaux, Aura Rosser, Mya Hall. By the time Crenshaw reaches the third name, almost all the audience members are seated, and by the time she reaches the fifth name, the only people left standing are those working on her campaign, #SayHerName.[56]

#SayHerName was founded in 2014 by Crenshaw to raise visibility regarding the number of Black women killed by the police. "Historically, Black women, girls, and femmes have not fit the most accessible frames of anti-Black police violence," Crenshaw says.

> Their precarity is buried beneath myths, stereotypes, and denial. But the heartbreaking truth is that Black girls as young as 7 and women as old as 93 have been killed by the police. They've been shot, beaten, and tasered to death for driving while Black, having a mental health crisis while Black,

being homeless while Black, and sleeping in their own beds while Black. They've been killed when they don't conform to gender stereotypes, and executed when their very existence strikes fear into the hearts of police officers. Many times, they're killed for simply "being" while Black.[57]

The #SayHerName campaign and its sister network, #SayHerName Mothers Network, launched by the African American Policy Forum (AAPF) and the Center for Intersectionality and Social Policy Studies (AAPF), breaks the national silence around the death of Black women at the hands of the police, bringing attention to the stories of the killings of Black women and trans folk that get overlooked because they fall outside the lines of a conventional narrative.[58]

When Officers Jonathan Mattingly, Brett Hankison, and Myles Cosgrove forced entry into an apartment in Louisville, Kentucky, on the night of March 13, 2020, they fired six bullets in a matter of seconds into twenty-six-year-old Breonna Taylor, killing her in her home. But the world didn't begin to pay attention to her case until June 2020. It felt initially like the death of another Black woman would pass by without nationwide recognition and outrage, but following the killings of Ahmaud Arbery and George Floyd and the corresponding haunting videos, Taylor's death and the events that led to it were quickly folded into the anger and demands for justice occupying the streets in the summer of 2020. Taylor became a household name, and her killing increased an awareness around the "no-knock warrant practice" that allowed Mattingly, Hankison, and Cosgrove to enter her apartment unannounced, so much so that Louisville officials have banned the use of no-knock warrants.[59] But like the memories of previous victims of police brutality, Taylor's memory and death were distorted, becoming part of the latest trend on social media.

"It's a great day to arrest the cops who killed Breonna Taylor," read the memes and captions on Twitter, Instagram, and Facebook. Taylor's death was turned into an almost jovial punchline. Lili Reinhart posted a tone-deaf naked Instagram post captioned "Now that my sideboob has gotten your attention, Breonna Taylor's murderers have not been arrested. Demand Justice." Etsy and Teepublic saw a staggering increase in the for-profit merchandise exploiting Taylor's name, selling T-shirts with checkboxes that read "Single, Taken, Entanglement, Arrest the cops that killed Breonna Taylor," as well as Breonna Taylor face masks. And posts such as "i love you

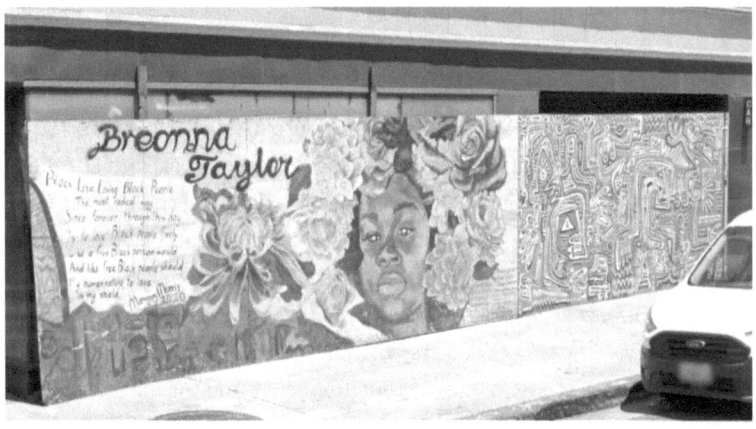

For Breonna Taylor (2021). 15th and Broadway, Oakland, Calif. Painted by the People's Conservatory. Image from Google Maps, 2024.

but I had to make it rhyme / roses are red / i use google chrome / arrest the bastards who murdered breonna taylor in her own home" lined the feeds of Twitter.[60] The statement "Arrest the cops who killed Breonna Taylor" was so easily disseminated that it became a catchphrase far removed from the reality and atrocities surrounding her death and, in turn, reduced her life to a single popular slogan.

So on June 6, 2020, in the streets of Oakland, following Taylor's twenty-seventh birthday, the People's Conservatory created a mural that resurrected the image of Breonna Taylor in a way that commemoratively honored her memory. At 15th and Broadway, Taylor's face is beautifully painted in rich brown tones, and her serene portrait is ornamented by a bouquet of purple, pink, and orange flowers, forming an almost halo-like wreath around her head. Shining out from her likeness are bright yellow sunbeams—her memory casts a light upon the community—and layered atop the rays of sun is a poem written by Mahogany Morris:

> Black Love, Loving Black People,
> The most radical way,
> Since forever through this day
> Is to love Black people freely,
>
> Like a free Black person would,
> And like free Black people should
> My human nature to love
> is my shield.

The poem, as a dedication to Blackness and Black love, shields Taylor's image in the same way Morris's "human nature to love" is her own shield. Although Taylor's memory and visual afterlife were warped through social media hashtags and popular soundbites, Morris and the People's Conservatory used the poem to impress on the community of Oakland how Taylor, her life, and her memory are loved and embraced. But the poem not only speaks to Taylor's life. It also speaks to George Floyd's, to Sandra Bland's, to Ahmaud Arbery's, and to the countless victims, mainly Black women and queer and trans people, whose names are not uttered around the dinner tables of households across the country. They are loved as well, and they are loved freely, radically, and unconditionally. Morris's poem of Black love, in tandem with the beautiful likeness of Taylor painted over a twenty-seven-hour period—each hour for each year of life she should have been living—offers a powerful commemoration of her. This community-made mural slowly recreated the memory of a Black woman whose life was cut short at the hands of the police and whose death became an uncomfortable and ubiquitous trend across social media.

But the propagation of Black death throughout the media is not the only way victims of police brutality are dehumanized. In the summer of 2020 a group of artists gathered at Cup Foods on 38th and Chicago in Minneapolis to paint a mural of George Floyd at the site where he was murdered by Derek Chauvin. The mural became a space for communal activism, and it marked the landscape where the world witnessed, once again, a modern-day lynching. In an interview, artist Cadex Herrera, who painted the mural with a group of Minneapolis-based artists, including Xena Goldman and Greta McLain, touched on another instrumental role played by Black Lives Matter murals. "A lot of the time, when things like this happen, the media tries to paint the victim as a criminal," he said, "so when I first thought of this idea, I instead wanted the mural to be something positive: I wanted it to be something that uplifted people and also uplifted George Floyd's memory. I wanted to portray him as a light in this community, as someone who was important to his family, as a human being."[61] So frequently, following the killing of a Black man or woman, their life and memory are castigated, criminalized, and dehumanized. The media and individuals on social media work tirelessly to show how these tragic fates, as Wesley Lowery suggests, were reserved for those "innately criminal who behave in a way we never would."[62] Murals, then, are in direct conversation with these racist acts

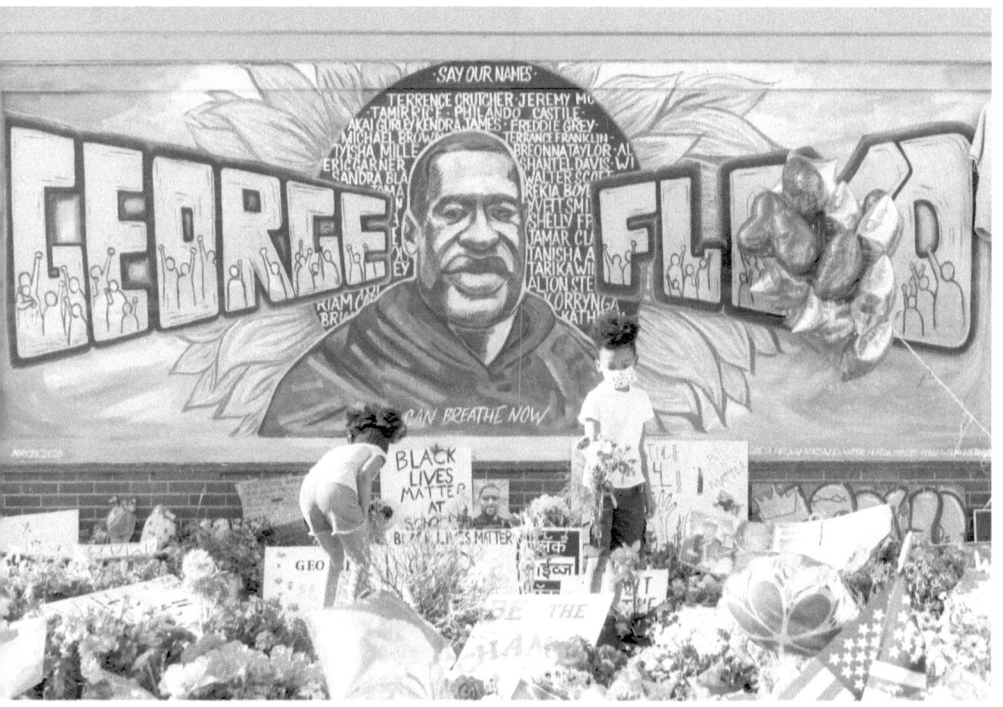

George Floyd (2020). Cup Foods, Chicago Avenue and E. 38th Street, Minneapolis, Minn. Painted by Xena Goldman, Cadex Herrera, and Greta McLain. Image from Flikr, taken by Chad Davis. CC BY-S 2.0. No changes made to image.

of dehumanization, creating a visual afterlife that seeks to counter mainstream misrepresentations and rehumanize the memories of those killed at the hands of the police.

Commonly after such acts of atrocity occur, victims are demonized and criminalized in a way to justify their deaths. Attacks on character, lifestyle choices, personal behavior, and previous criminal records are used to vindicate the acts of the police and reconcile these instances of Black death circulating on our news feeds. Trayvon Martin shouldn't have been wearing a hoodie. Elijah McClain shouldn't have been wearing a balaclava. Sandra Bland shouldn't have failed to signal at an intersection. Akai Gurley shouldn't have been living in housing projects or have a criminal record. For victims of police brutality, there is no margin for error.

Shortly after Michael Brown was killed by Darren Wilson in Ferguson, a suburb of St. Louis, Missouri, on August 9, 2014, Police Chief Thomas Jackson released a grainy video that depicted Brown stealing cigarillos from a local convenience store. At the time of Brown's death, Wilson was unaware of Brown's encounter at the shop, but the work of the tape had already been done. Brown, as Keeanga Yamahtta-Taylor suggests, had already been "transformed from a victim of law enforcement into a Black suspect whose death was probably justified."[63] Protests and demonstrations broke out in Ferguson as residents and people from across the country sought justice for the killing of Brown. On January 23, 2015, however, *New York Times* columnist Nicolas Kristof tweeted: "Activists perhaps should have focused less on Michael Brown, more on the shooting of 12-yr-old Tamir Rice in Cleveland," while subtweeting an article from *The New York Times* about the killing of Rice.[64] Kristof's reasoning? Brown's case was too ambiguous and uncertain to garner support for the movement.

In his 2017 book, *They Can't Kill Us All: The Story of Black Lives Matter*, Wesley Lowery speaks to this point by asking us, "Who is the perfect victim? Michael Brown? Kajieme Powell? Eric Garner? Sandra Bland? Freddie Gray? . . . Does it matter?"[65] Regardless of who the victim is, their character will continuously be lambasted throughout the media. In 2016 Calvin John Smiley and David Fakunle conducted a study for the *Journal of Human Behavior and Social Environment* that demonstrated the "demonizing process that happens to unarmed Black men posthumously."[66] Looking at the case studies of Eric Garner, Michael Brown, Akai Gurley, Tamir Rice, Tony Robinson, and Freddie Gray, Smiley and Fakunle used local, national, and international media coverage to reveal how these men were portrayed as "thugs and criminals to seemingly justify their deaths while simultaneously shifting blame away from law enforcement." Garner's representation in newspapers, for example, featured microinvalidations around his size and health issues: "a 400-pound asthmatic Staten Island dad," "the 350-pound Garner's poor health, including acute and chronic bronchial asthma; obesity; hypertensive cardiovascular disease." There was also a focus on his lifestyle and previous behaviors, such as "criminality and the perception of being a 'hustler' due to his propensity to sell single cigarettes, which is illegal yet not a felony in New York." These microinvalidations around his size and lifestyle were weaponized by the media to justify and scapegoat Garner's death. Similarly with Akai Gurley, the media posthumously castigated his character. Two international media sources ran Gurley's story alongside his mugshot. The *Daily Mail* ran a story with the headline "NYPD Rookie Officer Shot 'Innocent' Unarmed Father Dead in Brooklyn Stairwell by 'Accident' as Girlfriend Watched in Horror." The use of quotation marks around "innocent" and "accident" offers the implication that Gurley was not innocent and that his death was "not an accident but valid if he was not innocent."[67]

One thing Black Lives Matter murals do in communities today is extricate the memories of victims whose life is criminalized and devalued and whose death is framed as justified due to their behaviors and lifestyle choices. These murals line the streets of communities across the United States to rehumanize victims, to show how their lives mattered, and to show how they wrongfully died at the hands of the police. Artists create these works of art to show that whether victims had criminal records or not is irrelevant. George Floyd used a counterfeit twenty-dollar bill, yet instead of receiving a fine, he paid with his life. Much like Lowery writes of the demonstrations and protests in cities following these killings, these murals are not meant to "assert the innocence of every slain Black man and woman."[68] Instead, they are a way of highlighting a broken system that unjustly and inequitably brutalizes Black men and women. These murals exist in the streets to counter the racist, stereotypical, criminalizing perceptions of police brutality victims whose memory gets reduced to a certain moment, behavior, photograph, or act in their life.

The physical and personal life of Michael Brown was dehumanized repeatedly after his death. For four and a half hours his lifeless body lay out on the hot tarmac on Canfield Drive, baking in the August heat in front of residents as his blood stained the road. This would later be cited by local police officers as one of their major mistakes.[69] On the day Darren Wilson's name was released to the public, so too was the grainy video of Brown in the convenience store shortly before his death. Swiftly after his death, reports of Brown robbing the store took precedence in the overall narrative of an unarmed eighteen-year-old African American shot several times by police officer Darren Wilson, something Deron Lee, writing in the *Columbia Journalism Review*, believed was "designed to reverse perceptions about the young shooting victim."[70] In the days following his death, the national media litigated Brown as opposed to the shooting. "It was only a matter of time . . . before local media began attacking the character of a man whose blood was still seeping into the ground," activist Netta said.[71]

When Wilson's testimony was published a few months after Brown's death, his account added ballast to the dehumanization of the eighteen-year-old unarmed teenager. "When I grabbed him, the only way I can describe it is I felt like a five-year-old holding onto Hulk Hogan," Wilson said of their physical altercation, presenting Brown as a colossal and uncontrollable "wrestler-esque" figure. Both men stood at six feet four inches tall, with Wilson at 210 pounds and Brown at 292, placing them in the same weight class—heavyweight—in any professional boxing match.[72] Wilson continued degrading Brown by turning him into an animal who made "a grunting, like aggravated sound" as he "looked up at me and had the most intense aggressive face" before stripping away all sense of humanity from Brown, referring to him as "it": "It looks like a demon, that's how angry he looked."[73]

Given the incessant assassination of Brown's character as well as his body, following his death, murals emerged across the country to piece his memory back together again, slowly rehumanizing him in the streets of the United States to present him as he was: an eighteen-year-old unarmed Black teenager.

In Portland, Oregon, on November 25, 2014, two days after Darren Wilson's acquittal for the death of Michael Brown in Ferguson, muralist Ashley Montague painted a visually striking mural of Brown on the side of the well-loved eatery the Bonfire Lounge. Montague painted him standing in the center of the mural, palms upturned, and arms outstretched in homage to the increasingly popular slogan of the movement, #HandsUpDontShoot, and he is unarmed. He doesn't look like Hulk Hogan, grunting with a demonic facial expression, as Wilson described. Instead, he stands serenely with his eyes closed and face angled toward the sky as his hands glow with a light orange hue, casting a warm glimmering light onto his face. His heart lifts and pulses from his chest, enveloped by the same comforting glow, waiting to be carried by a dove to be protected. The double collar on the left-hand side of Brown's shirt looks almost page-like, and when coupled with his open, prayer-like pose, the collar takes the form of the Bible, with Brown seeking comfort and solace in his final hour. Alternatively, the page-like qualities of Brown's collar are also reminiscent of a school textbook, and when considering the colors used by Montague—a green top with a dark red color lining his left hand—the muralist subtly mirrors the colors of Brown's graduation robes in one of the few photographs released of him in the aftermath of his death, in which Brown stands before a camera in a green robe and a dark red sash. By playing on the importance of education, Montague reminds viewers that Brown was only eighteen years old, with his whole life ahead of him.

Positioned with his face tilted toward the sky and his arms open and unthreatening, Brown and his body language beg the question, "Why am I still being killed in 2014?" In the back of his mind, though, he literally knows the answer: the systemically racist policing and judicial system in the United States. Refraining from overtly violent imagery, Montague laced the mural with connotations of a videogame when the back of Brown's head crumbles into pixels and blocks. The police stand behind Brown, incongruously threatening to the messiah-like figure being killed at their feet. While Montague used warm, natural colors to envelop the face of the dying young Brown, the police counteract this image with an unnatural shade of bright purple to highlight their imposing and unnecessary presence. Montague omitted the likeness of Officer Darren Wilson from the mural and instead dressed the police in full riot gear, complete with shields, guns, and headwear to give them anonymity and invoke the memory of many officers who have killed Black people in the streets—Daniel Pantaleo, Johannes Mehserle, Derek Chauvin, Kim Potter, Blane Salamoni.

The presence of the police was a point of controversy when building owner George Kassapakis demanded Montague paint over the officers, frequently placing his garbage bins in front of the mural to obscure the message.[74] Shortly after these demands, however, the Bonfire Lounge changed owners, and the new owner, Travis Miranda, warned Montague of his plans to paint over the entire mural because, as Montague recalled of their conversation, the neighborhood apparently "fucking hated it."[75] Montague took to Facebook to garner support for his mural, and after five hundred shares and one hundred comments, local residents threatened to boycott all of Miranda's businesses.[76] The mural was an unnerving "representation of the beauty and violence in life mixed together . . . and in really white Portland, it's jarring to be faced with that reality," local Black activist Royal Harris suggested.[77]

As of August 2019, the mural, now attached to new building owners Baby Doll Pizza, remained half painted over—the two police officers had been removed and replaced with green hearts, and it was still largely obscured by dumpsters. Regardless of its current physical obfuscation, however, the purpose of the memorial was to remedy the slew of negative press defaming the life and memory of Michael Brown. Montague invoked a powerfully spiritual aesthetic that countered the misrepresentations of Brown's "hulking" size and aggressive face by instead reminding the world of the basic facts so easily forgotten in the media: He was an eighteen-year-old victim of police brutality who wanted to go to college and who thought he had his whole life ahead of him.

On August 21, 2018, a commemorative rehumanizing mural appeared in the streets of Manhattan. Nearly six years after the death of Trayvon Martin, a memorial depicting his likeness wearing a light gray hoodie emerged in New York's Lower East Side. Seventeen-year-old Trayvon Martin was fatally shot by neighborhood watchman George Zimmerman in Sanford, Florida, on February 26, 2012. Carrying only a packet of Skittles and a bottle of iced tea, Martin was profiled by Zimmerman as both suspicious and threatening as he passed through the Twin Lakes Housing Community at 7:09 p.m. with his hood up.[78] Seven witness calls to 911 and a fatal shot to Martin's chest later, Zimmerman was apprehended by the police and taken into questioning, only to be released five hours later under the remit of self-defense in accordance with Florida's Stand Your Ground statute.[79] The following year, in July 2013, Zimmerman was tried for the second-degree murder of Martin, as well as the lesser charge of manslaughter. Three weeks later, on July 13, 2013, he was acquitted of both. Protests ensued, and the sanctity of the American judicial system was brought into question for months after the trial.

On the night of Martin's death he was deemed "real suspicious" by his killer for wearing "a dark hoodie, like a gray hoodie," Zimmerman told the 911 operator before he shot Martin.[80] A few days later, *Fox News* commentator Geraldo Rivera ignited widespread criticism when he lambasted the victim: "The hoodie is as much responsible for Trayvon Martin's death as George Zimmerman was."[81] In the weeks and months following Martin's death, a litany of activists turned their attention to debunking the stereotypical potency of hoodies. Daniel Maree, organizer of the Million Hoodie March in New York in honor of Trayvon Martin, created the march to reclaim the stigma of hoodies today: "I've had experiences where I've been walking down the street in New York, and as an African American man in a hoodie, I can tell you it's seen as incredibly suspicious. . . . [S]ome people hold their purses a little tighter. When I heard Trayvon was wearing a hoodie, I thought, I've felt this before."[82] Bobby Rush, former SNCC and Black Panther Party member and U.S. representative for Illinois's First Congressional District, staged his own form of protest in the House of Representatives when he stated: "I applaud the people all across the land who are making a statement about hoodies, about the real hoodlums in this nation, particularly those who tread on our laws wearing official or quasi-official clothes. Racial profiling has to stop, Mr. Speaker. Just because someone wears a hoodie does not make them a hoodlum."[83] By making such a profound statement, Rush simultaneously removed his jacket to reveal a gray hoodie and shortly after put the hood up. He was immediately interrupted by Representative Gregg Harper and was forced off the House floor for disobeying a rule that stipulates no hats or covering of the head in the chamber.

While Trayvon Martin's character was assassinated in the immediate aftermath of his death for wearing a hoodie, Tatyana Fazlalizadeh created a rehumanizing memorial in New York City that reclaimed the obscured and forgotten elements of Martin's personality—that he was a seventeen-year-old teenager who happened to wear a sweatshirt with a hood. At around twenty feet tall, this simple portrait of Trayvon Martin from the waist up stands as a poignant work of art in the streets of Manhattan. A peaceful, mournful aesthetic laces the mural as petals and flower buds rain from the sky. Debunking the "suspicious" hoodie that was deemed "as much responsible for Trayvon Martin's death as George Zimmerman," Fazlalizadeh used an almost white shade of gray to extract any remaining connotations of dark, ominous, or threatening inferred from the garment. The hood, enveloping the back of Martin's head, is depicted as perfectly open at the front to ensure that his young face is fully visible because he has nothing to hide. He is, and was, no threat, as the viewers can see. He remains calm, with no hint of fear on his face, and his gaze breaks the fourth wall as he stares intimately into the heart, mind, and soul of the viewer, tapping into their emotions with his innocent expression.

As the viewer breaks gaze with the victim, their eyes drift down to the writing on his hoodie—"Trayvon" it reads. In an act of reclamation, Fazlalizadeh used the hoodie not as an accomplice that led to the death of Martin but instead as a politically charged item of clothing forever imbued with the innocent memory of Trayvon. As the commemorative flowers fall from the sky, they ornament his frame, with only one small bud caressing his cheek where his tears of anguish, pain, and sorrow should be. Instead, a red flower head kisses his cheek. His life may have ended, but his memory is now immortalized. As the mural wallpapers the streets of the Lower East Side, the omission of a complex narrative—akin to those of the 1970s—in tandem with the stoic presence of Martin makes the mural a visual gravestone. The mural's purpose is to show how Trayvon Martin was not a threatening figure

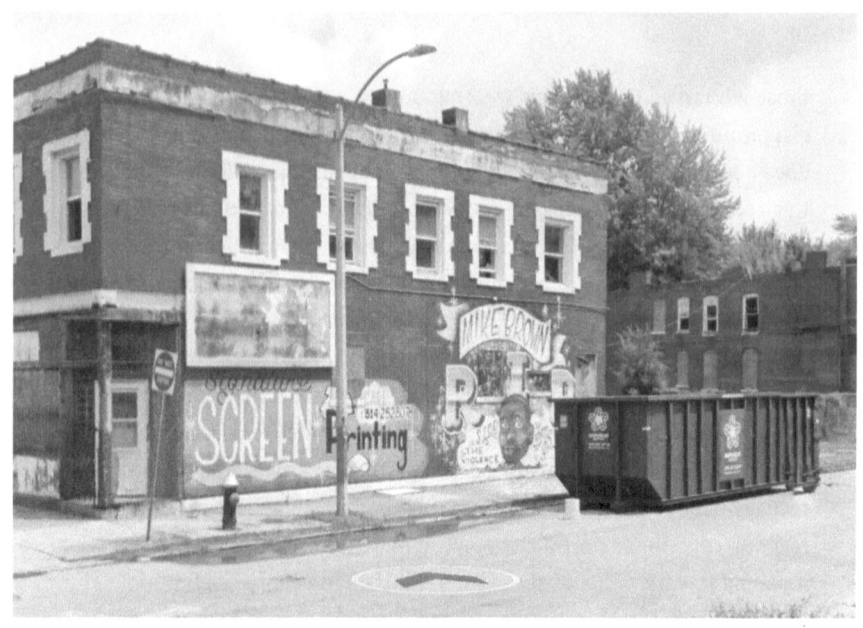

Michael Brown (2014). 1902 North Union Boulevard, St. Louis, Mo. Painted by Joe Ryan. Image from Google Maps, 2024.

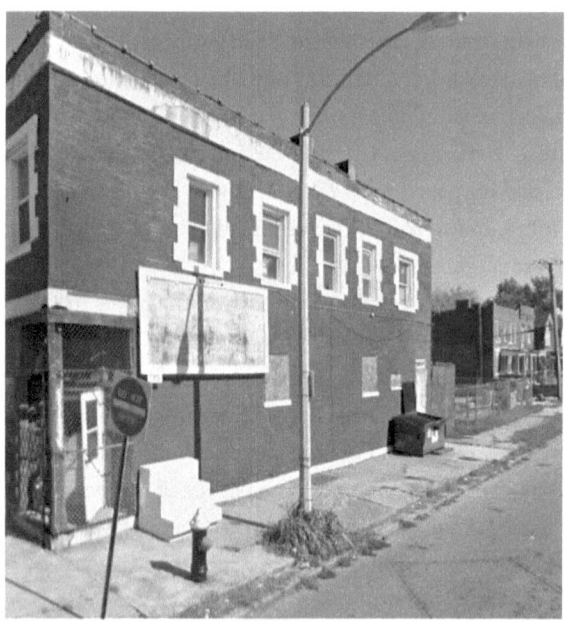

Blank wall. 1902 North Union Boulevard, St. Louis, Mo. Image from Google Maps, 2024.

who looked "real suspicious." Rather, he was a seventeen-year-old African American boy walking around the streets of his Twin Lakes Housing Community with a bottle of iced tea and a packet of Skittles, unaware that it was the last night of his life.

When doing research for this chapter, I often walked the streets of Google Maps to get a sense of each mural's location and to visualize where it stands. On a few instances, though, I was struck by something haunting. In Google Maps there is often a lapse in time when moving around the city. One minute the image could have been captured in 2021, while the next frame is in 2016. Playing with the temporality of the streets in this way and watching how they change over time is an interesting experience, but in the age of Black Lives Matter it is also an incredibly sobering one. When digitally standing on 1902 North Union Boulevard in St. Louis, looking up at a Michael Brown mural, I can see the mural at the intersection with Cote Brilliante Avenue. My screen tells me I'm currently in 2018. The mural looks colorful, proud, and untouched.

I move forward slightly to get a closer look. The mural vanishes.

My first thought is that the mural has been whitewashed and no longer exists. This wouldn't be surprising, given that murals are ephemeral, and their lifespan is occasionally only a few years long. It happens all the time, especially in the age of Black Lives Matter. But I glimpse the border of Google Maps and realize I'm in 2011. Right now, Michael Brown is still alive. At this moment in time on my screen, there's no mural here because his death is three years away and the world doesn't yet know his name or the untimely passing he will soon meet. I am struck by the painful reality of this moment and am reminded of a powerful statement from Michael Eric Dyson's *Long Time Coming*: "As is often the case for the Black dead, most of us got to know your name only after you were gone."[84]

In the streets of Black America—and not the Black corollary separated out from the rest of the country—Black lives are being lost at a vastly disproportionate rate. Wesley Lowery acknowledges that although several citizen journalists have attempted to count the number of people killed by police each year, it remains an insurmountable and near impossible task to undertake given the unavailability of data on national police violence.[85] But what remains undeniable is that the headlines of the Obama presidency read as a yearbook of Black death, speaking truth to what Dyson brings to our awareness: Most of us only know these names after acts of fatal violence.

But if the newspapers were the yearbooks, then so were the streets. When Oscar Grant was shot and killed by Johannes Mehserle in 2009, his death ushered in not only a new moment in a Black mural tradition arcing across the twentieth and twenty-first centuries but also a visual counterpart to the imminent Black Lives Matter movement yet to emerge after the killing of Trayvon Martin. Since 2009 the likenesses of victims such as Grant, Martin, Eric Garner, Freddie Gray, Alton Sterling, Sandra Bland, George Floyd, Elijah McClain, Ahmaud Arbery, and Breonna Taylor have wallpapered the streets across the country—and even across the world.

These murals, somewhat unintentionally, become part of the battleground for memory in America's streets, seeking to reclaim agency over the commemorative landscape currently plagued by the memories of white supremacy. These powerful murals curate spaces of communal activism in the streets, offering tangible rallying points for protests and demonstrations; and, more specifically, Black Lives Matter murals are often found at the sites of atrocity and death to embed the memory of police brutality victims back into their hometowns. And in response to the pervasive dehumanization and criminalization of police brutality victims, as well as the oversaturation and omnipresent circulation of Black death through social media and the news, murals in the age of Black Lives Matter undertake the important work of creating a visual afterlife that rehumanizes victims whose memory and life become distorted and denigrated.

Black Lives Matter murals are more than just paintings on a wall. They are someone's memory, someone's visual afterlife, and someone's unofficial gravestone embedded into the community in which they died. They are a memory layered onto the physical landscape of America demanding acknowledgment and offering a truthful reality about the disproportionate rate in which Black people are brutalized in the streets. Murals line walls to show the faces we only get to know after instances of violence, and they make sure we remember the names and faces of those lost lives. They physically mark the streets that are filled with the memories of civil rights marches and Black Power demonstrations, enveloping them with a message that throughout history has been demanded time and time again but that is still having to be shouted out today—that Black Lives Matter.

When Kimberlé Crenshaw tells her audiences of the overlooked stories of Black and trans women killed as a result of police and supremacist violence, she tells the listeners, "If we can't see a problem, we can't fix a problem." It is time for mourning and grief to become action and transformation, she continues. We must hold up these women, bear witness to them, and bring them into the light. "Do not allow her death to happen in silence. . . . [D]o not let them believe their lives were insignificant. . . . [T]he first step begins when we say her name."[86] Given the ubiquity of police and supremacist violence, it's near impossible to know every name lost to such injustice, but below are just some of the names of women that this book hopes to bear witness to, to bring into the light, and to take the steps to say their names.

Aiyanna Stanley Jones

Alberta Spruill

Alexia Christian

Atatiana Jefferson

Aura Rosser

Bettie "Betty Boo" Jones

Breonna Taylor

Charleena Chavonn Lyles

Danette Daniels

Darnisha Harris

Deborah Danner

Duanna Johnson

Eleanor Bumpurs

Frankie Ann Perkins

Gabriella Nevarez

Gynnya McMillen

India Beaty

India Kager

Janisha Fonville

Jessica Williams

Joyce Curnell

Kathryn Johnson

Kayla Moore

Kendra James

Kimani "KiKi" Gray

Kisha Michael

Korryn Gaines

Kyam Livingston

LaTanya Haggerty

Ma'Khia Bryant

Malissa Williams

Margaret LaVerne Mitchell

Meagan Hockaday

Michelle Cusseaux

Miriam Carey

Mya Hall

Natasha McKenna

Nizah Morris

Pearlie Golden

Ralkina Jones

Redel Jones

Rekia Boyd

Sandra Bland

Shantel Davis

Sharmel Edwards

Shelly Frey

Sheneque Proctor

Shereese Francis

Sonji Taylor

Symone Marshall

Tanisha Anderson

Tarika Wilson

Tyisha Miller

Yvette Smith

Telling the People's Story

Murals and the Movement for Black Liberation

Community public art practice was created to function as a public space
for symbolic free speech in neighborhoods—a space for expression.
    —*Kymberly Pinder*

The artist has an obligation to express his or her times, open up social
ills, express people's needs, community grievances—lay out the future
for the naked eye to see or not to see. Sometimes an individual has to go
to the wall many times before they see the message there, then the message or art becomes their property, something great to them. . . . Artists
are not to know when this happens, how could they? The job of painting
the mural is over and the artist has gone, only the painting remains, an
idea, or several ideas, some real, others unreal, to give one complete message to the people. If times change, and it will, and this mural does not
fill the needs of the people in the community, then I feel the mural should
be painted out and another one painted in its place.
    —*Mitchell Caton, artist (1975)*

I am doing what I am doing because I am trying to be worthy of my being.
I am trying to contribute what I can while I am here. . . . I wanted to be
worthy for being a part of humankind. . . . I wanted to be an artist to the
people. I've tried to do the best I could. I've tried to tell the truth.
    —*Bill Walker*

In the spring of 2022 I visited Chicago to finish my research for this book.
While I was there I met with journalist and mural documentarian Jeff Huebner. Because we shared an affinity for the power of murals, Jeff graciously
offered to drive me around the city to give me a glimpse into an artistic
past still gripping the city's cultural and environmental landscape. Weaving through block after block, we'd stop to contemplate Mexican, Puerto
Rican, Black, coalition, and corporate murals in neighborhoods across the

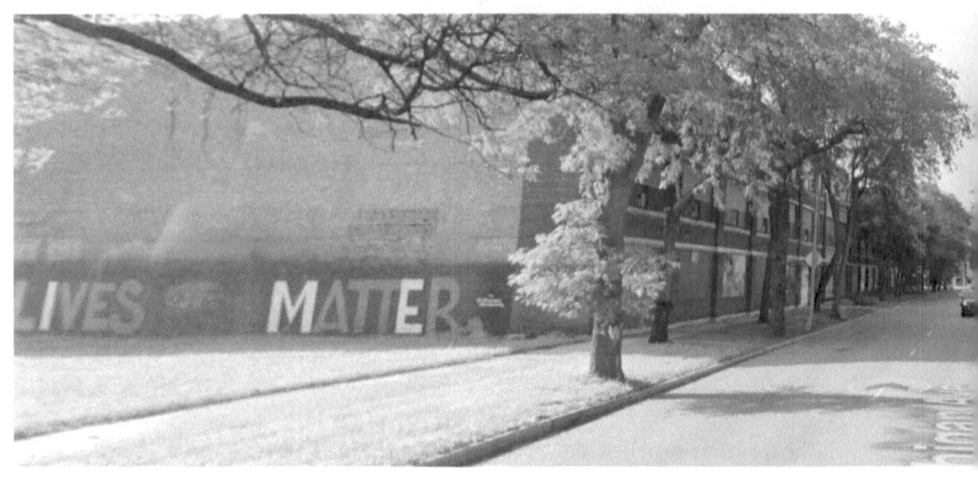

city—the Near North Side, Garfield Park, Wicker Park, Ukrainian Village, Near West Side, Pilsen, Chinatown, Bridgeport, Bronzeville. Jeff showed me around areas where murals such as Eugene "Eda" Wade's *Wall of Meditation* (1971) fell prey to gentrification and urban renewal in the city's Near North Side, and he showed me the sites where others such as Bill Walker's *All of Mankind: The Unity of the Human Race* (1971–74) had been whitewashed and removed from buildings and churches in the interest of business ventures and capitalistic gains. As we crossed the borders of the tessellating West Side neighborhoods, each with walls haunted by the ghosts (and sometimes faint outlines) of murals past, we found ourselves heading east into Bronzeville on the city's South Side. Jeff excitedly told me we were going to see some surviving murals from the heyday of Chicago's community mural movement in the 1970s and 1980s.

Crossing under the Dan Ryan Expressway, we made our way across the neighborhood until we reached 40th Street and Martin Luther King Drive. Pulling up at the side of the road next to a brightly colored wall, I contemplated it for a second before realizing it was C. Siddha Sila Webber's *Earth Is Not Our Home* mural from 1981. Although slightly reworked with new written statements and colors, the golden coin-like centerpiece was unmistakable. I had been writing about this mural from my office in Edinburgh, but I was finally standing right in front of it. I tore myself away for a moment to take in its surroundings. The streets were empty except for Jeff and me. Behind me stood another mural by Webber, his 1995 *Have a Dream* mural—only this time updated with an image of Obama. And faintly in the distance, as I glanced to my right-hand side northward up the city's concrete arteries, I

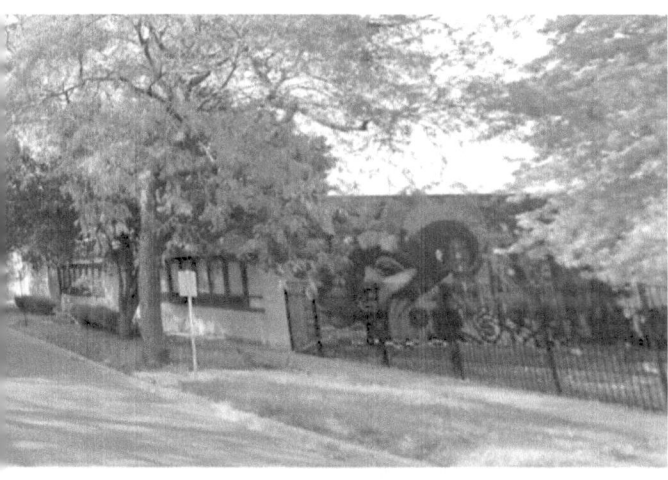

South Side Chicago street (2021), Elliot Donelley Youth Center, 3947 S. Michigan Avenue, Chicago, Ill. Image from Google Maps, 2024.

noticed the Willis Tower punctuating the city skyline. The skyscrapers and tourist traps of uptown Chicago felt incongruous to the historic murals of the Black South Side painted onto the walls in front of me.

We got back into the car; there was another stop to make, Jeff informed me. Driving back east along 40th Street, we stopped at the intersection with Michigan Avenue this time—a street that, if you let it carry you northward for five miles, will surround you with luxury apartments and high-end shops such as Burberry, Cartier, Rolex, and Tiffany & Company. But standing on Michigan Avenue next to the Elliot Donelley Youth Center in the heart of the South Side, I wasn't surrounded by commercial opulence. Instead, I felt like I was standing on the border of two moments of history. Looking northward along the tree-lined avenue, I was flanked by two murals. To my right, I could see a colorful purple and pinkish mural rising above the youth center's railings, painted on the back of the building, and facing a children's playground. It was Mitchell Caton and Calvin Jones's diasporic mural *Another Time's Voice Remembers My Passion's Humanity* from 1979, painted after the slow decline of the Black Power movement. And to my left, I could see a contemporary mural that included the words "Black Lives Matter" painted in green, red, and yellow lettering upon a black backdrop. The artist of this mural is anonymous, and the date it was created remains unknown—although it's likely to have been painted in the summer of 2020 after the murder of George Floyd.

Walking along a street in Chicago and being surrounded by two murals that live as part of the movement for Black liberation but that are temporally separated by forty years of history and protest felt striking. On one side of the road, *Another Time's Voice* offered a small glimmer into the aesthetic and visual context of the late 1970s and early 1980s. It was a time capsule of an earlier community mural movement. And on the other side of the road stood a reflection of the contemporary movement, artwork that holds up a mirror to society and gives the streets a stark and unshakeable reality check about the endemic racial violence stealing the lives of people of color today. Seeing these murals in direct conversation with one another drove home not only the longevity of the Black community mural movement throughout history but also its power and its demand. Murals are ephemeral. There's no permanence to them. They can vanish from the urban landscape without a trace. But they never do quite leave, because the people keep them alive.

This book isn't a finished product, and it couldn't possibly be. There's so much more work to be done to uncover the sheer volume of Black community murals in existence since the 1930s. But I hope this book inspires people not only to dig a little deeper into this astonishing artistic movement but also to stop and take in the murals of their local community—the ones that line their path on the way home, or on the way to work, or as they head to the shops. In a phone call with Eda in the early stages of writing this book, he told me how excited he was for it and how he hoped to read the finished product before he passes away—at eighty-one years old he wasn't getting any younger, he joked. The thought of someone telling his story by interviewing him and asking him about his life was, sadly, quite rare, he felt— only a handful of people had interviewed him, he told me, and sometimes people wrote about his life and story without even doing that. His emotional words were never far from my mind as I worked to complete this book, and it breaks my heart a little to think he was unable to read his story and his own words in print at last. Eda passed away in April 2021 on the day I signed the contract for this book. I hope I've been able to do justice to his words and to his work.

The movement for Black liberation is full of stories we don't yet know, and as time moves on, it takes the makers of history with it, so we need to seize these moments when we can. The muralists throughout this book—and the Black community mural movement more broadly—were and are brave, bold, and creative, and they sometimes placed their lives on the line to create artworks that inspired, empowered, and uplifted people. "We figure that, well, if we have to go out being shot or whatever, then OK," Eda told me of his time working on the *Wall of Truth* under the surveillance of the FBI. "We are committed to this, we aren't getting any money from it, but this is what we are committed to, so we are going to go ahead and do it. And if we have to go out whatever kind of way, OK, at least we got to do what we want to do."[1] Such dedication to art is rare, but from it beautiful work is born. These are artists who stood and still stand in the face of injustice, working with and for Black communities to create something powerful. Against the backdrop of Jim Crow, European Fascism, World War II, the Black Power movement, neoconservatism, the post–civil rights era, and Black Lives Matter, artists produced subversive, empowering, potent, heroic, historic, commemorative, revolutionary, groundbreaking, educational, challenging, poetic, and performative murals. These murals stood proudly on the walls of buildings to prove the sheer existence of Black life in America, and they expanded the imaginations of Black community members across the nation, transforming community walls, unquestionably, into monuments to Blackness.

NOTES

Introduction. The People's Art

Epigraphs are from Cederic J. Robinson and Elizabeth P. Robinson, preface to *Futures of Black Radicalism*, ed. Gaye Theresa Johnson and Alex Lubin (Verso, 2017), 3; Floyd Coleman, "Keeping Hope Alive: The Story of African American Murals," in *Walls of Heritage, Walls of Pride: African American Murals*, by Jim Prigoff and Robin Dunitz (Pomegranate Press, 2000), 10; Edmund Barry Gaither quoted in Prigoff and Dunitz, *Walls of Heritage*, 5.

1. East Side Voice of Independent Detroit, "ESVID Builds a New Wall: Detroit's Wall of Dignity," *The Ghetto Speaks*, April 22, 1968, copy courtesy of the Bentley Historical Library, University of Michigan, Ann Arbor.

2. Ibid.

3. Michael D. Harris, "Urban Totems: The Communal Spirit of Black Murals," in Prigoff and Dunitz, *Walls of Heritage*, 24.

4. Robin D. G. Kelley, *Freedom Dreams: The Black Radical Imagination* (Beacon Press, 2002), 10.

5. Ibid., 11.

6. Ibid., ix.

7. Quoted in Harris, "Urban Totems," 29.

8. Ibid.

9. For more information on these artistic forms, see Roland L. Freeman, *A Communion of the Spirits: African-American Quilters, Preservers and Their Stories* (Rutledge Hill Press, 1996); Gladys-Marie Fry, *Stitched from the Soul: Slave Quilts from the Antebellum South* (University of North Carolina Press, 1990); "A Description of William Wells Brown's Original Panoramic Views of the Scenes in the Life of an American Slave," Cornell University, https://digital.library.cornell.edu/catalog/ss:18167969; Laban Carrick Hill, *Dave the Potter: Artist, Poet, Slave* (Little, Brown Books for Young Readers, 2010); Michael A. Chaney, "Signifying Marks and the 'Not Counted' Inscriptions of Dave the Potter," *Arizona Quarterly* 72, no. 4 (Winter 2016): 1–25; Chaney, "Words, Wares, Names: Dave the Potter as American Archive," *Anglia* 138, no. 3 (2020): 449–67; and Chaney, *Where Is All My Relation? The Poetics of Dave the Potter* (Oxford University Press, 2018).

10. This was the same year Douglas was commissioned to paint a series of murals at Cravath Hall at Fisk University, Nashville. For an in-depth discussion of these murals, see Amy Helene Kirschke's chapter, "The Fisk Murals Revealed: Memories of Africa, Hope for the Future," in *Aaron Douglas: African American Modernist*, ed. Susan Earle (Yale University Press, 2007), 115–35.

11. Eva Cockroft, John Pitman Weber, and John Cockroft, *Towards a People's Art: The Contemporary Mural Movement* (E. P. Dutton, 1977), xxi.

12. Ibid.

13. Abdul Alkalimat, Romi Crawford and Rebecca Zorach, *The Wall of Respect: Public Art and Black Liberation in 1960s Chicago* (Northwestern University Press, 2017), 3.

14. Jeff W. Huebner, "William Walker's Walls of Prophecy and Protest," in *Art Against the Law*, ed. Rebecca Zorach (School of the Art Institute of Chicago, 2014), 31–46, 31.

15. Quoted in Janet Braun-Reinitz and Jane Weissman, *On the Wall: Four Decades of Community Murals in New York City* (University Press of Mississippi, 2009), xiv.

16. CNBC, "President Donald Trump on Charlottesville: You Had Very Fine People, on Both Sides," *YouTube*, 4:07, August 15, 2017, https://www.youtube.com/watch?v=JmaZR8E12bs.

17. Manning Marable, *Living Black History: How Reimagining the African-American Past Can Remake America's Racial Future* (Civitas Books, 2006), 22.

18. Ibid., 21.

19. Celeste-Marie Bernier, *Stick to the Skin: African American and Black British Art, 1965–2015* (University of California Press, 2018), 29.

20. Lippard quoted in ibid., 31.

21. Prigoff and Dunitz, *Walls of Heritage*, 8.

22. George Lipsitz, "What Is This Black in the Black Radical Tradition?," in *Futures of Black Radicalism*, ed. Gaye Theresa Johnson and Alex Lubin (Verso Books, 2017), 108–20, 111.

23. 1977, F10, Black Women's Mural Project (1), and 1977, F2.2, Black Women Emerging (11), DeVan, Chicago Public Art Group archives.

24. Southbank Centre, "Kimberlé Crenshaw—On Intersectionality—keynote—WOW 2016," *YouTube*, 30:46, 2016, https://www.youtube.com/watch?v=-DW4HLgYPlA.

25. Bernier, *Stick to the Skin*, 11.

26. Rebecca Zorach, *Art for People's Sake: Artists and Community in Black Chicago, 1965–1975* (Duke University Press, 2019), 7–9. In descriptions of Black or poor neighborhoods in the 1960s and 1970s, the term "ghetto" was often used, but today the term carries negative and racist connotations. While I use the term occasionally throughout this book, it remains only in quotation marks from direct statements from scholars, artists, and sociologists of the 1960s and 1970s.

1. Quoted in Stephanie Fox Knappe, "Chronology," in *Aaron Douglas: African American Modernist*, ed. Susan Earle (Yale University Press, 2007), 212.

2. Nico Wheadon, "Charles White: A Retrospective," *The Brooklyn Rail*, https://brooklynrail.org/2018/12/artseen/Charles-White-A-Retrospective.

3. Olive Jensen Theisen, *Walls That Speak: The Murals of John Thomas Biggers* (University of North Texas Press, 2010), 12.

4. Ibid., 13.

5. Ibid., 27.

6. James Prigoff and Robin Dunitz, *Walls of Heritage, Walls of Pride: African American Murals* (Pomegranate Press, 2000), 59.

7. Ibid., 26.

8. David Levering Lewis, *When Harlem Was in Vogue* (Penguin Books, 1979), 101.

9. Ibid., 102.

10. Amy Helene Kirschke, *Aaron Douglas: Art, Race & the Harlem Renaissance* (University Press of Mississippi, 1995), 39.

11. Quoted in Bridget R. Cooks, *Exhibiting Blackness: African Americans and the American Art Museum* (University of Massachusetts Press, 2011), 22.

12. Quoted in Cederic Dover, *American Negro Art* (New York Graphic Society, 1960), 31.

13. Nathan Irvin Huggins, *Harlem Renaissance* (1971; repr., Oxford University Press, 2007), 118.

14. Lewis, *When Harlem Was in Vogue*, 98.

15. Quoted in Kirschke, *Aaron Douglas*, 41.

16. Don McIlvaine quotation in Prigoff and Dunitz, *Walls of Heritage*, 66.

17. For an extensive examination into Walker's mural contribution across Chicago, see Jeff Huebner, *Walls of Prophecy and Protest: William Walker and the Roots of a Revolutionary Public Art Movement* (Northwestern University Press, 2019).

18. For more information on City Arts, see Eva Cockroft, John Pitman Weber, and John Cockroft, *Towards a People's Art: The Contemporary Mural Movement* (E. P. Dutton, 1977); and Janet Braun-Reinitz and Jane Weissman, *On the Wall: Four Decades of Community Murals in New York City* (University Press of Mississippi, 2009).

19. Alan Barnett, *Community Murals: The People's Art* (Art Alliance Press, 1984), 101.

20. Ibid., 78.

21. Ibid. For more information on the Chicano movement and the Chicano mural movement, see Eva Sperling Cockroft, *Signs from the Heart: California Chicano Murals* (University of New Mexico Press, 1993); Erin Curtis, Jessica Hough, and Guisela Latorre, *Murales Rebeldes! L.A. Chicana/Chicano Murals Under Siege* (Angel City Press, 2017); Mario T. García and Ellen McCracken, *Rewriting the Chicano Movement: New Histories of Mexican American Activism in the Civil Rights Era* (University of Arizona Press, 2021).

22. Barnett, *Community Murals*, 257.

23. Kymberly Pinder, *Painting the Gospel: Black Public Art and Religion in Chicago* (University of Illinois Press, 2016), 5.

24. Ibid., 24.

25. Barnett, *Community Murals*, 240.

26. Ibid., 229.

27. Ibid., 214.

28. Ibid., 215.

29. Ibid., 240.

30. Timothy W. Drescher, *San Francisco Murals: Community Creates Its Muse, 1914–1990* (Pogo Press, 1991), 36; Huebner, *Walls of Prophecy*, 214.

31. Cynthia Koch, "The Contest for American Culture: A Leadership Case Study on the NEA and NEH Funding Crisis," *Public Talk: Online Journal of Discourse Leadership* 2 (Fall 1998), https://www.upenn.edu/static/pnc/ptkoch.html.

32. Ibid.

33. Ibid.

34. Quoted in Braun-Reinitz and Weissman, *On the Wall*, xvii.

35. Michael D. Harris, "Urban Totems: The Communal Spirit of Black Murals," in Prigoff and Dunitz, *Walls of Heritage*, 38.

36. Quoted in ibid., 168.

37. Ibid.

38. Quoted in ibid., 177.

39. Quoted in ibid., 180.

40. Harris, "Urban Totems," 39.

41. Quoted in Prigoff and Dunitz, *Walls of Heritage*, 182.

42. Ibid.

43. Quoted in ibid., 110.

44. Ibid., 138.

Chapter 1. "I Had to Fight with My Brushes"

Epigraphs are from Stacy Morgan, *Rethinking Social Realism: African American Art and Literature, 1930–1953* (University of Georgia Press, 2004), 43; Lizzetta LeFalle-Collins, "Contribution of the American Negro to Democracy: A History Painting by Charles White," *International Review of African American Art* 12, no. 4 (1995): 39; Lizetta LeFalle-Collins and Shifra M. Goldman, *In the Spirit of Resistance: African American Modernists and the Mexican Muralist School* (American Federation of Art, 1996), 44.

1. The bondage over the economic mobility of African Americans in the 1930s is described by Paul Gardullo as "neo-slavery." See "'Just Keeps Rollin' Along': Rebellions, Revolts and Radical Black Memories of Slavery in the 1930s," *Patterns of Prejudice* 41, no. 3–4 (2007): 271–301, 272–75.

2. Susan Earle, "Harlem, Modernism, and Beyond: Aaron Douglas and His Role in Art/History," in *Aaron Douglas: African American Modernist*, ed. Susan Earle (Yale University Press, 2007), 5.

3. LeFalle-Collins, "Contribution of the American Negro," 40.

4. Morgan, *Rethinking Social Realism*, 43.

5. Oral history interview with Charles W. White, March 9, 1965, Archives of American Art, Smithsonian Institution.

6. Morgan, *Rethinking Social Realism*, 43.

7. "The Murals: Recreation in Harlem," Institute for Research in African-American Studies, http://iraas.columbia.edu/wpa/recreation.html.

8. Floyd Coleman quotation discussing Hale Woodruff's *Mutiny Aboard the Amistad 1839* (1939) in Michael D. Harris, "Urban Totems: The Communal Spirit of Black Murals," in *Walls of Heritage, Walls of Pride: African America Murals*, by James Prigoff and Robin Dunitz (Pomegranate Press, 2000), 24.

9. Alain Locke, *The American Negro: His History and Literature* (Arno Press and The New York Times, 1969), 43.

10. Alain Locke, *The New Negro: An Interpretation* (Albert and Charles Boni, 1925), 6.

11. Ibid., 14.

12. Ibid., 6.

13. Ibid., 11.

14. Gregory Sholette, "Review: Where Have All the Leftists Gone?," *Art Journal* 64, no. 4 (2005): 128; Mark Naison, *Communists in Harlem During the Depression* (University of Illinois Press, 2005), xvii.

15. Naison, *Communists in Harlem*, 11.

16. Mark Solomon, *The Cry Was Unity: Communists and African Americans, 1917–1936* (University Press of Mississippi, 1998), 234.

17. Jerry Adler, "1934: The Art of the New Deal," *Smithsonian*, June 2009, https://www.smithsonianmag.com/arts-culture/1934-the-art-of-the-new-deal-132242698/.

18. Jonathan Harris, *Federal Art and National Culture: The Politics of Identity in New Deal America* (Cambridge University Press, 1995), 14.

19. When the NRA aimed to eliminate cutthroat competition by bringing industry, government, and labor together to create "codes of fair practice," the codes themselves victimized African Americans. Throughout the South, the Urban League estimated that nearly three million Black workers were excluded through the manipulation of "loosely drawn codes and . . . the establishment of formal wage disparities in the South" (Solomon, *The Cry Was Unity*, 235).

20. Bill V. Mullen, *Popular Fronts: Chicago African-American Cultural Politics, 1935–46* (University of Illinois Press, 1999), 9.

21. Morgan, *Rethinking Social Realism*, 10; Mullen, *Popular Fronts*, 3. According to Paul Gardullo, the Black Belt thesis "stated that Blacks in the South comprised a separate nation over which they deserved total economic and legal control, whereas Blacks in the North had lost their southern folkways and required total assimilation into the working class. It appealed to many Blacks and attracted many of them into the orbit of the Communist Party" ("'Just Keeps Rollin' Along,'" 277n12). For a more in-depth analysis of the Black Belt thesis, see William J. Maxwell, *Old Negro, New Left:*

African American Writing and Communism Between the Wars (Columbia University Press, 1999).

22. Brian Dolinar, *The Black Cultural Front: Black Writers and Artists of the Depression Generation* (University Press of Mississippi, 2012), 3.

23. Ibid., 3.

24. Quoted in Morgan, *Rethinking Social Realism*, 42.

25. Aaron Douglas, "The Negro in American Culture," in *Artists Against War and Fascism: Papers of the First American Artists' Congress*, ed. Matthew Baigell and Julia Williams (Rutgers University Press, 1986), 83.

26. Ibid., 84.

27. Ibid., 83.

28. Ibid., 84.

29. In 1930 Douglas was approached by Fisk University in Nashville to create a series of murals in multiple rooms in the university's Cravath Library. These murals tell the story of Black life in Africa and America. For more information on these murals, see Amy Helene Kirschke's chapter "The Fisk Murals Revealed: Memories of Africa, Hope for the Future," in Earle, *Aaron Douglas*, 115–35.

30. Celeste-Marie Bernier, *African American Visual Arts* (Edinburgh University Press, 2008), 68.

31. Quoted in *Harlem Renaissance Reader*, ed. David Levering Lewis (Viking Penguin, 1994), 119.

32. Bernier, *African American Visual Arts*, 59.

33. Aaron Douglas—Writings—Lectures, "The Harlem Renaissance," March 8, 1971, roll #4520 Drawings, Aaron Douglas Papers, 1921–1973, Archives of American Art, Smithsonian Institution.

34. Earle, "Harlem, Modernism, and Beyond," 5.

35. Ibid., 41; Amy Helene Kirschke, *Aaron Douglas: Art, Race & the Harlem Renaissance* (University Press of Mississippi, 1995), 39.

36. Earle, "Harlem, Modernism, and Beyond," 27.

37. Kirschke, *Aaron Douglas*, 79.

38. Nathan Irvin Huggins, *Harlem Renaissance* (Oxford University Press, 2007), 85.

39. David Levering Lewis, *When Harlem Was in Vogue* (Penguin Books, 1979), 98.

40. Quoted in Lewis, *Harlem Renaissance Reader*, 120.

41. T. R. Poston, "MURALS and MARX," *New York Amsterdam News (1922–1938)*, November 24, 1934.

42. Ibid.

43. Quoted in Lewis, *Harlem Renaissance Reader*, 119.

44. Poston, "MURALS and MARX."

45. Ibid., 119. In 1931 nine African American teenagers were accused of raping two white women on a train in northern Alabama. A racially charged fight broke out on the train. The white men who started the fight were forced to leave the train. Enraged by this, they fabricated a fictitious story to instead place the nine African American teens at fault. Once the train reached Paint Rock, Alabama, it

was greeted by an angry mob, and the boys were charged with assault. Two white women riding the train faced charges of vagrancy and illegal sexual activity. To evade these charges, the nine boys were falsely accused of rape. The cases were tried in Scottsboro, Alabama, receiving national attention. Eight of the nine young men were sentenced to death, but this verdict led to protests throughout the North, leading the Supreme Court to overturn the convictions. After further retrials, the boys served a collective one hundred years in prison. The Communist Party ran a campaign to free the Scottsboro Boys: "Black and white Communists made the details of the Scottsboro case a part of the daily consciousness of the community until 'Scottsboro' became synonymous with southern racism repression and injustice" (Naison, *Communists in Harlem*, 57). For more information, see chapter 3 of Naison's *Communists in Harlem*; "The Scottsboro Boys," National Museum of African American History and Culture, March 15, 2017, https://nmaahc.si.edu/explore /stories/scottsboro-boys.

46. Poston, "MURALS and MARX."

47. Ibid.

48. Renée Ater, "Creating a Usable Past," in Earle, *Aaron Douglas*, 101. Ater has acknowledged how, coming at the height of the Great Depression, "these extravaganzas may have seemed inappropriate," but the fairs offered a sense of hope for the future. As author Robert Rydell argues, these fairs "were designed to restore popular faith in the vitality of the nation's economic and political system, and . . . in the ability of government, business, scientific and intellectual leaders to lead the country out of the depression to a new, racially exclusive, promised land of material abundance" (quoted in Ater, "Creating a Usable Past," 98).

49. Ibid., 100.

50. Ibid., 101.

51. Ibid., 102.

52. Ibid.

53. Jesse O. Thomas, *Negro Participation in the Texas Centennial Exposition* (Christopher Publishing House, 1938), 86.

54. Collectively, the four mural cycles depicted certain stages of the development and progress of African Americans in the United States. One mural depicted the African American role in the state of Texas, portraying Estevanico, a Black explorer who explored the early lands of Texas. There are no images of this mural, and the mural no longer exists. The other mural to survive, along with *Into Bondage*, is *Aspiration*. Depicting exceptional Black life in the United States, the mural shows the contributions African Americans have made in the fields of science, literature, and music. Douglas painted all four murals on site, but no information from Douglas exists on the series. Although he wrote extensively about his other mural cycles, he left no notes or descriptions on the Texas Centennial murals. See Thomas, *Negro Participation*, 102; Ater, "Creating a Usable Past," 105.

55. Ater, "Creating a Usable Past," 102.

56. Kirschke, *Aaron Douglas*, 124.

57. Douglas, "The Negro in American Culture," 83; Poston, "MURALS and MARX."

58. Quoted in Gardullo, "'Just Keeps Rollin' Along,'" 292.

59. Thomas, *Negro Participation*, 27.

60. Quoted in ibid., 26.

61. Ater, "Creating a Usable Past," 104.

62. Joel Bresler, "What the Lyrics Mean," Follow the Drinking Gourd: A Cultural History, accessed April 11, 2016, http://www.followthedrinkinggourd.org.

63. Gardullo, "'Just Keeps Rollin' Along,'" 277.

64. Quoted in ibid., 292.

65. Quoted in Celeste-Marie Bernier, "'The Slave Ship Imprint': Representing the Body, Memory, and History in Contemporary African American and Black British Painting, Photography, and Installation Art," *Callaloo* 37, no. 4 (2014): 990.

66. Quoted in Celeste-Marie Bernier, *Characters of Blood: Black Heroism in the Transatlantic Imagination* (University of Virginia Press, 2012), 56.

67. Aaron Douglas, letter, reel 4520, Aaron Douglas Papers, owned by Fisk University Special Collections, microfilmed by Archives of American Art, Smithsonian Institution.

68. Poston, "MURALS and MARX."

69. Jonathan Harris, *Federal Art and National Culture: The Politics of Identity in New Deal America* (Cambridge University Press, 1995), 14.

70. Gary Kamiya, "How Coit Tower's Murals Became a Target for Anti-Communist Forces," *San Francisco Chronicle*, September 23, 2018, https://www.sfchronicle.com/chronicle_vault/article/How-Coit-Tower-s-murals-became-a-target-for-11273933.php.

71. Quoted in Lizetta LeFalle-Collins and Shifra M. Goldman, *In the Spirit of Resistance: African American Modernists and the Mexican Muralist School* (American Federation of Art, 1996), 44, 12.

72. Ibid., 11.

73. Ibid., 12.

74. Quoted in ibid., 33. In 1933, at the Rockefeller Center in New York City, Diego Rivera painted his infamous mural *Man at the Crossroads*. The mural was controversial because of its inclusion of Lenin and a Soviet May Day parade. Nelson Rockefeller ordered the mural's destruction before it was even finished. For more information, see "Man at the Crossroads by Diego Rivera," Diego Rivera, https://www.diegorivera.org/man-at-the-crossroads.jsp.

75. Quoted in LeFalle-Collins and Goldman, *In the Spirit of Resistance*, 56.

76. Morgan, *Rethinking Social Realism*, 3.

77. Ibid.

78. For an expansive, comprehensive, and in-depth account of African Americans and social realism, see Stacy Morgan's unparalleled book *Rethinking Social Realism*.

79. The Chicago Renaissance is often overshadowed by the East Coast Harlem Renaissance, but from the 1930s to the 1950s, Black Chicago experienced a cultural

renaissance of flourishing art, literature, theater, poetry, music, and dance. It included people such as Arna Bontemps, Gwendolyn Brooks, Elizabeth Catlett, Walter Ellison, Gordon Parks, Charles White, and Richard Wright. For more information on the Chicago Renaissance, see Darlene Clark Hine and John McCluskey Jr., eds., *The Black Chicago Renaissance* (University of Illinois Press, 2012); Richard A. Courage and Christopher Robert Reed, eds., *Roots of the Black Chicago Renaissance: New Negro Writers, Artists and Intellectuals* (University of Illinois Press, 2020); Davarian L. Baldwin, *Chicago's New Negroes: Modernity, the Great Migration, and Black Urban Life* (University of North Carolina Press, 2007).

80. Quoted in Erik S. Gellman, "Chicago's Native Son: Charles White and the Laboring of the Black Renaissance," in Hine and McCluskey, *Black Chicago Renaissance*, 152.

81. While White didn't join the CPUSA, that didn't stop the FBI from opening surveillance files on him. Due to his political leanings and leftist friends, White was summoned to testify at a hearing of the House Un-American Activities Committee (HUAC), but this summons was revoked quickly and mysteriously. See "Charles White (1918–1979)," Michael Rosenfeld Gallery, https://www.michaelrosenfeldart.com/artists/charles-white-1918-1979.

82. Charles White, interview with Peter Clothier, September 1979, Altadena, California, quoted in Melanie Anne Herzog, *Elizabeth Catlett: An American Artist in Mexico* (University of Washington Press, 2000), 27.

83. LeFalle-Collins, "Contribution of the American Negro," 39.

84. This information comes from ibid. See also Breanne Robertson, "Pan-Americanism, Patriotism, and Race Pride in Charles White's Hampton Mural," *American Art* 30, no. 1 (2016); chapter 2 of Morgan, *Rethinking Social Realism*; and *Charles White: Art and Soul*, special issue of *Freedomways* 20, no. 3 (1980), https://www.jstor.org/stable/pdf/community.28037052.pdf.

85. Quoted in Morgan, *Rethinking Social Realism*, 48.

86. Richard J. Powell and Jock Reynolds, *To Conserve a Legacy: American Art from Historically Black Colleges and Universities* (Addison Gallery of American Art, 1999), 11.

87. Roll #3189, Charles W. White Papers, 1933–1987, bulk 1960s–1970s, Archives of American Art, Smithsonian Institution.

88. John Pittman, "He Was an Implacable Critic of His Own Creations," *Freedomways* 20, no. 3 (1980): 187.

89. Quoted in Bernier, *African American Visual Arts*, 130.

90. White oral history interview.

91. Bernier, *African American Visual Arts*, 131.

92. Morgan, *Rethinking Social Realism*, 56.

93. Kenneth S. Greenberg, ed., *Nat Turner: A Slave Rebellion in History and Memory* (Oxford University Press, 2003), xi.

94. Robertson, "Pan-Americanism," 52.

95. Morgan, *Rethinking Social Realism*, 64.

96. Quoted in Ruth Needleman, *Black Freedom Fighters in Steel: The Struggle for Democratic Unionism* (Cornell University Press, 2003), 1.

97. Morgan, *Rethinking Social Realism*, 67.

98. Quoted in Robertson, "Pan-Americanism," 72n48.

99. Morgan, *Rethinking Social Realism*, 67.

100. Quoted in LeFalle-Collins, "Contribution of the American Negro," 39; roll #3189, 8, White Papers.

Chapter 2. "The WALL Is for Black People"

Epigraphs are from Larry Neal, "Any Day Now: Black Art and Black Liberation," in *Black Poets and Prophets: A Bold, Uncompromisingly Clear Blueprint for Black Liberation*, ed. Woodie King and Earl Anthony (Signet Classics, 1972), 148; interviews of AfriCOBRA founders 2010, Archives of American Art, Smithsonian Institution; *Greater Milwaukee Star*, July 11, 1970, 7.

1. *Greater Milwaukee Star*, February 22, 1969, 15.

2. Ibid.

3. Rebecca Zorach, *Art for People's Sake: Artist and Community in Black Chicago, 1965–1975* (Duke University Press, 2019), 56.

4. Carol Adams quotation in Tony Smith, "BLACK IS BEAUTIFUL . . . (Reflections on the Wall of Respect)," YouTube, 00:24, May 6, 2015, https://www.youtube.com/watch?v=hvxSRfpRauc&t=1s.

5. While the *Wall of Respect* is often alluded to in passing detail in scholarship, in 2017 Abdul Alkalimat, Romi Crawford, and Rebecca Zorach edited a groundbreaking and comprehensive book on the history of the wall titled *The Wall of Respect: Public Art and Black Liberation in 1960s Chicago* (Northwestern University Press, 2017). Paralleling the rise of Black street muralism was the Chicana/Chicano mural movement. For more information, see Alan Barnett, *Community Murals: The People's Art* (Art Alliance Press, 1984); and Eva Sperling Cockcroft and Holly Barnet-Sanchez, *Signs from the Heart: California Chicano Murals* (University of New Mexico Press, 1990); Erin Curtis, Jessica Hough, and Guisela Latorre, *Murales Rebeldes! L.A. Chicana/Chicano Murals Under Siege* (Angel City Press, 2017); Mario T. García and Ellen McCracken, *Rewriting the Chicano Movement: New Histories of Mexican American Activism in the Civil Rights Era* (University of Arizona Press, 2021).

6. Peniel E. Joseph, *Dark Days, Bright Nights: From Black Power to Barack Obama* (Civitas, 2010), 4.

7. Peniel E. Joseph, "Rethinking the Black Power Era," *Journal of Southern History* 75, no. 3 (2009): 707–16, 710.

8. Rhonda Y. Williams, "Black Women, Urban Politics, and Engendering Black Power," in *The Black Power Movement: Rethinking the Civil Rights-Black Power Era*, ed. Peniel E. Joseph (Routledge, 2006), 79–103, 82.

9. Joseph, "Rethinking the Black Power Era," 715.

10. Michael Harris interview 2, interviews of AfriCOBRA founders, 2010, Archives of American Art, Smithsonian Institution.

11. Unstripped Voices, "One of Dr. Martin Luther King's SCARIEST Marches

(Chicago, 1966)," October 29, 2019, *YouTube*, https://www.youtube.com/watch?v=H1hTocshzQQ.

12. "MLK in Chicago," *Chicago Tribune*, January 18, 2010, *YouTube*, https://www.youtube.com/watch?v=BKbpYXCibzQ.

13. George Lipsitz, *How Racism Takes Place* (Temple University Press, 2011), 14.

14. Richard Rothstein, *The Color of Law: A Forgotten History of How Our Government Segregated America* (Liveright, 2017), 78.

15. Twin Cities PBS, "Redlining and Racial Covenants: Jim Crow of the North," August 4, 2019, *YouTube*, 8:00, https://www.youtube.com/watch?v=ymOaiWla3DU.

16. Ibid. It's important to note that while African American families are the main target of racially restrictive covenants, they weren't the only racial and minority group subjected to these practices. From the early twentieth century, racially restrictive covenants were used to also prevent Latinx, Asian American, Jewish American, and Middle Eastern families from purchasing or living in homes among white families. See "Racial Restriction and Housing Discrimination in the Chicagoland Area," Digital Chicago: Lake Forest College, https://digitalchicagohistory.org/exhibits/show/restricted-chicago/restrictive_covenants.

17. Zorach, *Art for People's Sake*, 34.

18. The Great Migration in the United States saw the movement of approximately six million African Americans from the South to the Northern, Western, and Midwestern states from roughly the 1910s to the 1970s. The catalyst for the migration was to escape the horrors of Jim Crow, lynching, and supremacist violence plaguing the South and to pursue the economic and educational freedom promised in the North.

19. Arnold Hirsch, *Making the Second Ghetto: Race and Housing in Chicago, 1940–1960* (University of Chicago Press, 1983), 10.

20. Chicago is commonly used as a case study for examining Black life, housing, and segregation in the post–World War II era. Scholarship such as St. Clair Drake and Horace R. Cayton's *Black Metropolis: A Study of Negro Life in a Northern City* (University of Chicago Press, 1945); Hirsch's *Making the Second Ghetto*; Mary Pattillo-McCoy's *Black Picket Fences: Privilege and Peril Among the Black Middle Class* (University of Chicago Press, 1999); Mary E. Pattillo's *Black on the Block: The Politics of Race and Class in the City* (University of Chicago Press, 2007); and Rashad Shabazz's *Spatializing Blackness: Architectures of Confinement and Black Masculinity in Chicago* (University of Illinois Press, 2015) all analyze Chicago's Black neighborhoods to understand how racial and spatial lines were drawn in a city that experienced one of the greatest increases in Black population during the Great Migration. Chicago becomes a prominent case study not just because it represented a pattern of segregation and urban renewal that was witnessed in other cities across the North but also because, as Hirsch identifies, Chicago was "a persistent pioneer in the developing concepts and devices that were later incorporated into federal legislation defining the national renewal effort. The tools that were developed to

control and mitigate the consequences of racial succession in Chicago were thus made available to the country at large," and many cities used these tools. The legal framework for the national urban renewal effort, suggests Hirsch, was forged by the racial struggles experienced in Chicago's South Side (*Making the Second Ghetto*, xxii, 10).

21. Ibid.

22. Rothstein, *The Color of Law*, 32.

23. "Part IX: Civil Rights and the Cities, Chapter 1—Civil Rights in the Urban Context," 29, January 1, 1961–December 31, 1961, folder 103963-004-0716, Civil Rights Movement and the Federal Government: Records of the U.S. Commission on Civil Rights, Police-Community Relations in Urban Areas, 1954–1966, https://www.archives.gov/findingaid/stat/discovery/453.

24. Aliyah Dunn-Salahuddin, "A Forgotten Community, a Forgotten History: San Francisco's 1966 Urban Uprising," in *The Strange Careers of the Jim Crow North: Segregation and Struggle Outside of the South*, ed. Brian Purnell, Jeanne Theoharis, and Komozi Woodard (New York University Press, 2019), 217.

25. Lipsitz, *How Racism Takes Place*, 7.

26. Kymberly N. Pinder, *Painting the Gospel: Black Public Art and Religion in Chicago* (University of Illinois Press, 2016), 141.

27. Hirsch, *Making the Second Ghetto*, xx.

28. Raúl Homero Villa, *Barrio-Logos: Space and Place in Urban Chicano Literature and Culture* (University of Texas Press, 2000), 5.

29. Lipsitz, *How Racism Takes Place*, 60.

30. Ibid.

31. Kenneth Clark, *Dark Ghetto: Dilemmas of Social Power* (Lowe and Brydone, 1965), 11.

32. Quoted in James Prigoff and Robin Dunitz, *Walls of Heritage, Walls of Pride: African American Murals* (Pomegranate Press, 2000), 124.

33. Barnett, *Community Murals*, 78.

34. Robin D. G. Kelley, *Freedom Dreams: The Black Radical Imagination* (Beacon Press, 2002), 11.

35. Larry Neal, "New Space: The Growth of Black Consciousness in the Sixties," in *The Black Seventies*, ed. Floyd Barbour (Sargent Porter, 1970), 12.

36. Ibid., 25.

37. Quoted in Don L. Lee, "Tomorrow Is Tomorrow If You Want One," in *Black Fire: An Anthology of Afro-American Writing*, ed. Amiri Baraka and Larry Neal (Black Classic Press, 1968), 245.

38. Larry Neal, "Any Day Now: Black Art and Black Liberation," in *Black Poets and Prophets: A Bold, Uncompromisingly Clear Blueprint for Black Liberation*, ed. Woodie King and Earl Anthony (Signet Classics, 1972), 154.

39. Quoted in Abraham Chapman, *New Black Voices: An Anthology of Contemporary Afro-American Literature* (Penguin, 1972), 560.

40. Ibid., 560, 563.

41. Neal, "New Space," 15.

42. Hoyt Fuller, "Towards a Black Aesthetic," in *The Black Aesthetic*, ed. Addison Gayle Jr. (Anchor Books, 1972), 8.

43. Ibid.

44. This quote comes from Ron Karenga's essay "On Black Art," in which he discusses the importance of revolutionary art. Ron Karenga, "On Black Art," Modern American Poetry, accessed March 20, 2018, http://www.english.illinois.edu/maps /blackarts/documents.htm.

45. David Driskell, "An Artist Recounts the Creative Lead and Move into the 1960s," box 1, Jeff Donaldson Papers, ca. 1960–2005, Archives of American Art, Smithsonian Institution.

46. Lipsitz, *How Racism Takes Place*, 60.

47. Murals were not the only cultural form emerging in Chicago during this period. The city was a hotbed of artistic activity from poetry, dance, theater, and artwork as well as writers, essayists, and street performers. For more information on the artistic landscape of Chicago in the 1960s and 1970s, see Rebecca Zorach's groundbreaking work *Art for People's Sake*.

48. OBAC was made up of three main arms, a visual arts workshop, a writers' workshop, and a drama workshop. For more information on OBAC, its inception, and its gender makeup, see chapter 2 of Jonathan Fenderson's book *Building the Black Arts Movement: Hoyt Fuller and the Cultural Politics of the 1960s* (University of Illinois Press, 2019); and Alkalimat, Crawford, and Zorach, *The Wall of Respect*.

49. Quoted in Zorach, *Art for People's Sake*, 21.

50. Fenderson, *Building the Black Arts Movement*, 104.

51. Jeff Huebner, *Walls of Prophecy and Protest: William Walker and the Roots of a Revolutionary Public Art Movement* (Northwestern University Press, 2019), 52.

52. Ibid., 5.

53. Author's telephone interview with Eugene "Eda" Wade, April 7, 2018.

54. Author's telephone interview with Eugene "Eda" Wade, June 1, 2017.

55. Alkalimat, Crawford, and Zorach, *The Wall of Respect*, 97.

56. Jeff Donaldson quotation in Margo Natalie Crawford, "Black Light on the *Wall of Respect*," in *New Thoughts on the Black Arts Movement*, ed. Lisa Gail Collins and Margo Natalie Crawford (Rutgers University Press, 2006), 26.

57. Jeff Donaldson Papers, ca. 1960–2005, Archives of American Art, Smithsonian Institution.

58. Elijah Muhammad complained about having his face displayed on a mural next to his former protégé, Malcolm X, who held a prominent position next to Marcus Garvey, Stokely Carmichael, and H. Rap Brown. Walker was asked by the Nation of Islam to paint over the prophet's likeness under threat of being sued. Crawford, "Black Light," 26.

59. Ibid., 25.

60. Julian Mayfield, "You Touch My Black Aesthetic and I'll Touch Yours," in *The Black Aesthetic*, ed. Addison Gayle Jr. (Anchor Books, 1972), 26.

61. Barbara Jones-Hogu, interviews of AfriCOBRA founders, 2010, Archives of American Art, Smithsonian Institution.

62. Wade interview, June 1, 2017.

63. The African Commune of Bad Relevant Artists (AfriCOBRA) was founded in 1968 by Jeff Donaldson, Barbara Jones-Hogu, Jae and Wadsworth Jarrell, and Gerald Williams. The focus of artwork from the arts collective was about creating "social content–message-oriented art" that included "traditional African art forms." Concerned with empowering Black communities under a collective "black aesthetic," AfriCOBRA wanted their art to "mean something for black people" and for it to be functional and to "communicate to its viewer a statement of truth, of action, of education, of conditions and a state of being to our people" (Robert L. Douglas, *Wadsworth Jarrell: The Artist as Revolutionary* [Pomegranate Artbooks, 1996], 28–29). For more information, see AFRICOBRA: *Experimental Art Toward a School of Thought* (Duke University Press, 2020).

64. According to Eda, the incident was something Walker felt guilty about until he passed away, and before Eda passed away in April 2021, he made attempts to reconnect with members of OBAC: "I did make peace with Wadsworth Jarrell, because we were lecturing together and he was disagreeing on everything I had said, and I was disagreeing on everything he had said and then the end result, I know he would never come up to me and tell me. I walked up to him and said, 'Look Wadsworth, perhaps in our next life, we can be brothers.' So that kind of broke the ice, and we started talking and we talked and we talked and we talked. . . . And Roy Lewis . . . was mad as hell with me also, and so I did the same thing with him. After we had finished discussing and talking, I walked up to him and said, 'Roy, you know, probably one day we can become brothers.' So we started talking and one thing led to another and before we left, because we were living in the same hotel they put us up in, he came over and we started talking and he wished me luck and whatever. But I would have done that with Jeff and all of them" (Wade interview, June 1, 2017).

65. Faheem Majeed quotation in Eugene Wade, "Eugene 'Eda' Wade Talk About the 2nd Phase of the Wall of Respect," *YouTube*, 03:43, June 7, 2015, https://www.youtube.com/watch?v=1A3UzjQVDMg.

66. Florynce "Flo" Kennedy is frequently omitted from discussions of Eda's section of the mural, with people focusing on Malcolm X, H. Rap Brown, and Stokely Carmichael, but during a phone conversation with Eda, after I asked about the female figure in his section, he said, "Nobody's ever said anything in reference to who that is or what she did. Perhaps I should have mentioned it before now, but you know, it was always Malcolm X and H. Rap Brown and Stokely Carmichael. . . . She was amazing. She helped defend H. Rap Brown one time in court. She also helped Bird—that is, Charlie Parker—with his royalties and those kinds of things. If you read about her, you'll see what she was about, and nobody ever asked about her, and up until recently I just started talking about her, and I know she's important in terms

of representative of the Black woman as well as in terms of her contribution, you see" (Wade interview, April 7, 2018). For more information on Kennedy, see Sherie M. Randolph, *Florynce "Flo" Kennedy: The Life of a Black Feminist Radical*, Gender and American Culture series (University of North Carolina Press, 2015).

67. Interviews of AfriCOBRA founders, 2010, Archives of American Art, Smithsonian Institution.

68. Crawford, "Black Light," 30.

69. Ibid.

70. Ibid.

71. Dan Cameron, Richard Powell, and Michele Wallace, *Dancing at the Louvre: Faith Ringgold's French Collection and Other Story Quilts* (University of California Press, 1998), 162.

72. The line "Afrikan velvet" skin comes from Gwendolyn Brooks's poem "An Aspect of Love, Alive in the Ice and Fire" (1971). She writes about how the African velvet skin is "a physical light in the room" (Crawford, "Black Light," 30–40n25).

73. Ibid., 30.

74. Wade interview, June 1, 2017.

75. Interviews of AfriCOBRA founders, 2010, Archives of American Art, Smithsonian Institution.

76. Ibid.

77. Alkalimat, Crawford, and Zorach, *The Wall of Respect*, 41.

78. Wade interview, June 1, 2017.

79. Zorach, *Art for People's Sake*, 5.

80. Ibid.

81. Oral history interview with William Walker, June 12–14, 1991, 33, Archives of American Art, Smithsonian Institution.

82. Alkalimat, Crawford, and Zorach, *The Wall of Respect*, 51.

83. Quoted in Smith, "BLACK IS BEAUTIFUL," 00:56.

84. Quoted in Huebner, *Walls of Prophecy and Protest*, 68.

85. Crawford, "Black Light," 26; Alkalimat, Crawford, and Zorach, *The Wall of Respect*, 108.

86. Norman Parish III, "The Wall of Respect: How Chicago Artists Gave Birth to the Ethnic Mural," *Chicago Tribune*, August 23, 1992, in Alkalimat, Crawford, and Zorach, *The Wall of Respect*, 323.

87. Walker oral history interview.

88. Tony Smith, "Dr. Haki R. Madhubuti . . . Hero's on the Wall of Respect," *YouTube*, 06:24, August 22, 2016, https://www.youtube.com/watch?v=fVqVOr6UHFE.

89. Wade interview, April 7, 2018.

90. Jeff Donaldson, "Upside the Wall: An Artist's Retrospective Look at the Original 'Wall of Respect,'" in *The People's Art: Black Murals, 1967–1976* (African American Historical and Cultural Museum, 1986).

91. Robert Sengstacke interview, interviews of AfriCOBRA founders, 2010, Archives of American Art, Smithsonian Institution.

92. Alkalimat, Crawford, and Zorach, *The Wall of Respect*, 30.

93. Jeff Donaldson in ibid., 295.

94. Fenderson, *Building the Black Arts Movement*, 68.

95. Group interview: Barbara Jones Hogu, Napoleon Jones Henderson, Howard Mallory, Carolyn Lawrence, Michael Harris, interviews of AfriCOBRA founders, 2010, Archives of American Art, Smithsonian Institution.

96. Alkalimat, Crawford, and Zorach, *The Wall of Respect*, 322.

97. Group interview, Archives of American Art, Smithsonian Institution.

98. Ibid.

99. Huebner, *Walls of Prophecy and Protest*, 110.

100. Quoted in Jeff Huebner, "Bill Walker and the Roots of a Revolutionary Public Arts Movement." This manuscript has now been published as Huebner's *Walls of Prophecy and Protest*. Some quotations from the manuscript may not appear directly the same in the published version of the book and hence have been quoted directly as the unpublished manuscript with the original working title.

101. Huebner, *Walls of Prophecy and Protest*, 110.

102. Ibid., emphasis in the original.

103. Quoted in Benjamin Looker, *Point from Which Creation Begins: The Black Artists' Group of St. Louis* (Missouri Historical Society Press, 2004), 26.

104. Ibid.

105. Ibid.

106. As Alan Barnett writes in his seminal work *Community Murals*, the sponsorship for these murals was one of the first instances of government support for murals, and upon seeing the prideful and radical imagery on the walls, government sponsorship quickly became more hesitant and deliberate about what it offered funding to. See Alan Barnett, *Community Murals: The People's Art* (Art Alliance Press, 1984), 58. For more information on the Summerthing program, see Maura Greaney, "The Power of the Urban Canvas," *New England Journal of Public Policy* 18, no. 1 (2002).

107. Quoted in Thomas H. Shepard, "Exodus Building Hub Artists Canvas," *New England News Clip*, July 25, 1968, Dana Chandler Papers, 1968–1993, Archives of American Art, Smithsonian Institution.

108. "Dana C. Chandler Jr., Pan-African Artist and Lecturer on Art, Sex, Politics, and Revolution," *Mindblower*, roll #3195, Charles W. White Papers, 1933–1987, bulk 1960s–1970s, Archives of American Art, Smithsonian Institution.

109. Ibid., 10.

110. Getty Research Institute, "Oral History on Painting: Dana Chandler, Nelson Stevens, William T. Williams, Randy Williams," *YouTube*, 03:30, April 7, 2020, https://www.youtube.com/watch?v=ZiAMuduzoHk&t=208s.

111. Barnett, *Community Murals*, 58.

112. Shepard, "Exodus Building Hub Artists Canvas."

113. "Dana C. Chandler Jr., Pan-African Artist."

114. Quoted in Prigoff and Dunitz, *Walls of Heritage*, 129.

115. Ibid.

116. Ibid.

117. Shepard, "Exodus Building Hub Artists Canvas."

118. *The Milean* (Miles College), October 1, 1969, box 1, Jeff Donaldson Papers, ca. 1960–2005, Archives of American Art, Smithsonian Institution.

119. Ibid.

120. Subhead is from "Emerging Black Woman: Dedicated," 1977, F.2—Black Women Emerging (11), DeVann, Chicago Public Art Group Archives.

121. Chenoa Baker, "Vanita Green: Occupying a Space on Her Own Terms," *Sixty Inches from Center*, January 20, 2022, https://sixtyinchesfromcenter.org/vanita -green-occupying-a-space-on-her-own-terms/.

122. Ibid. For more information on Vanita Green and her life, see Chenoa Baker, "Words, a Love Offering: Rosanna, Alexis, and Carmen's Account of Vanita Green," *Sixty Inches from Center*, March 20, 2023, https://sixtyinchesfromcenter.org/words-a -love-offering-rosanna-alexis-and-carmens-account-of-vanita-green/.

123. Baker, "Words, a Love Offering."

124. Kimberly Springer, "Black Feminists Respond to Black Power Masculinism," in Joseph, *The Black Power Movement*, 107.

125. Ashley D. Farmer, *Remaking Black Power: How Black Women Transformed an Era* (University of North Carolina Press, 2017), 4.

126. Rhonda Y. Williams, "Black Women, Urban Politics, and Engendering Black Power," in Joseph, *The Black Power Movement*, 81.

127. 1975, F10, Black Women's Mural Project (1), and 1977, F2.2, Black Women Emerging (11), DeVan, Chicago Public Art Group archives.

128. Ibid.

129. Ibid.

130. Ibid.

131. Bill Walker and Mitchell Caton helped DeVan with donations for the mural and the protection of it.

132. "Emerging Black Women, Dedicated, September 3, 1977," 1977, F2.2, Black Women Emerging (11), DeVan, Chicago Public Art Group archives.

133. Ibid.

134. Ibid., 2.

135. Ibid.

136. Ibid.

137. Farmer, *Remaking Black Power*, 4.

138. For more information on Black women and Black Power, see ibid.; Kimberly Springer, "Black Feminists Respond to Black Power Masculinism," in Joseph, *The Black Power Movement*, 105–19; and Rhonda Y. Williams, "Black Women, Urban Politics, and Engendering Black Power," in Joseph, *The Black Power Movement*, 79–103.

139. Lipsitz, *How Racism Takes Place*, 53.

140. Masequa Myers quotation in Tony Smith, "BLACK IS BEAUTIFUL."

141. Kelley, *Freedom Dreams*, 11.

142. Alkalimat, Crawford, and Zorach, *The Wall of Respect*, 318.

Chapter 3. "All Worship the Wall"

Epigraphs are from James Prigoff and Robin Dunitz, *Walls of Heritage, Walls of Pride: African American Murals* (Pomegranate Press, 2000), 24; Seitu Jones, "Public Art That Inspires: Public Art That Informs," in *Critical Issues in Public Art*, ed. Harriet F. Senie and Sally Webster (Smithsonian Books, 1998), 240; Amiri Baraka, *The Autobiography of LeRoi Jones / Amiri Baraka* (Freundlich Books, 1984), 242.

1. Rebecca Zorach, "C. Siddha Webber," in *Never the Same: Conversations About Art Transforming Politics and Community in Chicago and Beyond*, https://never-the-same.org/interviews/c-siddha-webber/.

2. Ibid.

3. Prigoff and Dunitz, *Walls of Heritage*, 24.

4. Zorach, "C. Siddha Webber."

5. Ibid.

6. Ibid.

7. Ibid.

8. Performing prayer at the site of murals during the Black Power movement was much less common than spoken word, dance, personal tours, poetry, music, and plays. *Home* is the only mural found to date where inherently religious acts were performed at its site.

9. "Wall of Meditation," *Chicago Tribune*, September 13, 1970.

10. Author's interview with Eugene "Eda" Wade, April 7, 2018.

11. "Wall of Meditation."

12. 1970, F3, Wall of Meditation (20), Eda, Chicago Public Art Group archives.

13. Alan W. Barnett, *Community Murals: The People's Art* (Art Alliance Press, 1984), 373.

14. This phrase comes from the author's telephone interview with Eugene "Eda" Wade, June 1, 2017.

15. Abdul Alkalimat, Romi Crawford, and Rebecca Zorach, *The Wall of Respect: Public Art and Black Liberation in 1960s Chicago* (Northwestern University Press, 2017), 34.

16. Gwendolyn Brooks, "The Wall" (1968), reprinted in Barnett, *Community Murals*, 52.

17. George Lipsitz, *How Racism Takes Place* (Temple University Press, 2011), 60.

18. Brooks, "The Wall," 52.

19. Ibid.

20. Ibid.

21. Haki Madhubuti, "The Wall," in Alkalimat, Crawford, and Zorach, *The Wall of Respect*, 40.

22. Ibid.

23. Jeff Huebner, "The Man Behind the Wall," *Chicago Reader*, August 28, 1997, http://www.chicagoreader.com/chicago/the-man-behind-the-wall/Content?oid=894264.

24. Alkalimat, Crawford, and Zorach, *The Wall of Respect*, 30.

25. Ibid., 28.

26. Ibid., 30.

27. There are three dates listed for the creation of *Rip-off* / *Universal Alley*, but all suggest that *Rip-Off* was painted first, with *Universal Alley* as the extension. See Eva Cockroft, John Pitman Weber, and John Cockroft, *Towards a People's Art: The Contemporary Mural Movement* (E. P. Dutton, 1977). Barnett, *Community Murals*, suggests the mural began in 1970 and was extended in 1974. Rebecca Zorach, *Art for People's Sake: Artist and Community in Black Chicago, 1965–1975* (Duke University Press, 2019), says that Caton had already painted a mural at the site in 1969 and that in 1970 it was extended with Webber to become *Rip-Off*. After the mural fell into slight disrepair in 1974, Caton repainted it and continued extending the mural down the wall. Prigoff and Dunitz, *Walls of Heritage*, suggests that the mural began in 1968 (the *Rip-Off* part of the wall) and was continually extended (the *Universal Alley* panels) until 1973. Their book has a quotation from Webber that says, "In 1968 we did a mural called *Universal Alley*" (Prigoff and Dunitz, *Walls of Heritage*, 68). For more information on the community reactions to the wall, see Zorach, *Art for People's Sake*, 242–50.

28. C. Siddha Sila Webber in Prigoff and Dunitz, *Walls of Heritage*, 68.

29. Barnett, *Community Murals*, 199; Zorach, "C. Siddha Webber."

30. Zorach, *Art for People's Sake*, 251.

31. 1974, F14, Universal Alley (3), Caton, Chicago Public Art Group archives.

32. Zorach, "C. Siddha Webber."

33. Cockroft, Weber, and Cockroft, *Towards a People's Art*, 252.

34. Zorach, "C. Siddha Webber."

35. Ibid.

36. 1974, F14, Universal Alley (3), Caton, Chicago Public Art Group archives.

37. Zorach, "C. Siddha Webber."

38. Ibid.

39. New York Public Radio, "The Brian Lehrer Show: Remembering the Harlem Riot of 1964," WNYC, July 16, 2004, https://www.wnyc.org/story/remembering-harlem-riot-1964.

40. Janet L. Abu-Lughod, *Race, Space and Riots in Chicago, New York, and Los Angeles* (Oxford University Press, 2007), 172; Fred C. Shapiro and James W. Sullivan, *Race Riots* (Crowell-Collier Publishing, 1964), 1–7.

41. Abu-Lughod, *Race, Space and Riots*, 172.

42. Ibid., 173.

43. Daniel Matlin, *On the Corner: African American Intellectuals and the Urban Crisis* (Harvard University Press, 2013), 2.

44. Peter B. Levy, *The Great Uprising: Race Riots in Urban America During the 1960s* (Cambridge University Press, 2018), 1.

45. Gerald Horne, *Fire This Time: The Watts Uprising and the 1960s* (University Press of Virginia, 1995), 2.

46. For more information on the Soldier Field Rally of Chicago and Martin Luther King Jr.'s demands for open housing, see Abu-Lughod, *Race, Space and Riots*; and

Amanda I. Seligman, "'But Burn-No': The Rest of the Crowd in Three Civil Disorders in 1960s Chicago," *Journal of Urban History* 7, no. 2 (2011): 230–55.

47. Scott Martelle, *Detroit [A Biography]* (Chicago Review Press, 2012), 193; John Hersey, *The Algiers Motel Incident* (Johns Hopkins University Press, 1968), ix.

48. Martelle, *Detroit [A Biography]*, 193.

49. Ibid., 193–95.

50. Ibid., 196.

51. National Advisory Commission on Civil Disorders, *The Kerner Report: The 1968 Report of the National Advisory Commission on Civil Disorders* (Pantheon Books, 1988), 2.

52. Kenneth Clark, *Dark Ghetto: Dilemmas of Social Power* (Lowe and Brydone, 1965), 11.

53. Jeff W. Huebner, *Walls of Prophecy and Protest: William Walker and the Roots of a Revolutionary Public Art Movement* (Northwestern University Press, 2019), 86.

54. While this chapter examines two murals painted on churches in the 1960s, one of which has religious iconography, see Pinder, *Painting the Gospel* (especially chapter 5), for a deeper examination into the relationship between Black murals and religion.

55. Huebner, *Walls of Prophecy and Protest*, 96.

56. "Detroit's Ditto," *Time*, June 13, 1969. Ditto was in Detroit a month before the riots after organizing in Chicago, and on July 23, when the rebellions broke out, he was at the Black Power conference in Newark, listening to speeches from H. Rap Brown and Amiri Baraka.

57. Huebner, *Walls of Prophecy and Protest*, 87.

58. For more information on Ditto, see Jeff Huebner, "In Search of Detroit's Lost Walls of Dignity, Freedom, and Pride," *Detroit Metro Times*, February 26, 2020, https://www.metrotimes.com/arts/in-search-of-detroits-lost-walls-of-dignity -freedom-and-pride-23943418.

59. Ibid.

60. Author's phone call with Eugene "Eda" Wade, January 20, 2018.

61. Ibid.

62. Josh Akers, "Map: Detroit Civil Disturbance July 1967," DETROITography, October 21, 2015, www.detroitography.com/2015/10/21/map-detroit-civil-disturbance -july-1967/.

63. East Side Voices of Independent Detroit, "ESVID Builds a New Wall: Detroit's Wall of Dignity," *The Ghetto Speaks*, April 22, 1968, copy courtesy of the Bentley Historical Library, University of Michigan, Ann Arbor.

64. *Colored People's Time*, January 22, 1969, https://abj.matrix.msu.edu/videofull .php?id=198-733-548.

65. Marlene Sanders quoted in "Power, Pride and Self-Help, Aiding Black Movement," *Abilene Reporter-News*, August 8, 1971; Wade phone call, January 20, 2018.

66. Quoted in Huebner, *Walls of Prophecy and Protest*, 87.

67. Barnett, *Community Murals*, 53.

68. Wade phone call, January 20, 2018.

69. Ibid.

70. "ESVID Builds a New Wall."

71. Ibid.

72. Ibid.

73. EMU School of Art and Design Gallery, "'Detroit's Black Power Murals as Public Art,' by Rebecca Zurier," *YouTube*, 1:26:56, October 19, 2021, https://www.youtube.com/watch?v=tzO9Xznf3LI.

74. East Side Voices of Independent Detroit, "ESVID Builds a New Wall."

75. Ibid.

76. Ibid.

77. Ibid.

78. Huebner, *Walls of Prophecy and Protest*, 87.

79. Prigoff and Dunitz, *Walls of Heritage*, 65; Wade phone call, January 20, 2018.

80. Wade phone call, January 20, 2018.

81. Quoted in Prigoff and Dunitz, *Walls of Heritage*, 65.

82. Barnett, *Community Murals*, 53.

83. Huebner, *Walls of Prophecy and Protest*, 87.

84. Quoted in ibid.

85. Ibid.

86. *Colored People's Time*.

87. Dedication booklet, *The Harriet Ross Tubman Memorial Wall*, folder 33, box 3, St. Bernard of Clairvaux, Detroit Parish Collection, Archives of the Archdiocese of Detroit.

88. "When Bill painted Elijah Muhammad on the first wall, they threatened to come and sue him because they didn't want him up there alongside a traitor like Malcolm X," Eda told me in an oral history interview. "What they did is they came in and they painted Elijah Muhammad's image completely out because he was beside Malcolm, and they painted the Holy Quran out of Malcolm's hand." Eda was vague when I pressed him with the question of who "they" were, but when asked if it was the Nation of Islam, he replied by saying, "Right, so Bill had to paint him out." Interviews with William Walker by Jeff Huebner suggest "they" referred to the Fruit of Islam, the security wing of the Nation of Islam. Father Kerwin called Walker and Eda once they had returned to Chicago to tell them about this defacement. When Walker offered to repaint the mural for free, Father Kerwin replied, "No, no—we want it to stay the way it is." Wade phone call, January 20, 2018; Huebner, *Walls of Prophecy and Protest*, 99; Huebner interview with Walker, October 22, 2010.

89. "Detroit's Wall of Pride Gives City Big Lift," *Detroit American*, August 9, 1968, 12.

90. Ibid.

91. Ibid.

92. Ibid.

93. Huebner, *Walls of Prophecy and Protest*, 90.

94. Peniel E. Joseph, *Waiting 'til the Midnight Hour: A Narrative History of Black Power in America* (Henry Holt and Company, 2006), 83.

95. Huebner, *Walls of Prophecy and Protest*, 92.

96. Ibid.

97. Ibid.

98. Ibid., 93.

99. Ibid., 95.

100. Ibid.

101. Ibid.

102. East Side Voices of Independent Detroit, "ESVID Builds a New Wall."

Chapter 4. "Africa Had No History, and Neither Did I"

Epigraphs are from Don L. Lee, "Tomorrow Is Tomorrow if You Want One," in *Black Fire: An Anthology of Afro-American Writing*, ed. Amiri Baraka and Larry Neal (Black Classic Press, 1968), 242; Andrea A. Burns, *From Storefront to Monument: Tracing the Public History of the Black Museum Movement* (University of Massachusetts Press, 2013), 1; Ossie Davis quotation in Matthew Siegfried, "James Baldwin Speaks! The Confessions of Nat Turner, with William Styron and Ossie Davis—May 28, 1968," *YouTube*, 55:25, May 25, 2015, https://www.youtube.com/watch?v=TCkpiRMoG4g.

1. Riverbends Channel, "James Baldwin Debates William F. Buckley (1965)," *YouTube*, 58:57, October 27, 2012, https://www.youtube.com/watch?v=oFeoS41xe7w.

2. Quoted in Susan E. Cahan, *Mounting Frustration: The Art Museum in the Age of Black Power* (Duke University Press, 2016), 1.

3. Ibid.

4. Ibid.

5. Bridget R. Cooks, *Exhibiting Blackness: African Americans and the American Art Museum* (University of Massachusetts Press, 2011), 53.

6. Burns, *From Storefront to Monument*, 5.

7. Ibid., 3; Janet Braun-Reinitz and Jane Weissman, *On the Wall: Four Decades of Community Murals in New York City* (University Press of Mississippi, 2009), 45.

8. McCannon was acutely aware of being the only female artist on the project, titling one of her murals *The Wall of Women Dedicated to Faith Ringgold*. In the mural, she criticized how the traditional portrayals of women confined them only to domestic settings and instead put forward the idea of women "looking out for one another." For more information on Dindga McCannon, see the 1971 exhibition *Where We At: Black Women Artists*. McCannon was selected as one of fourteen artists, and with fellow exhibition contributors Kay Brown and Faith Ringgold, the three female artists established the Where We At artists collective to remedy and correct the exclusion of Black female artists from Black male-dominated arts organizations. Braun-Reinitz and Weissman, *On the Wall*, 47.

9. Ibid., 45.

10. Ibid., 46.

11. Ibid., 47.

12. Babtunde Folayemi in ibid., 45–46.

13. Amy Abugo Ongiri, *Spectacular Blackness: The Cultural Politics of the Black Power Movement and the Search for a Black Aesthetic* (University of Virginia Press, 2009), 110.

14. Author's telephone interview with Eugene "Eda" Wade, June 1, 2017.

15. Author's telephone interview with Eugene "Eda" Wade, April 7, 2018.

16. Patrick S. Washburn, *The African American Newspaper: Voice of Freedom* (Northwestern University Press, 2006), xi.

17. *The Black Press: Soldiers Without Swords*, dir. Stanley Nelson Jr. (PBS Documentaries, 1999); Patrick S. Washburn, *The African American Newspaper: Voice of Freedom* (Northwestern University Press, 2006), xi. As a slogan popularized by the *Pittsburgh Courier* during World War II, the Double V campaign was a fight for both international victory against the Fascist forces in Europe and a domestic victory for African Americans against the supremacist, racist forces at home.

18. Washburn, *The African American Newspaper*, xi.

19. This quotation is from an interview with African American journalists for Henry G. La Brie III's 1973 study on the Black press. James D. Sullivan, *On the Walls and in the Streets: American Poetry Broadsides from the 1960s* (University of Illinois Press, 1997), 200.

20. Quoted in Jeff W. Huebner, *Walls of Prophecy and Protest: William Walker and the Roots of a Revolutionary Public Art Movement* (Northwestern University Press, 2019), 56.

21. Black communities are not monolithic, and this point is not to suggest that people only read these Black community newspapers at this time. This point is to highlight the growing presence of independent Black papers and magazines during the 1960s.

22. Wade interview, April 7, 2018.

23. Quoted in Huebner, *Walls of Prophecy and Protest*, 1.

24. Wade interview, June 1, 2017.

25. Jeff Huebner, "Bill Walker and the Roots of a Revolutionary Public Arts Movement." This book manuscript has now been published as Huebner's *Walls of Prophecy and Protest*. Some quotations from the manuscript may not appear directly the same in the published version of the book and hence have been quoted directly as the unpublished manuscript with the original working title.

26. Oral history interview with William Walker, June 12–14, 1991, 33, Archives of American Art, Smithsonian Institution.

27. "Black Jobless Rate Still Unchanged," *Chicago Daily Defender (Big Weekend Edition) (1966–1973)*, February 21, 1970.

28. Wade interview, June 1, 2017.

29. Walker oral history interview, 40.

30. "The Fontenelle Family, 1967," Gordon Parks Foundation, https://www.gordonparksfoundation.org/gordon-parks/photography-archive/the-fontenelle-family-1967?view=slider.

31. Ibid.

32. "History of Lynching in America," NAACP, https://naacp.org/find-resources/history-explained/history-lynching-america.

33. *Milwaukee Star*, December 20, 1969, 4.

34. Huebner, "Bill Walker," n.p.

35. Wade interview, June 1, 2017.

36. Huebner, "Bill Walker," n.p.

37. Wade interview, June 1, 2017.

38. Quoted in Rebecca Zorach, *Art for People's Sake: Artists and Community in Black Chicago, 1965–1975* (Duke University Press, 2019), 106.

39. Huebner, *Walls of Prophecy and Protest*, 106.

40. Quoted in Huebner, "Bill Walker," n.p.

41. Claude McKay, "If We Must Die" (1919), Poetry Foundation, accessed September 7, 2017, https://www.poetryfoundation.org/poems/44694/if-we-must-die.

42. Ward Churchill and Jim Vander Wall, *Agents of Repression: The FBI's Secret Wars Against the Black Panther Party and the American Indian Movement* (South End Press, 1988), 63–76. For more information on the assassination of Fred Hampton and the ways in which the COINTELPRO tried to dismantle the Black Panther Party, see Ward Churchill and Jim Vander Wall, *The COINTELPRO Papers: Documents from the FBI's Secret Wars Against Dissent in the United States* (South End Press, 1990); Jeffrey Haas, *The Assassination of Fred Hampton: How the FBI and Chicago Police Murdered a Black Panther* (Chicago Review Press, 2008).

43. Walker oral history interview, 40.

44. Emory Douglas, "Position Paper #1 on Revolutionary Art (1968)," It's About Time Black Panther Party, accessed June 12, 2017, http://www.itsabouttimebpp.com/emory_art/pdf/Position_Paper_on_Revolutionary_Art_No1.pdf; Colette Gaither, "What Revolution Looks Like: The Work of Black Panther Artist Emory Douglas," in *Black Panther: The Revolutionary Art of Emory Douglas*, ed. Sam Durant (Rizzoli, 2007), 96.

45. Douglas, "Position Paper #1."

46. Walker oral history interview, 41.

47. Huebner, *Walls of Prophecy and Protest*, 30.

48. "'Wall of Respect' Tumbles Down," *Chicago Daily Defender*, March 29, 1972.

49. For more information on the demise of the *Wall of Respect* and *Wall of Truth*, see Huebner, *Walls of Prophecy and Protest*, 111.

50. Ibid.

51. Burns, *From Storefront to Monument*, 72.

52. Ibid.

53. Ibid.

54. James Turner, "Black Students and Their Changing Perspective," *Ebony*, August 1969, 138.

55. Quoted in ibid., 139.

56. Peniel E. Joseph, "Dashikis and Democracy: Black Studies, Student Activism, and the Black Power Movement," *Journal of American History* 88, no. 2 (Spring 2003): 182–203, 188.

57. Kristina Rizga, "Black Studies Matter: How One of the Nation's Biggest—and Most Violent—Campus Protests Brought Diversity to the Rest of America," *Mother Jones,* May 19, 2016, https://www.motherjones.com/politics/2016/05/ethnic-studies -agents-of-change-documentary-san-francisco/.

58. *Agents of Change,* dir. Abby Ginzberg and Frank Dawson (Kovno Communications, 2016), DVD. At the time of his appointment to San Francisco State College, Hare was a Chicago-trained sociologist, and as the first coordinator to be hired for a Black studies program, he was often referred to as "the father of Black studies." Hare was fired after two semesters for refusing to break the five-month student strike, and soon after, he became the founding publisher of the *Black Scholar.* "Nathan Hare," African American Literature Book Club, accessed May 14, 2017, https://aalbc.com /authors/author.php?author_name=Nathan+Hare.

59. "Nathan Hare."

60. Turner, "Black Students," 138.

61. Peniel E. Joseph, "Black Studies, Student Activism, and the Black Power Movement," in *The Black Power Movement: Rethinking the Civil Rights–Black Power Era,* ed. Peniel E. Joseph (Routledge, 2006), 251–77.

62. San Francisco State College Strike Collection, "SF State: Associated Students Meeting & Amiri Baraka," San Francisco State College Strike Collection, accessed April 1, 2018, https://diva.sfsu.edu/collections/strike/bundles/187241.

63. David Hilliard, "Black Student Unions: Speech Delivered at San Francisco State College," in *The Black Panthers Speak,* ed. Philip Foner (Haymarket Books, 1970), 124.

64. While this case study specifically focuses on the murals of Dewey Crumpler, murals teaching about Black history were not just confined to those by Crumpler in San Francisco. In Chicago, Eugene "Eda" Wade was creating murals that also responded to the biases of school curricula. In a 2017 interview Eda said: "They didn't have that [Black history] in the curriculum because everything was and is dictated and created in the laws. . . . So what we felt we needed to do was to bring our own heroes and sheroes in and have them painted on the walls so we could explain. We did have our own heroes and sheroes that made a contribution that may not be included in a textbook because of whatever political or social reason." The idea of murals as a communicative tool for learning Black history therefore was frequently used as a motivation for their creation. Wade interview, June 1, 2017.

65. Arthur E. Hippler, *Hunter's Point: A Black Ghetto* (Basic Books, 1974), 17.

66. SFAI official, "Dewey Crumpler—CODE Black Futures Month: San Francisco Art Institute 2017," *Vimeo,* 50:03, February 8, 2017, https://deweycrumpler.com /videos/.

67. Author's telephone interview with Dewey Crumpler, February 22, 2018.

68. Quoted in James Prigoff and Robin J. Dunitz, *Walls of Heritage, Walls of Pride: African American Murals* (Pomegranate Press, 2000), 169; Crumpler interview, February 22, 2018.

69. Crumpler interview, February 22, 2018.

70. Dewey Crumpler, in SFIA official, "Dewey Crumpler."

71. The debate over the display of Arnautoff's murals is still very much alive today. In June 2019 the San Francisco School Board voted to destroy the Life of Washington series, citing the murals as triggering and violent and as depicting history from the colonizer's perspective. But as Crumpler argues, Arnautoff in his murals "is really trying to show us the problematic [sic], really critiquing this notion that this George Washington was a liberator. He liberated white people, he didn't liberate black people." The decision to erase these murals led to a national defense of Arnautoff's murals citing "First Amendment issues, the importance of historical memory, the failure to grasp the radical intent behind the mural series, and the absurdity of spending $600,000 that could have gone to fund arts education to destroy a work of art." After a debate on the national stage, a compromise was struck that would see the murals preserved and digitized but also hidden behind removable covers. For more information on the debates, see Robin D. G. Kelley, "We're Getting These Murals All Wrong," *The Nation*, September 10, 2019, https://www.thenation.com/article/archive/arnautoff-mural-life-washington/; Ariella Markowitz, "The Radical History of the Murals at George Washington High School," *Kalw*, August 2, 2021, https://www.kalw.org/arts-culture/2019-08-20/the-radical-history-of-the-murals-at-george-washington-high-school; Jillian Caddell, "The George Washington Murals Are Meant to Make Viewers Uncomfortable," August 22, 2019, https://www.apollo-magazine.com/life-of-washington-victor-arnautoff-san-francisco/; and Carol Pogash, "These High School Murals Depict an Ugly History. Should They Go?," *New York Times*, April 11, 2019, https://www.nytimes.com/2019/04/11/arts/design/george-washington-murals-ugly-history-debated.html.

72. Quoted in Prigoff and Dunitz, *Walls of Heritage*, 158.

73. Ibid.

74. Crumpler interview, February 22, 2018.

75. Ibid.

76. Quoted in Prigoff and Dunitz, *Walls of Heritage*, 158.

77. Ibid.

78. Crumpler interview, February 22, 2018.

79. Ibid.

80. Ibid.; Tim Drescher, "The Fire Next Time II," Public Art and Architecture, April 2, 2013, http://www.artandarchitecture-sf.com/tag/dewey-crumpler.

81. Crumpler interview, February 22, 2018.

82. Ibid.

83. Ibid.

84. Quoted in Tim W. Drescher, *San Francisco Murals: Community Creates Its Muse, 1914–1990* (Pogo Press, 1991), 35.

85. Crumpler interview, February 22, 2018.

86. Drescher, *San Francisco Murals*, 35.

87. Joanna Brooks, *American Lazarus: Religion and the Rise of African-American and Native American Literatures* (Oxford University Press, 2003), 10; Brian A. Wren, *Praying Twice: The Music and Words of Congregational Song* (Westminster John Knox Press, 2000), 196.

88. Crumpler interview, February 22, 2018.

89. James Baldwin, *The Fire Next Time* (Dial Press, 1963), 15.

90. Ibid., 16, 18.

91. Ibid., 25.

92. Quoted in Prigoff and Dunitz, *Walls of Heritage*, 169.

93. Drescher, *San Francisco Murals*, 35. In 1984 Crumpler extended *The Fire Next Time I* and created *The Fire Next Time II* on the adjacent gym at the recreation center. It continued similar motifs of African symbols and figures of Black history.

Chapter 5. "I Wanted the Wall to Scream"

Epigraphs are from *Style Wars*, dir. Tony Silver and Henry Chalfant (Public Art Films, 1983); "Reverend Jesse Jackson, March on Washington 1993," c-span, https://www.c-span.org/video/?c4462569/user-clip-eumi-rev-jesse-jackson; Brandan Odums, "Exhibit Be," BMike Brandan Odums, accessed June 11, 2019, http://bmike.com/project/exhibit-be/.

1. *Crack: Cocaine, Corruption and Conspiracy*, dir. Stanley Nelson Jr. (Oddball Films, 2021).

2. Elizabeth Hinton quoted in ibid.

3. Manning Marable, *Beyond Black and White: Transforming African-American Politics* (Verso, 1995), 26–32.

4. *13th*, dir. Ava DuVernay (Kandoo Films, 2016).

5. Silver and Chalfant, *Style Wars*.

6. Ibid.

7. Ibid.

8. Ibid.; Jeff Chang, *Can't Stop, Won't Stop: A History of the Hip-Hop Generation* (Random House, 2007). While it's important to acknowledge graffiti as a marker and movement on the public art landscape in the 1980s and 1990s, as well as how some Black murals were painted to cover up tagging and graffiti in neighborhoods in the 1960s, the process, practice, and principles of graffiti differ greatly from those of the community mural movement, so this book avoids ruminating on them. An in-depth discussion of the parallels, differences, and chronological overlaps requires its own in-depth study, but for information on graffiti, see *Style Wars*; Chang, *Can't Stop, Won't Stop*; Jack Stewart, *Graffiti Kings: New York City Mass Transit Art of the 1970s* (Abrams, 2009).

9. Jeff Huebner, *Walls of Prophecy and Protest: William Walker and the Roots of a Revolutionary Public Movement* (Northwestern University Press, 2019), 214.

10. Alan Barnett, *Community Murals: The People's Art* (Art Alliance Press, 1984), 240.

11. Ibid.; Huebner, *Walls of Prophecy and Protest*, 214.

12. Barnett, *Community Murals*, 240.

13. Ibid.

14. Timothy W. Drescher, *San Francisco Murals: Community Creates Its Muse, 1914–1990* (Pogo Press, 1991), 36; Huebner, *Walls of Prophecy and Protest*, 214.

15. Quoted in Huebner, *Walls of Prophecy and Protest*, 214.

16. Quoted in "Caton Unites People, Art," *Chicago Daily Defender*, January 8, 1973.

17. In 1984 the Philadelphia Anti-Graffiti Network (PAGN) was established to combat the spread of graffiti in the city. It was led by Tim Spencer, and the aim was to redirect the energies of graffiti writers into public arts projects. Two years later under a branch of PAGN, the Mural Arts Project (MAP), headed up by artist Jane Golden, emerged, which sought to create transformative art in public spaces. Today, MAP (now branded as Mural Arts Program) is the largest public art program in the nation. For more information, see Mural Arts Philadelphia, https://www.muralarts.org /ignite/; and Jane Golden, Robin Rice, and Monica Yant Kinney, *Philadelphia Murals and the Stories They Tell* (Temple University Press, 2002).

18. Quoted in Janet Braun-Reinitz and Jane Weissman, *On the Wall: Four Decades of Community Murals in New York City* (University Press of Mississippi, 2009), xvii.

19. Ibid.

20. Quoted in T. R. Poston, "MURALS and MARX," *New York Amsterdam News* (1922–1938), November 24, 1934. For more information on this, see chapter 1.

21. Quoted in Huebner, *Walls of Prophecy and Protest*, 214.

22. Ibid., 217.

23. Oral history interview with William Walker, June 12–14, 1991, 100, Archives of American Art, Smithsonian Institution.

24. Vanessa Swales, "When the O.K. Sign Is No Longer O.K.," *New York Times*, December 15, 2019, https://www.nytimes.com/2019/12/15/us/ok-sign-white-power .html. Under Reagan's presidency, there was an increase in supremacist activity and violence and, more specifically, an increase in Klan activity. In North Carolina, for example, Klansmen organized registration drives; state leader Glenn Miller ran in the democratic primary for governor on an openly pro-Klan and white supremacy platform; Klansmen in Georgia and Alabama succeeded in being named county deputy voter registrars; and many Klansmen worked for Reagan's reelection. Marable, *Beyond Black and White*, 40. For more information, see Baxter Smith, "Reagan and Repression," *Black Scholar: Journal of Black Studies and Research* 12, no. 1 (1981); Branko Marcetic, "Fighting the Klan in Reagan's America," *Jacobin Magazine*, August 25, 2017, https://jacobinmag.com/2017/08/greensboro-massacre-ku-klux-klan-far-right.

25. Manning Marable, *Race, Reform, and Rebellion: The Second Reconstruction and Beyond in Black America, 1945–2006*, 3rd ed. (University Press of Mississippi, 2007), e-book, unpaginated.

26. Huebner, *Walls of Prophecy and Protest*, 215.

27. Ibid., 217.

28. Walker oral history interview, 100.

29. Huebner, *Walls of Prophecy and Protest*, 219.

30. Marable, *Race, Reform, and Rebellion*.

31. Robin D. G. Kelley, *Yo' Mama's DisFUNKtional! Fighting the Culture Wars in Urban America* (Beacon Press, 1997), 7.

32. Marable, *Race, Reform and Rebellion*.

33. Ibid.

34. Nelson, *Crack*.

35. Marable, *Race, Reform and Rebellion*.

36. Ibid.

37. James Forman Jr., "The War on Drugs," in *Four Hundred Souls: A Community History of African America 1619–2019*, ed. Ibram X. Kendi and Keisha N. Blain (Penguin Random House, 2021), 353.

38. Ibid., 352.

39. Marable, *Race, Reform and Rebellion*.

40. Forman, "The War on Drugs"; Nelson, *Crack*.

41. Nelson, *Crack*.

42. Forman, "The War on Drugs," 354.

43. U.S. Department of Justice, "Violent Crime Control and Law Enforcement Act of 1994," *National Criminal Justice Reference Service*, October 24, 1994, https://www.ncjrs.gov/txtfiles/billfs.txt. Clinton's crime bill also included bans on the manufacture of nineteen military-style assault weapons; stiffer penalties for violent and drug trafficking crimes committed by gang members; enhanced penalties for alien smuggling, illegal reentry after deportation, and other immigration-related crimes; the doubling of the maximum term of imprisonment for repeat sex offenders; allowing victims of federal, violent, and sex crimes to speak at the sentencing of their assailants; strengthening federal licensing standards for firearms dealers; prohibiting the sale and possession of firearms by persons subject to violence restraining orders.

44. Angela Y. Davis, "The Crime Bill," in Kendi and Blain, *Four Hundred Souls*, 367.

45. Marable, *Race, Reform and Rebellion*.

46. Ibid.

47. Marable, *Beyond Black and White*, 205, xiii.

48. Marable, *Race, Reform and Rebellion*.

49. James Prigoff and Robin Dunitz, *Walls of Heritage, Walls of Pride: African American Murals* (Pomegranate Press, 2000), 151.

50. Brett Cook (Dizney), "Brett Cook on the Practice of Building Community," *Not Real Art*, June 8, 2021, https://notrealart.com/brett-cook/.

51. Ibid.

52. Quoted in Prigoff and Dunitz, *Walls of Heritage*, 153.

53. Ibid.

54. Ibid., 151.

55. Ibid.

56. Quoted in Marianne Garvey, "Portraits for the People Is Artist's Aim," *New York Post*, August 12, 2002, https://nypost.com/2002/08/12/portraits-for-the-people

-is-artists-aim/; Jeff Chang, *Total Chaos: The Art and Aesthetics of Hip-Hop* (Civitas Books, 2008), 334.

57. Cook, "Brett Cook on the Practice."

58. Quoted in Prigoff and Dunitz, *Walls of Heritage*, 151.

59. Ibid., 153.

60. Ibid.

61. Ibid.

62. Ibid., 151.

63. "Studio Check In with Brett Cook," Studio Museum in Harlem, https://studiomuseum.org/article/studio-check-brett-cook.

64. Ibid.

65. Arts Research Center, "Brett Cook—Embodying Liberation: A Dialogue on Community and Healing," *YouTube*, 1:27:06, November 28, 2014, https://www.youtube.com/watch?v=az-u8ACNarw&t=4324s.

66. LA 92, dir. Daniel Lindsay and T. J. Martin (National Geographic, 2017).

67. Anjuli Sastry Krbechek and Karen Grigsby Bates, "When LA Erupted in Anger: A Look Back at the Rodney King Riots," NPR, April 26, 2017, https://www.npr.org/2017/04/26/524744989/when-la-erupted-in-anger-a-look-back-at-the-rodney-king-riots.

68. Marable, *Beyond Black and White*, 178.

69. Bill Stout from CBS News in Lindsay and Martin, *LA 92*.

70. Olivia B. Waxman, "30 Years After the Rodney King Verdict, Why Advocates Believe 'Reforms Didn't Go Far Enough,'" *Time*, April 28, 2022, https://time.com/6169564/rodney-king-riots-beating-anniversary/.

71. Prigoff and Dunitz, *Walls of Heritage*, 186.

72. Mural Conservancy LA, "MCLA June 2012 Artist of the Month: Noni Olabisi," *YouTube*, 9:11, June 14, 2012, https://www.youtube.com/watch?v=DySjC8XDnJc.

73. Ibid.

74. Ibid.

75. Noni Olabisi, "Noni Olabisi: Fellowship for Visual Arts, Artist's Statement," California Community Foundation, https://www.calfund.org/nonprofits/featured-funds/fva/2010-gallery/noni-olabisi/.

76. Ibid.

77. Ibid.

78. Julian Mayfield, "You Touch My Black Aesthetic and I'll Touch Yours," in *The Black Aesthetic*, ed. Addison Gayle Jr. (Anchor Books, 1972), 26.

79. Brandan Odums quotation in TEDx Talks, "Art to inspire | Brandan Odums | TEDxNewOrleans," *YouTube*, 10:57, June 20, 2015, https://www.youtube.com/watch?v=gGz8BSVuZZQ.

80. Troy D. Allen, "Katrina: Race, Class, and Poverty: Reflections and Analysis," *Journal of Black Studies* 37, no. 4 (March 2007): 446.

81. Marable, *Race, Reform and Rebellion*, 3.

82. Brandan Odums, "Exhibit Be," BMike Brandan Odums, June 11, 2019, http://bmike.com/project/exhibit-be/.

83. Brandan Odums quotation in TEDx Talks, "Art to inspire."

84. Ibid.

85. Ibid.

86. Ibid.

87. Ibid.

88. NOLA.com, "Brandan Odums Puts Graffiti in a New Orleans Context at 'ExhibitBE,'" *YouTube*, 3:35, November 12, 2014, https://www.youtube.com /watch?v=s7L34_qocvw&t=215s; TEDx Talks, "Art to inspire."

Chapter 6. A Space to Have a Voice

Epigraphs are from Michael Eric Dyson, *Long Time Coming: Reckoning with Race in America* (St. Martin's Press, 2020), 44; Ta-Nehisi Coates, *Between the World and Me* (Text Publishing Company, 2015), 9; Tina M. Campt, *A Black Gaze: Artists Changing How We See* (MIT Press, 2021), 4.

1. "Final Report Internal Affairs Investigation, New Year's Day, 2009," Oscar Grant Internal Affairs Investigation Report CPRA Document, July 31, 2009, https://www.documentcloud.org/documents/7222786-Oscar-Grant-Internal -Affairs-Investigation.

2. Brakkton Booker, "California District Attorney Says Probe of Oscar Grant Killing Will Be Reopened," NPR, October 6, 2020, https://www.npr.org/sections/live -updates-protests-for-racial-justice/2020/10/06/920895464/california-district-at torney-says-probe-of-oscar-grant-killing-will-be-reopened; Sam Levin, "Officer Punched Oscar Grant and Lied About Facts in 2009 Killing, Records Show," *The Guardian*, May 2, 2019, https://www.theguardian.com/us-news/2019/may/02 /officer-punched-oscar-grant-and-lied-about-facts-in-2009-killing-records-show; Demian Bulwa, "BART's Shooting Probe Missteps," SF *Gate*, January 30, 2009, https://www.sfgate.com/bayarea/article/BART-s-shooting-probe-missteps-3174551. php#photo-2310191.

3. Dyson, *Long Time Coming*, 60.

4. Ibid., 19.

5. It is important to note that only a handful of victims are memorialized in murals due to the high-profile nature of their cases. There are countless other victims whose faces we don't see and whose names we don't say. Renée Ater has created an online memorial to honor these lives. Renée Ater, "In Memoriam: I Can't Breathe," *Renée Ater*, May 29, 2020, https://www.reneeater.com/on-monuments-blog/tag /list+of+unarmed+black+people+killed+by+police.

6. Barack Obama [@barackobama], photo of statement by President and Mrs. Obama, *Instagram*, April 20, 2021, www.instagram.com/p/CN58Ni5Ax8C /?igshid=YmMyMTA2M2Y=.

7. Dyson, *Long Time Coming*, 4.

8. Larry Buchanan, Quoctrung Bui, and Jugal K. Patel, "Black Lives Matter May Be the Largest Movement in U.S. History," *New York Times*, July 3, 2020, https://www.nytimes.com/interactive/2020/07/03/us/george-floyd-protests-crowd-size.html.

9. The National Advisory Commission on Civil Disorders, *The Kerner Report: The 1968 Report of the National Advisory Commission on Civil Disorders* (Pantheon Books, 1988), 2.

10. Jelani Cobb, "An American Spring of Reckoning," *New Yorker*, June 14, 2020, https://www.newyorker.com/magazine/2020/06/22/an-american-spring-of-reckoning.

11. Ibid.

12. Ibid.

13. Sabrina Moreno, "Projections at Lee Monument Offer Peace in Time of Violence," *Washington Post*, July 5, 2020, https://www.washingtonpost.com/local/projections-at-lee-monument-offer-peace-in-times-of-violence/2020/07/05/477f79c4-bec8-11ea-8908-68a2b9eae9e0_story.html.

14. For more information on the history of Confederate monuments, see Karen L. Cox, *No Common Ground: Confederate Monuments and the Ongoing Fight for Racial Justice* (University of North Carolina Press, 2021); Sanford Levinson, *Written in Stone: Public Monuments in Changing Societies* (Duke University Press, 2018); Kirk Savage, *Standing Soldiers, Kneeling Slaves: Race, War and Monument in Nineteenth-Century America* (Princeton University Press, 1997).

15. Cox, *No Common Ground*, 3.

16. Ibid.

17. Savage, *Standing Soldiers, Kneeling Slaves*, 5.

18. Arwa Haider, "The Art of Protest: The Street Art That Expressed the World's Pain," BBC, December 14, 2020, https://www.bbc.com/culture/article/20201209-the-street-art-that-expressed-the-worlds-pain.

19. Aimee Ortiz and Johnny Diaz, "George Floyd Protests Reignite Debate over Confederate Statues," *New York Times*, June 3, 2020, https://www.nytimes.com/2020/06/03/us/confederate-statues-george-floyd.html.

20. "The Story of the Black Lives Matter Mural," Murals DC Project, June 2020, http://muralsdcproject.com/mural/black-lives-matter/.

21. Kyle Chayka, "The Mimetic Power of D.C.'s Black Lives Matter Mural," *New Yorker*, June 9, 2020, https://www.newyorker.com/culture/dept-of-design/the-mimetic-power-of-dcs-black-lives-matter-mural.

22. Ibid.

23. Quoted in Maya King, "'It's Not Enough': Activists Say Black Lives Matter Murals Are Empty Gesture," *Politico*, July 19, 2020, https://www.politico.com/news/2020/07/19/black-lives-matter-murals-369091.

24. Quoted in Megan Sims, "Activists Say Black Lives Matter Street Murals Are 'Performative Support': 'They Don't Stop the Next Murder of a Mr. Floyd,'" *Yahoo*, July 17, 2020, https://shorturl.at/wDSYZ.

25. King, "It's Not Enough."

26. Chayka, "The Mimetic Power."

27. Victor Luckerson, "The Defacement and Destruction of Black Lives Matter Murals," *New Yorker*, November 19, 2020, https://www.newyorker.com/news/us-journal/the-defacement-and-destruction-of-black-lives-matter-murals/.

28. Dan Adler, Anthony Breznican, Kenzie Bryant, Michael Calderone, Arimeta Diop, Caleb Ecarma, Joe Hagan, Claire Landsbaum, Chris Smith, Abigail Tracy, and Erin Vanderhoof, "True Stories About the Great Fire," *Vanity Fair*, 2020, https://www.vanityfair.com/culture/2020/08/george-floyd-oral-history/.

29. Quoted in Haider, "The Art of Protest."

30. For a report on how this has been measured in a case study in Madison, Wisconsin, see Mike Andreas and Matthew McAllister, "Protest Murals and Community Formation in Madison, Wis.: An Atlas of Art and Ideology on State Street," https://minds.wisconsin.edu/bitstream/handle/1793/81087/Andreas%20McAllister.pdf?sequence=1&isAllowed=y.

31. Manning Marable, *Living Black History: How Reimagining the African-American Past Can Remake America's Racial Future* (Civitas Books, 2005), xii.

32. Ronald Lee Fleming, *The Art of Placemaking: Interpreting Community Through Public Art and Urban Design* (Merrell, 2007), 15.

33. Ibid., 15.

34. Joshua Berlinger, Nick Valencia, and Steve Almasy, "Alton Sterling Shooting: Homeless Man Made 911 Call, Source Says," *CNN*, July 8, 2016, https://edition.cnn.com/2016/07/07/us/baton-rouge-alton-sterling-shooting/.

35. Richard Fausset, "Baton Rouge Office Is Fired in Alton Sterling Case as Police Release New Videos," *New York Times*, March 30, 2018, https://www.nytimes.com/2018/03/30/us/baton-rouge-alton-sterling.html; Nicole Chavez, "Body Camera Show Officer Threatened to Shoot Alton Sterling Within Seconds," *CNN*, March 31, 2018, https://edition.cnn.com/2018/03/31/us/alton-sterling-police-videos-hearings/index.html.

36. Fausset, "Baton Rouge Office Is Fired."

37. Press release, "Federal Officers Decline Prosecution in the Death of Freddie Gray," United States Department of Justice, September 12, 2017, https://www.justice.gov/opa/pr/federal-officials-decline-prosecution-death-freddie-gray.

38. David A. Graham, "The Mysterious Death of Freddie Gray," *The Atlantic*, April 22, 2015, https://www.theatlantic.com/politics/archive/2015/04/the-mysterious-death-of-freddie-gray/391119/.

39. Ibid.

40. Ibid.

41. Ibid.

42. Alex T. Williams, "Did the Media Cover Only the Violent Protests in Baltimore?," *Washington Post*, May 13, 2015, https://www.washingtonpost.com/news/monkey-cage/wp/2015/05/13/did-the-media-cover-only-the-violent-protests-in-baltimore/?utm_term=.f2bfdb02c589.

43. Quoted in Rashad Robinson, "Media's Biased and Dehumanizing Coverage

of Baltimore Fails to Tell the City's Real Story," *The Root*, May 1, 2015, https://www
.theroot.com/media-s-biased-and-dehumanizing-coverage-of-baltimore-f
-1790859651.

44. "President Obama on Baltimore Riots (C-SPAN)," *YouTube*, April 28, 2015,
https://www.youtube.com/watch?v=AHOdPEFYUg4.

45. Fleming, *The Art of Placemaking*, 14.

46. Elizabeth Alexander, "The Trayvon Generation," *New Yorker*, June 15, 2020,
https://www.newyorker.com/magazine/2020/06/22/the-trayvon-generation.

47. Jelani Cobb, "The Death of George Floyd in Context," *New Yorker*, May 27, 2020,
https://www.newyorker.com/news/daily-comment/the-death-of-george-floyd-in-
context.

48. Dyson, *Long Time Coming*, 1.

49. Quoted in Kenya Downs, "When Black Death Goes Viral, It Can Trigger PTSD-
Like Trauma," PBS, July 22, 2016, https://www.pbs.org/newshour/nation/black-pain
-gone-viral-racism-graphic-videos-can-create-ptsd-like-trauma.

50. It's important to note that desensitization and dehumanization were also
felt during the Rodney King beating and trial in the 1990s. For more information,
see Kimberlé Crenshaw and Gary Peller, "Reel Time / Real Justice," *Denver Law Review: Colloquy—Racism in the Wake of the Los Angeles Riots* 70, no. 2 (1993): 283–96; and
Robert Gooding-Williams, *Reading Rodney King / Reading Urban Uprising* (Routledge,
1993).

51. Caelan Reeves, "Front of House: Social Media's Repackaging of Black Death,"
Student Life, April 29, 2021, https://tsl.news/black-death-social-media/.

52. Quoted in Hadia Shaikh, "Murals for Racial Justice: A Dive into the Artists'
Mind," *Nuvo News Nirvana*, December 31, 2020, https://nuvo.newsnirvana.com/arts
/visual/murals-for-racial-justice-a-dive-into-the-artists-minds/article_08adf012
-4b82-11eb-80b1-1fae45d0ef8a.html.

53. Luis Andres Henao, Nomaan Merchant, Juan Lozano, and Adam Geller,
"A Long Look at the Complicated Life of George Floyd," *Chicago Tribune*, June 11,
2020, https://www.chicagotribune.com/nation-world/ct-nw-life-of-george-floyd
-biography-20200611-cxmlynpyvjczpbe6izfduzwv54-story.html.

54. The People's Conservatory [@thepeoplesconservatory], "27 Hour Mural for Breonna," *Instagram*, June 6, 2020, www.instagram.com/p/CBHHG8JB2cL
/?igshid=YmMyMTA2M2Y=.

55. Kimberlé Crenshaw, "The Urgency of Intersectionality," *Ted*, 2016, https:
//www.ted.com/talks/kimberle_crenshaw_the_urgency_of_intersectionality
?language=en; Southbank Centre, "Kimberlé Crenshaw—On Intersectionality—
Keynote—WOW 2016," *YouTube*, 30:46, 2016, https://www.youtube.com
/watch?v=-DW4HLgYPlA.

56. Homa Khaleeli, "#SayHerName: Why Kimberlé Crenshaw Is Fighting for
Forgotten Women," *The Guardian*, May 30, 2016, https://www.theguardian.com
/lifeandstyle/2016/may/30/sayhername-why-kimberle-crenshaw-is-fighting-for-for
gotten-women.

57. Malika Saada Saar, "#SayHerName: A Q&A with Professor Kimberlé Crenshaw," *YouTube Blog*, March 13, 2021, https://blog.youtube/news-and-events /sayhername/.

58. "#SayHerName African American Policy Forum: Black Women Are Killed by Police Too," *African American Policy Forum*, https://www.aapf.org/sayhername. For the full report written by the #SayHerName Campaign and the African American Policy Forum, see Kimberlé Williams Crenshaw and Andrea J. Ritchie with Rachel Anspach, Rachel Gilmer, and Luke Harris, "Say Her Name: Resisting Police Brutality Against Black Women," https://44bbdc6e-0144-4a9a-88bc-731c6524888e.filesusr .com/ugd/62e126_9223ee35c2694ac3bd3f2171504ca3f7.pdf.

59. Richard A. Oppel Jr., Derrick Bryson Taylor, and Nicholas Bogel-Burroughs, "What to Know About Breonna Taylor's Death," *New York Times*, April 26, 2021, https://www.nytimes.com/article/breonna-taylor-police.html.

60. Aja Romano, "Arrest the Cops Who Killed Breonna Taylor: The Power and Peril of a Catchphrase," *Vox*, August 10, 2020, https://www.vox.com/21327268/breonna -taylor-say-her-name-meme-hashtag.

61. Anya Shukla, "'A Community Effort': Cadex Herrera Discusses the Mural at the George Floyd Memorial," *Colorization Collective*, June 16, 2020, https://www .colorizationcollective.org/blog/a-community-effort-cadex-herrera-discusses-the -mural-at-the-george-floyd-memorial.

62. Wesley Lowery, *They Can't Kill Us All: The Story of Black Lives Matter* (Penguin Random House, 2017), 36.

63. Keeanga-Yamahtta Taylor, *From #BlackLivesMatter to Black Liberation* (Haymarket Books, 2016), 22.

64. Nicolas Kristof, Twitter post, January 23, 2015, 11:00 p.m., https://twitter .com/nickkristof/status/558761095478145025.

65. Lowery, *They Can't Kill Us All*, 195.

66. Calvin John Smiley and David Fakunle, "From 'Brute' to 'Thug': The Demonization and Criminalization of Unarmed Black Male Victims in America," *Journal of Human Behavior and Social Environment* 26, no. 3–4 (2016): 350–66.

67. Ibid., 358.

68. Lowery, *They Can't Kill Us All*, 37.

69. Ibid., 29.

70. Deron Lee, "In Ferguson, Local News Coverage Shines," *Columbia Journalism Review*, August 20, 2014, https://archives.cjr.org/united_states_project/local _coverage_ferguson_michae.php.

71. Netta quotation in Lowery, *They Can't Kill Us All*, 42.

72. Terrance McCoy, "Darren Wilson Explains Why He Killed Michael Brown," *Washington Post*, November 25, 2014, https://www.washingtonpost.com/news /morning-mix/wp/2014/11/25/why-darren-wilson-said-he-killed-michael -brown/?noredirect=on&utm_term=.00b783d33c1c; Smiley and Fakunle, "From 'Brute' to 'Thug,'" 359.

73. Larry Buchanan, Ford Fessenden, K. K. Rebecca Lai, Haeyoun Park, Ali-

cia Parlapiano, Archie Tse, Tim Wallace, Derek Watkins, and Karen Yourish, "Q & A: What Happened in Ferguson?," *New York Times*, August 10, 2015, https://www .nytimes.com/interactive/2014/08/13/us/ferguson-missouri-town-under-siege -after-police-shooting.html; Jessica Glenza, "'I Felt Like a Five-Year-Old Holding On to Hulk Hogan': Darren Willson in His Own Words," *The Guardian*, November 25, 2014, https://www.theguardian.com/us-news/2014/nov/25/darren-wilson-testimony -ferguson-michael-brown.

74. Enid Spitz, "Can Federal Law Save This Threatened Black Lives Matter Mural?," *Willamette Week*, July 19, 2016, http://www.wweek.com/arts/2016/07/19/can -federal-law-save-this-threatened-black-lives-matter-mural/.

75. Ibid.

76. Ibid.

77. Ibid.

78. John Rudolf and Trymaine Lee, "Trayvon Martin Case Spotlights Florida History of 'Sloppy' Police Work," *Huffington Post*, April 9, 2012, http://www .huffingtonpost.com/2012/04/09/trayvonmartin-cops-botched-investigation_n _1409277.html.

79. Ibid.

80. Katherine Boyle, "Trayvon Martin's Death Has Put Spotlight on Perceptions About Hoodies," *Washington Post*, March 25, 2012, https://www.washingtonpost .com/lifestyle/style/trayvon-martins-death-has-put-spotlight-on-perceptions-about -hoodies/2012/03/24/gIQAwQ6gaS_story.html?utm_term=.7efb5fcd22ef.

81. Ibid.

82. Ibid.

83. PBS News Hour, "Rep. Bobby Rush Kicked Off House Floor for Wearing Hoodie in Support of Trayvon Martin," *YouTube*, 02:27, March 28, 2012, https://www .youtube.com/watch?v=KrMb-ZbngsY.

84. Dyson, *Long Time Coming*, 3.

85. Lowery, *They Can't Kill Us All*, 18.

86. Kimberlé Crenshaw, "The Urgency of Intersectionality," *Ted*, 2016, https: //www.ted.com/talks/kimberle_crenshaw_the_urgency_of_intersectionality ?language=en; Southbank Centre, "Kimberlé Crenshaw—On Intersectionality— keynote—wow 2016," *YouTube*, 30:46, 2016, https://www.youtube.com/watch?v =-DW4HLgYPlA.

Conclusion. Telling the People's Story

Epigraphs are from Kymberly N. Pinder, *Painting the Gospel: Black Public Art and Religion in Chicago* (University of Illinois Press, 2016), 14; "Forty Seventh and Calumet— the Wall of Daydreaming and Man's Inhumanity to Man," by Mitchell Caton, CPAG; Jeff W. Huebner, *Walls of Prophecy and Protest: William Walker and the Roots of a Revolutionary Public Art Movement* (Northwestern University Press, 2019), 56.

1. Author's telephone interview with Eugene "Eda" Wade, June 1, 2017.

INDEX

www.ingramcontent.com/pod-product-compliance
Lightning Source LLC
Chambersburg PA
CBHW020854180526
45163CB00007B/2505